SUSPECT SAINTS AND HOLY HERETICS

SUSPECT SAINTS AND HOLY HERETICS

DISPUTED SANCTITY AND COMMUNAL IDENTITY IN LATE MEDIEVAL ITALY

JANINE LARMON PETERSON

CORNELL UNIVERSITY PRESS

Ithaca and London

First published 2019 by Cornell University Press

Library of Congress Cataloging-in-Publication Data

Names: Peterson, Janine Larmon, author.
Title: Suspect saints and holy heretics : disputed sanctity and communal identity in late medieval Italy / Janine Larmon Peterson.
Description: Ithaca [New York] : Cornell University Press, 2019. | Includes bibliographical references and index.
Identifiers: LCCN 2019015734 (print) | LCCN 2019018065 (ebook) | ISBN 9781501742354 (pdf) | ISBN 9781501742361 (epub/mobi) | ISBN 9781501742347 | ISBN 9781501742347 (cloth ; alk. paper)
Subjects: LCSH: Christian saints—Cult—Italy—History—To 1500. | Christian saints—Cult—History of doctrines—Middle Ages, 600–1500. | Sanctification—Catholic Church. | Canonization. | Papacy—History. | Italy—Church history—476–1400. | Catholic Church—Italy—History.
Classification: LCC BX2333 (ebook) | LCC BX2333 .P48 2019 (print) | DDC 235/.2094509022—dc23
LC record available at https://lccn.loc.gov/2019015734

ISBN 978-1-5017-7590-1(pbk)

Cover illustration: detail from the Spiezer Chronik (1484/5).

To Larry

Contents

Tables and Illustrations

Tables

Illustrations

Acknowledgments

Research for this book was possible due to a number of wonderful friends, colleagues, and institutions over many years. I am grateful for support provided by the American Catholic Historical Association (John Tracy Ellis Dissertation Award); the American Historical Association (Bernadotte E. Schmitt Research Grant); the Center for Medieval Studies at the University of Notre Dame (Ambrosiana Microfilms Travel Stipend); grants and fellowships from the College of Arts and Sciences and the Department of History, Indiana University (Paul V. McNutt and Kathleen McNutt Watson Graduate Fellowship, College of Arts and Sciences Dissertation Year Research Fellowship, Andressohn Fellowship, and Valerie J. Gulick Fellowship); the National Endowment for the Humanities (NEH Summer Stipend); and Marist College (Dean of Faculty/VPAA of Academic Affairs Summer Research Grants). Most of this book was written (or rewritten) during two halcyon periods: as a Medieval Fellow at the Center for Medieval Studies at Fordham University in spring 2014 and on a summer research appointment at Marist-Italy in summer 2016.

I have deep gratitude for the generous help of archivists and librarians. In particular, I thank the staff of the Archivio di Stato di Firenze; the Archivio di Stato di Milano; the Archivio Segreto Vaticano and the Biblioteca Apostolica Vaticana, Vatican City; the Biblioteca Ambrosiana, Milan; the Bibliotheca Casanatense, Rome; the Biblioteca Nazionale, Florence; and the Biblioteca Nazionale Braidense, Milan. In addition, the interlibrary loan staff of the libraries of Indiana University, Fordham University, and Marist College located a number of hard-to-find printed texts, without which this book would have been incomplete. *Past and Present* and *Traditio* kindly allowed me to use portions of my work published as articles in their journals. Some sections of chapter 4 were published in "Holy Heretics in Later Medieval Italy," *Past and Present* 204 (2009): 3–31. Parts of chapter 3 previously appeared in "The Politics of Sanctity in Thirteenth-Century Ferrara," *Traditio* 63 (2008): 307–26.

I have been extremely fortunate to have had many knowledgeable individuals read portions or all of this manuscript, although any errors are, of course, mine alone. I would like to thank Kristin Bayer, Renate Blumenfeld-Kosinski, David Brakke, Louisa Burnham, Eileen Curley, Jennifer Kolpacoff Deane, Jay Diehl, Mary Harvey Doyno, Christine Dunn, Sally Dwyer-McNulty, Dyan Elliott, Mary Erler, Arnold Franklin, Alison Frazier, Gábor Klaniczay, Lauren Mancia, Nicholas Marshall, Sara McDougall, Catherine M. Mooney, Barbara Newman, James A. Palmer, Andrew Romig, Neslihan Şenocak, Leah Shopkow, and Dror Wahrman for their incisive and thoughtful comments. Many colleagues at various conferences provided invaluable feedback. Beatrice Arduini and Ben St. John helped with particularly thorny translations from Italian and Latin, respectively. I also owe a huge debt of gratitude to Mahinder S. Kingra, Cornell University Press' readers, and the press's editorial board. Their comments were invaluable for the publication of this book in its present (and much improved) form.

One cannot thrive without a tribe. Mine is an eclectic mix of friends and scholars that I can always depend on. First and foremost is Dyan Elliott. I could not have dreamed for a more attentive and supportive teacher, mentor, and friend. She constantly pushes me outside of my comfort zone and has done more than I can acknowledge to make me a better thinker and writer. Leah Shopkow is and has always been a bastion of support. Others not already named, such as Kristina Christian, Christine Dunn, Joanne Filippone, Mary Halbach, Jill Massino, José Najar, Jody Prestia, James G. Snyder, Joseph and Reneé Stubenrauch, and Jane Wickersham, have been there for me professionally and personally over the years it took to complete this book. I have benefited from many other scholars and friends in New York City, old and new, with whom I have been able to collaborate or reap the rewards of their knowledge.

Maryanne Kowaleski of Fordham University and H. Wayne Storey of Indiana University provided me invaluable mentoring as a young undergraduate student and well beyond. These remarkable teachers helped to foster my interest in the Middle Ages, encouraged me to go to graduate school and, in different ways, helped me to achieve that goal. Special thanks also to Richard Gyug, who advised me through my first published article long ago. Finally, it is not an exaggeration to say that I would not be publishing this book without the support of my parents, Karen and Bruce Larmon. I appreciate more than I can say the fact that they did not bat an eye when I announced I was going to college to major in Medieval Studies. And Larry Peterson, my partner of over two decades, cheerfully picked up and moved cross-country with me several times, joyfully took care of our increasing feline brood when I was off on research trips, and supported me every step of the way. *Para ti, tres besos en la boca y uno in la cachete.*

ABBREVIATIONS

AASS	*Acta Sanctorum quotquot toto orbe coluntur.* 65 vols. Antwerp-Brussels-Tongerlo-Paris, 1643–1940.
Acta S. Officii	*Acta S. Officii Bononie ab anno 1291 usque ad annum 1310.* 3 vols. Edited by Lorenzo Paolini and Raniero Orioli. Fonti per la storia d'Italia, 106. Rome: Istituto storico italiano per il Medio Evo, 1982–1984.
ASF	Florence, Archivio di Stato di Firenze.
ASV	Vatican City, Archivio Segreto Vaticano.
BAV	Vatican City, Biblioteca Apostolica Vaticano.
Eretici	D'Alatri, Mariano, ed. *Eretici e inquisitori in Italia: Studi e documenti.* 2 vols. Rome: Istituto storico del Cappuccini, 1987.
Itinerari	Zanella, Gabriele, ed. *Itinerari ereticali patari e catari tra Rimini e Verona.* Istituto Storico Italiano per il Medio Evo, Studi Storici, fasc. 153. Rome: Nella Sede dell'Istituto, 1986.
Meco	DeSantis, Antonio, ed. *Meco del Sacco, inquisizione e processi per eresia. Ascoli-Avignone 1320–1346.* Ascoli Piceno: A. DeSantis, 1982 [1980].
MGHSS	*Monumenta Germaniae Historica, Scriptores.* Hanover, Frankfurt, and Munich: Monumenta Germaniae Historica Institute, 1826–.
Milano 1300	Benedetti, Marina, ed. *Milano 1300: I processi inquisitoriali contro le devote e i devoti di santa Guglielma.* Milan: Libri Scheiwiller, 1999.
RIS	*Rerum Italicarum Scriptores.* 24 vols., series 2. Città di Castello—Bologna, 1917–1975.
Riti	Vatican City, Archivio Segreto Vaticano, Congregazione dei Riti.

SUSPECT SAINTS AND HOLY HERETICS

Introduction

In the late thirteenth century, the Franciscan chronicler Salimbene de Adam described the recent cult of a layman in Cremona named Albert of Villa d'Ogna (d. 1279). Albert was a humble wine carrier and a local saint who could have lapsed into obscurity if not for Salimbene's famous description of him and the dogged efforts of his community to canonize him, which resulted in a seventeenth-century canonization process. Thanks to these sources, scholars such as André Vauchez, Augustine Thompson, and Lester K. Little reignited interest in Albert and the circumstances of his veneration.[1] According to his contemporary Salimbene, Albert was a wine porter but also a drunk sinner. The bishops of Cremona, Parma, and Reggio promoted his devotion although his supposed miracles were false and "deceptive," including one instance in which Salimbene claimed citizens of Parma mistook a clove of garlic for a relic of Albert's toe.[2] Salimbene's ire at the fact that bishops allowed his veneration without papal authorization reveals two points of contention about the construction of sanctity in late medieval Italy. The first was what criteria should assess holiness and the relative weight of each factor when assessing "true" or "false" sanctity. In the context

---

1. Vauchez, *La sainteté en Occident*, cited throughout in English translation, *Sainthood in the Later Middle Ages*, 235–6; Thompson, *Cities of God*, 204–5; and Little, *Indispensible Immigrants*.

2. Salimbene de Adam, *Cronica*, 2:733–34, cited throughout in English translation, *Chronicle of Salimbene de Adam*, 512.

of Salimbene's critique of Albert's cult, should Albert's ignoble socioeconomic background, presumed less-than-noteworthy morality, and predilection for wine have greater import than the testimony of witnesses who experienced miraculous answers to their prayers upon supplication to this saint? The second was about the process of sanctification and how it should occur: at the diocesan level through communal consensus between the citizens and their bishops, as had been traditional until the twelfth century, or solely at the pontifical level, as the papacy established in the thirteenth century? Salimbene directs the reader's attention to this tension between competing authorities by berating those bishops who heeded "common report" about Albert's miracles and allowed his veneration instead of crushing the cult since the pope, who Salimbene thought should have the sole authority to judge signs of holiness and create cults, did not approve it.

This book is about those citizens of the Italian peninsula in the late Middle Ages—consisting of both men and women, wealthy and poor, laity and clergy—who created and promoted Albert's cult and who continued venerating him regardless of papal authorization or the disparagement of institutional insiders like Salimbene. It is about the people who did the same for roughly thirty other saints, some of whom individually faced excommunication or collectively faced interdict for their choice of holy patrons. It is about the church's efforts to stop, or at least discourage, devotion to the local saints these citizens favored. Most of all, it is about why these individuals persisted in their veneration when they had so much to lose and how they successfully challenged popes and papal inquisitors who tried to end their devotions. The answers to these questions lie in placing these discussions of religious culture within very localized political change in Italy in the late Middle Ages, which is the aim of this book.

Although the cults discussed in this book might be familiar to scholars of sanctity, heresy, and late medieval Italy, their grounding in specific local politics and how that affected the construction of sanctity in thirteenth- and fourteenth-century Italy differentiates this study from other scholarship, noted below, that mentions some of the same holy persons. The fact that this is a geographic study of many cults, rather than a chronological study of how a single new cult is politicized in a particular time (or over time), separates it from valuable recent hagiographical studies in other regions.[3] It is built on the foundation of the painstaking research of André Vauchez, who looked at over-

3. For the latter, see for example Birkett, "Struggle for Sanctity"; Oertel, *Cult of St. Erik in Medieval Sweden*; the essays in Camp and Kelley, *Saints as Intercessors*; and St. Lawrence, "Crusader in a 'Communion of Saints.'"

all trends in sainthood during the Middle Ages and posited increasing papal hegemony in sanctification, as well as newer scholarship such as that of Donald Prudlo, who examined how the papacy created a process that allowed popes to claim total control over canonizations through the introduction of the idea of papal infallibility. Ronald Finucane and Laura Ackerman Smoller, who used "thick description" for deep analysis of issues within the papal canonization process, shaped my approach to the microhistorical cases I examine. This book also is indebted to the research of Augustine Thompson, OP and Robert Bartlett, who looked closely at aspects of lay devotional practices in Italy and elsewhere, and to scholars such as Miri Rubin, who examined the ritualized nature of veneration in the creation of cults. The work of John Arnold, Dyan Elliott, R. I. Moore, and Elizabeth Makowski, among others, argued that a strict division between sanctity and heresy was a myth and depended upon one's perspective, which is an integral premise of this book. Christine Caldwell Ames and James Given explained how inquisitors intellectually dealt with this overlap and detailed the methods they used to enforce their perspectives on others, respectively. John Arnold's *Inquisition and Power: Catharism and the Confessing Subject* addressed how the modern scholar can read between the power dynamics, technologies that inquisitors used, and the layers of intervention in inquisitorial records to uncover differences in how inquisitors and witnesses understood and categorized the world. All these texts on the inquisitorial process provide a framework for many of the cases of contestation I discuss and my methodology in approaching the sources.[4]

What almost all of these earlier studies share is a focus on the institutional development of cult creation, sanctification, canonization, inquisition, and devotion. This view is most explicit in Ronald Finucane's argument that the term "saint" applies strictly to papally canonized holy persons.[5] There were many voices who contributed to constructing sainthood through memory, ritual, and language in the late Middle Ages. The process of negotiating consensus about holiness, two centuries earlier than Finucane's examples and before popes successfully centralized the canonization process, makes any distinction between saints with papally approved cults and saints without that sanction anachronistic. In fact, medieval popes did not canonize any of the cults I examine in depth. Each saint, however, experienced the same evaluative process of their merits and ultimately the same type of ritual veneration on the local level, whether a pope officially recognized them or not.

---

4. See the bibliography for the works of these scholars that are most relevant to this book.

5. Finucane, *Contested Canonizations*, 3–4; cf. Vauchez, *Sainthood in the Later Middle Ages*, and Thompson, *Cities of God*, which acknowledge other forms of sanctification in this period.

Donald Prudlo's recent study, *Certain Sainthood*, and Mary Harvey Doyno's monograph *The Lay Saint: Charity and Charismatic Authority in Medieval Italy, 1150–1350* lend nuance to the tendency to focus on the effect of the institution on the people, rather than vice versa or in a more collaborative way, by addressing how the laity influenced the church's intellectual ideas in what Prudlo calls an "organic" process.[6] Prudlo does so by focusing on how the laity's opposition to church doctrine and/or its concept of sanctity helped to shape doctrine and the process of canonization, specifically through the idea of papal infallibility. Doyno embarks on a similar task, looking instead at how lay religiosity shaped church views on what it meant to be part of a civic community, as well as of Christendom.[7] Both scholars question the idea of a calculated and hegemonic late medieval church that resonates through the work of Vauchez, and others such as Dyan Elliott and John Arnold, by fusing intellectual and cultural history. This book furthers their decentering approach by focusing on specific examples of communal and individual agency. It differs from them by examining these localized instances of cults within the context of how communities used them for political purposes. It examines the institutional developments of canonizations and inquisitions only to the extent necessary for explaining how these developments led popes and inquisitors to struggle with citizens of Italian towns who did not accept the church's new mandates. While many of the saints discussed are lay saints and many of the people who venerated them were part of the laity, this work also differs from Prudlo and Doyno by eliminating the assumption of a specific lay form of veneration. Instead, it addresses the politics of sanctity in communities that included many members of the clergy working in tandem with the laity to use cults as a tool for the political purpose of expressing a local identity that trumped vocational affiliation.

Within the framework of tracing the papal centralization of the canonization process and the development of the inquisitorial process, scholars tend to use the language of "resistance" for any challenges to that authority.[8] This term argues for a negative power differential that was constant for those of a subaltern group. It takes for granted that citizens were in a state of abject subordination and could only employ the "weapons of the weak" against the dominant culture.[9] My rejection of this term is twofold. First, it sets up a false

---

6. Prudlo, *Certain Sainthood*, 5–7.

7. Doyno, *Lay Saint*, introduction.

8. For example, Burnham, *So Great a Light*, 51–94; Friedlander, *Hammer of the Inquisitors*; Given, *Inquisition and Medieval Society*, 91–140; and Pegg, *Corruption of Angels*, esp. chaps. 2 and 10.

9. Scott, *Weapons of the Weak*.

dichotomy between elite and "popular" culture or religion.[10] It suggests there was a divergence in how the laity experienced, expressed, recognized, and understood religious belief in contrast to the clergy. The examples discussed throughout this book, especially in chapters 6, 7, and 8, prove that such a distinction is untenable since clergy and laity united in championing their hometown saints in the face of institutional censure. Second, I contend that local communities did not resist. Rather, lay citizens, bishops, canons, monks, and friars kept doing what they had always done. When papal or inquisitorial directives limited or attempted to prevent devotions, these individuals just persisted, albeit sometimes with new strategies. These included rituals that developed from the performative aspect of devotion for authorized and tolerated cults (chapter 3) or techniques appropriated from inquisitors to form what I call "oppositional inquisitorial culture" (chapter 8) to protect their own. Saints became pawns in a struggle for authority, but one of the papacy's making in its attempt to wrest power from local communities and diocesan authority in the construction of cults. Popes and inquisitors were the ones who experienced limitations to extending their authority, which occasionally they could not overcome, since the memory and veneration of some accused or sentenced heretics continued well into the early modern period and even today. I argue that, paradoxically, by trying to increase its spiritual authority through bureaucratic centralization and regulation of what constituted sanctity, the church absented itself from the development of cults on the ground and inadvertently encouraged the proliferation of local disputed saints. Members of communities challenged any opponent to their traditional prerogative to identify saints and to recognize heretics.

Notwithstanding the papacy's attempt to institute an "objective" process, papal canonizations and inquisitorial investigations were relatively new, highly subjective, and intrinsically tied to local politics and claims of authority. Thus, while I focus on the religious culture of late medieval Italy, I am equally concerned with its political cultures. This is another area in which this book diverges from recent work about the specific beliefs, practices, processes, or internal group dynamics of lay sanctity, heretical groups, and "civic" religion. The work of Carrie E. Beneš on how Italian towns placed saints within classical models for political purposes, and Mary Harvey Doyno's work on how

---

10. Literature on the debate over the existence of "popular religion" as part of "popular culture" is vast. Standard discussions include Burke, *Popular Culture in Early Modern Europe*; Chartier, "Culture as Appropriation"; and Schmitt, "Religion, Folklore, and Society." Premodern historians who reject the idea include Capp, "Popular Culture(s)"; and Kieckhefer, "Specific Rationality of Medieval Magic," 833. For a chronologically wider consideration of the term "popular culture," its alternatives, and its drawbacks, see Parker, "Toward a Definition of Popular Culture."

communities used charitably minded contemporary lay saints to create social aspirations and a civic identity, have helped to frame my discussion of the political uses of disputed saints. Members of communities recognized that by choosing to take part in an activity that hindered or foiled inquisitors, for instance, they were in fact questioning the legitimacy of inquisitorial power and, by extension, that of the pope, as discussed in chapters 6 and 7. This is very different, however, from the concept of "civic religion" that one finds in the historiography of later medieval Italy, which rests more easily within the Renaissance city-states than late medieval communes or signorial governments.[11] Civic religion, according to James Palmer, describes "efforts by municipal governments to develop associations between the sacred and their own authority."[12] Recent scholarship by Palmer and Andrew Brown challenge the usefulness of this term, with the latter pointing out that it creates another layer to the false division between lay/secular and clerical/ecclesiastical religion.[13] Local saints performed actions in the urban landscape that helped communities, but in the thirteenth and early fourteenth centuries, municipalities rarely constructed these cults as a conscious way to cement their political power. The political landscape was in a state of flux, with some towns having a communal government, some seeing the rise of *signori*, and some vacillating between political forms. These cults formed in a more fluid and organic way in a process of negotiation and consensus that included both lay and clerical members of a community, as chapters 1–4 and 8 in particular demonstrate. They served as a "symbol without a fixed meaning" that allowed whole communities, rather than certain social groups, to assert a collective identity through consensus on the holiness of the individual that had its foundation in the town's political context.[14]

This book explores the messy, complicated, and politicized process of creating saints. In late medieval Italy, a number of individuals simultaneously existed as both saint and heretic depending on the perspective of the observer. Saints and the creation of cults on the one hand, and condemnations and the destruction of cults on the other hand, both became weapons in a new war for religious and political authority in thirteenth- and fourteenth-century northern and central Italy, including the Papal States, Tuscany, the Romagna,

---

11. See, e.g., Chittolini, "Civic Religion and the Countryside"; D'Andrea, *Civic Christianity in Renaissance Italy*; and Terpstra, "Civic Religion."

12. Palmer, "Medieval and Renaissance Rome," 6–7.

13. See ibid. and Palmer, *Virtues of Economy*, as well as Brown, "Civic Religion in Late Medieval Europe," esp. 343–44.

14. Smoller, *Saint and the Chopped-Up Baby*, 2. For a contrasting study of the creation of specific social group identity versus this type of larger collective identity, see Maire Vigeur, *L'Autre Rome*, in English translation as *Forgotten Story: Rome in the Communal Period*, chaps. 3–5.

FIGURE 1. Map of Italy circa 1300 with centers of disputed saints' cults. Map by Bill Nelson.

and Piedmont. Figure 1 provides a schematic view of where these disputes occurred in a hierarchical layout of most contested (group 1) to least contested
(group 4) and inversely corresponds to the nomenclature I describe below.

These regions are not unique in producing examples of contested sanctity,
but they have been recognized for their large preponderance of unauthorized
local cults of saints, including twenty to thirty debated cases of recently deceased saints in the later Middle Ages. The predominant characteristic of all
cases of contested sanctity is that orthodox members of society supported and
participated in these cults, even after inquisitors condemned some of these

Table 1. Selected list of disputed saints

NAME	DATE OF DEATH	STATUS	LOCATION(S) OF CULTS	DISPUTED SANCTITY ON MAP	SOURCE(S)
Albert of Villa d'Ogna	1279	Lay	Parma, Cremona, Reggio	Tolerated (4)	Mendicant chronicle; canonization process (1744)
Amato Ronconi	1266 or 1292	Franciscan Third Order	Saludecio, Rimini	Suspect (3)	Canonization process (1733–1734)
Anthony Peregrinus	1267	Lay	Padua	Tolerated (4)	*Vitae* and *miracula*; mendicant chronicle; communal statutes
Armanno Pungilupo	1269	Lay	Ferrara	Heretical saint (2)	*Miracula*; inquisitorial testimony; letters to papacy; papal condemnation; civic chronicle
Bevignate of Perugia	Late 12th century	Flagellant	Perugia	Tolerated (4)	Civic statutes; canonization inquiry; artistic depictions
Cecco of Ascoli	1327	Lay	Ascoli, Spoleto	Holy heretic (1)	Inquisitorial condemnations; civic statutes
Cecco of Pesaro	1350	Possibly Third Order	Pesaro	Tolerated (4)	*Vita*
Clare of Rimini	1326	Franciscan Third Order	Rimini	Suspect (3)	*Vita*
Dolcino of Novara	1307	Lay	Vercelli	Holy heretic (1)	Civic chronicles; inquisitorial process (1291–1310); papal bulls; inquisitorial manual (Gui)
Facio of Cremona	1271	Lay	Cremona	Tolerated (4)	*Vita* and *miracula*
Henry ("Rigo") of Bolzano	1315	Lay	Cremona	Tolerated (4)	*Vita*; canonization process (1768)
Gerard Segarelli	1300	Lay	Parma, Spoleto	Heretical saint (2)	Mendicant chronicle; civic chronicles; inquisitorial process (1291–1310); papal bulls; inquisitorial manual (Gui)

Name	Date	Affiliation	Location	Classification	Sources
Guglielma of Milan	1281	Lay	Milan, Brunate	Heretical saint (2)	Inquisitorial process (1300–1302); inquisitorial manual; artistic depictions
Guido Lacha	Mid-12th century	Lay	Brescia	Holy heretic (1)	Mendicant chronicle; inquisitorial manuals
Margaret of Cortona	1297	Franciscan Third Order	Cortona	Tolerated (4)	*Vita* and *miracula*
Meco del Sacco	c. 1346	Lay	Ascoli	Suspect (3)	Letters to papacy; papal communications; inquisitorial materials; civic statutes
Michele Berti da Calci	1389	Spiritual Franciscan	Florence	Holy heretic (1)	*Vita*
Parisio of Treviso	1267	Camaldolese Order	Treviso	Tolerated (4)	*Vita* and *miracula*
Peter of Abano	c. 1316	Lay	Padua	Holy heretic (1)	Civic chronicles; civic statutes
Peter Crisci	1323	Third Order	Foligno	Suspect (3)	*Vita*; civic statutes
Peter Pettinaio	1289	Possibly Third Order	Siena	Tolerated (4)	*Vita*
Tommasuccio of Nocera	1377 or 1400	Third Order	Nocera Umbra, Foligno, Spello	Suspect (3)	*Vita* and book of his prophecies; relics and chapel; anonymous letter c. 1400

saints as heretics; consequently, devotees risked eternal damnation through excommunication or interdict. That any cases of this sort occurred at all is remarkable, considering that communities risked their own salvation and exposed themselves to papal retribution by taking part in these cults, especially when there were so many seemingly viable and less controversial saints.

This book examines how and why this occurred. Part I addresses four processes through which someone became a disputed saint. Its four chapters are not intended to present a typology of sainthood. As mentioned here and noted throughout, no disputed (or undisputed) saint fits seamlessly into certain expectations. These chapters present examples of saints whose holiness became contested through particular means rather than through certain characteristics. Some saints went through multiple processes—or overlapped in the defining characteristics of two of them—so these categories cannot be considered hermetically distinct. Table 1 provides the saints most often discussed, noting the process that produced each one. The first chapter describes "tolerated saints." Tolerated saints achieved local veneration but could have been subject to derision, such as that which Salimbene directed toward Albert of Villa d'Ogna. In other instances, such as those of Facio of Cremona (d. 1271) or Henry of Bolzano (d. 1315), disapproval came in the form of rejected canonization inquiries, although communities continued to venerate these saints without fear of reprisal. These so-called tolerated cults serve as a foundation for investigating the two intrinsic issues with which the papacy and communities were wrestling, namely, how and by whom sainthood should be conferred. The second chapter examines "suspect saints," who emerged when either the pope or papal agents publicly suspected a local holy person of heresy. The individual was the focus of a cult that popes undoubtedly preferred to discontinue, but a lack of evidence meant inquisitors could not condemn their veneration. The third and fourth processes resulted in more dramatic cases of official disapprobation and local indifference to papal mandates. "Heretical saints" (chapter 3) were individuals that people accepted as holy when living and venerated after death, even though inquisitors condemned them. The distinction between suspect saints and heretical saints is twofold. In the latter case, the aberrant behavior or beliefs of the saint's inner circle often prompted suspicion into the saint's orthodoxy, and that suspicion often led to a posthumous sentence for heresy. Chapter 4, which discusses "holy heretics," inverts the former process.[15] In these cases, inquisitors condemned a person as a heretic first and later communities decided the individual was holy. Local observers rejected the inquisitorial de-

---

15. Peterson, "Holy Heretics in Later Medieval Italy."

cree due to the demeanor and behavior of the condemned in the face of that person's imminent demise and came to a consensus that rather than being a dangerous heretic, he or she was in fact a saint who had suffered from unjust persecution.

The four chapters of Part II examine why citizens and communities were willing to suffer excommunication and interdict by retaining and creating cults that popes and inquisitors viewed of questionable merit. Chapter 5 looks at the motives of patronage and economics and how issues such as war and peace-making played a part in the contested cults of specific towns. Chapter 6 discusses inquisitors and the rise of anti-inquisitorial and antimendicant sentiments. Chapter 7 examines antipapal views that increased in the wake of popes' decisions to use the charge of heresy to achieve temporal as well as spiritual control over communities in northern and central Italy. Chapter 8 addresses the methods that individuals and communities used to thwart popes and their agents. Throughout, my approach is to discuss an aspect of a case study in-depth and use it to highlight a larger process to achieve what Carlo Ginzburg described as "a constant back and forth between micro- and macro-history, between close-ups and extreme long-shots, so as to continually thrust back into discussion the comprehensive vision of the historical process through apparent exceptions and cases of brief duration."[16] Thus the full stories of a saint's cult often unfold in the course of several chapters, although the specific points of the case study addressed in a single chapter can stand alone to support its main argument.

All of these discussions are grounded in local politics, which differed from town to town, although some larger generalizations may be useful to those less familiar with the Italian peninsula. What is generally known is that the term "Italy" when one is speaking about the Middle Ages is anachronistic. While some historians and literary scholars have argued that a sense of an "Italian" cultural or literary heritage existed by the Trecento, in a political sense the word only denotes a geographical area in the medieval period, which is how it is used in this study.[17] The northern and central regions of the peninsula were politically fragmented. The pope was the territorial lord of the Papal States, which circa 1300 stretched from Rome to the northeast, through Lazio, Umbria, and parts of the Marche and Emilia-Romagna. North and west of the Papal States the land was divided into dozens of polities consisting of governing cities and the countryside or *contado* under their control. Each of

16. Ginzburg, "Microhistory," 27.

17. Laura Morreale, "Chronicle and Community in Northern Italy"; and Porta, "L'urgenza della memoria storica." Cf. scholars who see the period rather as a case of divisive regionalism, such as Mundy, "In Praise of Italy," and Tabacco, "La genesi culturale."

these entities had its own political system. In the thirteenth century many towns were republican communes, although some (and more in the following century) became nascent city-states ruled by dynastic lords or *signori*. These leaders were concerned with expanding their power: the popes by asserting their authority over recalcitrant towns of the Papal States and against the encroaching *signori* to the north; the northern lords by engaging in territorial expansion of the areas under their domain through wars with other *signori*; and the communes by trying to keep their republican values and lands amid these power plays.

These ambitions led to a notably unstable political environment. In the Papal States many communities under the pope's jurisdiction opposed papal lordship. Cities such as Perugia, Spoleto, Assisi, Ascoli, and Ancona sought independent rule, a wish that the papacy was not willing to grant. The civic authorities of Spoleto were noncompliant with papal commands, resulting in Pope Alexander IV in 1260 ordering the Dominican bishop of Spoleto to send the town's highest civic authorities, the *podestà* and *capitano del popolo*, to a papal tribunal for aiding heretics.[18] The city of Ascoli was particularly recalcitrant and consistently refused to acknowledge the pope as its overlord. As a consequence it found itself under interdict three times within a century, attesting to a strong opposition to papal authority. The community's insubordination was such that the last interdict remained in effect for twenty-two years.[19] In signorial cities north of the Papal States, such as in Tuscany, Lombardy, and the March of Treviso, dynastic lords such as the Visconti, Este, Della Scala, and Montefeltro continually vied for power and territory. Northern and central Italy also served as the battleground for the Guelphs and Ghibellines, or the parties that came to represent papal interests as opposed to those of the Holy Roman Emperor to the north. From the inception of this political dispute in the twelfth century the papacy actively sought allies and became embroiled in local politics. This continued into the later thirteenth and fourteenth centuries, even though the initial cause of conflict had lost most of its original import (chapter 5).

Like all disputed saints, local contemporary saints, whose prestige derived from communal consensus, could help to unify members of these communi-

---

18. See discussion and documents in Mariano D'Alatri, "Accuse di eresia a Spoleto e a Narni negli anni 1259 e 1260," in *Eretici*, 1:297–312.

19. Innocent III placed Ascoli under interdict in 1202 for rebelling against Rome under Marcoaldo; in 1264 Urban IV did the same for being partisan to the Holy Roman Emperor Frederick II's son Manfred; and John XXII similarly punished the city in 1324 for its "eccessivo zelo" in a war against the rival city of Fermo (*Meco*, 5).

ties and heal the fractures in social networks because each saint had shared in the town's recent history and was exclusive to it. Many of the new saints in this period, such as Facio of Cremona or Margaret of Cortona (d. 1297), achieved renown for their efforts in reconciling factions and promoting regional peace. Communal statutes transformed private ritual devotions to these new saints into public displays of civic identity.[20] Bishops sought to preserve peace with the regime and protect their own interests. By controlling the cult, they could fight rising anticlericalism, decreasing episcopal power, and rival clergy, like the mendicants (chapter 6). A variety of citizens therefore felt a connection to their local men and women and believed them potent intercessors, while also recognizing the political expedient of having a saintly patron. To this end, communities refused to abandon local saints who became suspected of heresy or other faults or who impeded inquisitors, the administrative arm of the papacy (chapters 7–8). Conflict over cults of saints reflected spiritual disaffection with the new papal canonization process and also expressed autonomy from the papacy's political and social power.

Thus a larger implication of this book is how a disputed saint united the different social, economic, and political factions of a community into a cohesive, and often powerful, social body. While the term "community" implies a bounded group, defining those bounds is problematic. A community is not those living in a discrete geographical unit within town walls, or even the town plus the surrounding countryside under its control. Under such a definition the community often would include the very persons that the proponents of a disputed saint challenged, such as inquisitors and others from the same region who supported papal views against local cults. The term "community" also cannot presuppose a group that is unified by shared goals and values. That definition is untenable for towns grappling with political and social factionalism. Nor were loyalties divided along fault lines like those separating clergy and laity. David Sabean argued that "what is common in community is not shared values or common understanding so much as the fact that members of a community are engaged in the same argument, the same *raisonnement*, the same *Rede*, the same discourse, in which alternative strategies, misunderstandings, conflicting goals and values are threshed out."[21] I use the term "community" in this book in this sense of a shared spiritual discourse. The outsiders, those who did not help sustain this "argument" or who did not share the group's *raisonnement*, were the agents of papal authority. For example, in

20. Webb, *Patrons and Defenders*, 6.
21. Sabean, *Power in the Blood*, 29.

Italy a pope would often assign inquisitors to areas they knew well, presumably in the hope that their relationships with and knowledge of the inhabitants would assist in the pursuit of heterodoxy.[22] In this context, even a resident of long standing through lineage or other affiliations was an outsider because, as an inquisitor, he did not share in the discourse. Rather, he attempted to obliterate it with a condemnation.

The phenomenon of the disputed saint occurred primarily from 1250 to 1400. Beginning circa 1200, and influenced in large part by the Fourth Lateran Council in 1215, the papacy centralized its control over canonizations, changing it from a diocesan to a pontifical process; turned canonizations into a formal juridical procedure based on Roman law; imposed regulations on how Christians should behave; and created a judicial inquisitorial office to make sure people followed the new rules. These changes lessened the chance that a pope would recognize a regional saint's cult and prompted debates over who had the authority to recognize sainthood and what types of evidence had merit for identifying saints and heretics. This century and a half was also a time when the pope, both the spiritual head of the church and a landowner of a good portion of the central Italian countryside, had become a distant territorial lord, particularly during the papacy's move from Rome to Avignon for most of the fourteenth century. The Avignon papacy coincided with the strengthening of signorial rule in much of northern and central Italy, when the concerns of emerging dynastic lords often came into conflict with those of the pope. Prominent cases of contested sanctity declined by the end of the fourteenth century, when these *signori* had predominantly completed solidifying their rule and the papal seat was facing perhaps its greatest challenge in the advent of the Western Schism and the consequent conciliar movement. The papacy's efforts to cement its terrestrial power and expand its bureaucratic authority by implementing the papal canonization process and establishing the inquisitorial office were undermined following the attempt to return the papal seat to Rome in 1378. Between the early thirteenth-century endeavor to impose authority derived from the idea of the papal monarchy, and the late fourteenth-century derailment of papal power, saints' cults became a negotiating tool for the papacy's political ambitions as well as local communities' gambits to assert their autonomy. The loss of authority that the papacy suffered in the late fourteenth century resulted in fewer instances of disputed saints as other venues for power negotiations emerged.

The existence of unofficial local cults of any type demonstrated a spiritual disdain for papal authority and the pope's claim to be the ultimate arbiter of

---

22. Lansing, *Power and Purity*, 141; cf. Geltner, *Making of Medieval Antifraternalism*, 55.

holiness, one that was closely aligned with political concerns, as these case studies demonstrate. The chronologically and geographically localized process discussed here has a larger significance for scholarship on social identity and power relations. The veneration of contested saints crossed the supposed fissures dividing clergy and laity, orthodox and heterodox, men and women, rich and poor, and literate and illiterate. Individuals who were customarily divided by class, gender, or profession could become united in their struggle to create a saint. While some participants were part of the local clerical elite, such as bishops, canons, and abbots, others were outside the dominant power structure, which included in this period those who lacked civil rights and privileges and, in many cases, literacy and knowledge of Latin. As a result, the way in which northern and central Italian communities challenged papal authority participates in and informs the wider historical discourse on subordinate groups by problematizing the simple dichotomy of dominant/subordinate.[23]

Contested sanctity was the result of a combination of forces—religious, social, economic, and political—that worked in concert specifically during the thirteenth and fourteenth centuries. When communities chose to venerate condemned or suspect individuals and thus attempted to retain their right to identify holiness and establish saints' cults on a local level, they articulated their own civic identities and expressed a desire for autonomy. The different processes that produced disputed saints required a multifaceted approach to the sources. These include secular and clerical chronicles or narrative histories; saints' lives and lists of miracles composed (usually) by local clergy; inquisitorial processes and canonization inquiries, which include witness testimony complicated by levels of intervention; mendicant inquisitorial manuals; bulls, letters, and canon law produced by the papal bureaucracy; and civic statutes addressing the general treatment of heretics and the veneration of specific individuals. While a variety of these sources are sometimes present for a specific saint's cult, some types of sources predominate depending on the context. Table 1 provides an overview of what sources are extant for the most-discussed saints. I refer to all of these individuals as "local saints," which denotes persons from particular towns or persons who had more regional appeal in a few different communities, such as Albert of Villa d'Ogna. I use "town" and "city" interchangeably without reference to size or the existence of an episcopal seat. In both cases the *contado* or countryside under the city's dominion is included in the nomenclature. When a town was under the control of a

---

23. Some scholars have critiqued recent attempts to apply postcolonial theory to the Middle Ages by identifying the medieval church as a "colonial" church, composed of Christian missionary/conquerors expanding the borders of its cultural empire, Latin Christendom. See Bartlett, *Making of Europe*, 15; cf. Brown, "In the Middle"; and Dagenais and Greer, "Decolonizing the Middle Ages."

signore I prefer to use the phrase "signorial government" instead of "city-state," which connotes a different and later type of political entity. Saints' names are Anglicized as they usually appear in the English literature. The names of rulers or other elites are generally in Italian as they usually appear studies in both Italian and English. The names of others, such as inquisitorial witnesses, are generally kept in either the Latinized or Italianized versions of the primary sources in which they appear.

PART ONE

How

CHAPTER 1

Tolerated Saints

It was tough being a saint, but the "afterlife" of a new saint was even tougher. It was extremely difficult for someone to be officially recognized for holiness in the later Middle Ages. Although there were a large number of local saints during this period, popes did not sanction many of these cults. Out of the hundreds of venerated individuals that emerged between 1198 and 1431, popes canonized just thirty-five. Every one of these saints, except for two, were of royal birth or members of the clergy.[1] The saints whom popes approved were not necessarily saints that members of the laity preferred; for instance, the papal canonization of the assassinated inquisitor St. Peter Martyr (d. 1252) was largely greeted with apathy.[2] This led to many unauthorized cults, such as that of Anthony Peregrinus (d. 1267). His hagiographer maintained that Peregrinus "was famous . . . [though] the Roman Church did not permit him to be received into the catalog of the saints. Nevertheless he was held in the greatest veneration from that time in Padua . . . and it was established by municipal decree, that a day was solemnly fixed in his memory for solemn supplication, [which is] observed in all the shops of the city . . . not otherwise than if it had been mandated by the

---

1. Vauchez, *Sainthood in the Later Middle Ages*, 256, table 10.
2. Elliott, *Proving Woman*, 170.

supreme pontiff."[3] The idea that someone could be canonized in the people's eyes if not the pope's caused some institutional concern. The Franciscan chronicler Salimbene de Adam criticized what he perceived to be the credulity of Italian communities, claiming, "For no man's relics are supposed to be held in reverence unless he is first approved of by the Church and written in the catalogue of saints . . . [;] thus it is that a sinner or an infirm man goes badly astray by casting aside true saints and by praying to one who cannot intercede for him."[4] The only "true" saints for Salimbene were those whom popes canonized in accordance with new thirteenth-century directives. Outside observers, such as the English chronicler Matthew Paris, claimed that citizens of Italian towns were "semi-Christians" (semi-Christiani) for their veneration of unauthorized saints and seeming dismissal of institutional regulations about pious behavior.[5]

The many saints' cults in the later Middle Ages that failed to achieve official recognition resulted from changes in the canonization process rather than from the types of individuals that Italian communities chose to venerate or what traditional signs communities identified as holy. The papal bureaucracy expanded in the thirteenth century and instituted regulations on how the Christian laity should behave, outlined criteria to assess holiness, and decreed that popes had the ultimate say in assigning sainthood. Changes to the canonization process coincided with urban growth in Italy and the spread of the *vita apostolica*. This reform movement encouraged individual expressions of piety that were harder to regulate but captured the attention of members of the laity and some clergy. People embraced new saintly contenders, many from the male lay population, whom papal representatives viewed as unworthy due to their profession, activities, or ideology about how to live a virtuous life. The papacy's and the people's standards for sainthood no longer coincided. Popes nominally tolerated new local cults because there was not enough evidence for outright discouragement. This very veneration, however, was a challenge to papal authority through an indifference to papal authorization. It also constituted a conscious self-assertion in the prerogative of citizens and their local clerical representatives—bishops—to create saints.

Miracles and the Bureaucratization of Sanctity

André Vauchez's seminal *Sainthood in the Later Middle Ages*, the essays in the recent collection edited by Gábor Klaniczay, *Medieval Canonization Processes*,

---

3. Bernardino Scardeonio, *vita* of Anthony Peregrinus, *AASS* I, February 1, col. 265. All translations are my own unless otherwise noted.

4. *Chronicle of Salimbene de Adam*, 512–13.

5. Paris, *Chronica Maiora*, 170.

and Robert Bartlett's new sweeping study, *Why Can the Dead Do Such Great Things?*, all describe thirteenth-century changes to the canonization process and facets of Christian devotion.[6] The following brief overview is the foundation for the argument that these bureaucratic changes helped to produce a number of unauthorized saints, that in Italy many of these cults were for charitably minded laymen, and that these tolerated cults functioned to unify citizens without concerns about papal approval, which had repercussions for more controversial cults. In short, circa 1200 the papacy sought to establish itself as the sole authority for canonizing saints, divesting bishops of a role they had formerly possessed. Before the twelfth century, when a local community achieved a majority consensus that an individual was worthy of veneration, the bishop would investigate and, if he determined the person's holiness was genuine, would confer the title of saint with the ritualized translation of the new saint's relics. Diocesan canonizations were standard and usually based on the *vox popoli*, the voice of the people.[7] While popes in this early period ratified cults, the first formal pontifical canonization of a saint did not occur until 993, for Ulric of Augsburg. According to André Vauchez, the verb *canonizare* was not used until 1016 and then only infrequently until the middle of the twelfth century.[8] Papal canonization was not the only or even the primary route to official sanctity in the first millennium of Christianity.

This process changed in the latter half of the twelfth century as the papacy centralized its administration and established itself as the sole authority for canonizing saints. Pope Alexander III decreed in 1173 that people could venerate only saints whom the church recognized, even if others seemed to perform miracles. In 1200 Pope Innocent III confirmed this decision in a papal bull.[9] The new emphasis on papal canonizations required the implementation of a new evaluative procedure. In the wake of the Fourth Lateran Council (1215) the papacy adopted the inquisitorial procedure from Roman law, the *inquisitio*, to adjudicate canonization and inquisitorial inquiries (discussed in chapter 2). Its purpose was to discern between the holy and the ordinary, the ordinary and the heretical, and the holy and the heretical.[10] This investigatory

---

6. Vauchez, *Sainthood in the Later Middle Ages*, 33–58; Klaniczay, *Medieval Canonization Processes: Legal and Religious Aspects*; and Bartlett, *Why Can the Dead Do Such Great Things?*, 57–84.

7. Molinari, "Saints and Miracles," 291.

8. Vauchez, *Sainthood in the Later Middle Ages*, 22. Scholars debate the exact process and when the papacy officially asserted the supreme authority for canonizations; see Kuttner, "La réserve papale"; cf. Kemp, *Canonization and Authority in the Western Church*, 99–104.

9. Innocent III, *Cum secundum*, 3. IV. 1200, in Petersohn, "Die Litterae Papst Innocenz III."

10. Blaher, *Ordinary Processes in Causes of Beatification and Canonization.* For the similarities between canonization and inquisitorial processes, see Cazanave, "Aveu et contrition," and Elliott, *Proving Woman*, 119–79.

technique mandated more exacting criteria and rigorous judicial guidelines, requiring skilled investigators to question witnesses. Miracles were still a crucial component for determining sanctity, although there were now stricter standards. Popes required evidence of posthumous miracles to ensure that they came from divine power rather than human sleight of hand, sensory misjudgment, or diabolical agency. From the reign of Pope Innocent III forward, a saint also had to exhibit *virtus morum*—or the "heroic virtues" of faith, hope, charity, prudence, temperance, and justice—to help substantiate the evidence of miracles.[11]

Other new requirements for sainthood made papal authorization harder to achieve. The existence of a local cult was no longer enough. The prospective saint's reputation, or *fama*, had to be widespread, with devotees that transcended the geographic bounds of one region. The odds were de jure stacked against a local saint obtaining papal recognition, and de facto it was even more difficult, since the new regulations and procedures made the canonization process very expensive and time consuming. The procedure required that communities gather necessary documentation and hire a procurator to initiate a canonization inquiry, which took time, money, and resources many communities in war-torn late medieval Italy did not have at their disposal.[12] Representatives had to travel to the papal seat, a difficult undertaking particularly in the fourteenth century when popes resided in Avignon. Moreover, if a new pope was elected during this process, as often occurred in the late thirteenth century, the petition had to begin anew. Many saints therefore failed to achieve official endorsement because the process faltered on account of the prohibitive cost, demanding criteria, and time and effort it took to complete. In other cases, communities voluntarily neglected to pursue a canonization process because of these same considerations or because they still relied on their own judgment rather than on the new interrogatory methods that led to papal recognition. Saints' cults were also at the mercy of the larger political scene, as the following factors (addressed in detail in later chapters) demonstrate. Frequent wars meant frequent promotion of different, new saintly contenders as towns searched for the most effective holy protector. A proliferation of requests from a single town could suggest an undiscerning approach and lessen the

---

11. Weinstein and Bell, *Saints and Society*, 141–43. Pope Innocent III was the first to require both a virtuous life and the performance of miracles in his bull of 12 January 1199 canonizing Homobonus of Cremona (Hageneder and Haidacher, *Die Register Innocenz' III*, 1:762; see Goodich, *Vita Perfecta*, 23). Evidence of the heroic virtues was not standardized until the early seventeenth century in the *Caelestis Hierusalem cives* of Pope Urban VIII, 5 July 1634 (*Bullarum diplomatum et privilegiorum sanctorum*, 436–40). On distinguishing the diabolical, see Dinzelbacher, *Heilige oder Hexen?*, and Kieckhefer, "Holy and the Unholy."

12. Vauchez, *Sainthood in the Later Middle Ages*, 64–70.

overall chances for canonization for any candidate. In addition, if the cult was in a town that had rebelled against the forces of the papacy or a pope perceived its government to be an opponent of his authority, the saint could become tainted by association and the continued existence of his or her previously tolerated cult put in jeopardy.

Many regional saints consequently failed to achieve official authorization. This fact did not deter towns from deciding an individual merited veneration and promoting a cult of an uncanonized saint. Citizens did not scrutinize sanctity in the same way as the papacy. saint placed great value on their own personal knowledge of the saint and experience of his or her powers. A consensus on a prospective saint's merits had previously galvanized episcopal canonizations. Communities thus viewed the new pontifical canonization process, in the words of André Vauchez, "as . . . largely superfluous procedures, since, in their eyes, the result was known in advance."[13] From citizens' perspective, a papal canonization merely confirmed the community's assessment of who was worthy of veneration. The power to evaluate and designate sainthood remained in the control of those who knew the saint best: those who had observed his or her virtues in life and experienced his or her miracles.

Miracles were an essential factor for the obstinacy that communities showed in their devotion to a local but unauthorized cult. Peter Brown argued that during the twelfth century medieval society's relations with the supernatural world changed. Formerly, supernatural phenomena had reflected the "objectified values" of the community, such as in the use of trial by ordeal. A shift occurred in the twelfth century, whereby the interaction between humans and the spiritual world no longer represented the ethical and judicial standards of a communal consensus; instead it became imbued with subjective meaning.[14] Yet miracles of personal intercession, particularly miraculous cures of illnesses that had flummoxed earthly doctors, had always articulated the concerns of individuals. Miracles, many of them thaumaturgic, had been the foundation for diocesan canonizations in Christianity's first millennium. Posthumous miracles were critical for later papal canonizations as well, but proving to the pope that one had occurred that could meet the burden of proof of the new *inquisitio* was no easy task. By the thirteenth century, a commission of cardinals or other papal curates examined a canonization dossier of testimony that included witnesses to the prior affliction and

---

13. Ibid., 99. On the process and power of communal consensus, see Kleinberg, "Proving Sanctity," 191–97.

14. Brown, "Society and the Supernatural," 325.

the miraculous cure. The panel would scour statements for contradictions and assess the veracity of the witness accounts. Not even the miracles of such popular royal saints as Louis IX were exempt from exacting eyes. Successfully substantiating a miracle became even more difficult in the fourteenth century.[15] In contrast, an individual supplicant's personal experience of a miraculous cure was, for him or her, a simple and obvious sign of sanctity.

Although manifested through the corporeal, the healing power of the saint fulfilled a genuine spiritual function: to dispense God's grace on those who most needed his aid. It is not surprising that miracles of healing became the mainstay of saintly intercession.[16] The limited capacity of humoral theory for understanding the transmission and prevention of disease, as well as the dearth of investigative dissections to understand the internal mechanisms of the human body, ensured that a significant portion of the population suffered from some type of illness in the Middle Ages.[17] Furthermore, from the late thirteenth century forward, universities curtailed the activities of local midwives and healers as physicians attempted to obtain complete control over the profession.[18] As a result, the treatment options for various afflictions rapidly narrowed in the late Middle Ages, while the ability of physicians to heal illnesses did not substantively progress. As Patrick Geary noted, the thaumaturgical saint "provided the point of contact between mundane existence and the divine world . . . [and] provided the only recourse against the myriad ills, physical, material, and psychic, of a population defenseless before an incomprehensible and terrifying universe."[19] In such a setting, for many people miraculous cures were the decisive factor in establishing holiness.

Local saints renowned for performing healing miracles were thus in high demand. When Peter Crisci died in 1323 the number of people who congregated at the church of San Feliciano in Foligno hoping he would bless them with a healing miracle delayed his burial for several days.[20] The commune of Treviso attested that after Henry of Bolzano died, "[when] a cleric of the cathedral went to move his body, so many people crowded inside, that one was hardly able to exit the room: [the body] was followed through the street by

---

15. Vauchez, *Sainthood in the Later Middle Ages*, 481–98.

16. Weinstein and Bell, *Saints and Society*, 143–44.

17. Carlino, *Books of the Body*, 5; French, *Dissection and Vivisection*, 35; Green, "Integrative Medicine"; Jacquart, "Medical Scholasticism," 212; Katherine Park, "Life of the Corpse."

18. *Chartularium universitatis Parisiensis* (Paris: Delalain, 1889–1897), 1:488–90, translated in Thorndike, *University Records and Life*, 83–85. The king enforced the restriction by publishing his own royal ordinance at the behest of Paris's faculty of medicine in 1352 (*Chartularium universitatis Parisiensis*, 3:16–17; Thorndike, *University Records and Life*, 235–36).

19. Geary, *Furta Sacra*, 22.

20. Gorini, "Beati Petri de Fulgineo Confessoris," 369.

many, who through his intercession then were liberated of various infirmities."[21] Healing miracles comprised a rough average of 68 percent of all miracles in eighteen canonization processes between 1201 and 1417 (75 percent from 1201 to 1300 and 61 percent from 1301 to 1417). That number rises to an average of 84.75 percent (90.2 percent in the first period and 79.3 percent in the second) when including healing of mental illness and help with fertility and birth.[22] The lists of miracles appended to the *vitae* of uncanonized local saints display a similar concern. In many of these instances, the recipients of the miracles stressed that they had first gone to a succession of doctors. This testimony sought to address the new canonization standards, but it also signaled that the miracle was "beyond the powers of nature," demonstrating that medieval society recognized a hierarchy of treatment.[23] Patients first sought the advice of the local physician; when these knowledgeable individuals failed, people turned to a regional holy man or woman. For instance, when a horse ran over the foot of the son of a certain Iohannes Albertini Pegoloti, resulting in bleeding that would not cease, Anthony Peregrinus healed the boy three days after the latter had gone to the saint's tomb and vowed to serve him. The vow was necessary since "medicines brought about nothing, human remedies were worth nothing."[24] When the Cistercian abbot of the monastery of St. Columba in Piacenza, who had "both reverence of age and sanctity of life, [and was] venerable and rich," suffered from an abscess that doctors could not heal, he too turned to Anthony Peregrinus. God, "who is the true and good doctor," worked through Anthony and freed the monk of his ailment.[25] The Cistercian abbot ultimately found recourse through a saint of a nascent cult after trying earthly cures and presumably praying to traditional saints and ones connected to his order. In another example, a woman named Ziliana had suffered a painful abscess on her foot for fourteen years, which seven doctors could not heal. Ziliana finally appealed to Facio of Cremona. Facio told her to bandage her foot and not to accept any medicine, only God's grace. He cured her by making the sign of the cross and blowing on her feet.[26] Thus it was the saint alone who was able to heal when all human intervention failed.

Moreover, new saints could be particularly responsive to intercessory prayers. The supplicant's emotional outpouring of faith and the spiritual, and at times physical, hardship he or she endured during the process of petitioning

---

21. *Riti*, proc. 3021 (Henry of Bolzano, 1768), article 8, p. 40 (contemporary pagination).
22. Vauchez, *Sainthood in the Later Middle Ages*, 468, table 31.
23. Bartlett, *Natural and the Supernatural*, 11–12.
24. Sicco Polenton, "Vita Beati Antonii Peregrini," 423.
25. Ibid., 424.
26. Vauchez, "Sainteté laïque aux XIIIe siècle," 44.

could forge a personal partnership between the saint and supplicant and establish mutual ties of dependency. Thomas Head noted the similarities between the contractual nature of feudalism and the bond between saints and their devotees in eleventh-century Francia and the Holy Roman Empire.[27] Thirteenth-century Italian cities differed greatly from the rural French villages that were the setting for Head's study. The political and social arrangements usually referred to as feudal relationships were never the prevailing system in Italy.[28] Nonetheless, social bonds based on pledges of fidelity and promises of service in return for protection remained an integral facet of urban life, present in the relationship between a merchant and his traveling assistant, or a master and his apprentice, or the *capitano del popolo* and the people of his commune. Although the historical context was different, the oath of loyalty to the saint was the foundational avowal of service, expressing the supplicant's intense need for protection and the safeguarding of his or her health. In return, the devotee lobbied for the saint's holiness and defended his or her *fama* against detractors by attesting to the efficacy of the person's miracles.

Several examples illustrate the saint-supplicant relationship in Italian urban centers and the importance of a public performance of faith to receive a miraculous response. The process of supplication usually comprised a journey to the saint's shrine, a vow made to the postulant saint and to God, and offerings such as candles or wax images.[29] Benvenuta from Mestre (near Venice), whose left side was paralyzed, traveled to Anthony Peregrinus's sepulchre in Padua to enlist his aid. After this pilgrimage her full motor skills returned.[30] A certain Albertinus of Parma from the noble Palaciola family, studying law at the university of Padua, rapidly failed in his studies when "he lost [his] speech and the use of either of his hands" due to a nerve problem. After he made a vow and presented wax statues to "God and Peregrinus," however, he regained his health.[31] Armanno Pungilupo (d. 1269) relieved the soldier Marinellus of gout after Marinellus undertook a vigil in front of Armanno's tomb all Christmas Day, "right up to after nones humbly and devoutly and supplicating God, so that He should free him by the merits of blessed Armanno from the gout which held him, and in the hour of the ringing of the bell for divine office he

27. Head, *Hagiography and the Cult of the Saints*, 151. Cf. Peter Brown, who saw the relationship between saint and supplicant as more one-sided: "The saint's power held the individual in a tight bond of personal obligation" (Brown, *Cult of the Saints*, 118).

28. Foote, *Lordship, Reform, and the Development*, 30–34; and Wickham, *Mountains and the City*, chap. 11.

29. Vauchez, *Sainthood in the Later Middle Ages*, 453–62.

30. Polenton, "Vita Beati Antonii Peregrini," 423.

31. Ibid., 422.

perceived himself without the usual pain of the ankles and hips and legs."[32] Ritualized pilgrimages and vigils showed the sincerity of the intercessory plea and cemented the personal bond between saint and supplicant.

Two stories from the *vitae* of tolerated saints illustrate a specifically contractual nature of the supplicant-saint relationship that resonates with a "cost-benefit analysis" of intercession that prevailed in later medieval Italian *miracula*.[33] Mathaeus gained Facio of Cremona as his personal protector through the usual process of supplication. Suffering from a grave illness, Mathaeus sought Facio, who was considered holy prior to his death. Mathaeus was healed and became a devotee. Some years later he required another thaumaturgical miracle. Once again healed, "brother Mathaeus, with his entire will along with all his kin, was converted to God on account of this miracle, and afterwards he stayed faithful right up to his death."[34] Mathaeus became Facio's faithful servant with "his entire will" only after two miraculous demonstrations. Mathaeus pledged not only his own loyalty but that of "all his kin," thereby publicizing the saint's merits and expanding the circle of devotees. After he committed himself to Facio's service in perpetuity, Mathaeus followed the holy man across Europe on pilgrimages to holy sites for eighteen years. Facio, in turn, became Mathaeus's patron and protector, again miraculously saving him, this time from shipwreck, on two further occasions.

The account of Petrus, a devotee of Armanno Pungilupo, delineates the potential quid pro quo nature of these relationships. Petrus's left side had been paralyzed for two years when he heard of Armanno's death. As soon as the canons of the cathedral had formally translated his body to the cathedral for burial, Petrus immediately went to the saint's tomb "and offered to him his likeness in wax in the same place and [the vow that] for one year he would serve him in ringing his bells."[35] Armanno subsequently freed Petrus from his affliction in response to this promise. Petrus's swift recognition that Armanno could be a saint suggested desperation and an overwhelming desire to be healed. More importantly for unauthorized cults, the episode reveals that both parties were to benefit: Petrus's pledge to the saint had a price. Petrus expected that if he served Armanno by ringing his bells, his health would be restored in recompense. But the ties between saint and supplicant could be conditional in Italian urban life, or at least could be contractually limited: Petrus placed a time limit of one year on his bell-ringing service. After that period, or presumably if his health deteriorated, Petrus could withdraw from his devotion, for

---

32. *Itinerari*, 74.
33. For the term, see Camp, "The Sunday Saint," 46–47.
34. Vauchez, "Sainteté laïque aux XIIIe siècle," 47.
35. *Itinerari*, 80.

Armanno would have broken the contract. The condition that Petrus placed upon his loyalty perhaps also reflects ambivalence about the authenticity of Armanno's sanctity. According to the testimony of several local mendicants, there were rumors that Armanno had been a relapsed heretic (chapter 2).[36] Petrus may not have wanted to forge an indissoluble bond with a person who might turn out not to be one of God's elect. In this case, however, both sides fulfilled their promise of mutual aid. Petrus regained his health and testified to that fact before the canons of Ferrara, who were sponsoring Armanno's canonization. Armanno granted Petrus a miracle in return for his supplication and service, and Petrus promoted the sanctity of Armanno by affirming that he was indeed holy.

The demonstration of miraculous power did not just create a relationship between the saint and one devotee but was the foundation for establishing a community of believers.[37] The miracle functioned as a symbolic rite of passage in which the postulant saint experienced a change in status if the community came to a consensus that the miracles were in fact valid. A successful repackaging of the history of a newly recognized saint provided the community with a valuable patron. If a town achieved a consensus that went unchallenged by popes or inquisitors, the saint's cult could provide it with monetary benefits, social prestige, and spiritual patronage (chapter 5). A flourishing cult helped to unify the community by prompting ritual devotion on a larger scale. This course of events did not always occur, for citizens of medieval Italy were not indiscriminate in their choice of saints. Sometimes miracles were witnessed by a numerically insignificant proportion of the population. On other occasions the evidence for holiness rested upon the postulant saint's virtues rather than miraculous occurrences. In these situations, a resolution could only occur when members of the community proselytized on the individual's behalf. If successful, the result was a devotional cult around a new locally venerated saint. If they did not achieve a consensus, the process of negotiation could begin anew with a different prospective saint. Since local saints articulated the community's spiritual needs and were a repository of its conceptions of the holy, the stakes were high. In this way, the subjective relationship of the individual informed the objective values of the community in the later Middle Ages.

While miracles were the foundation for late medieval official canonizations, there were several factors that limited their efficacy for official sanctification. Healing miracles were individual, personal occurrences, not experienced by a

---

36. *Itinerari*, 48–49.
37. Weinstein and Bell, *Saints and Society*, 145.

multitude or those in an official investigatory capacity, such as cardinals and curial insiders. While both communities and the papacy adhered to similar notions of the importance of posthumous miracles, the shift in the canonization procedure created a point of divergence between the traditional communal recognition of a saint and the new papal requirements: the personal experience of the supplicant and communal consensus that the miracles had occurred, as opposed to a judicial decision by an outside party. The saint-supplicant bond was a fundamental part of the customary means of identifying saints and establishing cults. New, papally authorized saints, however, were not supposed to "belong" to an individual or town. Their holiness was to transcend geographical proximity and exemplify the awesome power of divine grace. For local communities in the thirteenth and fourteenth centuries, the personal experience of miracles that produced a protector and patron trumped papal authorization. This conviction in the value of subjective experience contributed to the many unauthorized cults. Thus miracles themselves served as a main point of contention in the cases of dramatically contested sanctity examined in later chapters.

The Ordinary versus the Extraordinary Saint

A number of local cults emerged in Italy during the same time the papacy was discouraging regional saints. Many of the saints who emerged in Italy between 1200 and 1400 were recently deceased and had lived in the communities that subsequently championed their holiness. Vauchez asserted that the popularity of hyperlocal saints in this period was because people believed holy persons who were temporally and spatially proximate were more accessible.[38] The lives of these individuals were comparable to those of much of the population of northern and central Italy; these were pious yet often seemingly ordinary laypeople. This was in contrast to the more ascetic saints who garnered the attention of high-ranking prelates and curial supporters in the period. In his life of the early thirteenth-century beguine Marie of Oignies (d. 1213), Jacques de Vitry proposed that people should admire rather than imitate saintly behavior.[39] His view, which became the prevailing one, presupposed that true saints were exceptional, disengaged from mundane existence, and released from the normal bounds of conduct. As Richard Kieckhefer's work on

---

38. Vauchez, *Sainthood in the Later Middle Ages*, 133 and 278. See also Kleinberg, *Prophets in Their Own Country*, 1–20; and Zarri, "Living Saints."

39. De Vitry, *The Life of Marie d'Oignies*, 1.12, 54–55.

fourteenth-century saints, *Unquiet Souls*, detailed, the extraordinary nature of sanctity became equated with extreme behavior such as long hours of prayer, rigorous asceticism, constant tears, excessive confession, and habitual reception of the Eucharist.[40] Instead of existing as icons for admiration like the more somatic saints of the period, humble laypersons of Italian towns provided a model for imitation and offered hope for the salvation of the average man or woman.

This fact appears to be at the crux of both these saints' appeal and their failure to attain canonization. Contemporary lay saints did not conform to the papacy's criteria for sainthood: they were too "ordinary" for official recognition and seemingly too plebeian and secular as well. Of the thirty-five individuals whom popes officially canonized between 1198 and 1431, the postulants of choice were bishops, members of royal families, and well-educated mendicants.[41] Popes only canonized two lay saints not directly related to royalty: Homobonus of Cremona (d. 1197, canonized 1199) at the extreme early boundary of this study, and Elzéar of Sabran (d. 1323, canonized 1369).[42] Homobonus had a conversion experience after which he dedicated his life fully to the contemplation of God, although he never joined a clerical order. His rejection of the world differentiates him from most of the lay saints that emerged in the two centuries after his death who, in contrast, continued to participate in civic life. His eremitical proclivity helps to explain the anomaly of his papal canonization. Elzéar was from the ruling elite and became the Baron of Ansouis and the Count of Ariano. His experience as a powerful lord, albeit a pious one who became a Franciscan tertiary and yearned for the monastic life, seems to place him within either the royal or mendicant canonization trajectory.

Many local cults in later medieval Italy formed around laymen of modest means from the artisan class who became involved in charitable pursuits even after a conversion experience. Despite Jacques de Vitry's warning, members of Italian towns preferred saints with whom they could identify as products of a similar social background. The booming success of the Italian cities before the onset of the Black Death in 1348 produced a number of rich merchants

---

40. Kieckhefer, *Unquiet Souls*, 14 and 120; see also the case studies on pp. 21–49. See Vauchez, *Sainthood in the Later Middle Ages*, 190–92, on the rise in ascetic or penitential saints in Italy; see also Weinstein and Bell, *Saints and Society*, 73–86.

41. Vauchez, *Sainthood in the Later Middle Ages*, 249–84.

42. Ibid., table 18, 264. To this perhaps could be added Sebald, an eleventh-century Franconian saint canonized in 1425 whose biography is shrouded in mystery but for whom there was a tradition he was descended from the king of Denmark. Catherine of Siena's canonization process opened in the early fifteenth century, but she was not canonized until 1461, outside the chronological boundary of Vauchez's typology.

whose wealth and importance rivaled that of the nobility. This wealth depended upon the artisans, laborers, and minor tradesmen who provided merchants with materials and were the basis for the economic survival of these communities. The emergence of saints from this latter group directly relates to the expanding numbers of individuals in this social stratum. Thus the thirteenth and fourteenth centuries saw a rise in contemporary laypersons from the lesser merchant and artisan classes, such as Albert of Villa d'Ogna, who was a wine porter; Facio of Cremona, who was a goldsmith; Peter Pettinaio (d. 1289), who was a comb merchant; Henry of Bolzano, who worked as a notary; and Asdente of Parma (d. late thirteenth century), who was a shoemaker. Many inhabitants of a city could identify with a saint from the *popolo minuto*, the lesser artisans and merchants, who comprised most of the population in Italian towns. Lay candidates from this demographic were far more popular in northern and central Italy than in other European countries, perhaps due to the urban and mercantile development that the region experienced in the eleventh and twelfth centuries.[43]

When persons who practiced a trade came to be considered holy, they had a built-in support group to champion their cause. For instance, the guild of goldsmiths in Cremona adopted Facio, himself a goldsmith, as its patron.[44] The cult of Albert of Villa d'Ogna, the wine porter, shows how a local cult could emerge because of someone's association with a particular trade, and how those who shared that vocation could benefit from the cult. Albert's veneration spread first among the wine carriers of Parma, who promoted his holiness with the aid of local clerics. The success of this endeavor led the wine carriers themselves to be considered special by virtue of sharing his profession. Salimbene de Adam, who lived in Parma at the time of Albert's death, recorded that following his decease, "all the *brentatores*, that is, the wine carriers of Parma congregated in the church, and blessed was that man who could touch them or give them something."[45] Vocational affinity with a saint engendered a sense of ownership toward a holy person from a certain constituency and became a powerful catalyst for a local cult.

The male lay saint from the artisan class encapsulated the belief that God could bestow his grace on anyone who was morally worthy. Sainthood was not limited to royalty, the rich and powerful, or members of the ecclesiastical orders, providing hope that God did not discriminate against His more humble petitioners. These local saints made manifest the ideal that the meek truly

---

43. Vauchez, *Sainthood in the Later Middle Ages*, table 6, 184.

44. Vauchez, "Sainteté laïque aux XIIIe siècle," 20.

45. *Chronicle of Salimbene de Adam*, 512; for discussion, see Little, *Indispensible Immigrants*, 23–32.

could inherit the earth merely by living a pious life as a "witness" to God, a powerful message in the hierarchical society of the Middle Ages.[46] It would be a mistake, however, to construe these cults as the products of a Marxist class struggle. Just because the *popolo* supported a saint from within their ranks does not mean that the citizens of a town identified themselves as a socioeconomic "class" and sought to overturn the power structure. The cults of new saints were to exist alongside those of the town's older, traditional saints, who were mostly of noble extraction. There are also some exceptions to the above generalizations: Anthony Peregrinus was from the nobility of Padua; Amato Ronconi (d. circa 1266 or 1292) was from a wealthy family of Saludecio and a Franciscan tertiary; and Parisio of Treviso (d. 1267) was not a layman but a Camaldolese monk.[47] In addition, the local clerical support these saints garnered makes it difficult to regard their cults as a direct challenge to the papacy's preference for canonizing notable and noble mendicants, bishops, and royalty.

Perhaps the most significant reason why these individuals had such appeal, one that spoke to clerical and lay members of an Italian community alike, was that the thirteenth- and fourteenth-century local saint was overwhelmingly an active member of the community who lived fully "in the world." One common theme that hagiographers stressed was the act of pilgrimage. Anthony Peregrinus, as his name suggests, made several journeys to Jerusalem, Santiago de Compostela, and Rome; Facio of Cremona traveled to various churches in Italy and Spain; and Albert of Villa d'Ogna had been on pilgrimage.[48] The purpose of this *topos* was to emphasize the piety and humility of the saint, but it also reveals a particular concept of holiness. These individuals were candidates for sainthood because they were active participants in society, living in the world rather than removed from it. This characteristic is even clearer in the emphasis given to performing good works that benefited the community, such as easing factional strife, donating money and goods to churches, and establishing charitable institutions.

There are many examples of charitably minded or socially active sanctity. Ambruogio of Siena (d. 1287) helped to reconcile his town with the papacy after Guelph partisans assassinated the bishop.[49] Facio tried to ease tensions between his birthplace of Verona and the rival town where he settled, Cremona.[50] Their

---

46. Ranft, "Concept of Witness."

47. *AASS* I, February 1, col. 265A. Anthony Peregrinus may have also joined the Camaldolese of Sta. Maria di Porcilia as an oblate after his peregrinations (Goodich, *Vita Perfecta*, 195). For Amato, see *Riti*, proc. 89 (Amato Ronconi, 1733–1734); for Parisio, see *AASS* II, June 11, col. 484D; for Italian Camaldolese saints in the late Middle Ages, see Vauchez, *Sainthood in the Later Middle Ages*, 193–94.

48. *AASS* I, February 1, col. 264F; *AASS* II, January 18, col. 211; *AASS* II, May 7, col. 281B.

49. *Cronache Senesi*, 71.

50. Vauchez, "Sainteté laïque aux XIIIe siècle," 37.

actions demonstrate an active political conscience, prompting actions that would help to heal communal divisiveness and the negative economic, social, and spiritual effects of war. Charitable activities are another venue for this performative holiness. Albert of Villa d'Ogna, for instance, gave all he had to the poor.[51] Amato Ronconi founded a hospital for pilgrims.[52] One of Peter Crisci's disciples named Cecco of Pesaro (d. 1350) restored churches and founded the confraternity of Santa Maria d'Annunziata in Pesaro.[53] Facio of Cremona worked tirelessly to help his adopted town of Cremona. As a goldsmith he crafted items for poor churches in the area and he established the charitable confraternity of the Fratres de Consorti Sancti Spiritus. Facio also visited incarcerated citizens, consoled the ill and exhorted them to have patience, and received and fed poor pilgrims.[54] André Vauchez observed in his discussion of Facio's life that what distinguished Facio—and the majority of the other holy persons discussed here—from Homobonus of Cremona, the only lay saint not of the nobility to achieve canonization in the later Middle Ages, is that Facio continued to work after his conversion experience.[55] While Homobonus dedicated himself to a spiritual life that had no room for professional activities, Facio and other later saints like him used their skills in the name of God for the benefit of the community.

The personal spirituality of these saints also would have been familiar to many citizens. Rather than exhibiting extreme behavior that would have immediately made them exceptional figures in society, their expressions of spirituality were quite restrained. The hagiographers of Facio of Cremona, for instance, were hard-pressed to include concrete examples of Facio's asceticism, despite their claims he led an austere life. Both of his *vitae* merely note in passing that Facio spent his days and nights in prayer.[56] The *vita* of Peter Crisci of Foligno depicts him as showing merely a moderate amount of asceticism, yet with somewhat more rigor than other local saints, as befitted his final years as an anchorite attached to the church of S. Feliciano in Foligno. He repudiated doctors, even during his final illness, because Christ had appeared to Crisci and assured him that he would go to Heaven eight days hence.[57] Otherwise, the hagiographer claimed, Crisci confessed often, habitually cried in compunction, and flagellated himself in penitence.[58]

---

51. *AASS* II, May 7, col. 281B.

52. *Riti*, proc. 89 (Amato Ronconi, 1733–1734), f. 17v.

53. *AASS* I, August 3, 660C–662D.

54. Vauchez, "Sainteté laïque aux XIIIe siècle," 39.

55. Ibid., 30.

56. *AASS* II, January 18, col. 211; Vauchez, "Sainteté laïque aux XIIIe siècle," 39.

57. Gorini, "Beati Petri de Fulgineo Confessoris," 366.

58. *AASS* IV, July 19, col. 665E and 667C.

As discussed above, miracles were the primary sign of holiness and the cement that bound the local saint and his or her supplicants. Unsurprisingly, in the *vitae* of lay saints there are a high proportion of thaumaturgical miracles to the exclusion of almost all other types of supernatural intercession. Every single one of Anthony Peregrinus's miracles exhibited his healing powers.[59] All but two of Armanno Pungilupo's were miraculous cures, as were most of Parisio of Treviso's and Henry of Bolzano's. Papally canonized saints also exhibited healing powers, but the *vitae* of tolerated saints focus on these to the exclusion of almost any other supernatural performance. Occasionally this curative faculty extended to healing the soul from demonic possessions, as it did with Armanno (two miracles), Facio (two miracles), and Peter Crisci (an unknown number).[60] In contrast, while power over the elements is a recurring theme in the lives of canonized saints, only Facio's *vita* describes an ability to control nature (three miracles).[61] Prophetic miracles also occur in tiny numbers; Peter Crisci foresaw his death (albeit through his vision of Christ, arguably the true miracle), and Facio predicted peace between his birthplace of Verona and his adopted town of Cremona.[62] The miracles of these new local saints were not those that emphasized the glory of the saint as one of God's chosen elect, such as by overcoming severe physical hardship, the power of clairvoyance, or the ability to control nature. Rather, just like the actions of these saints during their lifetimes focused on helping the poor and needy, so too did their miracles after death center upon aiding the sick and infirm citizens of their communities. The miracles of these lay contemporary saints demonstrate that the citizens preferred saints whose acts benefited members of their own community.

Paradoxically, healing miracles did not do much to persuade authorities, since they could be faked or be misinterpretations of physical processes. Other holy signs went further to convince popes that a particular saint was extraordinary or different.[63] Manifestations like the "odor of sanctity" or an unearthly radiance from the putative saint's corpse were stronger evidence of God's favor, since he gave the saint's remains the power to defy normal human lim-

---

59. Polenton, "Vita Beati Antonii Peregrini"; "Miracula Beati Antonii Peregrini."

60. Peter Crisci's *vita* only states "liberantur demoniaci" (Gorini, "Beatri Petri de Fulgineo Confessoris," 369). All of these examples are of freeing women from demons. For the belief in women's propensity toward possession, see Caciola, *Discerning Spirits*, 130–35, and Newman, "Possessed by the Spirit," 733–70.

61. Facio's fifty or so postmortem miracles are in the "Vita Beati Facii," Cremona, Archivio di Stato di Cremona, Archivio di Santa Maria della Pietà, sez. Iᵃ, cass. 11, ff. 16v–33v.

62. Gorini, "Beati Petri de Fulgineo Confessoris," 366–67; Vauchez, "Sainteté laïque aux XIIIe siècle," 38.

63. Weinstein and Bell, *Saints and Society*, 143.

itations.[64] Of the saints here discussed, only Peter Crisci's body underwent this kind of change. His hagiographer described that "he appeared shining in body after death, because more and more often he had been speaking with God in the sphere of the sun . . . from which a wonderful odor in such a manner and so greatly breathed forth from his most holy body."[65] Overwhelmingly, however, these signs of sanctity were absent for local saints, which distinguishes them from their papally sanctioned counterparts. Instead of God's grace being manifested by visible signs on the body of the saint, the *vitae* emphasize that God revealed his grace through the charitable and personal impact of the local saint on the citizens of the saint's town.

In sum, the local saint was a pious individual with a social conscience. His or her support came from the *popolo* and the secular clergy who wanted to claim the individual as the patron of the prospective saint's adopted or birth city. For example, the commune and bishop of Treviso jointly requested canonization inquiries for both Parisio of Treviso and Henry of Bolzano, requests that popes did not grant. Notwithstanding the popularity of local saints, their ordinary characteristics and utilitarian qualities often undercut their candidacy as postulants for official sainthood. The ostensible mediocrity of these men led popes and the prelates who heard of their cult or examined their *vitae* to view them as unworthy of an official inquiry, as occurred, for instance, for Peter Crisci, Facio of Cremona, and Anthony Peregrinus, as well as for Henry of Bolzano and Parisio of Treviso. In a real if limited sense, their holiness became disputed. Members of communities, believing in the efficacy of their patron saints, refused to accept the detractors of their holy intercessors. They continued to venerate their saints, believing (as did the hagiographer of Anthony Peregrinus) that although the pope had not canonized them on earth, Jesus had received them into the catalog of saints in heaven. While communities continued to view these persons' charitable and pious deeds as venerable, thus creating a new existence for them as extraordinary examples of Christian perfection, late medieval popes saw only ordinary piety at work.

Gender, the *Vita Apostolica*, and Unregulated Penitents

Two distinct characteristics emerge from the overview above: many unauthorized local saints traveled and lived the life of a penitent outside, or only

---

64. Ibid., 149–50; Vauchez, *Sainthood in the Later Middle Ages*, 427.
65. Gorini, "Beati Petri de Fulgineo Confessoris," 369.

loosely tied to, the institutional church, and they were largely male. The second trait helps to explain the first. The religious fervor termed the *vita apostolica* that spread across Europe in the twelfth century and became exemplified in the early thirteenth century in the establishment of the Franciscan Order, among other mendicant orders, called for a penitential life of wandering, begging, and preaching to live like the apostles. Both society and the church strongly dissuaded or explicitly prohibited women from doing these activities, and so they were restricted in how they could take part in an apostolic life. Clare of Assisi (d. 1253), St. Francis's intimate, fought to provide her community of Poor Ladies with the strict avowal of poverty that the *vita apostolica* demanded, finally receiving papal approval on her deathbed in 1253. It was the only concession; the Rule of St. Clare had strict injunctions for a cloistered and silent existence.[66] This differed greatly from the new Franciscan Rule, the *Regula bullata*, which Pope Honorius IV confirmed in 1223 and provided for an itinerant existence and a life of begging, not just receiving alms, for Francis's male followers.[67] Tolerated local saints in later medieval Italy predominantly were either laymen who lacked mendicant support because of their unregulated activities outside of a rule, or laywomen with mendicant spiritual directors who sponsored their cults.

Paradoxically, it is perhaps the institutionalization of the Franciscans and the Dominicans, and their consequent negotiation of how to remain within the apostolic tradition, that led communities to focus their attention on members of the laity who seemed to have a more unadulterated understanding of the *vita apostolica*. In his seminal work *Religious Movements in the Middle Ages*, Herbert Grundmann posited that the mendicant orders "became rich and powerful, withdrawing from the world in all too monastic a manner to satisfy the religious forces and needs of the laity. . . . The threatening growth of heresy . . . only becomes understandable through this disavowal by the new orders, which alienated them from the religious movement which had given them birth."[68] Both the Franciscans and Dominicans faced challenges

---

66. See "The Rule of Saint Clare," esp. chaps. 1, 6, and 8, in Armstrong and Brady, *Francis and Clare*; see also the introductory notes on pp. 209–25. Catherine M. Mooney traces this "resistance" of Clare and other penitent women to a church trying to regulate them in *Clare of Assisi*; see also Knox, "Audacious Nuns."

67. *Regula bullata*, in Armstrong and Brady, *Francis and Clare*, 136–45. The initial acceptance of Pope Innocent III of a proposed manner of life or "primitive rule" in 1209 or 1210 was the justification for Honorius IV's acceptance of the *Regula bullata* in his bull *Soluet annuere* of 1223, although the Fourth Lateran Council had placed a ban on new orders in 1215 (Tanner, *Decrees of the Ecumenical Councils*, vol. 1, canon 13, p. 242). On mendicant spirituality, see Rosenwein and Little, "Social Meaning in the Monastic and Mendicant Spiritualities."

68. Grundmann, *Religious Movements in the Middle Ages*, 226. For a discussion of how the desire to live like the apostles manifested itself in Italy, see Dal Pino, *Il laicato italiano*.

as a result of the institutionalization that their popularity prompted. The Franciscans became embroiled in a controversy over apostolic poverty, leading to a split in the order between a radical reform wing called the Spirituals and the Conventuals, who had a more moderate view of what the order could "possess" and "use."[69] The Dominicans quickly became a primary administrative arm of the papacy as inquisitors, a role that generated much antipathy in the Italian peninsula (chapter 6). It was not until the later fourteenth century that the Dominicans underwent a reform movement under Raymond of Capua that was influenced by a growing mystical tradition, thus revitalizing aspects of its apostolic roots.[70] The mendicant orders thus had become more traditionally "monastic-seeming," or at least institutionalized, during the period of this study.

Outside of the mendicant orders there existed few other authorized avenues to participate in the apostolic mission. Men and women who had the will to live the *vita apostolica*, but not the wherewithal or the desire to join an official order, could become part of the lay alternative to the mendicants as *conversi* or tertiaries. *Conversi*, known as *pinzocheri* or *bizochi* in Italy, were "converts" who voluntarily embarked on living the life of a penitent with no institutional affiliation. Tertiaries were lay member of a tertiary order, also called the mendicant Third Orders. They took limited vows of poverty and chastity in accordance with apostolic ideals, but remained members of the laity and did not live under a specific rule or in a community.[71] They often worked to support themselves and to provide resources for their charitable endeavors. They were frequently indistinguishable from the *conversi*, at least until the first quarter of the fourteenth century.[72] Although the Franciscans and Dominicans theoretically managed the conduct of their tertiaries, in reality many tertiaries seem to have functioned with little official supervision until the very end of the thirteenth century.[73] Many local saints have been identified (with varying degrees of persuasiveness) as members of a Third Order, including Luchesio of Poggibonsi (d. 1260), Novellone of Faenza (d. 1280), Peter Pettinaio, John Pelingotto of Urbino (d. 1304), Amato Ronconi, Peter Crisci, Francis "Cecco" of Pesaro, and Tommasuccio of Nocera (d. 1377). While women could be *conversae*, their existence as tertiaries is often easier to

---

69. For a general history of the Spirituals, see Burr, *Spiritual Franciscans*, and Burr, *Olivi and Franciscan Poverty*.

70. Kieckhefer, *Unquiet Souls*, 48.

71. Prior to 1289, the Third Orders were called the Orders of Penitence. See Meersseman, *Dossier de l'Ordre*; Vauchez, *Laity in the Middle Ages*, 119–27; and Vauchez, "Pénitents au Moyen Âge."

72. Thompson, *Cities of God*, 69–102; and Sensi, "Anchoresses and Penitents."

73. More, "Institutionalizing Penitential Life," 302–3; and Lehmijoki-Gardner, "Dominican Penitent Women."

trace since their male confessors encouraged them to formalize their relationship with a Third Order, as occurred for Umiliana dei Cerchi (d. 1246) and Angela of Foligno (d. 1309). Even for women the distinction between a *conversa* and a tertiary is unclear. Jacques Dalarun persuasively argued that Clare of Rimini (d. 1326) was a *conversa* whom the Franciscans later appropriated and claimed as a member of their Third Order because a friar had been her spiritual director. Other women, such as Seraphina of San Gimignano (d. 1253), became associated with an order because a mendicant later wrote or revised a female saint's *vita*.[74]

Unsanctioned male lay saints realized their spiritual goals by living a meager existence, wandering about, and helping their fellow beings. The only aspect of the mendicant lifestyle barred to them was public preaching, although they could exhort others to live a pious life, as Tommasuccio of Nocera did to his detriment, ultimately rousing the ire of the visiting vicar of the Papal States, whose character he impugned (chapter 2). Their expressions of spirituality took a slightly different form than that of the friars, one that speaks to a heightened social consciousness as outlined above. While both lay penitents and the friars adhered to the apostolic ideal of poverty, the lay penitents who became local saints had particular appeal in their communities for how they embraced their poverty and turned their piety toward helping those in need. Through their charitable activities, these saints focused on the bodies of the involuntary poor—those impoverished through circumstance, not by choice—rather than on saving souls through exhortation. The willingness of these saints to accept their God-given poverty by extension suggested a meaningful existence for anyone who was destitute but still had apostolic fervor.

This characteristic is in contrast to the wealth and power that the mendicant orders came to epitomize. Many of the canonized mendicant saints were born into affluence and had undergone a conversion experience that prompted the distribution of their wealth. One's moral virtues, an important element in the papacy's profile of holy persons, became embodied in the sacrificial act of becoming voluntarily poor.[75] The story of St. Francis immediately conjures up images of this paradigm, when the rich merchant's son stripped naked and

---

74. Benvenuti Papi, "Mendicant Friars and Female Pinzochere." Compare Clare of Rimini's fourteenth-century *vita* to the chronicle of the Franciscan Order written by Mariano of Florence circa 1515 (Dalarun, *"Lapsus linguae": La légende de Claire de Rimini*, 19–54; cf. Mariano of Florence, *Compendium chronicarum ordinis Fratrum Minorum*). Seraphina's main *vita* is by Johannes of San Gimignano, a member of the Dominicans (*AASS* II, March 12, cols. 236C–242E).

75. Kleinberg, *Prophets in Their Own Country*, 126–48; on the lack of a liminal conversion in the *vitae* of female saints, see Bynum, "Women's Stories, Women's Symbols"; cf. Weinstein and Bell, *Saints and Society*, 52.

threw his money into the middle of a piazza.[76] The hagiographer of Elzéar of Sabran, a Franciscan tertiary and the only male lay saint not of royal lineage besides Homobonus to achieve canonization between 1200 and 1400, described him as particularly pious because he had wealth and power that he used for charity.[77] Instead of a transformative experience to the *vita apostolica* that led to a socioeconomic change in status, the majority of local saints were born into poverty or the lesser merchant class and had little opportunity for a dramatic conversion, for it was only the rich who had the ability to show their rejection of wealth by giving it all away.[78] In addition, popes and their agents could view these saints' itinerant existence as an occupational hazard resulting from jobs like wine carrier or comb merchant rather than from a conscious choice. The elision between voluntary and involuntary poverty and itinerancy perhaps helped to eliminate these saints from serious consideration for papal recognition. In contrast, members of Italian communities opted to support cults of individuals whose charity seemed more present and difficult, as it came from a place of continuous poverty yet was tangibly seen and felt in those saints' continued active existence in their towns.

The unmonitored piety of local male lay saints could undermine the authority of the mendicants, reducing the potential for a sanctioned cult. Pope Innocent III's canonization of Homobonus of Cremona could have encouraged devotion to lay saints, but it did not lead to future popes formally recognizing the holiness of later lay candidates. Many later Italian tolerated saints carried out their activities without institutional oversight, even if they were members of a Third Order. This situation contributed to the problem of papal recognition. The lax supervision of tertiaries and the existence of *conversi* outside an institutional order led to concerns about their piety and obedience and, as discussed in the next three chapters, their orthodoxy.[79] Institutionally, the church attempted to tighten control over a flourishing lay spirituality, for instance in the formulation of specific regulations for penitents and the late thirteenth-century requirement that *conversi* must attach themselves to some religious society or order.[80] Under the best of circumstances, popes tolerated

---

76. Thomas of Celano, "First Life of St. Francis," 229–37.

77. *Vita* of Elzéar of Sabran, *AASS* VII, September 27, cols. 576D–577D.

78. Exceptions include Anthony Peregrinus, who spurned his father's wealth, and Peter Crisci, who left his parents' home and distributed all of his goods after he underwent a conversion experience at the age of thirty. On the tendency for wealthy men to remain unmarried at home until their thirties, see Herlihy and Klapisch-Zuber, *Tuscans and Their Families*, 221. For the relationship between money and the apostolic ideal, see Little, *Religious Poverty and the Profit Economy*, 3–18 and 146–70.

79. Goodich, *Vita Perfecta*, 186.

80. Fourth Lateran Council 1215, canon 3, in Tanner, *Decrees of the Ecumenical Councils*, 1:242; Vauchez, *Laity in the Middle Ages*, 119–27.

these lay saints or considered them of suspect spiritual mettle but allowed their cults to continue.

Disputed sanctity as a whole also displayed an interesting gender divide, one in which being a (presumably) superior male became a strike against one for canonization if one was not a cleric. As discussed above, male lay saints did not focus on asceticism as a way to express their devotion to Christ. Their piety was familiar and easily understood because they were not very ascetic. In contrast, many of the "extraordinary" lay saints of the late Middle Ages that garnered papal and mendicant support (if not official canonization) were women.[81] Women sought other avenues to express their religious fervor since they were denied the ability to wander and preach and had little control over personal wealth. As a result, women more often retreated into relative solitude and demonstrated extreme behavior as mystics and ascetics, as Caroline Walker Bynum famously analyzed.[82] Franciscans and Dominicans were the confessors for these female tertiaries or *conversae*. They were thus more firmly under male tutelage than the male saints, and the confessors who recorded their visions and somatic experiences had a vested interest in promoting their cults.[83]

This interpretation may seem contrary to the late medieval narrative of a "feminized" sanctity that is prevalent in Bynum's work and argued in André Vauchez's influential study, and to Renate Blumenfeld-Kosinski, Nancy Caciola, and Dyan Elliott's claims that church authorities increasingly demonized women because of their increasingly visible spirituality.[84] The focus on Italy, however, adds a localized element to augment these scholars' discussions about later medieval spirituality, the parameters of institutional support, and acceptance of holiness. Both this historiography of late medieval female sanctity and the argument about the predominance of active, urban, male lay saints who lacked papal and mendicant support were true and existed in tandem in Italy. There was a focus on ascetic and mystic experiences associated with women or a "feminization" of sanctity, and these women became the focus of local cults more than ever before. Female "palliative

---

81. Vauchez, *Sainthood in the Later Middle Ages*, 350–56.

82. On the predominantly female nature of immoderate penitence and asceticism, see Bynum, *Holy Feast and Holy Fast*, esp. 73–186, and Bynum, "Female Body and Religious Practice"; cf. Bell, *Holy Anorexia*. For a study that connects female asceticism in the late Middle Ages to earlier manifestations of female piety, see McNamara, "Need to Give"; see also Casagrande, "Note su manifestazioni"; and Weinstein and Bell, *Saints and Society*, 37–38, 234–36.

83. See Coakley, "Gender and the Authority of Friars"; and Vauchez, *Sainthood in the Later Middle Ages*, 207–12 and 379–80.

84. Bynum, *Holy Feast and Holy Fast*, 20–23; Blumenfeld-Kosinski, *Strange Case of Ermine de Reims*, esp. 127–50; Caciola, *Discerning Spirits*, 14–19; Elliott, *Proving Woman*, 2–3; Elliott, *Bride of Christ Goes to Hell*, esp. 174–279; and Vauchez, *Sainthood in the Later Middle Ages*, 267–69.

saints," who engendered "healing communities" were immensely important to late medieval religious life, as Sara Ritchey has detailed, and can be seen in Italy in the hagiographies of Umiliana dei Cerchi and Zita of Lucca (d. 1278), among others.[85] While there was no direct equivalent in Italian towns to the Parisian beguinages that Tanya Stabler Miller described, with their communal spirituality and charitable and economic endeavors, the *vitae* of laywomen penitents like Margaret of Cortona suggest female social networks that offered comparable means of religious expression and produced similar outlets for active engagement in their communities.[86] At the same time, as other scholars have argued, mendicants and other authorities monitored these women more closely as the Middle Ages progressed because their spirituality seemed threatening in some way, and this ironically led to mendicant promotion of their cults. All of these factors were clearly present in the number of new cults of female saints in late medieval Italy.

While women publicly expressed an influential mystical or somatic religiosity more than ever before, their confessors, often Franciscans or Dominicans for reasons already noted, attained access to the divine by proxy. The male friars' relationship with these female saints allowed them both to explore the limits of their own authority and to make up for the deficiencies in that authority by promoting their protégés' sainthood. John Coakley noted that the female mystic posed no real challenge to her confessor's ecclesiastical or sacerdotal authority.[87] Female sanctity, therefore, did not constitute a palpable threat to male power. While many of these women failed to achieve canonization by a medieval pope and had to wait centuries later for papal recognition, members of the powerful Franciscan and Dominican orders supported them. Friars served as papal administrators, both for inquisitorial and canonization inquiries. They also had immense influence over the urban landscape and therefore the ritualized manifestation of local cults, in Italy as elsewhere. They tended to promote candidates from their own ranks or others over which they had tight spiritual rein: the women for whom they served as confessors. The likelihood was slim that a humble male Italian lay penitent

85. Ritchey, "Affective Medicine." On Umiliana, see *AASS* IV, May 19, cols. 386D–401D, English translation in Webb, *Saints and Cities*, 97–140. For her cult, see Benvenuti-Papi, "Umiliana dei Cerchi"; and Schlager, "Foundresses of the Franciscan Life." On Zita, see *AASS* III April 27, cols. 499B–527A, English translation in Webb, *Saints and Cities*, 160–90; and also *Riti*, proc. 1315 (Umiliana dei Cerchi, 1694–1695). For discussion, see Doyno, *Lay Saint*, and Benvenuti Papi, "*In castro poenitentiae*," 263–303; see also Goodich, "*Ancilla Dei*."

86. Miller, *Beguines of Medieval Paris*. For Margaret, see discussion below.

87. Coakley, "Gender and Authority," 449–59; see also *Women, Men, and Spiritual Power*. For specific examples of these relationships between male confessors and female mystics, see the essays in Mooney, *Gendered Voices*. For a discussion of the association between women and confession in the late Middle Ages, see Elliott, "Women and Confession."

would achieve mendicant or papal support for canonization. It was difficult to shape and channel the spirituality of such men, even if they were tertiaries, because they refrained from the type of mystical behavior that demanded interpretation and because sexual and social norms made it possible for them to be mobile, hard to track, and potentially figures of ecclesiastical authority. Lay male saints who lived in the world following the *vita apostolica* could test the friars' claims to spiritual perfection as occurred with Gerard Segarelli (d. 1300), discussed in chapter 3.

The life of Margaret of Cortona shows both the possibilities and limitations of this framework. Her story reveals fluidity between the typology of male saints and female saints and that the hermeneutical categories of tolerated saints versus canonized saints could quickly change. It therefore demonstrates the continued place for specific, localized studies to accompany sweeping narratives about the contested nature of late medieval sanctity for both men and women. Margaret was a Franciscan tertiary who voluntarily distanced herself from the order toward the end of her life after a somewhat lackluster reception from all Franciscans except her spiritual adviser and hagiographer, Giunta Bevegnati. Bevegnati tried to rally the friars to support her and her growing reputation. Instead it was secular clergy and the citizens of Cortona who promoted her cult until the Franciscans subsequently claimed her as one of their own.

In her youth Margaret had run away from her family to live with her noble lover, to whom she bore a son.[88] Someone murdered her lover when her son was nine. His parents banished Margaret from their property and her own family subsequently rejected her. She fled to Cortona, where two women took her in. These dramatic events served as the impetus for a conversion experience, and Margaret soon asked the Franciscan convent to accept her as a tertiary. According to her hagiographer and former confessor, Bevegnati, the friars were reluctant because they thought she was too beautiful and too young. Ultimately the convent acceded, and Margaret spent most of her subsequent life in the mold of the "lay charitable activist" like many of the tolerated male saints already described. She founded a hospice and confraternity (the Fraternitas Sanctae Mariae de Misericordia); granted baptisms to infants (purportedly until God, perhaps with some prompting by Franciscan prayers, told her not to); and counseled peace among warring factions. In her later years Margaret desired a more reclusive life. Frà Giunta Bevegnati persuaded her to stay

---

88. This overview is from Bevegnatis, *Legenda de vita et miraculis*, cited in English translation: Bevignati, *Life and Miracles of Saint Margaret of Cortona*. Secondary sources discussing Margaret include Cannon and Vauchez, *Margherita of Cortona and the Lorenzetti*; Coakley, *Women, Men, and Spiritual Power*, 130–48; Doyno, "Particular Light of Understanding"; Pryds, *Women of the Streets*; and Schlager, "Foundresses of the Franciscan Life."

near Cortona, but in 1288 at the Franciscan provincial chapter some friars apparently criticized her and, possibly, her relationship with Bevegnati. Margaret moved to a cell on the outskirts of the town, and the chapter ordered that her confessor could only visit her every eight days. The *vita* does not elaborate on the cause for this restriction, but the convent sent Bevegnati to Siena in 1289 or 1290. Margaret obtained a new confessor, a priest from the church of S. Basilio near her new home and where she ultimately was buried.

The commune and its secular clergy initially promoted Margaret's cult. Cortona rapidly took up donations for the building of a new church of S. Basilio. The bishop of Chiusi, whose diocese included the small town of Laviano where Margaret was born, granted a forty-day indulgence to those who contributed.[89] The Casali family, an emerging power dynasty, supported these efforts. The community's rapid promotion of her holiness is probably due to the fact that she did not fit the typology of the mystical female saint but her endeavors healed and unified the community in many of the same ways as the male saints discussed above. It was also her public actions, both before and after her conversion, that seem to have made the Franciscan convent reluctant to closely associate with her. Only after her death did the mendicants emphasize her Franciscan connections, something they did not promote before her popular cult emerged. Ultimately, the mendicants fought to attain her body, purportedly promised to their convent, and they secured it in 1392.[90]

Margaret of Cortona's history shows that mendicant convents did not always promote female saints and that wider secular support was not exclusive to male saints. It was the male saints with civic cults, however, that predominantly garnered the money and assistance to request a canonization inquiry. Margaret of Cortona is the only Italian lay female saint between 1200 and 1400 who had an official request for a canonization inquiry, which the town of Cortona and its secular clergy submitted jointly in 1318. In contrast, the communities where Anthony Peregrinus, Parisio of Treviso, and Henry of Bolzano had lived all paid to compile materials and formally submit a request, while the records of Armanno Pungilupo and the early *vita* of Facio of Cremona, among others, suggest that their towns were on the same path.[91] All of these efforts failed, and the candidates joined the substantial ranks of late medieval Italian saints with unauthorized but nominally tolerated cults. Although popes did not condemn the veneration of these holy persons (with the exception of Armanno, discussed in chapter 2), in a real sense their sanctity was contested.

---

89. Ludovico Da Pelago, II, *Registro*, no. 6, 162, cited in Cannon and Vauchez, *Margherita of Cortona*, 30.

90. Bornstein, "Uses of the Body," 167–70.

91. Vauchez, *Sainthood in the Later Middle Ages*, 72–73, table 4.

There was a public debate over the authenticity of their holiness: citizens celebrated feast days and prayed to the saints' relics, while popes rejected requests for canonization inquiries or observers denigrated these persons' virtues.

Several changes occurred circa 1200 that contributed to the rise in tolerated but unsanctioned cults. The papacy's appropriation of canonizations, centralization of the process, and implementation of the inquisitorial procedure served as a reductive force whereby more than ever only the wealthy and powerful—the elite, royalty, or preferred clergy such as bishops and mendicants—obtained a papal hearing. These developments coincided with a proliferation of local urban lay saints in Italy, a group that had little chance of successfully negotiating the canonization process because of the cost, time, and effort it demanded. The papacy's new articulation of what behaviors and actions designated holiness instituted a higher burden of proof, and many of the local saints' virtues and miracles did not impress popes as much as they did the citizens of towns who had known the saints and had enjoyed their intercessory gifts. Many of the new cults in northern and central Italy were of people whose very ordinariness could undermine the warning to "admire, not imitate" the officially canonized saints. The church had problems regulating late medieval Italian male saints within lay expressions of the *vita apostolica*, and so the saints could be perceived as a threat to institutional authority and papal control of lay piety. This led to disapprobriation, if not outright suspicion, of their nominally tolerated cults. In contrast, most tolerated female saints had a mendicant supporter in their confessor and thus faced less disapproval from other clerical authorities.

The number and variety of unofficial tolerated saints demonstrates how communities privileged their own experience of the postulant saint, their understanding of the signs of sanctity, their needs as a community, and their right to determine who was worthy of sainthood. The hagiographer of Facio of Cremona made this perspective clear when he asserted that "if he [Facio] is not canonized in the Church Militant . . . he is canonized above in the Church Triumphant."[92] While in general popes seldom hindered devotion to these holy persons, the saints' holiness was still contested. The contemporary Franciscan chronicler, Salimbene de Adam, ridiculed the cult of Albert of Villa d'Ogna on this point: "At that time his image was painted not only in the churches, but also on many walls and porticoes of cities, villages, and castles. Those bishops, therefore, who allow such abuses to be practiced in their diocese merit removal from office. . . . But there is nobody to correct those errors and

---

92. Vauchez, "Sainteté laïque aux XIIIe siècle," 36.

abuses."[93] People could venerate any deceased individual with the bishop's permission, and there were no restrictions on creating images of saints that the pope did not canonize.[94] Salimbene, however, conceivably channeled the dismay of others, including popes attempting to centralize the canonization process, who also viewed collective consensus and episcopal support as insufficient, and perhaps even insubordinate, for public displays of local devotion.

Communities expressed disagreement regarding who deserved sainthood and how the process should occur when they venerated certain saints when a pope had not officially endorsed a cult, when papal agents rejected a request for a canonization inquiry, or when local mendicant observers such as Salimbene dissuaded the growth of the saints' cults. This implicit dispute within unauthorized cults became an explicit debate when a local saint was suspected of being not just spiritually unworthy but potentially heterodox.

---

93. *Chronicle of Salimbene de Adam*, 512.
94. Vauchez, *Sainthood in the Later Middle Ages*, 86.

CHAPTER 2

Suspect Saints

The papacy did not challenge cults of unauthorized saints as long as there were no allegations of immorality, misconduct, or unorthodox actions or opinions. If inquisitors suspected a venerated person of grave faults, then the situation changed. Doubts about doctrinal error led to the concern that the saints were pious pretenders, or "wolves in sheep's clothing" (Matthew 7:15). Pope Boniface VIII used this specific biblical imagery in his 1301 posthumous condemnation of Armanno Pungilupo of Ferrara. In it he stated, "While he [Armanno] lived he pretended, giving holy and lively conversation, although under the aspect of a sheep he carried the cunning of a wolf and under a certain aspect of piety he concealed the wickedness of impiety."[1] Armanno and other saints like him became suspect saints, either during their lifetime or after their death. In most cases inquisitors could not resolve the ambiguity regarding the object of devotion's orthodoxy and/or holiness. Armanno is an exception, as discussed below. In general, popes did not endorse them, yet inquisitors did not obtain enough evidence to secure a condemnation.

A crucial difference distinguishes tolerated saints from suspect saints: church authorities actively tried to condemn the latter and discourage their cults. Clerics had to identify whether a venerated individual was a "wolf" or a "sheep,"

---

1. *Itinerari*, 91.

since duplicitous or false prophets put other Christian souls in jeopardy. The recognition of sanctity or heresy involved the detection of certain signs and the determination of whether they were produced by holy, human, or diabolical means. The papacy established inquisitors and implemented the *inquisitio*, or the inquisitorial procedure, to help in this endeavor. As a result, inquisitors scrutinized actions differently, as the problem with the *inquisitio* was how to assess external behavior to determine internal personal beliefs. Just as communities questioned the efficacy of using the *inquisitio* to judge the worth of candidates to sainthood, so too did they challenge its usefulness to determine heretics. The identification of someone as holy, heterodox, or an ordinary exponent of orthodoxy was itself a negotiation. Communities and inquisitors disagreeing about their assessment of a saint greatly complicated the situation and raised the stakes for both sides. Examples such as Peter Crisci of Foligno, Tommasuccio of Nocera, Meco del Sacco (d. circa 1346), and Armanno Pungilupo demonstrate how the construction of sanctity became contested after inquisitors took on the role of papal disciplinarians, due in part to diverging standards regarding how and by whom heresy, no less than holiness, should by judged. The result was competing ideas regarding the spiritual worth of these saints. Inquisitors questioned Peter Crisci, incarcerated Tommasuccio, and condemned Meco and Armanno, both of whom went through an appeal process. Inquisitors failed to secure lasting condemnations for all of these saints except Armanno Pungilupo. The problems inherent in the system of discerning heresy allowed the continued existence of their cults, especially when communal consensus challenged the effectiveness of the *inquisitio*.

Discernment and the *Inquisitio*

Developments in the papal bureaucracy at the turn of the thirteenth century included centralization of control over canonizations and the regulation of Christian behavior—the physical and observable expression of faith—and created an inquisitorial office to monitor it. These changes were possible by the adoption of the *inquisitio*, the judicial tool intended to discover "truth." The *inquisitio* was not the brainchild of the curia or canon law faculty; rather, it was the product of Roman civil law. Reimagined and reapplied, it became the tool to identify who was a threat to Christianity and who was not. While papal emissaries and popes used this procedure during the inquiry stages of papal canonizations, it was also the instrument *par excellence* for combating heterodoxy, meant to protect Christians by ensuring that no wolves threatened the flock. Its implementation was a direct response to the perceived threat of heresy to

Christian souls, a threat that inquisitors and several popes thought permeated northern and central Italy in particular during this period.

Church Fathers battled with heresy—or more specifically, decided what constituted heresy—in the period of doctrinal formation. By the seventh century, councils had largely determined the tenets of Christian belief, and heretical ideas seemed to be on the wane. The homogenizing process of Christian missionary work appeared successful, for by the eleventh century most of Europe was Christian. Shortly thereafter, however, Western Europe saw a proliferation of ideas deemed heretical in the wake of reform movements. The precise reasons how and why heterodox beliefs reappeared are contested, leading two influential scholars on the subject, Malcolm Lambert and R. I. Moore, to revise over time their widely influential respective views.[2] The salient point is that by the twelfth century the papacy saw heresy as a menace and started to address how to identify and combat it. The seemingly holy person seduced the faithful, co-opting the orthodox unwittingly into heretical belief, polluting their souls and jeopardizing their salvation. Heresy as disease quickly became a *topos*, since, as anthropologist Mary Douglas argued, ideas about pollution are intrinsically tied to perceived threats to one's own power and status.[3] Thus the Fourth Lateran Council in 1215 ordered each secular ruler to "cleanse his territory of this heretical foulness" so that heresy could be "exterminated" and Christian lands preserved "in the purity of faith."[4] Later inquisitorial manuals such as that of Bernard of Luxembourg equated heresy with leprosy, another feared contagion.[5]

Canon law came to codify heresy as "whosoever understands Holy Scripture, prescribed by the Holy Spirit, other than in the sense the Holy Spirit demands, although he does not separate himself from the Church."[6] A heretic was a person who deliberately denied Christian revelatory truth of the Gospels or maintained or taught beliefs not sanctioned by the pope. Despite this concise legal definition, it was difficult for medieval authorities to determine who fell into the heterodox camp. How could humans, denied God's omniscience, establish who held unorthodox beliefs and who did not? The central issue was the "discernment of spirits" (1 John 4:1 and 1 Corinthians 12:7–10):

---

2. Compare, for instance, the first and third editions of Lambert's *Medieval Heresy* or the first and second editions of Moore's *Formation of a Persecuting Society*; see also Moore, *War on Heresy*.

3. Douglas, *Purity and Danger*, 3. See Moore, "Heresy as Disease."

4. Tanner, *Decrees of the Ecumenical Councils*, 233–34; for discussion, see Sackville, *Heresy and Heretics in the Thirteenth Century*, 88–92.

5. Bernard of Luxembourg, *Catalogus haereticorum*, f. 4v.

6. *Corpus iuris canonici*, vol. 2, 998, C. 24 q. 3 c. 27; for an alternate English translation, see Lerner, "Ecstatic Dissent," 33. See also Arnold, *Inquisition and Power*, 59–61; Hamilton, *Medieval Inquisition*, 13; and Shannon, *Popes and Heresy in the Thirteenth Century*, 4–5.

the ability to differentiate between true miracles divinely wrought and those
that were falsely produced, either by human or diabolical simulation. The fact
that such canonists as Pope Innocent IV (d. 1254) and Hostiensis (d. 1271) addressed the subject shows that it was a concern, as was the ritual request that
people pray lest the pope was in error during the canonization ritual.[7] But how
to determine who had been graced with this divine gift?

Pope Innocent III, a savvy canonist, promoter of papal sovereignty, and
pope during the Fourth Lateran Council, formulated the boundaries. Donald
Prudlo's recent work on the connection between papal canonizations and the
concept of papal infallibility traces how later thirteenth-century popes expanded Innocent's idea that the pope was God's only "true" human representative on earth.[8] Innocent III's move to dispense with episcopal canonizations,
making only papal ones official, suggests this belief. Heretics, however, had
become much more pervasive. Whether this was the case in reality or only in
the church's perspective as it waged a new "war" on heresy starting in the
late twelfth century, as R. I. Moore argued, popes alone could not oversee
every inquiry.[9] The papacy needed a clerical brigade of trained and trusted
papal agents to dispense spiritual justice in their name. At the Fourth Lateran
Council in 1215, Pope Innocent III spearheaded a solution to the dual problem
of how to discern heresy and who was qualified to do so. The council mandated the behavior of a pious Christian in order to monitor orthodoxy via
one's external or public acts. Christians had to attend church regularly, confess
once a year, and reject all association with suspected heretics. If not, orthodox
members of the community exposed themselves to charges of heterodoxy or
the punishment of excommunication for being a receiver (*receptor*), defender
(*defensor*), or supporter (*fautor*) of heretics. The threat of excommunication
was harsh; by the early twelfth century Honorius Augustodunensis described
the excommunicated as "morally dead" and compared them to the physically
dead in their inability to be present at masses for the living.[10] Eventually, inquisitors included under these labels those who provided shelter to, ate with,
or even formally greeted someone suspected of heresy. The souls of those who

---

7. Elliott, *Proving Woman*, 127–28; cf. Kleinberg's discussion in "Proving Sanctity," 197, where he
claims these authors were "not bothered" by this potential problem. For a general introduction to this
topic, see François Vandenbroucke, "Discernement des esprits au moyen âge"; for a study of discernment in relation to female mystics, see Caciola, *Discerning Spirits*, 1–14. In contrast to the idea that
discernment of spirits was a mystical gift, Jean Gerson considered it a privilege of the learned priest;
see Elliott, "Seeing Double," 34–35.

8. Prudlo, *Certain Sainthood*, 122–50; see also Pope Innocent III, *Tertia compilatio* 1.5.3, cited in
Pennington, "Innocent III and the Divine Authority," 4.

9. Moore, *War on Heresy*, 7–9.

10. McLaughlin, "On Communion with the Dead," 24.

venerated a potential "wolf in sheep's clothing," even if done with good and orthodox intentions, were infected with heresy and in spiritual jeopardy. Moreover, canon 21 of Lateran IV mandated that secular authorities must seek and punish heretics or be susceptible to charges of heresy themselves.[11] Local rulers, like those in southern France in the early 1220s, proved to be unreliable, resulting in the Albigensian crusade. Subsequent popes therefore established a trusted judicial arm by creating the inquisitorial office.

Christine Caldwell Ames and Jennifer Kolpacoff Deane have recently traced the creation of the inquisitorial office.[12] The Dominicans were the first mendicants to serve as inquisitors, although Franciscans soon joined them, and in 1254 Pope Alexander III divided the office of inquisitors in Italy between the two orders. Inquisitors, answerable only to the pope, had considerable autonomy and authority and so circumvented church hierarchy since they functioned directly as papal agents.[13] This new judicial arm of the papacy needed a procedure to help with the process of discernment. That procedure was the *inquisitio*, which popes also adopted for canonizations. It was to provide authorities with the means for judging the veracity of deponents' testimonies by comparing the responses of witnesses to their own knowledge of heretics, derived from personal experience or from the descriptions provided in inquisitorial manuals.[14] In the hands of a skilled questioner, the *inquisitio* was supposed to neutralize the problem of exaggerated, biased, or faulty testimony. The method produced an inquisitorial reality through "productive discourse," a "formation of a knowledge of heresy, transgression, and identities," thus creating a reality from personal fears.[15]

While an inquisitorial inquiry focused on the evidence of one's actions, which was within the purview of human ability to assess, it was not long before inquisitors appropriated tools, or "technologies of power" as James Given described them, to examine internal belief and place others at their mercy. The church sanctioned the use of torture to "persuade" people to tell the "truth" about their actions, identify other supposed heterodox individuals, and force them to express their personal religious tenets less than forty years after the

---

11. Tanner, *Decrees of the Ecumenical Councils*, 233–35.

12. Ames, *Righteous Persecution*; Deane, *History of Medieval Heresy and Inquisition*. See also Douais, *L'Inquisition, ses origines, sa procédure*; and Lea, *History of the Inquisition*, vol. 1.

13. On the Franciscans as inquisitors, see Pope Gregory IX, *Excommunicamus*, in *Les Registres de Grégoire IX*, vol. 1, no. 539. For discussion of the division, see D'Alatri, *L'inquisizione francescana*, 17–18.

14. *Corpus iuris canonici*, vol. 1, 999, c. 24 q. 3 c. 29. On the chronological development and discussion of some of these inquisitorial manuals, see Dondaine, "Le manuel de l'inquisiteur." Many of the texts are extant in two manuscripts in Rome, Biblioteca Casanatense, ms. 969 and ms. 1730.

15. Arnold, *Inquisition and Power*, 11; see also Given, "Inquisitors of Languedoc," 351.

establishment of the inquisitorial office.[16] Following Greek and Roman precedent, a confession extracted by torture could be the sole grounds for conviction without further substantiation, even if the person later recanted his or her confession.[17] Its adoption shows the limitations of the *inquisitio* in contrast to its promise. Inquisitors could interpret a single act in multiple ways, different inquisitors could grant different weight to evidence used to assess heterodoxy (or orthodoxy), or the actions of a single suspect could conflict.

The supporters of a local saint who became the subject of inquisitorial scrutiny clearly did not consider that person a heretic, much less as a dangerous threat to Christianity or the social order. At the center of the conflict, again, were miracles. Miracles served as a unifying force to create a community of believers, as seen in the previous chapter on tolerated saints, but they could also be a divisive force between those believers and inquisitors in the cases of suspect saints. Both sides believed miracles were a sign of sanctity, but conflict occurred when there were different interpretations of the cause. The *inquisitio* could not discern real from false miracles. At least, inquisitors could not convince the community of its ability to do so, as is illustrated in the account of Guido Lacha of Brescia (d. mid-thirteenth century). Lacha had a reputation for being a holy man, yet inquisitors believed he had held heterodox beliefs and posthumously condemned him as a heretic. Although these circumstances differ from those of suspected saints discussed in this chapter, the events at the exhumation of his bones delineates the problem of discerning heresy and sanctity through the *inquisitio*'s ability to evaluate the veracity of external signs such as miracles.

While later commentators like Bernard of Luxembourg and Luis de Paramo listed Guido Lacha among their catalogs of heresiarchs, it is unknown whether inquisitors questioned Lacha during his lifetime, what type of heretical beliefs he held (if any), or even what year he died.[18] The lone contemporary source suggests that he had a cult of unknown scope when a council condemned him and exhumed him in 1279 in order to burn his bones. This was a standard process for condemned heretics, so that their physical remains would not continue to "pollute" Christian society or be considered relics.[19] At that point,

---

16. In 1254 Pope Clement IV sanctioned the use of torture in his bull *Ad extirpanda* (Paolini, *Il "De officio inquisitionis"*, 1:23, 2:66).

17. Shannon, *Popes and Heresy*, 70; on the classical idea of the body as the site of exacting truth, see DuBois, *Torture and Truth*, 6–14.

18. Bernard of Luxembourg, *Catalogus*, f. 20v; de Paramo, *De origine et progressu*, 299.

19. Hamilton, *Medieval Inquisition*, 55; Wakefield, "Burial of Heretics in the Middle Ages"; Russell, *Dissent and Order in the Middle Ages*, 57.

his bones were thrown into the fire in the presence of the people, and at once demons lifted the bones from the fire and held them suspended in the air just like a tower [i.e., upright] so that all the people saw the bones suspended so in the air, yet they could not see the demons. Then the people began to cry out, saying, "the bishop with his friars who, out of jealousy, wanted to burn God's saint should die, look how Our Lord does not wish it." Then the bishop was afraid. However, certain brothers comforted him, saying, "My lord, we are here for the defense of faith, [so] prepare yourself for mass because God may show some miracles lest one's faith is lost."[20]

This passage reveals the powerful effect that a miracle had on its observers and the difficulty inherent in interpreting such an event. Lacha's floating remains immediately led the Brescian onlookers to conclude that he was a saint. The miracle manifested God's anger over the decision to burn Lacha's remains. It engendered a belief in Lacha's holiness by signifying that the officials were mistaken in their judgment. Thus the burning of the deceased heretic's body, the ultimate rejection of any claims to his sanctity, backfired. For observers, the posthumous miracle in fact proved that God had ruled in Lacha's favor.

The bishop and friars in this case interpreted the miracle differently from the onlookers, ascribing the levitating bones to a diabolical imitation of divine intervention. These authorities believed they could discern the difference between a miracle and other supernatural phenomena that created the erroneous belief and dangerous illusion that a sinner, or even a heretic, was holy. It required another miracle to counter the effect of the "false" sign conveyed by Guido's bones and to reassert God's (and their own) authority. The inquisitor encouraged the bishop, who was cringing in fear of either this sign of God's displeasure or of his now-unruly parishioners, to get ready for mass. He assured the bishop that a true miracle, the transformation of Christ's physical body and blood into the Eucharist, would follow. The bishop consequently said mass. Faced with the divine power of the Eucharist, "the demons in the air cried out, 'O Guido Lacha, we have defended you as long as we were able, but now we no longer can, because one approaches who is higher than us, namely Christ.' And at once they dropped the bones in the fire."[21] The two miracles in this account are parallel: just as demons elevate the body of the dead heretic, a priest elevates the body of the living Christ. The demonic miracle was to convince the credulous observers that Lacha was a saint, while

---

20. Philippe de Ferrara, OP, "Liber de introductione loquendi," f. 94v, cited in Creytens, "Le manuel de conversation de Philippe de Ferrare, OP," 120–21.

21. Ibid., 121.

the bishop's mass was to persuade those who had been deceived to reaffirm their faith in the divine mystery. In the end the miracle of the mass generated a miracle of its own: the dispersal of the demons.

The author, a Dominican like the inquisitor in Brescia, ascribed the miracle of Guido's dancing bones to the devil's agents. He ended the account with the inquisitors vindicated and in triumph after God's will manifested itself in the Eucharist, prompting the demons to drop the remains. While the inquisitor was unsympathetic to the Brescian bystanders' perspective, his story reveals their contrasting interpretation from his own of the extraordinary event. Since the source of the miracle was concealed, the observers disagreed upon which power, divine or diabolical, was responsible for this visible supernatural sign. For the inquisitor, the mass was an exorcism, revealing the event's demonic source and banishing the diabolical influence. It confirmed what the inquisitor "knew": namely, that Lacha was a heretic.

This example demonstrates that inquisitors suspected the validity of miracles while others assumed that supernatural occurrences came solely from God, as testimony from inquisitorial registers from Bologna also suggests. One witness stated that, after the burning of several heretics in Mantua around 1300, "great lights appeared above them and they worked miracles and wonders. Having been asked if he believed it to be so, he responded that yes, because he strongly believed that heretics can work wonders and miracles."[22] Whether or not the witness believed these men were actually heretics, as inquisitors deemed them to be, is irrelevant. The deponent assumed God could give anyone the power to perform miracles, even those that inquisitors claimed were heretics, for only God knew who was truly saintly. A suspected follower of the condemned heretic Gerard Segarelli (discussed in chapter 3) displayed a similar conviction: "He believes and believed the said Gerard to be and to have been a good man, and believes that God made miracles through the merit of the said Gerard. Having been asked how [this] may be, he responded that [although] he was not present, nevertheless he heard that the saint Gerard miraculously healed certain ill persons of Milan and also a certain sick boy in Bologna, and the witness himself believes that it was so."[23] The perceived performance of a miracle justified one's subsequent devotion.

The conviction that supernatural events with a positive outcome that occurred after someone's death could only come from God was in fact a very orthodox construction in keeping with theological developments. As noted in chapter 1, popes granted special status to postmortem miracles, arguing that

---

22. Testimony of Iulianus, *Acta S. Officii*, vol. 1, no. 20, 11 May 1299, 46.
23. Testimony of Petrus Bonus, *Acta S. Officii*, vol. 1, no. 79, 18 November 1299, 114–15.

they were the only type that assured God was the source. Members of the community, in relying on these visible events as the main signifiers of holiness, were in accordance with this institutional emphasis. Once again, however, the miracle could be problematic and divisive to assess both sanctity and heresy. Miracles could strengthen the faith of a suspect saint's devotees, as occurred in the case of Guido Lacha, and even inspire belief in skeptics.[24] Their power to do so undermined belief in the value of the *inquisitio*, leading to suspect saints and other examples of disputed sanctity.

Conflicting Interpretations

Attaining enough indisputable evidence to condemn a saint and prohibit a cult was not always easy. The suspect saint Peter Crisci of Foligno is an illustrative case. Crisci had been an anchorite attached to the church of S. Feliciano in Foligno.[25] According to his *vita* by Johannes Gorini, some citizens of Spoleto and Assisi "falsely accused" him of holding Spiritual Franciscan beliefs, identifying him as part of the observant faction of the Franciscan order that had been condemned by Pope John XXII in 1317.[26] His hagiographer, Joannes Gorini, claimed that Crisci was brought to the inquisitors of Spoleto on an ass to produce abject humiliation. Crisci instead was overjoyed because he was ready to die for his faith like Christ. Gorini draws a parallel between Christ and Crisci, for "just as Our Savior Jesus Christ came to suffer death sitting on an ass, just so this man was thinking to die in a similar way."[27] He did not, however, die at that time, for inquisitors released him. The hagiographer attributes this result to the man's spiritual worth, asserting that "confessor Peter [was] an especially loyal and prudent servant of God, who was found so perfect in catholic faith that those who envied and falsely accused him were rightly defeated with confusion."[28] Crisci's perfect faith confounded and exposed his false accusers. From the inquisitorial perspective, it is possible that suspicions remained, but there was just not enough evidence to support a condemnation. By 1340, seventeen years after Crisci's death, Foligno's government recognized public feasts in his honor. Popes and inquisitors allowed his cult to continue

---

24. McCready, *Signs of Sanctity*, 33–64.

25. *AASS* IV, July 19, col. 665. Part of the same *vita* by Joannes Gorini is published in "Beati Petri de Fulgineo Confessoris," 358–69.

26. *AASS* IV, July 19, col. 663; Gorini, "Beati Petri de Fulgineo Confessoris," 365. On the Spiritual Franciscans, see Burr, *Spiritual Franciscans*, and Robson, *Franciscans in the Middle Ages*, 119–40.

27. Gorini, "Beatri Petri de Fulgineo Confessoris," 365.

28. Ibid.

even though his orthodoxy had been suspect.[29] A similar situation occurred for Amato Ronconi of Saludecio. His 1733 canonization process praised his deep piety, dedication to poverty, and generosity in founding a hospital for pilgrims. It also noted that the money and riches Amato gave to the poor angered his sister-in-law, who then accused Amato of incest with his sister Chiara. Charges of sexual deviancy often accompanied accusations of heresy. There was an investigation until a miracle convinced the official that Amato was innocent as well as holy.[30] Ultimately, Pope Francis canonized him in 2014.

A more shocking example is Tommasuccio of Nocera (d. 1377), who was a thorn in the side of many clerical authorities who suspected him of heresy yet could not secure a conviction.[31] Although inquisitors questioned and/or imprisoned Tommasuccio three times on suspicion of heresy, none of the charges stuck. His subsequent cult nevertheless flourished in the towns of Nocera, near where he was born, and Foligno, where he died.[32] According to a fourteenth-century hagiography by his disciple Giusta della Rosa, Tommasuccio was the fifth child of a poor farmer and a pious mother from the countryside of Valmacinaia outside Nocera. An angel told his mother, Madonna Bona, that she was pregnant with a son who would be close to God. The angel dictated that upon birth the child be named "Tommasuccio." Tommasuccio fulfilled his birthright, taking a vow of chastity at twelve and leaving his family at twenty-four to live with a hermit, Brother Piero, on nearby Monte Gualdo. After three years of living as an anchorite, God called him to go to Tuscany and preach. Since Tommasuccio did not want to leave his hermitage, God gave him a nudge: through the "permission and commandment of God," an anonymous friar close to Tommasuccio betrayed his friend and told the bishop of Nocera that Tommasuccio had not gone to confession for three years.[33] The basis of the accusation was that he had deviated from the Fourth Lateran Council's injunction that all Christians must confess at least once a year.[34] The

29. Ibid., 359.

30. *Riti*, proc. 89 (Amato Ronconi, 1733–1734), f. 17v.

31. His name is variably spelled "Tomasuccio," and occasionally secondary literature refers to him as Tommasuccio of Foligno. In Lea's work he is called Tommasino di Foligno. His birth name may have been Tommaso Unzio, although Michele Faloci Pulignani, who edited his vita and a collection of prophecies attributed to him, claimed this was merely a misreading of his given name (*La leggenda del beato Tommasuccio da Nocera*, 7). The overview of Tommasuccio in this chapter is based on the *vita* in Milan, Biblioteca Ambrosiana, cod. I.115, edited by Pulignani. See also D'Alatri, "Movimenti religiosi popolari umbri il Beato Tommasuccio e l'inquisizione," in *Eretici*, 2:219–32, and the essays in Pazzelli, *Il B. Tommasuccio da Foligno.*

32. Lea, *History of the Inquisition*, 2:281.

33. Pulignani, *La leggenda del beato Tommasuccio da Nocera*, chap. 7, p. 23.

34. Fourth Lateran Council, 1215, canon 21, in Tanner, *Decrees of the Ecumenical Councils*, 259–60.

bishop investigated but released him after the hermit, Brother Piero, attested that Tommasuccio had confessed to him every month. The experience, however, was enough for Tommasuccio to heed God's will and leave the area. Within the context of the *vita*, this episode introduces several recurring themes: mendicant jealousy of Tommasuccio; consequent attempts to ruin his reputation by impugning his orthodoxy; and God's subsequent intervention that, unsurprisingly, protects him from condemnation.

Following his first questioning, Tommasuccio spoke to God and, as St. Francis before him, expressed his desire to go overseas to preach to the Saracens and be martyred there. God rejected his request, responding, "I will have you well martyred in Tuscany; [if] you believe in me, turn towards Tuscany to preach, as I have told you, and you shall foretell their tribulations and trials, and judge that they will reform their sin[ful ways] [for] if they do not I will send them war, famine, and tribulation for their horrible sins that they continue to do and think without fear of me."[35] Unsurprisingly Tommasuccio capitulated to God's will and traveled in the Tuscan countryside preaching and dispensing prophecies. His rhetorical skills garnered a following, which included his hagiographer, Giusto della Rosa. He even persuaded a Jew in Arezzo to convert to Christianity. His renown increased as he forecasted the wrath of God, predicted destruction, and harangued those persons, clerics in particular, who he viewed as corrupt. When in Perugia, for example, he publicly lectured on the sins of Gerald, abbot of Marmoutiers, who was also the papal vicar of the Papal States.[36] In the *Profezie*, a collection of prophecies supposedly by Tommasuccio, he identified himself as a vehicle for divine justice whose mission was to purge the world of iniquity and persuade the church to return to focusing on the pastoral care of souls.[37]

These actions did not endear him to everyone, particularly the subjects of his orations. His successful predictions engendered reverence in some who thought he was a prophet; for others, they provided a justification for eventual incarceration. In Siena, for instance, Tommasuccio preached that God would punish unrepentant sinners through a devastating frost. When a terrible frost soon occurred, "malignant men" went to the Franciscan inquisitor and accused him of sorcery. Officials imprisoned and tortured him, but he was later let go. While it is unclear how Tommasuccio secured his freedom, his *vita* claims an angel visited him in prison and promised he would be released

---

35. Pulignani, *La leggenda del beato Tommasuccio da Nocera*, chap. 10, p. 26; cf. Thomas of Celano, "First Life of St. Francis," 277.

36. Pulignani, *La leggenda del beato Tommasuccio da Nocera*, chap. 15, p. 32. For the identification of the unnamed abbot with Gerald of Marmoutiers, see Bonazzi, *Storia di Perugia*, 485.

37. *La profezie del Beato Tommasuccio di Foligno*, chap. 13, vv. 48–51, p. 67.

from his physical suffering. Henry Charles Lea, the author of a foundational history of the medieval inquisition, interpreted this passage as implying that God's grace miraculously healed Tommasuccio's wounds, which convinced inquisitors of his innocence.[38] He then moved to Florence but again encountered problems with the authorities, who imprisoned him for three days and denied him even bread and water. Once again, this favorite of God enigmatically escaped the clutches of inquisitors. While the surviving Milanese manuscript copy claims the inquisitor pardoned him, the 1510 incunabula edition from Vicenza that includes Giusto's *vita*, as well as the 1626 edition of the text by Lodovico Iacobilli, both assert that some soldiers pressured the inquisitor to release him because he was just a "barefoot crazy person" (*pazzo scalzo*).[39] Persons deemed insane were not responsible for their words or actions; inquisitorial manuals often discussed how heretics would fake insanity to avoid condemnation.[40] It is possible that at some point a scribe added this explanation to the *vita* in order to place Tommasuccio within the "holy fool" tradition and further emphasize the similarities between him and St. Francis.[41]

Tommasuccio had survived three interrogations, including two incarcerations, on suspicions of heterodoxy. Despite these serious challenges to his reputation, his hagiographer, Giusto, firmly believed in his sanctity. His text reiterates the theme that Tommasuccio was holy, chosen by God to be a martyr for dealing with such impediments to his pious mission. Giusto's claim is not surprising, considering that in one of Tommasuccio's last visions an angel declared, "Take yourself to Foligno and remain there until your death; therefore God wishes that your relics, that is your bones, ought to remain there."[42] More surprising, perhaps, is that people besides those in Tommasuccio's circle venerated him. While the extent of his cult is unknown, it must have been as substantial as that of Peter Crisci or Amato Ronconi. The communities of Nocera, where Tommasuccio was born, and Foligno, where he died, publicly celebrated him as a saint. Nocera adopted Tommasuccio as its "advocate" (*avvocato*), or patron and intercessor, and there was even an unsuccessful attempt at opening a canonization inquiry.[43] In addition, there survives in

38. Lea, *History of the Inquisition*, 2:282.

39. Pulignani, *La leggenda del beato Tommasuccio da Nocera*, chap. 40, pp. 59–60.

40. For example, see Eymerich, *Directorium inquisitorum*. For feigned madness, see Given, *Inquisition and Medieval Society*, 95–96.

41. Consider the description of St. Francis as the "fantastical fool" (Ugolino, *Little Flowers of St. Francis*, book 2, chap. 1, p. 141).

42. Pulignani, *La leggenda del beato Tommasuccio da Nocera*, chap. 41, pp. 60–61.

43. According to Lodovico Iacobilli's late seventeenth-century panegyric of Tommasuccio, "Santo Tommasuccio beatissimo vostro cittadino, et avvocato singolare della vostra città da Nocera" (St. Tommasuccio is the most blessed of our citizens of Nocera and remarkable advocate of our city) (quoted in the introduction to *La profezie del Beato Tommasuccio di Foligno*, 23).

Siena's Biblioteca Comunale an anonymous letter from circa 1400 in which the author expressed concern that the text of Tommasuccio's prophecies, the *Profezie*, had been corrupted in its transmission.[44] The letter demonstrates continued interest in Tommasuccio and belief in his prophetic powers in the early years after his death.

The survival of Tommasuccio's cult into the sixteenth and seventeenth centuries in the region of his birth attests to the fact that popes tacitly accepted veneration of this thrice-suspected heretic. Both Peter Crisci and Tommasuccio of Nocera had been anchorites who became the targets of purportedly jealous individuals. It is possible that Crisci's accusers were Franciscan, as he was targeted for being a member of the radical and condemned branch of the order that came to be known as the Spiritual Franciscans. Similarly, a "friar" first brought Tommasuccio to the attention of the authorities; interestingly, the hermit with whom he lived for three years is called a *fraticello*, the term used for Spiritual Franciscans in Italy. Tommasuccio existed within a prophetic tradition associated with the Franciscans rather than the Dominicans, thanks to the legacy of writers such as Joachim of Fiore (d. 1202) and Gerardo Borgo san Donnino (d. 1276), who influenced the more mystical wing of the Spiritual Franciscans.[45] Although tenuous, there is a refrain of jealous Franciscan accusers of influential men who specifically disdained to join an order and instead led a solitary if somewhat peripatetic life. The accusations leading to inquisitorial questioning and/or incarceration, however, differentiates them from the likes of Peter Pettinaio, Albert of Villa d'Ogna, or other saints discussed in the first chapter. Both Crisci and Tommasuccio were stained with the taint of heresy, at least for a time making them a target of papal agents. That there were two opposing opinions of these men produced overt contestation over their identity. Were they saints or heretics? Inquisitors' expectations were such that where heresy was alleged, heresy existed, and they would prove it to be so through procedure. Yet in both cases the *inquisitio* "failed." Inquisitors could not ascertain from their questioning that Crisci held any heterodox ideas. Even the probable use of torture on Tommasuccio did not produce evidence persuasive enough to justify his condemnation. Both Crisci and Tommasuccio were suspect saints who gained that status due to the limitations of the inquisitorial procedure, which did not have an effective way to discover internal beliefs. The *inquisitio* produced tolerated saints when there was not enough evidence to secure a papal canonization; conversely it produced suspect saints when there was not enough evidence to secure an inquisitorial condemnation.

---

44. Ibid., 25–26.
45. Reeves, *Influence of Prophecy*, 187–189.

Competing Inquiries

The account of Guido Lacha's dancing bones demonstrates how a single act could be interpreted in multiple ways. The *vitae* of Peter Crisci and Tommasuccio of Nocera show that evidence based on public behavior could be inconclusive and internal beliefs hard to uncover. The histories of Meco del Sacco and Armanno Pungilupo further exhibit the inherent tension between private beliefs and public acts and raise another problem with the inquisitorial process regarding what to do when someone's behavior seemed contradictory. Both Meco and Armanno's identities as holy men suffered due to this evidentiary issue. As a result, Meco, three times condemned as a heretic and twice exonerated, is the poster child of the suspect saint, a local holy person forever tainted with the stain of heterodoxy. Armanno was the focus of a decades-long battle between popes, bishops, inquisitors, parish priests, Benedictine monks, and the citizens of Ferrara. His case exemplifies how the suspect saint became an object of contestation when there were two different views of an individual's merits at the same time because the evidence was inconclusive. Armanno's ultimate condemnation for heresy allows him to serve as a bridge between the suspect saints of this chapter and the heretical saints discussed in the next chapter.

A struggle over the living saint Meco del Sacco occurred in the 1330s and 1340s in Ascoli, a town in Le Marche that was part of the Papal States. Bishop Rainaldo IV of Ascoli, the Augustinian convent in town, and a notable segment of the local population venerated Meco del Sacco of Ascoli, or Domenico Savi as he is also known. Yet between 1334 and 1344 the Franciscan inquisitors of the March of Ancona condemned Meco for heterodoxy three times. Meco's life has to be pieced together somewhat more than usual for late medieval saints, suspect or otherwise. There is no canonization inquiry, no *vita* or list of miracles, and even his inquisitorial sentences are no longer extant. What survives are responses to his appeals and court documents from the Augustinians who were overseers of his property, which provide an unusual perspective.

Meco went through a conversion experience similar to that of Peter Valdes (d. circa 1205) and St. Francis. Like Valdes, Meco was married before turning to the spiritual life; he and his wife, Clarella, had at least two sons, Angelo and Pietro.[46] Unlike his predecessors, however, Meco sought an eremitical existence

---

46. This discussion is based on *Meco*, which includes all extant documents. Meco's son Angelo was named rector of the church and hospital that Meco established in 1344 (*Meco*, 187). Lea incorrectly identifies 1337 as the year of Meco's conversion. This date is impossible, as inquisitors already had questioned him in 1334 (Lea, *History of the Inquisition*, 3:124).

rather than an itinerant one. In 1334 an inquisitor determined that he disseminated heterodox beliefs in written form. Meco abjured and was reconciled with the church. Church authorities burned his treatises, and he was forbidden to write more. Records concerning Meco's first condemnation are no longer extant, but the early modern historian F. A. Marcucci claimed the books were "one in French about the Psalms, and two in the vernacular about the Gospels and the Apocalypse."[47] The surviving documents from his appeals reveal that inquisitors ascribed to him an eclectic mix of heterodox beliefs. They accused him of maintaining that he was the son of God, suffered as Christ through death and resurrection, possessed the stigmata, and could expel demons and produce miracles. They also claimed that Meco and his followers thought God would save babies who died before baptism through the faith of their parents, women could be publicly naked if flagellating themselves, wives were only bound to have sex with their husbands once a year, laypeople could absolve others of sin, and neither usury nor sexual contact up until the point of orgasm was sinful.[48] Inquisitors considered Meco not just a heretic but a heresiarch, for "deceiving and seducing the people in various ways."[49] Leaving aside the charge that Meco believed himself Christ, the accusations suggest that Meco and his followers had an overwhelming concern with ensuring that all Christians would achieve salvation, conceived within an antisacerdotal and anticlerical framework. The variety of these beliefs has led to trouble classifying him. Lea believed Meco was a member of the so-called *spiritus libertatis*, or "Free Spirits," while Lea's contemporary, Cesare Cantù, described him as a Spiritual Franciscan, or *fraticello*. Both theories are specious. Lea based his ideas on a text in one manuscript purporting to describe the tenets of the Free Spirit but that had no connection to Meco del Sacco or Ascoli, while Cantù cites no evidence to substantiate his claim.[50]

Although by abjuring Meco effectively admitted to heresy, the bishop of Ferrara, Rainaldo IV, granted him permission to build an oratory on nearby

---

47. Marcucci, *Saggio di Cose Ascolane*, cited in *Meco*, 162.

48. The documents are transcribed in *Meco*, appendix 11, 297–98; for a list and discussion of the charges, see 69–108.

49. *Meco*, appendix 11, 297.

50. Lea, *History of the Inquisition*, 3:125; Cantù, *Gli eretici d'Italia*, 133. The short text of Free Spirit beliefs is in Rome, Biblioteca Casanatense, ms. 1730. Lea also claimed the Free Spirit were closely "allied" to the Dolcinists and "formed a link between them and the German Brethren of the Free Spirit" (Lea, *History of the Inquisition*, 3:124). Whether such a group as the "Free Spirit" actually existed in fourteenth-century Italy is unclear, although several contemporary chroniclers mentioned people who called themselves by that term. The existence of the Free Spirit as a cohesive sect with a distinct ideology has been called into question, most notably by Lerner (*Heresy of the Free Spirit*). There was some suggestion of a connection between the *spiritus libertatis* and the Spiritual Franciscans; Pope Clement V inquired into this very matter in 1310 (Burr, *Spiritual Franciscans*, 113–16).

Monte Polesio.[51] Meco lived there as a lay penitent, attracting an unknown number of followers to the retreat. He also increased his profile as a philanthropist: for instance, building a hospital in town near the Tufillo gate that catered to pilgrims.[52] Unsurprisingly, Meco's growing acclaim did not allow him to remain under the inquisitorial radar for long. In 1337 inquisitors questioned him for the second time, condemned him as a relapsed heretic, and put him in prison. Authorities let Meco out on bail, a surprising development considering he was then a relapsed heretic, a condition that required harsh punishment, if not death. His release strongly suggests that Bishop Rainaldo was pressuring the inquisitors, since he was the one who could exert that kind of coercion on the Franciscan convent.[53] Meco left Ascoli to appeal his sentence to the pope. In his absence the Augustinians served as overseers of his hospital, located near their convent. Meco asserted to the pope that the Franciscan inquisitor had falsely accused him on account of "hatred and jealousy against him, and because his said hospital and church were more frequented by the faithful of Christ and His mother than their [own] place."[54] Ultimately Pope Benedict XII overturned Meco's second condemnation and absolved him. This is another startling element to the story, since Ascoli was under interdict during these events for rebelling against the pope, and one would assume the pope would not be sympathetic to a suspected heretic from a disobedient town exiled from the church.[55] The success of Meco's appeal suggests that the charges against him were trumped up.

Meco's orthodoxy was established again, but soon it would be challenged for a third and final time. A bull of Pope Clement VI dated August 1344 indicates that inquisitors condemned Meco for heresy once again and sentenced him to a fine of sixty gold florins and two years in exile. Meco appealed this sentence on the same grounds as before. The lead inquisitor, Peter da Penna S. Giovanni, ignored an order to take no further action while the case was being examined. He excommunicated Meco and led a group of armed men to confiscate his goods. These actions prompted the pope to convene a special commission, which ordered that Meco be given restitution in 1345, and in 1346 he absolved Meco of the charges and reinstated him in the church.[56] Unfortunately,

---

51. *Meco*, appendix 10.

52. *Meco*, appendix 4; Andreatonelli, *Historiae Asculanae*, 289.

53. Peterson, "Episcopal Authority and Disputed Sanctity," 210–12.

54. *Meco*, appendix 4. Meco's oratory became the property of the Augustinians after his death until the Napoleonic suppression (*Meco*, 36 and 53).

55. Ascoli was under interdict for displaying excessive violence during its last skirmish with the rival town of Spoleto (Capponi, *Memorie storiche della Chiesa Ascolana*, 52, cited in *Meco*, 12–13).

56. *Meco*, appendices 11–13.

Meco apparently died in the intervening time, although it is unclear when and from what cause.[57]

It is easy to lose sight of Meco's history as a saint in the midst of the drama of his contest with inquisitors, even though the Ascolani, including two bishops and the local Augustinian convent, took Meco's side throughout this debate (discussed further in chapter 6). In 1889 the town renamed a street after him in honor of his role as "a writer and reformer of the fourteenth century."[58] Celebrating Meco has continued, as the Festival dell'Appennnino in Ascoli Piceno in 2012 promoted visits to the church erected on the site of his oratory on Monte Polesio. Across the peninsula and far south in the town of Furore in Campania, a local website proudly proclaimed that the city served as the refuge for Meco's followers, the "Sacconi," who supposedly fled there in 1348 after a new inquisitor investigated the community on Monte Polesio for sexual irregularities.[59] However, many scholars of medieval saints have surrendered his story to their colleagues working on medieval heresy, firmly placing him in the category of heterodox sinner as opposed to holy saint. Not even André Vauchez's exhaustive discussion mentioned him.

Meco's dual identity as a heretic and holy reformer, in both the fourteenth century and today, results from conflicting interpretations of his behavior. For the Ascolani, including both members of the laity and secular and regular clergy, his charitable activities and penitential lifestyle demonstrated that he was holy and worthy of respect or even devotion. For inquisitors, Meco entranced the laity through his charitable activities in order to spread heretical beliefs. These papal agents maintained that the Christian flock could not be trusted to differentiate between the wolves and the sheep and to distinguish between authentic and fraudulent signs of sanctity. For many medieval theologians, canonists, and popes, the laity and even local clergy were unlearned and theologically untrained, and thus incapable of such discrimination, thereby justifying the establishment of the inquisitorial office.[60] Some modern schol-

---

57. The fact that Meco's son was named rector of his father's institutions in 1344 suggests that Meco was deceased by that year. Most scholars, excepting the eighteenth-century Augustinian L. Pastori and his twentieth-century disciple and editor of the documents, Antonio DeSantis, agree that Meco was burned in 1344 or 1345 since no references to Meco's activities exist between 1344 and 1346. DeSantis tenuously supported his argument by two points: that Meco was actually absolved of his final condemnation and given restitution, and that a chronicle of Ascoli Piceno does not mention that he was burned, while documenting similar fates of other notable citizens, such as Cecco D'Ascoli, who was burned in Florence in 1327 (*Meco*, 52–55).

58. The naming was done under the direction of the "commissione incaricata dal Sindaco di Ascoli Piceno" (*Meco*, 29–30).

59. *Meco*, 79–97; "Ascoli Piceno—A Polesio sulle tracce di Meco del Sacco e dei Sacconi"; and "Furore."

60. Kleinberg, "Proving Sanctity," 184.

ars have accepted this view, to the point of making the generalization that it was unlikely local bishops had the ability to recognize doctrinal error and so crack down on cults by calling on inquisitors.[61] In Meco's case, however, popes twice upheld the bishop's assessment of Meco's orthodoxy over that of the Franciscan inquisitors, so such a generalization is untenable. We see a similar situation in the next example, that of Armanno Pungilupo, in the early years of the dispute over his orthodoxy. Suspect saints emerged through a failure of the *inquisitio* to determine truth and of inquisitors to impose their will on those citizens, rather than due to mistakes by illiterate and untrained citizens.

Like Meco, Armanno Pungilupo suffered from contrasting views of his merits. He even became the focus of two simultaneous inquiries, one to canonize him as a saint and one to condemn him as a heretic. Immediately after his death in 1269, the canons of Ferrara carried Armanno's body in a public procession to the cathedral, buried him, and erected an altar over his tomb.[62] Members of the community and pilgrims from such towns as Padua, Parma, and even as far as Trieste gathered at Armanno's sepulchre hoping that their prayers of supplication would result in a miracle. They were not disappointed, and the new saint healed many visitors of such afflictions as partial paralysis and gout. The canons soon began to collect testimony from the recipients of these miracles, and the bishop of Ferrara initiated a diocesan inquiry into his spiritual merits. The bishop, Alberto Prandoni, himself presided over the collection of testimony. Not only did they question witnesses to miracles, but they also interrogated witnesses to the supplicant's previous affliction, in order to further validate the authenticity of the miraculous events. These actions demonstrate that the bishop and canons were eager to adopt a new holy patron and that they anticipated that Armanno would be acceptable to the Ferrarese. While the emphasis on the legitimacy of Armanno's miracles reflects the papacy's growing demands for the canonization of saints, it could also suggest that Bishop Alberto knew that there were dissenting opinions regarding Armanno's worthiness.

Within eight months of Armanno's death, the inquisitor of Lombardy and the March of Genoa began an investigation to determine if Armanno had been a relapsed heretic. Frà Aldobrandino had been involved in an inquiry in 1254 in which Armanno had confessed to being a Cathar, the dualist belief that had become popular in certain areas of southern Europe in the twelfth and thirteenth centuries. After Armanno abjured heresy, frà Egidio, the inquisitor of

---

61. Weinstein and Bell, *Saints and Society*, 142.

62. This overview is indebted to *Itinerari*; for further discussion, see Peterson, "Politics of Sanctity in Thirteenth-Century Ferrara."

Lombardy, absolved him and imposed a fine of 100 Ferrarese *librorum*. While Armanno subsequently seemingly led the life of a good Christian in Ferrara, some years before Armanno's death Aldobrandino questioned several heretics in Sermione who mentioned Armanno. Aldobrandino asked an inquisitorial official of Verona, a man named Nicolaus, to inquire "diligently" into Armanno's beliefs. Nicolaus discovered that Armanno had supposedly received the Cathar *consolamentum*, or ritual laying on of hands that signified entrance to the role of a *perfectus*, or full participant in the Cathar community. He informed Aldobrandino, who missed the communication because he had already left for Rome. There the inquiry ended until Armanno died and his cult began.

Competing inquiries into Armanno's holiness and into his heterodoxy ensued. Bishop Alberto started collecting testimony from Armanno's supplicants, who praised his many healing miracles in December 1269. Frà Aldobrandino began to question witnesses about Armanno's heterodoxy in August 1270. These deponents testified that Armanno continued to ascribe to Cathar doctrine after his confession and had tricked the Ferrarese into believing him holy. The inquisitor's witnesses, mostly Cathars themselves, testified that Armanno frequently gave reverence to Cathars in the ritual greeting called the *melioramentum*. Through interrogation the inquisitor learned that Armanno purportedly had received the *consolamentum* only two years before his death (although this dating conflicts with the witnesses from Sermione, who stated he had received it when they were questioned eight years prior to his death).[63] Armanno's presumed status as a *perfectus* made him a particularly dangerous recalcitrant heretic, for he had the power to perform the rite of *consolamentum* on others.[64] Further testimony was similarly damaging to Armanno's reputation. One witness asserted that Armanno had stayed in the homes of known Cathars and visited imprisoned Cathars in both the episcopal and communal palaces of Ferrara. Other deponents claimed he made fun of the host and the doctrine of transubstantiation and claimed that only Cathars would be saved. Several local friars also stated it was public knowledge that Armanno had retained Cathar beliefs. Nevertheless, there was a dissenting viewpoint

---

63. *Itinerari*, 50–52 and 59, respectively.

64. For an overview of Cathar beliefs, see Lambert, *Cathars*. For the medieval view of Cathars, see the series of treatises edited by Ilarino da Milano: "La 'Manifestatio heresies catharorum,'" "Disputatio inter catholicum e paterinum haereticum," "La 'Summa contra haereticos,'" and "Le 'Liber supra Stella.'" See also Dondaine, *Un traité néo-manichéen du XIIIe siècle*; this edition also includes Rainerio Sacconi's "Tractatus de Catharis sive Paterinis," extant in Milan, Biblioteca Ambrosiana A129 inf., ff. 153r–186v, and edited by Charles Molinier: "Un traité inédit di XIIIe siècle."

among the inquisitor's deponents, for one admitted heretic claimed that Armanno was a traitor (patharenus) to Cathar beliefs.[65]

As a result of this investigation, in 1271 the inquisitor Aldobrandino ordered the cathedral chapter to exhume and destroy Armanno's body. Aldobrandino claimed that Armanno came from a long line of heretics and that "his father, mother, and wife had all been consoled heretics [i.e., Cathars]."[66] Bishop Alberto refused. In response, the inquisitor excommunicated him, and the canons and placed Ferrara under interdict, in which the clergy were not allowed to administer to the spiritual needs of the citizens. In essence, the interdict also condemned the community of Ferrara as aiders (fautores) and receivers (receptatores) of a heretic, namely, Armanno Pungilupo. In modern parlance, the citizens were identified as "accessories" to the crime of heresy and were denied access to the spiritual healing of Christian rites.[67] The cathedral chapter of Ferrara fought back, compiling the list of Armanno's miracles and testimony asserting that his actions after his 1254 abjuration were those of a faithful Christian. The evidence the bishop gathered in 1272 specifically addressed Armanno's behavior, thus counteracting the inquisitor's evidence with testimony from seven priests of parish churches attesting to Armanno's orthodoxy. The clerics testified that Armanno habitually confessed, was always penitent, and frequently sought communion outside of the yearly one required at Easter.[68] The cathedral chapter sent this evidence, along with Armanno's miracula, to Cardinal Giovanni Gaetani Orsini and asked him to lift the excommunication and interdict. This request was subsequently granted.[69]

Appeals to the pope from both sides continued. Inquisitors took further testimony against Armanno in 1273, 1274, 1283, 1285, 1288, and 1289. The bishop's notaries obtained further evidence of his miracles in 1280, and then in 1286 had notaries verify the earlier testimony from 1269–1270. In 1301 the standoff finally ended after lasting thirty-two years and engaging three different popes, four inquisitors, and three bishops respectively (table 2).

---

65. Itinerari, 49, 50–51, 55, 57, 59, 62.

66. Itinerari, 59.

67. Clarke, Interdict in the Thirteenth Century, 21–28 on collective guilt, 59–74 on types of interdict, and 130–68 on the terms of an interdict; Stantchev, Spiritual Rationality, esp. 90–116.

68. Itinerari, 86–88.

69. The papal chair had been empty from 1268 until Pope Gregory X was elected in December 1271. Gregory X was not consecrated until 27 March 1272; in the meantime, Cardinal Orsini appears to have remained in charge of the situation in Ferrara (Benati, "Armanno Pungilupo nella storia religiosa," 99–100). Orsini was later elected pope in 1277, taking the name Nicholas III. The order was read on 4 June 1272 in the chapter of the Dominicans at Bologna (Ferrara, Biblioteca Comunale Ariostea, MS Cl. I, 445/2, 321–23, 286r–287v; transcribed in Benati, "Frater Armannus Pungilupus," 43–44; and Itinerari, 105–7).

Table 2.   Authorities involved in the dispute over Armanno Pungilupo

BISHOPS OF FERRARA	INQUISITORS (OP)	POPES (DIRECTLY INVOLVED IN BOLD)
Alberto Prandoni (r. 1257–1274)	Frà Aldobrandino	**Gregory X** (1271–1276)
	Frà Egidio	
Giacomo (r. 1274–1290)	Frà Florio	(3 short pontificates, 1276–1277)
		Nicholas III (1277–1280)
		Martin IV (1281–1285)
		Honorius IV (1285–1287)
Federico (r. 1290–1303)	Frà Guido of Vicenza	Nicholas IV (1288–1292)
		Celestine V (1294)
		Boniface VIII (1294–1303)

Factions both for and against Armanno's holiness sent delegates to the curia in 1300 to plead their cases.[70] Pope Boniface VIII refused to receive the agent of the bishop of Ferrara. He appointed the bishop of Bologna and a Dominican friar of the same city to oversee a special commission of experts in canon and civil law who would adjudicate. On the advice of the commission, Boniface condemned Armanno in 1301 as a relapsed heretic. The pope ordered the bishop to destroy all images and statues and warned that if the cathedral chapter disobeyed he would excommunicate them, strip them of their offices, and once again place an interdict on Ferrara.[71] The sentence of condemnation prompted a covert mission to gather Armanno's remains in a way that would present the recalcitrant community of Ferrara with a *fait accompli*. Under cover of darkness one night in March 1301, the inquisitor of Lombardy and the March of Genoa, along with some of his Dominican brothers, secretly entered the cathedral of Ferrara. They exhumed and burned Armanno Pungilupo's bones and dispersed his remains in the river Po. The next morning when the canons discovered the act, a full riot ensued. Citizens vowed to wreak vengeance on the inquisitor, Guido of Vicenza. According to a chronicle written in the 1370s, "Without doubt he [the inquisitor Guido] would have been taken, and perhaps killed, if the Marquis Azzo [d'Este] with many armed men had not run to the place, and made each one turn back."[72] The Ferrarese never received their wish, for when the reigning bishop of Ferrara, Federico, died in 1303 Pope Boniface VIII appointed frà Guido to the episcopal seat, perhaps as a reward for a deed well done. The contradictory testimony about Armanno

---

70. *Itinerari*, 72.
71. *Itinerari*, 93–97.
72. Bartolomeo of Ferrara, *Libro del Polistore*, 707.

Pungilupo's actions prompted the dramatic scene in Ferrara. The Dominican inquisitors had gathered enough material to condemn Armanno as a heretic under normal circumstances. Yet the situation in Ferrara was not normal: the evidence that "proved" Armanno's heterodoxy was countered by testimony of clerics that "proved" Armanno's orthodoxy. Thus there was a deadlock until Boniface VIII stepped in. The events demonstrate the problems of the *inquisitio* for establishing holiness or heterodoxy.

Armanno's history epitomized the theme of the heretical "wolf in sheep's clothing." In the Middle Ages wolves symbolized avarice, lust, and pride. People believed that wolves stalked their victims at night, terrified them by making loud noises, and concealed their approach by spitting on their paws, which hushed their footsteps.[73] The wolf's very body was deadly, according to Albertus Magnus, who claimed that their eyes infected the surrounding air with poison.[74] Only the saint and lover of animals, Francis of Assisi, could befriend and tame one of these rapacious animals, the wolf of Gubbio.[75] The connection between wolves, heresy, and disease was prevalent in inquisitorial literature. Just as the wolf's eyes polluted the air with poison that could not be seen, so too did the pious pretender endanger the salvation of Christians by stealthily infecting them with the religious pollution of heterodoxy. Conversely, lay members of the community who were hostile to clerics also utilized the image of the wolf, interpreting for themselves the image of the Dominicans as the "hounds of the Lord" (*domini canes*). Whereas the Dominicans celebrated their role as hunting dogs, as one fresco in the Spanish Chapel of the Florentine Dominican convent of Santa Maria Novella suggests (figure 2), local communities instead reviled the brothers as wolves in their midst, or wild dogs ready to rip out a jugular.[76] An inquisitorial register of Bologna makes this point clear; deponents attested that the inquisitors were "worse than dogs," while according to a certain Ala Raimondini, the inquisitors were the children of a she-wolf.[77]

The dichotomous identity of those who were identified with wolves overlaps with the dichotomous views of Armanno Pungilupo in an interesting way. Armanno's last name means "wolf killer." Depending upon one's inclination, this could be interpreted to mean that Armanno was a destroyer of heretics, as befitted a holy man, or that he was a predator of inquisitors and other "false"

73. "Wolf," in Metford, *Dictionary of Christian Lore and Legend*, 265.

74. Magnus, *Questions concerning Aristotle's "On Animals,"* VIII.24.296.

75. Ugolino, *Little Flowers of St. Francis*, book 1, chap. 21, pp. 48–49.

76. On the image in S. Maria Novella, see Meiss, *Painting in Florence and Siena*, 97–98; for the wolf in both inquisitorial and popular discourse, see Ames, "Does Inquisition Belong to Religious History?," 32.

77. *Acta S. Officii*, vol. 1, no. 467, p. 270, and vol. 1, no. 543, p. 289, respectively.

FIGURE 2. Detail of Andrea da Firenze, *The Way to Salvation* (1348–1355), Spanish Chapel, Santa Maria Novella, Florence. Photo by author.

clerics, as suited an unrepentant heretic. One inquisitorial witness testified that Armanno had claimed Christian clerics were wolves who did not do God's work and deceived souls.[78] His surname became apropos during the competing inquiries into his merits, when the citizens of Ferrara, both clerical and lay, supported his cult against the Dominican "wolves" who were trying to destroy his memory. Yet ultimately, as Pope Boniface VIII's condemnation makes clear, the "wolf killer" Armanno, who denigrated the mendicant "wolves" and almost bested those inquisitors who tried to destroy his cult, was transformed into a wolf himself for posterity by papal decree. His story, as well as the opposing usage of the term "wolf" to describe both heretics and those who sought them out, demonstrate how perception was the essential issue in cases of disputed sanctity.

Conflicts about suspect saints seem worthy of a Boccaccio story. For popes, inquisitors, or other papal agents, these local saints were Boccaccio's *ser* Ciappelletto in the flesh. The author's tale presents a man erroneously championed as a saint. Ciappelletto was concerned that the magnitude of his transgressions would result in his being denied a church burial. Consequently, during his

78. *Itinerari*, 54; see also 50, 64.

deathbed confession he omitted his offenses and embroidered upon his virtues so that his friar confessor would grant him absolution. Ciappelletto successfully pulled the wool over the unsuspecting friar's eyes only too well, for
the cleric posthumously promoted Ciappelletto as a saint based upon the humility he had displayed during his false confession. Ciappelletto's friends, cognizant of the deception, were overcome with mirth at the cleric's credulity.
Boccaccio moralizes at the end:

> It was thus, then, that *ser* Ciappelletto of Prato lived and died, becom-
> ing a Saint in the way you have heard. Nor would I wish to deny that
> perhaps God has blessed and admitted him to His presence. For albeit
> he lived a wicked, sinful life, it is possible that at the eleventh hour he
> was so sincerely repentant that God had mercy upon him and received
> him into His kingdom. But since this is hidden from us, I speak only with
> regard to outward appearance, and I say that the fellow should rather
> be in Hell, in the hands of the devil, than in Paradise. And if this is the
> case, we may recognize how very great is God's loving kindness towards
> us, in that it takes account, not of our error, but of the purity of our
> faith, and grants our prayers even when we appoint as our emissary one
> who is His enemy.[79]

Boccaccio's scandalous *ser* Ciappelletto demonstrates the problem of determining "true" as opposed to "false" sanctity based solely on external behavior. The resulting conflicting perceptions in this story are not merely a literary
device; they also reflect the reality of contested sainthood. The tale exemplifies how in the late Middle Ages the line demarcating the saint and the heretic, or the remarkable and the ordinary, could shift depending on how an
observer interpreted the actions, conduct, and words of a saint. The subjective nature of such assessments could give rise to separate and seemingly dichotomous realities.

In Boccaccio's story the friar was the one who considered Ciappelletto holy
based on his words and demeanor, while in contrast representatives from the
community viewed him as a fake based on their own knowledge of his prior
deeds. Boccaccio's moral synopsis illustrates the belief that only God knows
true spiritual merit and purity of intention. Outward appearance, the only
litmus test available to mere mortals, is a distant second-best. The relative
impossibility of differentiating true and false sainthood—and by extension,
true and false heterodoxy—is highlighted by the fact that it is the authority
figure, the friar, who mistakenly considers Ciappelletto holy. Boccaccio's

---

79. Boccaccio, *Decameron*, first day, first story, 36–37.

quasi-carnivalesque story of the duplicitous Ciappelletto thus inverts traditional power relations by portraying a cleric as the person who is hoodwinked.[80]
Such instances are also present in historical records. Sibylla of Metz, for example, deceived authorities into believing she was a saint before they discovered she was a fraud who simulated fighting off demons and only pretended
to fast for long periods of time. Cases like Sibylla's testify to the extreme difficulty of ascertaining sanctity, even for the clerical elite.[81] Unsurprisingly
most sources, written by this same clerical elite, present communities as the
parties that were regularly fooled and so venerated individuals hiding grave
faults, as the chronicler of Guido Lacha's dancing bones portrayed. Identifying heresy was difficult, as the failure of inquisitors to establish Meco del Sacco's guilt showed.

The examples in this chapter reveal that analyzing external signs to discern
sanctity was insufficient, since they could be interpreted in a manner that corresponded to an individual's desires and prejudices. The subjective nature of
such assessments could give rise to separate realities for suspect saints. The
line demarcating the saint and the heretic or the pious and the impious, just
like the one dividing the remarkable and the ordinary as discussed in chapter 1, could shift depending on how an observer interpreted the actions, conduct, and speech of the person in question. The problems inherent in this
process of recognizing sanctity, or heresy, is exemplified in suspect saints. The
contest between local communities and inquisitors regarding who was worthy of veneration shows that the *inquisitio* often fell short as a means of assessing spiritual worth. Even members of the clerical elite did not believe in
the power of inquisitors and their tools to identify heterodoxy. The bishop
and Augustinians who shielded Meco del Sacco and fought on his behalf, as
well as the secular clergy of Ferrara who promoted Armanno Pungilupo's cult
for thirty years, clearly demonstrate this fact. If inquisitors claimed to recognized heresy based on their knowledge of behavior, lay and clerical members
of communities maintained they could recognize sanctity in very much the
same way.

---

80. Boccaccio's tale of *ser* Ciappelletto cannot be characterized as carnivalesque proper, since its
premise is a secret ruse, known only to a few, rather than a popular ritual whose purpose is "grasp
reality" (Bakhtin, *Rabelais and His World*, 212). Nonetheless, resonances of carnivalesque inversion are
found in the narrator's "gleeful admiration" of Ciappelletto's trickery and its exploration of the "par-
adoxes and inconsistencies of the established social order" (G. H. McWilliam, introduction to Boccaccio, *Decameron*, cxxi).

81. Richer of Sens, *Richeri Gesta Senoniensis ecclesiae*, in *MGHSS*, XXV, 308–10; see the discussion
in Caciola, *Discerning Spirits*, 87–98, and Elliott, *Proving Woman*, 194–97. Most of these aspiring saints
were women, perhaps because it was women who were considered more susceptible to the devil's
attacks (Caciola, *Discerning Spirits*, 134).

CHAPTER 3

Heretical Saints

Guglielma of Milan (d. 1281) was a lay penitent posthumously condemned as a heretic. In 1300 inquisitors exhumed her body and burned it. Guglielma had garnered a following among a circle of devotees and in the wider community, including the monks of the prominent Cistercian monastery of Chiaravalle outside Milan's city walls, where she had been interred. Some of these devotees, however, such as a serving woman named Taria, ascribed more than mere holiness to Guglielma. During the questioning of Guglielma's followers, the inquisitorial process records that "having asked this Taria if she herself wishes to deny that the stated holy Guglielma was not the Holy Spirit, she responded that she did not want to deny or affirm [it], but she very much wished that this Guglielma was the Holy Spirit."[1] After the Milanese inquisitors learned of these questionable beliefs among her followers, Guglielma herself became the focus of attention.

As noted in the previous chapter, identifying true from false piety was of grave import. At stake was the fate of Christian souls: for inquisitors, this took the form of fear that heretics would seduce the faithful into error; for believers, it was of hope for salvation through intercessory prayers. While always an issue, this problem became particularly poignant in the thirteenth century amid a renewed fervor to live the *vita apostolica*, or apostolic life. The church

---

1. *Milano 1300*, 152.

recognized some, such as Francis of Assisi, for engaging in the apostolic mission as it was then understood, through preaching and living in poverty as a mendicant in imitation of the apostles. It condemned others, such as Peter Valdes, whose unauthorized preaching was not supported by a local bishop (and future pope), as Francis's would be.[2] As already noted, regulation in the thirteenth century forced those who were intent on living like Jesus' early followers to conform to an approved rule or to live in the world as lay penitents. The latter option became increasingly popular yet was a perilous venture as the thirteenth century progressed and the papacy's determination to eradicate nonconformity increased in step with its ability to do so through the establishment of inquisitorial offices. While the existence of unsupervised lay penitents made the papacy uncomfortable, others admired these men and women who adhered to the ideals of the apostolic life. Seemingly intensely pious persons attracted followers and resulted in regional devotion, such as occurred for Guglielma and another lay penitent who achieved a significant following named Gerard Segarelli. Both attained orthodox veneration and clerical approbation, yet inquisitors deemed them relapsed heretics and destroyed their nascent cults.

As discussed in the previous chapter, the establishment of the inquisition led to a new scrutiny of saints. As a result, locally venerated holy persons could suffer a fall from grace and become condemned heretics, particularly those who were not members of established clerical orders. Inquisitors viewed these men and women as pretenders because they did not recognize their followers as part of an orthodox association. A group's way of life could therefore only seem to be penitent and the leaders only purportedly show the characteristics of saintly perfection. What distinguishes heretical saints from suspect saints is that their ultimate condemnation primarily was based on the behavior of their followers. It was the time-honored rituals of devotion and the fervor of their admirers that caught the attention of the inquisitorial eye. The unmonitored religious movement, so feared by the papacy, resulted in these saints' official condemnation as they became tainted by the actions of their ardent devotees.

The Rise to Fame

Information about Guglielma of Milan and her posthumous cult is limited to the evidence her followers provided during an inquisitorial inquiry in 1300.[3]

---

2. Lambert, *Medieval Heresy*, 147–71.

3. The inquisitorial process is published in *Milano 1300* and is the basis for this overview. Recent scholarship on the Guglielmites and their beliefs is extensive; the most substantial published studies include Benedetti, *Io non sono Dio*; Costa, *Guglielma le Boema*; Istoft, "Divinity Manifest in a Female

She came to Milan circa 1260 with a son, whose existence is only briefly mentioned in the records. Deponents testified that she was the daughter or, according to one person, the sister of the king of Bohemia. Current scholarship posits that Guglielma was the daughter of King Ottokar I of Bohemia and Constance of Hungary. If this surmise is correct, Guglielma was related to Elizabeth of Hungary (d. 1231), Margaret of Hungary (d. 1270), and Agnes of Bohemia (d. 1282). All of these women were involved in the thirteenth-century blossoming of lay piety.[4] The fact that devotees believed Guglielma descended from a royal family whose lineage included several women recognized or revered as saints undoubtedly assisted in the perception of her as a holy woman, since she is not noted for being either extraordinarily ascetic or a mystic. Rather, Guglielma seems the archetypical lay penitent, living simply and acting humbly, clothing herself in a simple brown tunic and surrounding herself with like-minded individuals. She gave moral counsel to others; for instance, she instructed one Bonadeo Carentano to "keep yourself clear from oathbreaking and deception and usury."[5] She displayed none of the somatic experiences that emerged among female penitents in the thirteenth century, nor the characteristics of the mystic that would become prevalent during the fourteenth century.

Despite Guglielma's ordinariness outside of her presumed royal birth, she quickly became the focus of local devotion after her death on 24 August 1281.[6] Her body was moved to Chiaravalle after a short delay due to a war between Milan and Lodi that had rendered the roads impassable. Guglielma had promised the abbey her remains in exchange for providing her with a place to live in her final years, in a house that the monks purchased in the parish of S. Pietro all'Orto. This fact strongly suggests that the monastery planned to promote Guglielma's holiness well before she died. Once her body was interred at Chiaravalle, the abbey held feasts in her honor attended by roughly 120 citizens besides the monks, constructed an altar over her burial place that they kept continually lighted, and had a fresco of Guglielma painted above her tomb. Other churches and organizations supported Guglielma's sainthood. For

Body"; Muraro, *Guglielma e Maifreda*; and the following studies by Barbara Newman: "WomanSpirit, WomanPope"; "Heretic Saint"; and "Agnes of Prague and Guglielma of Milan." See also Peterson, "Social Roles, Gender Inversion,"; and Wessley, "Thirteenth-Century Guglielmites."

4. Guglielma's real name would have been Blažena Vilemína (Polc, *Agnes von Böhmen*, 11–18, cited in Newman, "WomanSpirit, WomanPope," 185n13. Cf. Marina Benedetti, who argued that there was no real evidence that Guglielma descended from Bohemian royalty (Benedetti, *Io non sono Dio*, 23). For a discussion of the "genealogy" of sainthood in thirteenth-century Eastern Europe, see Klaniczay, *Uses of Supernatural Power*, 95–110; and Klaniczay, *Holy Rulers and Blessed Princesses*.

5. *Milano 1300*, 182; see also the testimony of Giacoma da Coppa on p. 190.

6. Cf. Wessley, who placed her death two years earlier, in 1279 (Wessley, "Thirteenth-Century Guglielmites," 301n60).

instance, the monks of Chiaravalle fought with the church of S. Pietro all'Orto, where her body had lain before her translation to the monastery, for possession of her original coffin. In addition, the Humiliate house of Biassono erected an altar and commissioned a fresco of Guglielma and Jesus freeing captives while the parish churches of Sta. Maria Minore and Sta. Maria Mater Domini, and the ancient basilica of Sant'Eufemia, also commissioned images of Guglielma and celebrated her feast day, although the scope and extent of these devotions are unknown.[7]

While clerics rallied orthodox support for Guglielma's cult in the years following her death, an inner circle of devotees, comprised of many of Guglielma's close companions during her life, took this veneration to a new level by worshipping her as the incarnation of the Holy Spirit. The line between sectarian and devotee was porous; one witness told inquisitors he had "attended parties, congregations, and festivities for the devotion and veneration of the aforesaid deceased Guglielma . . . namely in the house of the aforementioned Amico Toscani and Carabella his wife . . . and in the house of the aforementioned Master Iacobus many times, and in [the monastery of] Chiaravalle many times, in which place they ate together; and many times this witness went with [other] devotees with candles to a solemn ceremony and the tomb of the said former Guglielma."[8] Although part of the inquisitorial register is missing, seventy-five people were named or implicated in addition to several monks who helped to protect the deponents with whom they had close relationship.

Two sectarians, Andrea Saramita and Maifreda da Pirovano, spearheaded the dissemination of the Guglielmite heresy. Andrea taught others that the Holy Spirit was reincarnated on earth "on account of the sins of false Christians and of those who crucified Christ."[9] The Holy Spirit had opted to return as a female for this earthly sojourn to prevent a repetition of what occurred during the Holy Spirit's/Christ's previous terrestrial manifestation. Andrea predicted that Guglielma would effect a Second Coming on Pentecost 1300. Her devotees would establish a new apostolic church in which all the Jews, Saracens, and those "outside the church" (presumably heretics, apostates, and those who had been excommunicated) would be saved. Since the Holy Spirit had chosen to appear in female form, the Guglielmites thought the pope of this new age should likewise be female. Andrea Saramita thus appointed Maifreda da Pirovano to this anticipated position.

---

7. *Milano 1300*, 72, 80, 96, 135, 144, 146, 148, 160, 184, 188, 190, 222, 236, 240, and 304.
8. *Milano 1300*, 240.
9. *Milano 1300*, 72.

The questionable beliefs of the Guglielmites first came to the attention of authorities in 1284 when the Dominican inquisitor Maifredo da Dovera questioned several sectarians who recanted their heterodox beliefs. Subsequently, a different inquisitor, Tommaso da Como, questioned another follower in 1296. After the pope removed da Como from office for overstepping his authority in another investigation, the men who replaced him, Guido da Cocconato and Rainerio da Pirovano, began an earnest inquiry into the group in 1300. It is possible that internal dissension within the Guglielmites after the failure of Guglielma to reappear on Pentecost of that year might have reignited the inquisitors' interest. They called the first deponent, Maifreda da Pirovano, on 18 April 1300. The outcome of the process was a foregone conclusion since devotees had been under the inquisitorial microscope for years. Inquisitors handed over to the secular arm for punishment as relapsed heretics those sectarians who previously had confessed and received absolution for holding heretical beliefs, while they sentenced other members of the group who abjured to wearing large crosses on their clothes or paying fines as forms of penance. Finally, they burned Guglielma's bones to prevent further veneration and undoubtedly ordered local churches to destroy their frescoes.[10]

Scholars have portrayed the Guglielmite sectarians as protofeminist reformers and simple religious nonconformists. Luisa Muraro argued that sectarians wanted to change the status of women in the Christian church but not dismantle the institutional structure. Although the group had composed a new liturgy and sacred writings and had chosen the future pope and some of a new

---

10. Inquisitors sentenced Giacoma da Nova, a relapsed heretic, to be burned. This decision forms part of the process, but it is the only one of its kind; the other sentences are all for monetary fines or yellow crosses (*Milano 1300*, 202). Although judgments for Andrea and Maifreda are not extant, Luisa Muraro, for one, claimed Andrea was burned between 2 and 9 September 1300. On 9 September, inquisitors questioned Riccadona, Andrea's wife (not to be confused with his mother, who was similarly named). Inquisitors referred to Andrea on this occasion as "quondam Andreas," suggesting he was no longer among the living. They also asked Riccadona how much wine was in the house at the time they detained Andrea, which Dyan Elliott suggested was for the purpose of determining the extent of his property that they could confiscate (*Milano 1300*, 222; Elliott, *Proving Woman*, 154). The confiscation of a relapsed heretic's property was part of standard procedure (Hamilton, *Medieval Inquisition*, 55). The destruction of Guglielma's remains probably took place early in September 1300. On 9 September, the notary no longer referred to her as "Guglielma, who is buried (*sepulta est*) in Chiaravalle" but as "Guglielma, who was buried (*sepulta erat*)" (noted by Grado Giovanni Merlo, "Inquisitori a Milano: intenti e techniche," in *Milano 1300*, 23). Inquiry into the monk Marchisio Secco in 1302 also attests to the destruction of Guglielma's remains; inquisitors asked, "Si ipse male dixit de illis qui fecerunt comburi corpus dicte Guillelme vel si credidit eos male fecisse" (*Milano 1300*, 304). Evidence for Maifreda's fate derives from a 1322 letter written by Pope John XXII to the archbishop of Milan, in which the pope accused the Vicar of Lombardy, Matteo Visconti, of aiding his cousin Maifreda during the trial of 1300. In the letter, John XXII identified Maifreda da Pirovano as the one who was burned with Guglielma, substantiating the destruction of Guglielma's remains and the ultimate fate of Maifreda (BAV, ms. 3937, published in part in Tocco, *Guglielma Boema e i Guglielmiti*, 30n1).

college of cardinals, Muraro argued that the rituals practiced by the sectarians imitated Roman rites, suggesting a respect for and belief in the orthodox institution. Barbara Newman, in contrast, asserted that the sectarians exhibited "common piety intensified to the point of deviance" but that ultimately their group posed a threat to orthodoxy only on the "theoretical plane."[11] It is true that this small group of radicals posed little imminent danger to the sitting pope's preeminence or to a schism, such as would occur three centuries later with Martin Luther. Nevertheless, the Guglielmites created a theological justification for a new church based on the need for female spiritual leadership, and so inquisitors found no difficulty in condemning the sectarians for heresy. Not even the support of orthodox members of the church hierarchy, including the monks of Chiaravalle, a monastery founded by St. Bernard of Clairvaux himself, could save Guglielma's cult.

The inquisitorial process of the Guglielmites is a rich source compared with other heretical saints. Information about Gerard Segarelli and Dolcino of Novara (d. 1307), the successive leaders of a thirteenth-century lay apostolic reform movement, must be pieced together from a variety of texts. Reconstructing their beliefs, actions, and veneration is hampered because medieval commentators such as Bernard Gui and Salimbene de Adam conflated the two men. Both chroniclers viewed the apostolic movement begun under Segarelli and continued under Dolcino as a natural progression and consequently attributed identical ideas to them and their respective followers. Unfortunately, modern scholars too readily have accepted this portrayal instead of examining them as distinct individuals.[12] The nature of Segarelli's movement altered drastically once he was executed and Dolcino stepped into the vacant executive role. The appellations by which members identified themselves demonstrate this point. One of Segarelli's followers testified to Bolognese inquisitors eight months before Segarelli's demise that they called themselves "*pauperes Christi*" or "*minimi*," but that "they were accustomed to be called apostles" (*consueverant appellari apostoli*) by others.[13] The terms "the poor of Christ" and "the insignificant ones" mimic Franciscan antecedents and emphasize apostolic poverty. The name "Apostles," in contrast, may have become favored under Dolcino's leadership. "Apostles" is more self-consciously aggrandizing; under Dolcino they also called themselves "[those of the] heavens" (*celorum*).[14] The attitude of church officials also differentiates the

---

11. Newman, "WomanSpirit, WomanPope," 191 and 189, respectively.

12. See Pierce, *Poverty, Heresy, and the Apocalypse*, 7–23.

13. Testimony of brother Gerardinus in *Acta S. Officii*, vol. 1, no. 77, 14 November 1299, p. 111.

14. Testimony of Nascinbene Iohannis Bixellini de Plumatio, in *Acta S. Officii*, vol. 2, no. 679, 29 July 1304, p. 461; see also no. 684. Some observers referred to Dolcino's group as "sgarmigliati" (testi-

men. Inquisitors initially tolerated Segarelli and his followers, and some high-ranking members of the clergy supported him. In contrast, religious authorities perceived Dolcino as a heretic from the beginning. Segarelli was a perceived pious individual whom inquisitors subsequently identified as heterodox, while Dolcino was a heresiarch who had an inner cult of supporters yet attained wider admiration after his execution. I therefore distinguish between the two men and the two manifestations of the group, using the term *pauperes Christi* for the movement under Segarelli and the designation "Apostles" or "Order of Apostles" for the group under Dolcino's leadership. Although the boundaries between types of disputed sanctity are fluid, as the example of Armanno Pungilupo in the previous chapter attests, Segarelli is addressed in this chapter as a heretical saint and Dolcino in the next as a holy heretic, since the circumstances of their veneration and the cause of their demise differ significantly.

According to Salimbene de Adam, whose chronicle is a primary source of information, Segarelli was "of base family, an illiterate layman, ignorant and foolish."[15] Salimbene had met Segarelli and was acquainted with a friar who had left the Franciscan order to join Segarelli's followers. When Salimbene was living at the Franciscan convent in Parma, Segarelli had tried to join the community but was rejected for reasons unknown. Undeterred in his desire to follow the *vita apostolica*, Segarelli grew his hair long, dressed himself in sandals and a rough garment, and sold his possessions. He took the money he had made from the sale of his goods and threw it into a crowded piazza, thus imitating the conversion experience of his model, Francis of Assisi.[16] He then embarked on an itinerant existence in Emilia-Romagna. Segarelli soon gathered a significant following of people who shared his determination to experience the *vita apostolica*. Those who became followers, or members of the *pauperes*

---

mony of sister Margarita, in *Acta S. Officii*, vol. 2, no. 675, 4 July 1304, p. 455). This term probably can be equated with the word "scarmigliato," meaning unkempt or disheveled. In modern Italian, "scarmigliato" refers mainly to one's general appearance, but it can also suggest someone who's appearance expresses a rejection of mainstream society or a more negative connotation of a disorderly (i.e., heretical) mind. I thank Dr. Beatrice Arduini for this suggested translation.

15. *Chronicle of Salimbene de Adam*, 250. The following summary comes from 249–69, 273, 275–79, 282–84, 286–87, 289–93, 570, and 626–27. For discussion, see Carniello, "Gerard Segarelli as the Anti-Francis"; Goodich, *Vita Perfecta*, 198–203; Lambert, *Medieval Heresy*, 219–22; Lea, *History of the Inquisition*, 3:103–9; Pierce, *Poverty, Heresy, and the Apocalypse*; and Stephen Wessley, "Enthusiasm and Heresy," 214–59.

16. Celano, "First Life of St. Francis," 229–37. Salimbene attempted to counteract this comparison by remarking that Segarelli, an illiterate fool, gave his money to the riff-raff who were gambling in the square rather than to the poor (*Chronicle of Salimbene de Adam*, 250). For how the papacy perceived St. Francis in comparison to others such as Segarelli or Valdes whose similar views on the apostolic life were deemed heretical, see Lambert's section on the Waldensians in *Medieval Heresy*, 147–71.

Christi, gave up their possessions, lived in common, and kept only one robe to wear. They survived by collecting alms while preaching the Gospels to others, although Salimbene claimed they did so without the "knowledge of the Scripture required, or the common sense."[17] One chronicler recounted that seventy-two postulants passed through Modena in 1284 on their way to join Segarelli in Parma. There is evidence that by 1287 the group had made it to Würzburg, where city officials found the need to prohibit citizens from giving the *pauperes Christi* food on the grounds that they were undesirable vagrants.[18] While some local governments viewed the movement as a social problem, Segarelli had gained the support of the bishop of Parma, Obizzo Sanvitale; the bishop of Spoleto, Rolando Taverna; and the abbot of the Cistercian monastery of Fontanaviva.[19]

Although peaceful and publicly orthodox, there were aspects of the group's beliefs that caused concern in some clerical circles. The apocalyptic tone of the *pauperes Christi* was problematic for some observers, as was the excessive adherence to early Christian practices, leading them purportedly to engage in the testing of their chastity by lying naked with a member of the opposite sex all night in order to see if they could restrain themselves in the face of temptation. This practice engendered the disapproval of inquisitors and mendicant commentators alike, who did not think anyone preserved their chastity on these occasions.[20] When authorities prosecuted three *pauperes Christi* in 1286 for deceiving a woman into having sex with them, clerical support for Segarelli and the *pauperes Christi* eroded. The group appeared to be acting like a religious order, although there had been a ban on new orders since the Fourth Lateran Council. No one was monitoring their public organization and preached interpretation of the Gospels. In the early 1280s Bishop Obizzo Sanvitale of Parma, formerly a supporter of Segarelli, imprisoned him for a short period.[21] Segarelli's brief incarceration was a harbinger of things to come. Pope Honorius IV in 1286 issued the bull *Olim felicis recordationis*, which condemned

17. *Chronicle of Salimbene de Adam*, 277.

18. Lea, *History of the Inquisition*, 3:105 and 106, respectively.

19. Lambert, *Medieval Heresy*, 221; Carniello, "Gerard Segarelli as the Anti-Francis," 227–28; and Wessley, "Enthusiasm and Heresy," 36–37.

20. *Chronicle of Salimbene de Adam*, 264, 265, 253. On the history of testing chastity, see Pierce, *Poverty, Heresy, and the Apocalypse*, 89. By Bernard Gui's time, the perception was that the group did not think it a sin to have intercourse "in order to put an end to temptation" (Guidonis, *Practica inquisitionis heretice pravitatis*, translated in part in Wakefield and Evans, *Heresies of the High Middle Ages*, 406).

21. *Chronicle of Salimbene de Adam*, 260. Lea stated that it was in 1286 that Obizzo imprisoned Segarelli (Lea, *History of the Inquisition*, 3:107); cf. Carniello, "Gerard Segarelli as the Anti-Francis," 228n8, who argued that the bishop protected him until 1295, when he left Parma to become archbishop of Ravenna.

the *pauperes Christi* and required secular officials to aid clerics in prosecuting them. In March of that same year the pope sent a letter to all the Italian bishops asking them to force the members of the group to transfer to an approved order.[22] Bishop Obizzo followed the pope's directions and ultimately expelled the *pauperes Christi* from Parma.[23] Papal pressure increased when in 1290 Pope Nicholas IV issued the bull *Dudum felicis recordationis*, which ordered inquisitors to imprison and question all *pauperes Christi* who would not join an approved order.[24] The year 1294 was a watershed for the group as inquisitors in Parma, the center of the movement, fulfilled the papacy's demands: they burned two male and two female *pauperes Christi*, and the bishop, Obizzo Sanvitale, imprisoned Segarelli for the second time.[25] Segarelli's whereabouts between 1294 and 1300 are unclear, outside of a reference that Pope Boniface VIII ordered Segarelli transferred to Ravenna in 1295.[26] At some point he must have confessed to heresy and possibly was released, because in 1300 the Dominican inquisitor of Parma, frà Manfredo, sentenced Segarelli as a relapsed heretic. He was burned on 18 July 1300.[27]

The *pauperes Christi*'s concept of how one should pursue the *vita apostolica* was similar to that of the mendicant orders: they believed in itinerancy, poverty, and popular preaching. Consequently, they received general approbation and the support of bishops and other religious authorities. It was the group's more radical understanding of the apostolic life—including unauthorized calls to penance and encouragement of testing one's chastity—that led to inquisitorial investigations. Both Guglielma of Milan and Gerard Segarelli had attained significant local support from members of the secular and regular clergy as well as from the laity. For both, however, it was the actions of their devotees that prompted a sharper look from inquisitors and ultimately turned these saints into heretical saints.

The Ritual of Discovery

Private rituals performed within small groups of devotees helped to forge bonds among a saint's supporters. These actions had a mediating influence, during which participants from various backgrounds could engage in a dis-

---

22. *Les registres d'Honorius IV*, xcix, 223; Goodich, *Vita Perfecta*, 202.

23. *Chronicle of Salimbene de Adam*, 627.

24. *Les registres de Nicholas IV*, 625, no. 4253; Goodich, *Vita Perfecta*, 202.

25. *Annales parmenses maiores*, 713.

26. *Les registres de Boniface VIII*, 260–61; Wessley, "Enthusiasm and Heresy," 231.

27. *Additus ad Historia fratris Dulcini*, 450.

course on how best to venerate their saint. Communal devotions expressed this negotiation and served as nonverbal articulations of spiritual solidarity. Rituals served as a nexus where "some pair of opposing social or cultural forces comes together."[28] In the religious arena, those forces are belief and behavior. Yet since external actions are performative, they do not necessarily represent internal belief. Maifreda da Pirovano, the Guglielmite leader, recognized this possibility when she berated sectarians at one luncheon, stating, "You all eat of one [loaf of] bread and drink of one [bottle of] wine, but you are not all of one heart and one will."[29] Asked what Maifreda meant by these words, the deponent, Danisio Cotta, explained that she was referring to those gathered at the feast who did not believe Guglielma was the Holy Spirit. Another follower recalled Maifreda proclaiming at the same lunch, "Our lady [Guglielma's spirit] said to me that I should tell you that she [is] the Holy Spirit, and I say to you there are among you many [Doubting] Thomases, that is unbelievers."[30] While persons engaged in this discourse might identify dissent below the surface, outsiders only saw the performance of communal solidarity trying to protect a saint's cult. Thus it was the ceremonies themselves that often provoked an unwelcome interest and led to inquisitors' fatal scrutiny.

Dress, rituals, and verbal catchphrases were among the customs that regulated the Guglielmites and the *pauperes Christi*. Dress, whether voluntarily assumed or involuntarily imposed, came to identify one's religious beliefs: Jews wore a special badge, heretics a yellow cross, penitents a tunic of undyed wool, and the mendicants a robe in the color associated with their order. The thirteenth-century introduction of sumptuary laws similarly attempted to designate members of certain social groups through clothing, thus marking boundaries to retain "purity" between groups. Dress is a convenient symbolic shorthand that allows one to label individuals and situate them within a recognizable spiritual and/or social hierarchy. The aesthetic element of dress allows it to "be understood as ideological, its function to resolve formally, at the imaginary level, social contradictions that cannot be resolved."[31] People expressed the ideal of apostolic poverty through simple clothing as a protest to the perceived luxuries of the elite, both lay and clerical. When the mendicant orders became institutionalized, the color and cut of their apparel became regulated as an external symbol of religious ideals.[32] Thus while clothing

---

28. Bell, *Ritual Theory, Ritual Practice*, 16.

29. *Milano 1300*, 248.

30. *Milano 1300*, 234.

31. Wilson, *Adorned in Dreams*, 9; see also Dwyer-McNulty, *Common Threads*, 1–15. Like other ritual symbols, fashion allows the participants to "act out" belief and inscribe dress with meaning (Bell, *Ritual Theory*, 28).

32. Klaniczay, *Uses of Supernatural Power*, 70–75.

choices are private and individual, they assume a performative aspect as people publicly observe them. They express one's values and allow others to identify and categorize the wearers.

The followers of Gerard Segarelli consciously acknowledged the performative element of garments by enacting a ritual that viscerally represented their choice of a life of poverty when they became members of the movement. The *pauperes Christi* would undress and place their clothes in the middle of the room. Then they would put on white robes, the only clothing allowed from that time forward, and call out to Segarelli, "Father, father, father!" The female members would then distribute the old clothes to the poor.[33] The ritual symbolized the rejection of the person's old life and his or her entrance into the apostolic life and admission into the community of *pauperes Christi*. The subsequent similarity of dress would allow the penitents—and others—to identify them as members of the movement. It was also a liminal experience for group members as a rite of passage, marked by separation from one's old life, transition, and incorporation into a new life. It functioned to separate the individual from the prevailing social structure and forge, in Victor Turner's term, *communitas*, or "a spontaneously generated relationship between leveled and equal total and individuated human beings, stripped of structural attributes."[34]

The Guglielmites likewise adopted distinguishing dress, a simple brown tunic that mimicked that which Guglielma had preferred. The plain garment allowed the Guglielmites to identify each other, to distinguish themselves from the general population, to express their devotion to Guglielma by imitating her manner of dress, and, most importantly, to place the sectarians on the same social footing. Many of the Guglielmites were laymen and laywomen of high social standing, either of the lesser nobility or the wealthy merchant class, but the group also included serving women, clerics, Humiliate, and tertiaries. Thus the humble dress that most of the Guglielmites donned served as an expression of equality and fraternity for devotees of disparate backgrounds. As a result, sectarians called themselves a family (*tota familia*), had frequent gather-

---

33. *Chronicle of Salimbene de Adam*, 259–60; Pierce, *Poverty, Heresy, and the Apocalypse*, 79.

34. Turner, "Pilgrimages as Social Processes," 202. For the underlying principle of equality in the idea of *communitas* as expressed through ritual, see Klaniczay, *Uses of Supernatural Power*, especially 1–50; on the transient nature of *communitas* and the potential destabilizing nature of ritual, see Rubin, *Corpus Christi*, 2 and 265–66. This ritual of the *pauperes Christi* conformed to Turner's requirement that *communitas* needed universality, for the point was to engage all in the apostolic mission. On rites of passage, see Rubin's study based on the theories of the ethnographer Arnold Van Gennep ("Introduction: Rites of Passage," 10–12).

ings in which they shared meals, and thought of themselves as a "congregation" (*congregatio*).[35]

Other private rituals that served as a unifying force could also publicly signify special devotees. The *pauperes Christi*'s supposed testing of one's chastity was a private custom that had a public component. Successfully negotiating the minefield of sexual temptation indicated not just devotion to the *vita apostolica* but also membership within an elite group. Other members of the movement or even the community at large needed to recognize the experiment publicly, since the purpose of the *pauperes Christi* was to inspire a penitential process in others. Their processions during which they would walk through towns shouting, "Do ye penance!" also were expressions of private uniformity that served to publicly "perform" their beliefs.[36] The Guglielmites had different rituals, but ones that similarly unified the devotees. Sectarians adopted the practice of naming their children Paraclitus, Paraclitollus, Filixollus, and Filixolla after Guglielma, the "Paraclete" whose supposed real name was "Felice" in Italian.[37] They also engaged in private rituals that occurred in public spaces. Maifreda da Pirovano, the appointed future pope, would preach to the devotees at various gatherings. These took place in sectarians' homes but also elsewhere, such as the female Humiliate house of Biassono.[38] Male sectarians would "consecrate" hosts on Guglielma's tomb, which Maifreda would distribute to the faithful.[39] This required the sectarians to first obtain the wafers and then to perform a ritual at Guglielma's public gravesite on the grounds of the monastery of Chiaravalle. Finally, a vial containing the water used to wash Guglielma's body resided on an altar dedicated to Guglielma in Biassono, which Andrea had collected and given to Maifreda. Maifreda would anoint the Guglielmite faithful with it and dispense it to heal those who were ill.[40] Once again this was a private ritual signifying membership among a certain group of followers but one they performed, at least in part, in front of nonsectarians.

While these practices unified followers, they also allowed outsiders to identify devotees as a cohesive group. Frà Guido Cocconato, one of the primary inquisitors of the Guglielmites, focused on the fact that the sectarians all dressed in brown tunics. To the inquisitor, the group's identical clothing looked suspiciously like the Guglielmites were acting like an unapproved order. This

35. *Milano 1300*, 254, 230, and 234, respectively.

36. *Chronicle of Salimbene de Adam*, 251–52.

37. *Milano 1300*, 66, 80, 84, 92, 106, 110, 114, 118, 120, 144, 184, and 254.

38. *Milano 1300*, 66, 80, 84, 92, 106, 110, 114, 118, 120.

39. For consecrating hosts, see *Milano 1300*, 72; for Maifreda's distribution of them, see 78, 106, 114, 118, 124, 142, 156, 164, and 216.

40. *Milano 1300*, 180.

was dangerous after the Fourth Lateran Council banned the creation of new orders, as the history of Segarelli's followers also demonstrates. The *pauperes Christi's* similar dress, processions, and specific ritualized practices signaled to authorities that they were acting like an unauthorized religious community. One of Salimbene's major complaints against the *pauperes Christi* was that they rivaled the Franciscans and Dominicans by acting like an order when they did not have sacerdotal responsibilities and were not papally approved.[41] This concern eventually precipitated Pope Honorius IV's command that the movement disband and followers join an official order, as well as Pope Nicholas IV's subsequent condemnation of the group.

The Guglielmites in particular demonstrate how customs and rituals intended to create a community of devotees could prove to be a group's undoing and subsequently turn a saint into a heretical saint. The sectarians' practice of calling their children names that reflected the belief that Guglielma was the "Paraclete," or Holy Spirit, suggested to inquisitors that they worshipped Guglielma rather than venerated her. Moreover, their religious rituals proved dangerous for their existence, particularly their preparations for Guglielma's predicted Second Coming, expected on Pentecost 1300. Andrea Saramita collected money to buy vestments and hangings for the celebration. For her Advent, sectarians planned a public mass at Sta. Maria Maggiore in Milan and Maifreda's subsequent planned ascension to the Apostolic See. Part of these plans took place. They set an altar with candles, hosts, water, and wine. After Andrea read the Gospels and Franceschino Malconzato the "epistles" (presumably the new scriptural works written by the Guglielmites), Maifreda officiated over mass, distributed hosts, and gave a benediction. The witnesses never said where the Paschal mass took place. It must have been enclosed in order for the participants to hang the draperies bought for the feast and perhaps took place on the grounds of Chiaravalle, where there was a stone-covered sepulchre for Guglielma's remains.[42] Guglielma's absence from the proceedings apparently moderated the fervor to continue the procession to Sta. Maria Maggiore and Rome. Some scholars have conjectured that it was the Paschal mass that aroused inquisitorial interest and led to the first questioning of Maifreda on 19 April 1300.[43] The danger of making such activities public was not

---

41. *Chronicle of Salimbene de Adam*, 249, 263, 276; discussion in Pierce, *Poverty, Heresy, and the Apocalypse*, 92.

42. *Milano 1300*, 58–60, 92, 94, 106, 164, and 214. Marina Benedetti included a photograph of the purported site in her book *Io non sono Dio*, although there is no way to tell exactly where Guglielma was interred. The monastery's English guidebook notes that it was in the second *aedicula* (Facchin, *Chiaravalle Abbey Milan*, 22).

43. Lea, *History of the Inquisition*, 3:98. In contrast, Luisa Muraro suggested that it was only after the death of Andrea and Maifreda in fall 1300 that the Guglielmites felt free to discuss this ceremony,

lost on Maifreda, who instructed the sectarians not to discuss it. Talking about Guglielma's saintliness in private homes was one thing. Presiding over a mass, with the simulacrum of the sacerdotal responsibilities that entailed, was another. Maifreda warned Beltramo da Ferno, "You should not care about this and beware lest you say the truth, because Andrea Saramita and myself will die."[44] Except for one brief mention, Guglielmite sectarians did not reveal any details about this ceremony to the inquisitors until five months after the investigation started.

Although communities of believers performed many of the private rituals that symbolized inclusion in public arenas, groups like the Guglielmites recognized that, if interpreted "incorrectly" by outsiders, their customs and behaviors could lead to prosecution and ultimately the destruction of their saint's wider cult. A saint's special devotees, whose piety may have been aroused to the point of "deviance" in Barbara Newman's words, recognized that if they achieved support for their saint from powerful members of the community, then a private sect could live on borrowed time, shielded by the public cult. The connection between Guglielma's resting place of Chiaravalle and many of the sectarians was obviously close. Andrea Saramita served as the procurator when the abbey arranged for Guglielma to live in the house it owned in S. Pietro all'Orto, and he also assisted in the translation of her body to Chiaravalle. Furthermore, Andrea went to the abbot for advice when the inquisitorial inquiry began (discussed in chapter 8).

Private rituals and devotions were hard to keep private. As in all places and times, people notice recurrent actions. When the purpose of the rituals was to express faith in the devotee's understanding of the *vita apostolica*, the performative aspect was a necessity. A central tenet of the apostolic life was to spread teachings that would supposedly result in salvation. Thus Segarelli's followers did not hide their preaching that proclaimed their mission. The Guglielmites did not hide a lot of their activities, particularly from the monks on whose property much of it took place. Some members of sectarian groups did understand the danger inherent in public actions, as evidenced by Maifreda da Pirovano's warnings to other sectarians to stay quiet. If the *inquisitio* failed as a useful way to determine inner belief for individuals, its ability to monitor the external behavior of Christians made it successful when dealing with a larger numerical group. Inquisitors noticed conduct that suggested lay devotees were acting like

and that its existence was unknown to the inquisitors until then (Muraro, *Guglielma e Maifreda*, 95); cf. testimony mentioning it before then (*Milano 1300*, 92) and Newman, who suggested that Maifreda's presumed death sentence was not carried out until 1301 when Matteo Visconti lost some of his control over Milan (Newman, "WomanSpirit, WomanPope," 194).

44. *Milano 1300*, 212.

an order, through their dress or otherwise, which the church prohibited, or through their physical participation in behaviors dissonant with the church's view of orthodoxy. As a result, inquisitors focused on those who venerated the saint and, consequently, on the saint himself or herself.

The Fall from Grace

The veneration of contested saints such as Guglielma and Segarelli encapsulated two opposing yet intertwined forces, what Gábor Klaniczay identified as centripetal and centrifugal trends. The private devotions and rituals of special devotees were centripetal, inexorably drawing the participants in toward a center of shared values and the creation of *communitas*. Simultaneously, the broader devotion these saints attained was centrifugal, veneration that whirled outward in ever-increasing circles, touching layers of the wider lay and clerical orthodox population, who engaged in public rituals enmeshed within the traditional structure of the Roman Church.[45] Due to the close association of these forces, the rituals of communal veneration of a few unorthodox devotees of a saint could lead to the punishment of the many once inquisitors turned their attention upon the group. The condemnation of a saint's followers had a ripple effect, with waves of suspicion radiating out to touch many strata of society. Everyone with whom the sentenced heretics came in contact was tainted by association, including the saints themselves. They suffered a fall from grace from which they could never recover. Once inquisitors condemned them there was to be no more orthodox veneration, and their public cults were dismantled upon threat of excommunication. Just as clearly, communities did not easily abandon their holy patrons.

Suspected devotees needed unity to survive the inquisitorial threat. Miraculous events often helped achieve solidarity. At one memorable luncheon of Guglielmite sectarians, Allegranza dei Perusi recalled that Maifreda da Pirovano had announced that Guglielma appeared to Maifreda in a vision and told her she was the Holy Spirit, "truly God and truly human," instructing Maifreda to convey this knowledge to the group.[46] A woman named Adelina da Crimella responded to this pronouncement by declaring that she, for one, believed Guglielma was crucified in the same flesh as Christ. Her husband, Stefano, reprimanded her for making this statement. Allegranza then described the miracle that ensued. Another woman, Carabella Toscano, "[had] sat down on her

---

45. Klaniczay, *Uses of Supernatural Power*, 35.
46. *Milano 1300*, 224.

mantle and, when she lifted it up, she found that in her belt, or the cord of her mantle, three knots were made in the said belt that were not [there] before; and from this [there] was astonishment and murmuring among them. And many believed from these things and the witness herself [thought] that it was a great miracle."[47] The exact chronology of these events is unclear from the testimony, but it seems likely that Maifreda made her announcement, to which Adelina professed her faith and her husband chastised her. The miracle of the belt followed. Allegranza's account thus juxtaposes the faithless Stefano da Crimella with the faithful believers, including his wife, who maintained Guglielma's divinity. The latter were rewarded for their own belief through a miracle that confirmed Guglielma's sanctity and deepened their faith in her holiness. This incident also exemplifies how miracles could function to convert unbelievers. The miracle had the effect that "many people believed *from* these things" (i.e., the miraculous knots) that Guglielma was indeed divine. The incredulity of Stefano da Crimella provoked an answer authenticating Guglielma's holiness and silencing the Doubting Thomases.

Cults like Guglielma's survived thanks to the devotees whose silence was protection and permitted wider veneration. When this unity broke down, as occurred when the Guglielmites first came to the attention of the inquisitors, the saint was in trouble with the authorities along with the sectarians. The question of whether the inner devotees bear the sole responsibility of inquisitorial condemnations of heretical saints is difficult to resolve. There is no simple answer to whether some of these saints only became heretics by virtue of their aberrant followers, or if they themselves actively promulgated schism or heresy. With a condemnation came the excision of all evidence connected to the saint except for the inquisitorial process. Scribes and notaries translated and transcribed witness testimony from the vernacular to Latin, generally revising the first-person question-and-answer procedure into a third-person account, resulting in potential misinterpretations. Officials often administered torture to produce confessions that may or may not have been truthful, or they otherwise manipulated deponents to say what they wanted to hear. The notary was supposed to record if officials used torture to obtain confessions. In some cases, such as that of the accused heretic Bernard Délicieux in Languedoc, the record does attest to the use of force.[48] More commonly, notaries neglected to include such information, leaving the scholar to posit torture based on what appears as a sudden turnaround in witness testi-

47. *Milano 1300*, 226.
48. Friedlander, *Processus Bernardi Delitiosi*, 143 and 179–80; see also Friedlander's study of the trial in *Hammer of the Inquisitors*, 190 and 264.

mony. Henry Charles Lea, for example, argued that inquisitors tortured the two Guglielmite leaders, Andrea and Maifreda, to account for their switch from staunch denial to confession, although the inquisitorial process did not record its use.[49]

Guglielma and Segarelli both knew and advised some of their followers who were later sentenced for heterodoxy. This fact begs the question of whether these holy *cum* heretical saints played a role in forming the unorthodox beliefs inquisitors ultimately attributed to them. The evidence for both is contradictory. In Guglielma's case, Maifreda da Pirovano testified that she had heard Guglielma had once been cited for heresy and questioned by inquisitors and that Guglielma was the first to teach Andrea Saramita his heretical beliefs.[50] Stronger "proof" came from Andrea himself, who confessed that Guglielma had informed him that she was the Holy Spirit.[51] Another devotee, Francesco da Garbagnate, substantiated this testimony, stating that Andrea and Maifreda asserted that Guglielma had once told them "[that] the body of Christ [i.e., the Eucharist] was no longer sacrificed or consecrated alone, but with the body of the Holy Spirit that was Guglielma [herself]; whence Guglielma said that she no longer wished to see the body of Christ sacrificed because [in it] she would see herself."[52] The statement implies that Guglielma believed she was the Holy Spirit and thus of the same nature as the other parts of the Trinity, although Stephen Wessley contested this interpretation and asserted that it referred to the interdict Milan was under from 1262 to 1277 and, thus, to a consequent distrust of the validity of the sacraments that inefficacious priests performed.[53]

Other testimony conflicted, with some witnesses claiming that Guglielma vehemently denied she was the Holy Spirit.[54] A deponent recounted one scene in which several female followers believed they saw the stigmata on Guglielma on her deathbed. Guglielma reputedly told them, "You believed [that you would] see what you will not see on account of your incredulity."[55] The statement is enigmatic at best. While these women obviously believed in Guglielma's holiness, *incredulitatem* could be translated as either "incredulity" or "disbelief,"

49. Lea, *History of the Inquisition*, 3:100. On the problems with using inquisitorial sources, see Arnold, *Inquisition and Power*, 3 and 23–90; see also Ginzburg, "Inquisitor as Anthropologist," 161; and Scott, *Domination and the Arts of Resistance*, 3–6. On the ability to discern the "real" voice of a witness, see Biddick, "Devil's Anal Eye."

50. *Milano 1300*, 102.

51. *Milano 1300*, 102, 214, 254; for Andrea's own admission to the inquisitors on this point, see 196.

52. *Milano 1300*, 220.

53. Wessley, "Thirteenth-Century Guglielmites," 297–98.

54. *Milano 1300*, 102, 172, 190, 228, 278.

55. *Milano 1300*, 170.

providing two very different interpretations. Barbara Newman noted, "Guglielma could have meant that her devotees were mistaken to think that she bore the stigmata, but they themselves might have thought they could not see them because they lacked faith."[56] The problem of interpretation demonstrates how the inquisitorial procedure was more successful in ferreting out living heretics than discovering "false" saints or suspected heretics after their death.[57]

Living witnesses could implicate themselves to inquisitors. Whether inquisitors used force or coercive imprisonment to obtain confessions, the fact remained that a confession justified their condemnation. For instance, the inquisitors of Bologna questioned a man named Bonigrinus of Verona, who freely confessed to heterodox beliefs. Bonigrinus claimed that all good men, not just priests, could absolve people from sin. He also stated there were seventy-two faiths just as there were seventy-two languages, and that there was only one God but that the Devil created the material things of this world.[58] Bonigrinus had abjured heresy once before, so inquisitors labeled him a Cathar by focusing on the last point and ignoring the rest. They handed Bonigrinus over to the secular arm to be burned as a relapsed heretic on 10 September 1297.

There was greater difficulty in discovering theological error when the subject of investigation was deceased. Since there is no record of Guglielma's own supposed inquisitorial interrogation, and with no other evidence outside of the process, the modern case against Guglielma remains unresolved. No similar impasse occurred in 1300. The inquisitorial process of the Guglielmites shows how inquisitors transformed a locally venerated saint into a heretic without solid proof that the person had held heterodox beliefs. The steps leading to the determination that a saint was actually a heretic were fraught with uneven boards and faulty carpentry. Inquisitors did not appear to consider Guglielma a heretic until they discovered the heterodox tenets of the sectarians, after which they fashioned her into a heresiarch. She became tarnished by virtue of association with her zealous devotees. The process is discernable in how the notaries referred to Guglielma during the investigation. In the process, at first inquisitors called her "holy Guglielma" (*sancta Guillelma*), which devolved into "lady Guglielma" (*domina Guillelma*), then "Guglielma," and finally "that Guglielma" (*ipsa Guillelma*, with the definite negative connotation).[59]

---

56. Newman, "Agnes of Prague," 571.

57. Elliott, *Proving Woman*, 252–54.

58. Testimony of Bonigrinus, *Acta S. Officii*, vol. 1, no. 4, 13 October 1296, p. 14.

59. Examples in the process are, respectively, *Milano 1300*, 68, 144, 160, and 246. Marina Benedetti first noted this shift in description (Benedetti, *Io non sono Dio*, 82).

Guglielma was no longer holy, and that was how she would live on in infamy. Bernardino Corio in his history of Milan described her as a heretic who pretended to be holy. With no evidence from the inquisitorial process to support it, he added a common accusation leveled at heretics and claimed that she was the leader of a group of sexual deviants.[60]

A similar difficulty occurs in assessing the role of Segarelli in promoting behavior that inquisitors saw as heretical, even though in this case his condemnation was not posthumous. Segarelli advocated the testing of one's chastity, which had a long tradition, but perhaps even members of the movement believed that Segarelli did not abstain from sex. One follower testified to a Bolognese inquisitor in 1299 that, "having been asked if he heard it said or believed that the aforesaid Gerard Segarelli busied [himself] and did filthy and shameless touching with women and young boys, he responded that he well heard this and believed that he did such things and other similar ones."[61] Of course, the man could have been answering truthfully that he heard detractors say Segarelli was sexually active. The practice only heightened suspicions of deviancy that all supposed heretics faced. Salimbene noted that many "rascals, seducers, deceivers, thieves, and even fornicators" joined the group in order to more easily persuade women to have sex with them.[62] Whether or not this account is true, considering that similar tales appear in *fablieaux* and the stories of Boccaccio and Chaucer, is less important than the point that contemporaries (including members of the group) seem to have been receptive to the idea that some chicanery went on during these vigils of temptation. Undoubtedly, such an apparent readiness to believe that Segarelli and some *pauperes Christi* engaged in nefarious seductions did not assist in changing inquisitorial perceptions of them. Salimbene is also the author of a tale of three *pauperes Christi* who were hung in Bologna in 1286. The men supposedly convinced a young groom not to sleep with his bride on their wedding night until they gave him leave, thus proving his spiritual worth. All three men promptly had sex with his new wife, masquerading as her husband in the dark. When her husband finally joined her in bed, she protested at a fourth interlude. The groom realized the trick and notified the authorities, although the behavior of a few followers tells little about that of Segarelli himself.[63]

When one or two *pauperes Christi* publicly erred, the entire community suffered the consequences precisely because papal authorities viewed them as an organized sect. The actions of several inspired the punishment of all and led

---

60. Corio, *L'historia di Milano*, 367–68.

61. Testimony of Petrus Bonus, *Acta S. Officii*, vol. 1, no. 79, 18 November 1299, p. 115.

62. *Chronicle of Salimbene de Adam*, 286.

63. Ibid., 626–27.

to the loss of former institutional support. When authorities hung the three *pauperes Christi* in 1286 for cuckolding the husband, Segarelli fell out of favor with his former protector, Bishop Obizzo of Parma.[64] Bishop Rolando Taverna of Spoleto and the abbot of the monastery of Fontanaviva, both of whom originally encouraged Segarelli in his vocation, also distanced themselves around the same time.[65] The consequences quickly followed upon each other until inquisitors identified Segarelli as a heresiarch, even though he had early on relinquished control over his followers because such a position and its attendant responsibilities would hinder his ability to follow the *vita apostolica* and was counter to his concept of a communal life.[66] Internal dissension soon split the ranks when two followers, Guido Putagio and Matteo of Ancona, fought for control of the position that Segarelli himself refused to assume. At one point, Matteo's faction tried to kidnap Segarelli, who was living with Putagio, in the hopes that "possession" of the man would engender support for Matteo's bid for leadership.[67] Although it was Matteo who prevailed, it was Segarelli that inquisitors considered the leader and burned. Later authors described Segarelli as the promulgator of a "malignant and presumptuous sect having been spread by a devil."[68] The penitential spirit of his movement was reinterpreted as a demonic, polluting miasma of the disease of heresy.

The inner beliefs of Guglielma of Milan and Gerard Segarelli and their intentions for their circle of followers will never be determined. Nevertheless, the simplicity and ordinary aspects of these penitents' lives served as a soft surface upon which others could easily etch heterodox beliefs. Both saints attracted devotees not just because they advocated the *vita apostolica* but also because they represented a radical alternative to the current mendicant spirituality. They symbolized the possibility of a perfected life, one that would hearken in a "new age" of Christian spirituality.[69] This idea was appealing in light of the thirteenth-century popularity of the ideas of Joachim of Fiore (d. 1202), whose eschatology promised just such a possibility. Joachim's apocalyptic exegesis described three ages or *status* of the world, which could be divided into seven *tempora*, or eras in the history of the Christian Church.[70] Joachim be-

64. Wessley, "Enthusiasm and Heresy," 232.

65. Lambert, *Medieval Heresy*, 221; Carniello, "Gerard Segarelli as the Anti-Francis," 18–19; and Wessley, "Enthusiasm and Heresy," 36–37.

66. There is in this action again a similarity to Francis of Assisi, who also gave up the reins of power over his own nascent movement. On Francis's renunciation of leadership, see the *Scripta Leonis* in *Scripta Leonis, Rufini*, sections 76, 87, and 105.

67. *Chronicle of Salimbene de Adam*, 255–56.

68. Ehrle, "Die Spirituellen, ihr Verhältnis," 131.

69. Goodich, *Vita Perfecta*, 198.

70. For a description of Joachim of Fiore's eschatology, see Daniel, "Joachim of Fiore," and McGinn, *Calabrian Abbott*.

lieved that the world was entering the third *status*, the age of the Holy Spirit. During this time a new order would attain the ultimate heights of spiritual understanding and would transmit this knowledge to the public. Joachim also thought that the church soon would cross the threshold of the seventh *tempus*. This final *tempus* would be heralded by the coming of the Antichrist, to be followed by a time of peace. A number of individuals, particularly Franciscans, adopted Joachimite beliefs. Some extrapolated from his writings that an "angelic pope" would inaugurate the period of amity and would achieve Christian harmony by purifying the church. Although Joachim himself did not define the year in which the seventh *tempus* would begin, this did not deter some of his overzealous proponents from fixing a date and attempting to discern the Antichrist in the contemporary church.[71] The papacy condemned some of Joachim of Fiore's writings in 1215. After that date, the application of Joachim's ideas to current conditions was spiritually risky, not the least because it was politically foolhardy to identify notable contemporaries as the Antichrist. Elements of Joachimite thought became a signal to inquisitors that a potential holy reformer could in fact be a dangerous revolutionary.

Joachimite thought resonated throughout the Guglielmite heresy. Guglielma was the personification of the *status* of the Holy Spirit, as her incarnation viscerally embodied the advent of the Joachimite Third Age. Maifreda da Pirovano was the "angelic pope" who would purify the Christian church and lead it into a spiritual *renovatio*. The Antichrist, whose persecutions would precede the accession of the new pope, was the controversial Pope Boniface VIII. This equation was apt, for it was Boniface VIII's inquisitors who ultimately "persecuted" the Guglielmites. Similarly, Segarelli's calls to repent, in conjunction with his conversion experience in the year 1260 (the year that Joachimite commentators had predicted would inaugurate the third *status*), led certain followers to believe that Segarelli was the harbinger of the new age.[72] To combat these views, Salimbene asserted twice that Joachim said the Dominicans and Franciscans were prefigured in the Old Testament while the *pauperes Christi* were not.[73] Still, some *pauperes Christi* believed that, like St. Peter, Segarelli

71. Salimbene toyed with Joachimism in his early years (*Chronicle of Salimbene de Adam*, 229–41). For discussion on Joachim's impact on Franciscanism, see West, "Reformed Church and the Friars Minor," and West, "Education of Fra Salimbene." The concept of the "angelic pope" was an interpretation of thirteenth-century commentators (Reeves, *Influence of Prophecy*, 47).

72. Many early commentators believed Joachim thought the seventh *tempus* would begin in 1260, in which year Frederick II, whom they identified as the Antichrist, would die. Frederick defeated these predictions by dying early in 1250 (Reeves, *Influence of Prophecy*, 59).

73. *Chronicle of Salimbene de Adam*, 287 and 293.

could walk on water.[74] By identifying Segarelli with Peter instead of Christ, some followers evidently viewed their leader as Peter's successor, thereby making him Christ's current vicar on earth. One *pauper Christi* testified to inquisitors after Segarelli's death that the man should have been made pope while he was alive.[75]

Inquisitors targeted Guglielma and Segarelli primarily because of some devotees. As a result, orthodox members of communities who participated in their cults became implicated in heresy as well. While the most notable aspects of these heretical saints are undoubtedly their radical followers, what makes their holiness truly contested is that orthodox members of the population shared in the ritual devotions. The clergy of parish churches and religious houses in Milan supported Guglielma's cult. Her feast days, celebrated at the Cistercian monastery and officiated by the monks, drew a respectable number of participants. Although inquisitors only questioned about thirty to forty members of the Guglielmite sect, one witness recalled that about 129 people attended Chiaravalle on one of her feast days. That number is significant and demonstrates a wider base of veneration, considering that Chiaravalle was outside the city walls (figure 3).[76]

Today it is a fairly easy subway plus bus ride to travel from Milan's Stazione Centrale to the abbey, a trip that takes roughly fifty minutes. The cemetery where Guglielma was interred is two bus stops farther away, past fields and a stream that once belonged to the abbey. According to Google Maps, it is a two-hour walk each way to Chiaravalle from the slightly closer neighborhood of Brera, in Milan's city center and near where many of the sectarians resided. The effort that both the monks and Milanese citizens went through in order to celebrate Guglielma suggests a deep if not wide basis of veneration beyond the small group of sectarians.

Institutions like Chiaravalle became suspect on account of their interaction with sectarians; the investigation of the sect and their devotional practices prompted the inquisitors to cast a wider net. For instance, two years after inquisitors sentenced the sectarians and burned Guglielma's remains, they questioned Marchisio Secco, who lived at the abbey of Chiaravalle where she had been buried. They asked him in what manner the monks regarded Guglielma. Marchisio claimed that Guglielma was a good woman, admitted that the monastery had provided for her and supported her cult, but stated that they never

---

74. Testimony of brother Gerardinus speaking of Guidone Cistelas, *Acta S. Officii*, vol. 1, no. 77, 17 November 1299, p. 111). The account of Peter is in Matthew 14:22–34.

75. Testimony of Blasius speaking of Zacharias, *Acta S. Officii*, vol. 2, no. 604, 18 August 1303, p. 381.

76. *Milano 1300*, 184.

FIGURE 3. The church of the Abbazia di Chiaravalle, outside Milan. Photo by author.

believed in the heretical doctrines of the Guglielmites or participated in their private rituals.[77] Likewise, both regular and secular clergy initially supported Segarelli. Bishop Obizzo Sanvitale even regarded Segarelli as something of a personal favorite. He had pronounced a forty-day deferment of penance to those who gave charitable contributions to a group of female *pauperes Christi*. Segarelli's inspired calls for penitence even appealed to Franciscan friars like Salimbene's acquaintance who became a *pauper Christi*, and his early followers included Tripia and Guido Putagio, siblings of the *podestà* of Bologna.[78]

Citizens who admired these saints did not willingly relinquish their devotion. Barbara Newman recently discussed a fresco dating from around 1450 in the main church of Sant' Andrea Apostolo in Brunate. Brunate is a small village directly above the city of Como on Lake Como, which would have been quite remote and difficult to access without the modern inventions of the car and the funicular. Taking the mountain path down the hill to Como is a two-hour hike; going up to Brunate would be considerably longer. Yet this small church contains a fresco with a woman Newman identified as Guglielma

77. *Milano 1300*, 302–4.
78. Pierce, *Poverty, Heresy, and the Apocalypse*, 82.

Figure 4. A fresco identified as Guglielma blessing the sectarians Maifreda da Pirovano and Andrea Saramita in the Chiesa di Sant'Andrea Apostolo, Brunate. Photo by author.

blessing a female dressed as a nun and a man, purportedly Andrea and Maifreda (figure 4).[79]

In addition, a fourteenth-century sketch of an uncompleted fresco in the abbey of Vibaldone in Milan also suggests the continuation of Guglielma's cult. The drawing depicts the Trinity with an embodied Holy Spirit that has assumed female form.[80] Both images attest to more than just communal memory of a once-revered saint, but the continued existence of a cult for a woman who was condemned as a heretic.

Evidence for an orthodox if covert cult for Segarelli is more difficult to establish, but people did continue to venerate him as holy after his death. An inquisitorial record from Bologna between 1291 and 1310 confirms that his movement survived under its new leader, Dolcino of Novara. Dolcino did not entirely eclipse Segarelli, however, as one follower testified in 1303, "the Church was in [the time of] Gerard Segarelli and is now in [the time of] the said Dolcino and his followers good, pure, poor, and persecuted, just as in the time of Christ."[81] Sympathy for Segarelli and those who followed his version of the *vita apostolica* is tangible in the record, even years after Segarelli's execution and the condemnation of the movement under Dolcino. One person the Bolognese inquisitor questioned was a priest who had absolved some excommunicated members of Dolcino's group. He admitted to hearing from them that Dolcino and Gerard Segarelli were good men. When asked if he believed they were, the priest refused to answer, saying, "I don't know and I don't want to say another thing."[82] This type of response demonstrates that even some clerics did not

---

79. Newman, "Heretic Saint," 1–3.

80. Caciola, *Discerning Spirits*, 57–60; and Caciola, "Guglielmite Trinity?"

81. Testimony of Blasius speaking of Zacharias, *Acta S. Officii*, vol. 2, no. 604, 18 August 1303, p. 381.

82. Testimony of presbyter Corvolo, chaplain of the church of S. Sismondo de Monçorgio, *Acta S. Officii*, vol. 2, no. 606, 19 August 1303, p. 384.

accept the official condemnations of local saints and their cults and could be complicit in protecting their constituents who still sought the type of "purified" spirituality that these contested saints represented.

Sainthood de facto required the establishment of a cult. Once this occurred, wider acceptance of the cult was dependent upon the saint's devotees. Communities had a major role in this process with their ability to increase the base of veneration and subsequently lobby for the canonization of a local saint. The community's power, however, could also jeopardize the saint's reputation if the rituals of some devotees attracted inquisitorial attention, which occurred particularly when they seemed to be acting as an unauthorized order. The external actions of these groups signaled to inquisitors that they may have held internal heretical ideas. In the process of investigating a saint's followers, inquisitors reconstructed the saint as a heretic. All who might have accepted that person's holiness became supporters (*fautores*) of heresy if they did not cease venerating the person immediately. Yet this official decree was not always successful. If inquisitors believed that some locally accepted saints were dangerous "false prophets," the communities that sheltered and supported them perceived their pursuit of a perfected Christian life as the ultimate sign of holiness, testifying to the deep-seated disaffection with the spiritual authority of the papacy that was already suggested by the cults of tolerated and suspect saints.

CHAPTER 4

Holy Heretics

In 1389 a man named Michele Berti da Calci was immolated in Florence as a relapsed heretic. The bishop and inquisitors had condemned Calci as a Spiritual Franciscan who was recalcitrant in his heterodox beliefs, but the public execution engendered an unintended reaction. Some observers of the event regarded his demeanor when facing certain death as fitting into the traditional framework of martyrdom. As his hagiographer described, "And dead, many said, 'It seems [he is like] a saint,' objecting to opponents . . . and when the people returned home, to the greater part it seemed an evil [deed], and they could not grow tired of saying evil things about the clerics, and there were people who said, 'He is a martyr,' and who [said], 'He is a saint,' and who said the contrary. And thus there was never a greater noise in Florence."[1] The sentences of medieval inquisitors, just like those of Roman officials during the early Christian persecutions, could have an unforeseen result. The expanding role of inquisitors and their zeal in fulfilling their duty led to many condemnations in the thirteenth and fourteenth centuries. Yet when a sentenced individual did not conform to the expectations of how he or she should behave, it was possible for communal consensus to transform heretics into saints. While a saint became a heretic when inquisitors contested communal veneration, the reverse occurred when communities challenged in-

---

1. Piazza, "La passione di frate Michele," 256.

quisitorial decrees: a heretic became a local saint. In this process these communities not only rejected inquisitorial authority but also, since inquisitors served as papal agents, by extension rejected the papacy's authority to determine sanctity and heresy.

Such overt contestation occurred under certain conditions. Members of a community had to perceive an individual as suffering from unjust persecution. That person had to exhibit behaviors that contradicted expectations of how heretics behaved. People had to observe and discuss the situation. Finally, once onlookers achieved a majority consensus, they had to express a rejection of the inquisitorial sentence by some kind of devotional practice. This process occurred for Peter of Abano (d. 1316), Cecco of Ascoli (d. 1327), Dolcino of Novara (d. 1307), and Michele Berti da Calci. These four saints loosely fall into two groups. Peter and Cecco were learned men who had held powerful positions as court physician and astrologer, respectively. Inquisitors accused both men of sorcery based on their scholarly work, which they each refused to repudiate. Their fame led their communities to protect them against inquisitors whose prosecution seemed to overstep their limits. Calci and Dolcino were leaders of apostolic movements: Dolcino was the heir to Gerard Segarelli's *pauperes Christi* and provided the group a more radical eschatological character, while Calci was what one might call the overseer of a "cell" of Spiritual Franciscans. Both astrologers and unauthorized penitential leaders posed a direct threat to central tenets of Christianity and to papal authority. The fact that communities risked the serious spiritual punishments of excommunication and interdict by disobeying inquisitorial injunctions that these men were heretics brings into sharp relief the dissatisfaction with the papacy and communal wishes for autonomy present throughout the whole spectrum of contested sanctity.

Prosecution versus Persecution

Inquisitors had the responsibility to seek out and prosecute heretics. Paradoxically, however, it was this very attempt to eradicate heresy that resulted in contested definitions of who were the persecuted and who the persecutors. Persecution was easy to recognize during the Decian and Diocletianic purges of the third century, when Christians who refused to make sacrifices to Roman gods were executed in public spectacles.[2] In the later Middle Ages, citizens

---

2. On the nature of Christian executions as public spectacles, see Bowersock, *Martyrdom and Rome*, 48–52. For the persecutions of Decius and Diocletian, see Frend, *Martyrdom and Persecution*, 285–323 and 351–92.

witnessed the orthodox Christian tribunal in the form of inquisitors step-
ping into the role once performed by pagan Roman officials. In this new historical context, identifying the orthodox and heterodox and differentiating
between righteous prosecution and unjust persecution was not so easy. In the
growing battle against heresy, both inquisitors and those they prosecuted became casualties of religious belief and had the potential to be considered martyrs to the cause. In this context, sometimes that group included someone
learned or of good repute who seemed to be unfairly targeted or treated during
an inquiry against them.

While the application of the term "martyr" to condemned heretics in the
later Middle Ages may seem highly controversial, it is merely one more instance of how the meaning of the word shifted to fit the historical context.
During the Roman Empire it meant "witness," in the sense of being a witness
to something and/or for someone. Initially all Christians were martyrs, or witnesses, to and for God.[3] Some early Christian theologians, such as Clement
of Alexandria (d. circa 215), believed that all faithful Christians would break
free of the regulations and codes of society and achieve moral perfection
through an ascetic lifestyle.[4] Not all Christians, however, shared Clement's op-
timism or penchant for self-denial. After the onset of Christian persecutions,
church fathers reinvented its meaning, and martyrs became exceptional individuals.[5] As G. W. Bowersock and Patricia Ranft have demonstrated, in the
third century Christian writers such as Cyprian, Origen, and Clement of
Alexandria attempted to restrict the use of the term specifically to individuals
who were persecuted, and consequently died, because of their faith. For many
of these early theologians, persecution was crucial for authentic martyrs: they
could not be persons who simply wanted to die (the suicidal) or persons who
actively sought situations in which they could die for their faith (voluntary martyrs), especially as the latter was linked to Montanism, which the church
deemed heretical.[6] Martyrs remained popular subjects of veneration even after
the spread of Christianity in western Europe made persecution of Christians
mostly obsolete.[7] It was the eleventh-century emergence of heresy in western Europe that allowed the ranks of martyrs to swell once again in any numerical significance.

---

3. Hahn, "Speaking without Tongues," 162; Frend, *Martyrdom and Persecution*, 87–89.
4. Clement of Alexandria, *Miscellanies, Book VII*, 87.
5. Smith, *Fools, Martyrs, Traitors*, 362.
6. Bowersock, *Martyrdom and Rome*, 2–4, 17–19, and 59–74; Frend, *Martyrdom and Persecution*,
291–94; and Ranft, "Concept of Witness," 12. On the Montanists, see Salisbury, *Blood of Martyrs*, 195.
7. For exceptions, see Peterson, "Holy Heretics," 3n3.

The rise in what was deemed heterodoxy in the later Middle Ages had the potential for providing the church with a new kind of martyr, the martyred inquisitor. These types of cults, however, were not popular. St. Peter Martyr (d. 1252), the inquisitor murdered in Milan, suffered from lackluster support outside of his order even after his canonization. In southern France, cults of other inquisitor-saints, such as Martin Donadieu (d. 1299) and Peter of Castro (d. 1208), never took off.[8] In contrast, when inquisitors in southern France burned Spiritual Franciscans, or beguins, some who shared their beliefs considered them martyrs. The inquisitor Bernard Gui claimed that the beguins of Provence, Narbonne, and Toulouse asserted that their friends who had been burned for heresy were "condemned unjustly and because they defended the truth, and that they were not heretics but Catholics and are glorious martyrs in the presence of God."[9] After the beguine Esclarmonde Durban and some of her colleagues were immolated, her brothers scavenged through the ashes to retrieve body parts as relics.[10] In the Italian peninsula members of the Order of the Apostles, followers of the heretical leader Dolcino of Novara, passed relics of their executed brethren among themselves. Soon after Dolcino's own execution in 1307 Bolognese inquisitors asked suspected sympathizers if they loved or believed in any member of the Apostles or if they loved or believed in "any person who has any relics of [these] heretics, such as hair or bones or clothes or nails, or any other relics."[11] These situations described supposed members of heretical sects venerating one of their own as a martyr. The more problematic situation for inquisitorial and papal authority was orthodox veneration of sentenced heretics that cut across the boundaries of social status, background, or spiritual beliefs. This type of martyr saint resulted from inquisitors whose actions seemed misguided and unnecessarily persecutory.

An issue for modern scholars no less than for medieval observers is whether inquisitorial prosecution can be differentiated from inquisitorial persecution. The distinction is difficult to make on even a procedural level. Popes themselves provided the scope of prosecutorial powers. It was incumbent upon inquisitors that if someone's behavior was brought to their attention, they must investigate it. In their general sermons, they also asked citizens to come,

---

8. Elliott, *Proving Woman*, 170 and 61; see also chap. 8 below.

9. Guidonis, *Practica inquisitionis heretice pravitatis*, part 5 chap. 14, English translation in *Inquisitor's Guide*, 104.

10. Given, *Inquisition and Medieval Society*, 76–78; Burnham, *So Great a Light*, 77–80.

11. *Acta S. Officii*, vol. 2, no. 728, 4 July 1307, pp. 515–16. Waldensians did not seem to engage in similar instances of cult construction. Mariano d'Alatri argued that this situation is due less to a theological rejection of sainthood per se than a refusal to venerate the material remains of individuals (*Eretici*, 1:40; see contemporary descriptions of Cathar beliefs regarding saints in Wakefield and Evans, *Heresies of the High Middle Ages*, 253, 332, and 697, and of Waldensians [ibid., 349, 372, and 391]).

confess, and be reconciled with the church, with no fear of reprisal beyond the required, and presumably desired, imposition of penance. Heretics were handed over to the secular justice to be burned only if they were contumacious. These were mostly relapsed heretics, or persons who returned to heterodox behavior and/or belief after having abjured and received the cleansing gift of absolution.[12] Nevertheless, medieval inquisitors had wide-reaching prosecutorial powers, and the subjects of an inquiry lacked the apparatus to spearhead a defense. It was not until the very late thirteenth century that suspected heretics were granted some recourse to counteract any possible abuse of the inquisitorial office or its juridical procedure.[13]

The fact that orthodox observers did not consider all individuals convicted as heretics as worthy of veneration is strong evidence that medieval communities distinguished between prosecution and persecution. Christine Caldwell Ames argued that inquisitors themselves recognized this tendency and employed strategies in their preaching to preempt challenges to their authority.[14] There are cases, however, in which a purported heretic's treatment seemed particularly unjust and raised the concern of inquisitorial harassment and belief in an erroneous conviction. This is not to suggest that people automatically considered these controversial figures to be holy. They had to display proper Christian behavior as understood by other members of the local community, although this often differed from how inquisitors viewed their actions. There had to be signs that the prosecution was "unjust" and therefore was in fact persecution, such as if they seemed singled out. Bystanders also had to identify elements of their spiritual worth and benefit to the community. Then members of the community at large could venerate these individuals even though they may not have shared their alleged heterodox beliefs.

Peter of Abano and Cecco of Ascoli were two individuals who fit this model. Inquisitors charged both of these men with sorcery because of their astrological ideas and condemned them as heretics, while their communities subsequently lauded them as saints. Astrologers walked a very fine line between commendation and condemnation. They were renowned for their power to read the stars and make predictions. They played an important role in late medieval politics when amid frequent wrangling, rulers looked to the stars for advice on what action to take. Although the University of Paris prohibited the study of astrology in 1270 and 1277, secular leaders still hired astrologers as close advisers.[15] The predictions astrologers made could set off warning sig-

---

12. Lea, *History of the Inquisition*, 1:371–73 and 534–50.
13. Given, "Inquisitors of Languedoc," 339; Shannon, *Popes and Heresy*, 88.
14. Ames, *Righteous Persecution*, 41–46.
15. See Lea, *History of the Inquisition*, 3:379–491, esp. 434–53.

nals to inquisitors. If they were too successful in their outcomes, they could be charged with sorcery. If they made predictions too bold, they could be charged with heresy for denying free will or God's omnipotence for ascribing events to the movement of the stars as entities without a master. Yet what inquisitors could view as works of the Devil, communities could regard as divine inspiration.[16]

Peter of Abano (d. circa 1316) was a learned physician who believed astrology was a major component of medicine and who served as Pope Honorius IV's (d. 1287) personal physician.[17] According to accounts such as that of Michele Savonarola (the grandfather of the famous preacher Girolamo Savonarola), the people of Padua regarded him as a great magician because of both his medical skills and his knowledge of the stars, although whether this was the case in the early fourteenth century or not until the mid-fifteenth century when Savonarola was writing is debatable.[18] Peter claimed that the history of the world was cyclical and that the nature of the "state" and the church transformed every 960 years due to new alignments of the planets and stars. In his work *Conciliator differentiarum quae inter philosophos et medicos versantur* (1303), he expressed a belief in the power of astrological alignments forcefully enough that inquisitors believed he denied God's power. He was questioned on several occasions: possibly for the first time around the publication of the *Conciliator*; for the second time when he returned to Padua in 1306 or 1307, when he recanted; and again in 1315. He seemingly died of natural causes before this inquiry was over, thus narrowly escaping immolation since he was posthumously sentenced as a relapsed heretic.[19]

Cecco of Ascoli's (d. 1327) history follows a similar path.[20] A scholar renowned for his knowledge of astronomy, Cecco accepted his fame and proclaimed himself the greatest astronomer since Ptolemy. His predictions of the future led prominent secular leaders such as Louis of Bavaria, Castruccio Castrucani, and Charles of Calabria (the son of Robert of Naples) to use his skills for their own fortunes. Cecco became Charles of Calabria's court astrologer until he injudiciously predicted that one of Charles's daughters would

16. Bailey, *Magic and Superstition in Europe*, 93–99.

17. This description is indebted to Lea, *History of the Inquisition*, 3:440–41, and Thorndike, *History of Magic and Experimental Science*, 2:874–947. See also Thorndike, "Relations of the Inquisition," and Thorndike, "Peter of Abano and the Inquisition."

18. Savonarola, *Libellus de magnificis ornamentis*, part 15.

19. Peter of Abano, *Conciliator*. Modern historians of science are more sympathetic regarding his position on the role of astrology; see Marangon, "Per una revisione dell'interpretazione"; Paschetto, *Pietro d'Abano medico e filosofo*, 28–32; Prioreschi, *History of Medicine*, 5:375–77; and Vescovini, "Peter of Abano, the 'Conciliator.'"

20. Cecco's birth name was Francesco degli Stabili. This description is indebted to Lea, *History of the Inquisition*, 3:441–44, and Thorndike, *History of Magic*, 2:948–68.

"sell her honor."[21] Upon leaving Charles's court, Cecco traveled to Bologna, where he taught at the university and wrote a commentary on John Sacrobosco's *Sphera*, in which he described how he could read men's thoughts and predict their futures by reading the position of the stars on the date of their birth. He illustrated his skill in the commentary by showing how Christ's horoscope made his Passion, poverty, wisdom, and birth in a manger inevitable. For inquisitors, Cecco's astrology seemed to deny both free will and God's omnipotence. In 1324 the Dominican inquisitor of Bologna, frà Lamberto da Cingoli, questioned Cecco. He abjured, his commentary was burned, and he was forbidden to teach. Cecco moved to Florence, where he wrote a poem called *L'Acerba* that again affirmed the power of the stars. In 1327 the Franciscan inquisitor of Florence, frà Accursio de' Bonfantini, questioned Cecco and condemned him as a relapsed heretic. He was handed over to the secular authorities and was burned near Santa Croce (perhaps in the same piazza as Michele Berti da Calci sixty-two years later) along with copies of his works.

Inquisitors targeted these men due to the theological implications of their work, which suggested that the world's history was discoverable in the alignment of stars and planets. There is evidence they were not diligent in their efforts to understand those implications. For instance, the Florentine inquisitor frà Accursio obtained a copy of Cecco of Ascoli's previous sentence and abjuration to ensure that he had the evidence to sentence Cecco as a relapsed heretic. He did not bother to read Cecco's commentary on the *Sphera* himself, however, and announced this fact in Cecco's sentence of condemnation, which he read aloud to the public.[22] This admittance created a problem and the suggestion of procedural transgression. A divergence from inquisitorial protocol or a questionable justification for a condemnation could cement the interpretation that inquisitors persecuted Cecco.

Ritual, ceremony, and procedure were ingrained and constantly observable in religion and daily life. Inquisitorial processes were a part of both in late medieval Italy. While most people in the Middle Ages were illiterate, they were not undiscerning. In Lunel in southern France, for instance, when inquisitors refused to read a deponent's confession at her own request, the people vocally questioned the justice of her sentence.[23] Some citizens of Bologna rioted when inquisitors refused to give a condemned heretic the communion he desired

---

21. Lea, *History of the Inquisition*, 3:442.

22. Ibid., 441–44. Cecco's 1327 sentence exists in later vernacular copies; the fullest edition is in Beccaria, *Le redazioni in volgare*, 10–30. Antonio DeSantis published the most complete transcription of Cecco's 1324 abjuration (*Meco*, appendix 1, 277–79). For a discussion of Cecco and his works, see the essays in Albertazzi, *Studi stabiliani*.

23. Given, *Inquisition and Medieval Society*, 77.

before the execution of his sentence.[24] The alleged comments of one Iohannes describe how the community viewed the event: "How could this be? He seemed to be a good Christian. I saw heretics despise the body of Christ [i.e., the host] and this one seeks it, so how could he be a heretic, since he sought the body of Christ? It is not possible."[25] Specific procedural transgressions engendered suspicions of more generalized inquisitorial misconduct. Moreover, they promoted the view that the person suffered from an erroneous judgment. The result was that some communities interpreted the deaths of certain sentenced heretics as cases of unjust persecution, as long as some of the other signs of sanctity were present.

Both Peter of Abano and Cecco of Ascoli acquired civic cults after they were sentenced as contumacious heretics. André Vauchez argued that in the late Middle Ages there was a propensity to venerate those who suffered a violent death, whether they were persecuted or not. Murdered "holy innocents" fit into this schema, as does Vauchez's category of "suffering kings," or even the famous saintly dog, St. Guinefort. More dubious examples of sanctity include two monks struck dead by lightning in 1368 and subsequently venerated in the Romagna.[26] Vauchez's contention could hinder looking at sainthood in a nuanced manner. Except perhaps for the unlucky monks, moral virtue and some form of unjust persecution are constants in all of these saintly examples, not just violent death. Robert Bartlett invoked Augustine's remonstrance that one must have suffered unjustly, not just suffered violence, in his discussion of later medieval martyr saints, such as those produced from accusations of ritual murder or "political martyrs."[27] In the case of holy heretics, sainthood could only happen if people considered them unjustly persecuted because they were sentenced criminals and supposed enemies of the church. Violence and suffering was not enough; citizens had to believe that these men (and, theoretically, women) were virtuous and worthy and had been mistreated. With these same characteristics at the foundation of officially recognized martyrdom, it did not require a leap of faith for the orthodox to recognize and apply the same standards of holiness to those in their communities that seemingly misguided or corrupt papal agents deemed heterodox. The perceived powers

---

24. Testimony of lady Bolnexe (filia condam Cunte piscatoris), *Acta S. Officii*, vol. 1, no. 156, 18 May 1299, p. 167. This was a common refrain; see also nos. 166, 167, 173, 174, 184, 208, 211, 218, 219, 226, 227, 233, 234, 239, 248, 249, 260–63, 272, 275, 277, 282–85, 290, 293, 322, 334, 339, 346, 348, 366, 411, 414, 417, 419, 437, 456, 458, 463, 472, 477–79, 481, 490–92, 516, 518–20, 523, 526, 549, 550, 551, 553, and 555.

25. *Acta S. Officii*, vol. 1, no. 152, 18 May 1299, p. 156.

26. Schmitt, *Holy Greyhound*; for the other examples, see Vauchez, *Sainthood in the Later Middle Ages*, 151–52, 158–66, and 89, respectively.

27. Bartlett, *Why Can the Dead Do Such Great Things?*, 179–85.

of Peter and Cecco, who healed the sick and/or predicted future events through their knowledge of the stars, were persuasive factors for how citizens assessed their spiritual worth.

Peter of Abano's history provides material evidence of how his contemporaries valued him, rejected the inquisitor's decrees, and then venerated him. Scholars assume that Peter died just before his condemnation as a relapsed heretic, hence his posthumous sentence. There is one account that upon his death sympathizers secretly buried his body so that unsuspecting inquisitors only burned an "effigy" of him.[28] The burning of bones provoked distress; following one such incident in Bologna in 1299 a number of citizens declared nothing was gained by destroying remains and doing so was foolish. One woman commented, "[Burning bones] was evil and it was better to burn the living than the dead."[29] Implicit in her remark is a belief that the annihilation of the body was analogous to the death of the soul. By the thirteenth century, theologians thought that after death the soul resided either within physical remains, which was why body parts of saints were relics, or suffered in purgatory until the Last Judgment, when God would resurrect the body and unite it with the soul.[30] This testimony suggests the woman thought that burning the living was a punishment by consigning a soul to the purgatorial fire, while burning the dead destroyed the possibility of a resurrected body by impeding God from granting salvation due to inquisitors sending a soul to the eternal fire. The burning of physical remains could therefore be considered not only evil but also the definitive act of persecution. The protection of Peter's body thus was a willful act of recalcitrance. It suggests that supporters viewed him as special, unjustly condemned, and his body consequently imbued with spiritual power. The bodies of saints were considered miracle-working relics, full of the presence of the saint and imbued with holiness. As John Arnold, Patrick Geary, and Peter Brown have all discussed, the power of a saint was thought to be focused in a physical space. The hiding of Peter's remains thus locates them in a protective space that becomes conferred with symbolic meaning.[31]

It is hard to determine how widespread the perception was that inquisitors engaged in persecutory instead of prosecutory actions, although this topic will

---

28. Naudé, *Apologie pour Tous les Grands Hommes, soupçonnez de Magie* (Amsterdam: chez Frédéric Bernard, 1712 [1625]), chap. 14; reprinted as *Apologie pour Tous les Grands Hommes: Qui Ont Este Accusez de Magie*, Classic Reprints (London: Forgotten Books, 2018).

29. *Acta S. Officii*, vol. 1, no. 239, 19 May 1299, p. 193; discussion in Lansing, *Power and Purity*, 154–55.

30. Bynum, *Resurrection of the Body*, 318–34, and Le Goff, *Birth of Purgatory*, 289–333.

31. Arnold, *Belief and Unbelief in Medieval Europe*, 86–87; Geary, *Furta Sacra*, 5–9; and Brown, *Cult of the Saints*, 1–22.

be explored further in chapters 6 and 8. What is clear is that condemned heretics such as Cecco of Ascoli and Peter of Abano achieved recognition as holy in their towns. According to a chronicler of Ascoli Piceno who recorded the deaths of notable citizens, Cecco became a spiritual patron of both Ascoli and Spoleto after he was executed in Florence in 1327.[32] Citizens protected—or wanted to protect—Peter's body from inquisitorial flames. In 1420 the city of Padua inscribed an epitaph for Peter of Abano on the gate of the Palazzo della Ragione.[33] Federico da Montefeltro, the duke of Urbino, later erected a bust of Peter in the town.[34] These acts physically inscribed approval of both Peter's work and his spiritual worth. Today Cecco of Ascoli too has a monument in his honor, erected in Ascoli Piceno. Although civic governments embraced these men, the extent of their veneration is unknown. It was probably very small and very local. All of these acts, however, were an outright defiance of inquisitorial judgments and the papal authority that had sanctioned them. Communities valued external signs of spiritual merit and moral worth, such as the astrological and medical arts of learned and respected men. Peter and Cecco became saints due to their standing in the community and the perception that not only did they not deserve execution but also that the investigation itself was unjust. In Cecco's case, the inquisitor admitted that he himself had not read the text that supposedly contained heretical doctrine. In Peter's case, the inquisitor posthumously declared him a heretic and attempted to burn his bones. Those who observed saw inquisitorial actions as persecutory instead of justified and transmitted that belief through communal memory to change the legacy of both men.

Late Medieval Heretical Martyrs

The visual elements of martyrdom also had the power to transform a heretic into a saint. Courage, physical fortitude, and steadfastness in the face of death had the potential to win over observers to the condemned heretic's side. The deaths of early Christians resulted in converts to the faith. While the death of a condemned heretic rarely led to mass conversions to heresy, it could produce sympathy and even veneration from orthodox members of society. Dolcino of Novara and Michele Berti da Calci were condemned heretics who exhibited behavior that mimicked that of the early Christian martyrs

---

32. Cited in *Meco*, 52–55.
33. Ronzoni, *Della vita e delle opere*, 537; for discussion, see Paschetto, *Pietro d'Abano*, 48–49.
34. Thomasini, *Patavini illustrissimi virorum elogia*, 23.

during their gruesome deaths for their beliefs. As a result, they became seeming saints and provoked rejections of inquisitorial authority.

Dolcino of Novara became the leader of the group called the *pauperes Christi* in 1300 after Gerard Segarelli was burned as a relapsed heretic. Segarelli's concept of how one should pursue the *vita apostolica* was like that of the mendicant orders: he believed in itinerancy, poverty, and popular preaching. His group's disregard for institutional support, unauthorized calls to penance, and encouragement of testing one's chastity, as described in chapter 3, all testified to a more radical understanding of the Christian life than the papacy would accept. Dolcino of Novara pushed papal tolerance to the limit with his apocalyptic ideology and vocal opposition to the institutional church. The Order of Apostles, the name used for the movement under Dolcino's leadership, transformed Segarelli's aspiration to live like the apostles into the goal of establishing a whole new church. To achieve this, Dolcino directly attacked the clergy and, above all, the pope with Joachimite polemic that unequivocally called for the destruction of contemporary ecclesiastical structures. The testimony of one follower, Vivianus Grandonis, a canon of Sta. Maria de Montebellio in Bologna, claimed that "just as God placed Adam and Eve in Paradise and as God renewed the world in the time of Noah through water and even renewed the world in the time of Moses and afterwards renewed the world in the time of Christ, just so it shall be renewed through those Apostles."[35] A significant number of Dolcino's followers were willing to fight to their deaths behind his battle cry of spiritual renewal.

Dolcino was possibly the son of a priest named Guilio of Trontano in the Val d'Ossola in the diocese of Novara.[36] He was educated, supposedly at the church of Sta. Agnese in Vercelli. It is unclear how he became involved with Segarelli, but one month after the latter's execution Dolcino wrote a letter claiming he was the mouthpiece of God and the new leader of the movement. Whereas there was only a thin veneer of Joachimite thought in the beliefs of Segarelli's *pauperes Christi*, Joachimism was the foundation for the Apostles' spiritual philosophy and its militant opposition to the contemporary church. Members of the Apostles questioned by inquisitors in Bologna in 1303–1304

---

35. Inquisitorial condemnation of Vivianus, *Acta S. Officii*, vol. 2, no. 597, 22 November 1304, p. 371).

36. The main sources that discuss Dolcino's life and the beliefs of the Apostles are an anonymous *Historia fratris Dulcini*, Bernard Gui's addition to this text, and his section on the apostles in his inquisitorial manual, the *Practica inquisitionis* (*Historia fratris Dulcini* and *Additus ad Historia Fratris Dulcini*, 15–36 and 449–53; Gui, *Practica*, in Wakefield and Evans, *Medieval Heresies*, 404–8; this synopsis of Dolcino's early life is from *Additus*, 449–53). Recent secondary works include Pierce, *Poverty, Heresy, and the Apocalypse*; Mornese and Buratti, *Fra Dolcino e gli apostolici tra eresia*; Orioli, *Fra Dolcino*; Orioli, *Venit perfidus heresiarcha*; Orioli, "Ancora su Fra Dolcino"; and Vercellino, *Frà Dolcino*.

identified four ages of the church: "[God] renewed the world in the time of Moses when He gave the New Law. Then He wished to renew the world in the time whereby blessed Christ came into the world. Then He wished to renew [it] in the time of St. Sylvester. Then . . . in the same way [God] wishes to renew the world in those who are [called] Apostles."[37] Segarelli was the "offshoot" of God who betokened the advent of the fourth age, in accordance with the Joachimite fixation on 1260 as a crucial year.[38] The events of this last age would include the immanent appearance of the Antichrist and a saintly pope.

Dolcino preached to his followers that during the fourth age all clerics would die because they were unworthy of their vocation. Following the Donatist legacy of Segarelli, they asserted that they could worship God anywhere they wanted, since the churches were defiled by corrupt priests and the pope had no power to excommunicate or bind or loose. Members of the Order of Apostles refused to take oaths and believed they were justified in lying to and deceiving inquisitors about their beliefs. In the words of a Sienese chronicler, Dolcino "put forward that the pope and cardinals and other rectors of the holy Church did not observe that which they ought for an evangelical life" and that the clergy were messengers of Satan.[39] Apostles maintained that the church was not the real church but a Babylon that had "forsaken the faith of Christ."[40] It was the Order of Apostles that was the "true" church of God because they lived in perfection just as the first apostles and thus were subject only to God.

The beliefs of the Apostles, publicly articulated, provoked the papacy to a strong response. In 1303, after several itinerant years in Lombardy and Piedmont gathering recruits, Dolcino wrote an epistle in which he claimed that sometime after 1304 Frederick of Trinacria (i.e., Frederick III of Sicily) would become the Holy Roman Emperor and would destroy the cardinals and the pope. The Apostles then would unite with the "spirituals," be given the grace of the Holy Ghost, and establish their renewed church. These "spirituals" should probably not be identified with the Spiritual Franciscans but rather with the Joachimite notion of the "spiritual men" who would guide the church in

37. Testimony of brother Vivianus, *Acta S. Officii*, vol. 2, no. 698, 14 August 1304, p. 479; see also p. 399). These beliefs came from a series of letters written by Dolcino, whose purported contents were described by Bernard Gui (Gui, *Additus*; see also *Chronique latine de Guillaume de Nangis*, 1:357). The structure diverges from Joachimism, which identified only three ages (Reeves, *Influence of Prophecy*, 16–27).

38. Guidonis, *Practica inquisitionis heretice pravitatis*, translated in Wakefield and Evans, *Heresies of the High Middle Ages*, 405; discussion in Lea, *History of the Inquisition*, 3:109–10. The year 1260 was also when Segarelli supposedly underwent his conversion experience.

39. *Cronache Senesi*, 293.

40. Guidonis, *Practica inquisitionis heretice pravitatis*, 405–6; see also testimony of Francischa speaking of a certain Bona, *Acta S. Officii*, vol. 2, no. 796, 6 June 1305, pp. 587–88.

its last age.[41] These assertions brought a more dangerous level of attention. In 1304 Dolcino, with supposedly 1,400 to 6,000 followers, fled to the area of the Valsesia, near Vercelli in the modern region of Piedmont. Inquisitors were hot on their heels. Local lords and villagers assisted Dolcino and his Apostles, hiding them in the mountains. The group raided villages when their supplies ran out, which somewhat quelled the initial sympathy of local inhabitants. Matters came to a head in 1305 when Pope Clement V called a crusade against the Order of Apostles on the grounds that they had rebelled openly against the pope by ignoring the 1290 bull that required members of Segarelli's movement to join an approved order or present themselves to inquisitors. At the behest of inquisitors and Bishop Rainerio of Vercelli, the local lords, no longer so amenable after the pillaging of their lands, raised an army and attacked Dolcino's mountain camp.[42]

For two years the Apostles fought a guerrilla war against the armies fighting under the crusading banner of the Holy Roman Church. On Holy Thursday in 1307, the fourth crusade called against Dolcino and his followers finally achieved victory. The pope's troops advanced on Dolcino's last stronghold at Monte Rubello. Salimbene's account of the confrontation is chilling: "On that day more than a thousand of the heretics perished in the flames, or in the river, or by the sword, the cruellest [sic] of deaths. Thus they who made sport of God the Eternal Father and of the Catholic faith came . . . to shame and disgraceful death, as they deserved."[43] Bishop Rainerio captured and imprisoned Dolcino, his companion Margherita of Trent, and one of his close associates, Longino Cattaneo. Inquisitors condemned all three to death. Secular officials first tortured Longino and burned Margherita for all to see, but they saved the most shocking public punishment for Dolcino. They forced him down the road while systematically tearing his body apart with hot pincers in a public exhibition of ritualized torture.

Supposedly, Dolcino never showed a sign of pain during this ordeal beyond a single shiver and one sigh. His reaction impressed onlookers. A hallmark of the early Christian martyr was not feeling pain when under physical torment. Those sympathetic to the Christian cause explained such fortitude by claim-

---

41. On the use of this word, see Burr, *Spiritual Franciscans*, 39–41 and 68. Some medieval writers interpreted Dolcino's remarks as referring to Franciscans; Angelo Clareno, himself troubled by charges of insubordination and widely considered one of the spokesmen for the Franciscan Spirituals, claimed in his history of the Franciscans, composed circa 1323, that both Gerard Segarelli and Dolcino had been possessed by a devil named Furio (Clareno, *Liber chronicarum, sive, tribulationum*, 650–52; for the source of the reference to Furio, see Mark 5:9 and Luke 8:36).

42. *Additus ad Historia fratris Dulcini*, 428–34; Lea, *History of the Inquisition*, 3:114.

43. *Chronicle of Salimbene de Adam*, 117; the following description of their deaths is from the same source (117–19).

ing that the individual had received God's aid by being released from physical suffering. The second-century chronicler of Polycarp's martyrdom explained, "[The martyrs] reached so high a pitch of nobility that no sound or groan escaped them, making manifest to all that in the hour of their torture the martyrs of Christ were absent from the flesh, or rather that the Lord was present and of their company."[44] A person could only withstand extreme physical torment without acknowledging pain if he or she had been liberated from the constraints of the human body and spiritually united with Christ. A similar interpretation occurred in the later Middle Ages: if a condemned heretic could silently endure debilitating pain while refusing to acquiesce to authorities, the person must have received God's grace and therefore was wrongfully put to death.

Dolcino was revolutionary, even in the context of medieval heretical movements.[45] He and his followers were committed to the idea of a renewed church, cleansed of corruption and sin, which would lead Christians to perfection and their ultimate salvation. Heavily influenced by Joachimite thought, Dolcino actively sought to hasten the onset of the new age, fulfilled through calls to shed the blood of undeserving clerics. It is this belief that engendered the carnage of his vision, although ultimately it was the bodies of the members of his own Order of Apostles that lay slain on the battlefield. His followers sacrificed themselves, inspired by Dolcino's conviction. One Apostle inquisitors questioned in 1303 asserted, "The Church was in [the time of] Gerard Segarelli and is now in [the time of] the said Dolcino and his followers good, pure, poor, and persecuted just as in the time of Christ. And [he spoke] of the destruction of the Roman Church and its clerics, and of the exaltation of the said Apostles, and [said] that now the said Dolcino was the foremost and greatest among them."[46] The inquisitorial register of Bologna attests that after 1307 inquisitors still questioned suspected sympathizers and followers. Yet even as radical as Dolcino was, he garnered support from the orthodox population. Not only members of his movement but also orthodox citizens of the mountainsides above Vercelli viewed him as a holy but persecuted individual. For three years the nobles near Vercelli, known to be antipapal politically but orthodox religiously, aided him. Circumstances such as starvation

---

44. "Martyrdom of Polycarp," 32–33.

45. In contrast, Jerry B. Pierce argued that Dolcino's vision, while apocalyptic and deemed heretical by authorities, was no more radical than any other reform movement ("Forced into an Apocalyptic Corner: Violence, Resistance, and the Order of Apostles," 40th International Medieval Congress, Kalamazoo, MI, 4 May 2005). He altered this view somewhat in his subsequent book (*Poverty, Heresy, and the Apocalypse*, 119).

46. Testimony of Blasius speaking of Zacharias, *Acta S. Officii*, vol. 2, no. 604, 18 August 1303, p. 381.

and desperation led his group to take advantage of their hospitality. Even after his death, and because of the way he went to his death, his legacy in the region was as a religious reformer. This view has persisted into the twentieth century. In 1907 a monument was erected to Dolcino on Monte Rubello. It was destroyed by Mussolini's blackshirts in 1927, but a replacement was erected in the early 1970s. Its dedicatory plaque mentions Dolcino's "martyrdom."[47]

Frà Michele Berti da Calci was less revolutionary, although papal decree similarly condemned the beliefs ascribed to him. Michele was a Spiritual Franciscan, a *fraticello* as they were called in Italy. The Spiritual Franciscans believed their order should possess nothing, individually or in common, in keeping with how they interpreted Francis's Rule and the principles of apostolic poverty. Popes and other Franciscans, called Conventuals, perceived them as a dangerous force in the fourteenth century. In 1317 Pope John XXII ruled in favor of the Conventuals. Those friars who refused to bow to papal directives became enemies of the church and declared heretics.[48] Michele purportedly was a member of an underground group of *fraticelli* that secretly met in the Anconian March.[49] In 1388 he was sent to Florence to preach. After gaining a number of followers, five women who ostensibly had "converted," led by one named Gulia, betrayed him to the bishop and the inquisitors. Frà Antonio Bindi, the episcopal vicar, imprisoned Michele for preaching that people should read the Gospels themselves to discover the truth, rather than listen to clerics. They questioned Michele, but he refused to recant his beliefs and in 1389 was burned.

The fullest account of these events comes from an anonymous author who wrote of Michele Berti da Calci's *"passione,"* or symbolic torture of imprisonment (rather than physical torture by civil officials). The author, or rather hagiographer, presented himself as a witness, reporting Michele's direct responses to inquisitors. He presumably was a close companion of the friar and personally viewed his execution; perhaps he was one of the two fellow friars

47. Pierce, *Poverty, Heresy, and the Apocalypse*, 143–44.

48. On the history of the *fraticelli*, see Douie, *Nature and the Effect*; on the difference between the Spiritual Franciscans of southern France and northern Italy, see Burr, *Spiritual Franciscans*, 202. An Italian treatise against the *fraticelli* is in Rome, Bibilioteca Casanatense, ms. 132. For Pope John XXII's condemnation, see Burr, *Spiritual Franciscans*, 196–99; for the persecution of Spirituals for heresy, see Lambert, *Medieval Heresy*, 208–305.

49. This and the following paragraphs on frà Michele are from the contemporary account of his death, edited by Piazza as "La passione di frate Michele." G. De Luca edited a less critical edition as "Il supplizio di frà Michele da Calci (1389)" in his *Prosatori minori del Trecento*, 1:213–36. Part of the process against him can be found in ASF, Capitano del popolo, n. 1775, ff. 118r–122r. A copy of his final sentence is in ASF, Capitano del popolo, n. 1782, ff. 25r–29r, transcribed in D'Ancona, *Varietà storiche e letterarie*, vol. 1, appendix 1, 345–55. For discussion, see Piazza, "La *via crucis* di frate Michele"; and Baker, "Death of a Heretic, Florence 1389."

who inquisitors also questioned but who abjured. Based on the account, Michele's answers to the inquisitor were characteristic of Spiritual Franciscans. He believed Pope John XXII was a heretic because, although he was obligated to defend the bulls of prior popes, he had overturned Pope Nicholas III's 1279 bull *Exiit qui seminat*. In this decree, Nicholas III declared that the Franciscan order should live as the apostles and affirmed that the apostles possessed nothing, individually or in common, and only had de facto use of property.[50] On account of John XXII's ruling, all subsequent bishops were "Pharisees" who had lost their rights and privileges, although the sacraments themselves still were valid. John XXII's papal successors were *fautores* or aiders of heresy, and the canonizations performed by John XXII (for instance, of St. Thomas Aquinas) were invalid. In addition, Michele asserted that people should believe only what is written in Scripture and read the Gospels themselves to steer clear of false prophets. These false prophets were all the clergy during and after John XXII's pontificate.

Unsurprisingly, inquisitors condemned Michele Berti da Calci as a contumacious heretic. The most compelling part of the text describes his punishment, which was an hour-long walk through the streets of Florence to the site of his immolation outside the gate of the Porta alla Giustizia, which was near Piazza Piave before it was demolished in 1864.[51] The route took him through the center of the city and past Piazza Santa Croce. It ended at the small church and cemetery established by the confraternity of Santa Maria della Croce al Tempio in 1361 as a place of preparation and prayer for the condemned who would be laid to rest outside the walls in the nearby cemetery.[52] As his body was set ablaze, Florence itself ignited in chatter. Michele's demeanor in the face of certain death persuaded many citizens that he must have been holy to remain so steadfast in his beliefs, as described in the opening quote of this chapter. Some onlookers asked if they could take his remains to bury them. The soldier in charge allegedly allowed this, against regulations.[53]

Although very different ideologically, Michele and Dolcino were radical reformers who sought a return to an apostolic church to renew the faith. Both men's conviction in their message and behavior during their executions

---

50. *Exiit qui seminat*, 7 (Franciscan Archive, https://franciscan-archive.org/bullarium/exiit-l.html [accessed 28 August 2016]). John XXII condemned Nicholas III's understanding of evangelical poverty in a series of bulls between 1322 and 1324: *Ad conditorem canonum* (1322), *Cum inter nonnullos* (1323), *Quia quorundam* (1324), and *Quia vir reprobus* (1324). The most important of these was *Quia quorundam*; for an English translation and commentary, see Heft, *John XXII and Papal Teaching Authority*, 33–166.

51. Artusi, *Le antiche porte di Firenze*, cited in "Porta alla Giustizia."

52. Felice, *La Compagnia de' Neri L'arciconfraternita*, 35.

53. Piazza, "La passione di frate Michele," 256.

identified them as contemporary martyrs for the faith. "Le passione di frate Michele" even intentionally imitates the early Christian *Acts of the Martyrs*, describing him as a "witness" to Christian truth, a willing and necessary human sacrifice to God. While the author is partisan, the story illustrates how observers identified certain behaviors within traditional frameworks, such as martyrdom, and so consciously rejected inquisitorial condemnations in favor of their own interpretation. Like Dolcino's, Michele Berti da Calci's comportment was persuasive evidence that officials had made a mistake and that these convicted heretics might actually be holy, for it was saints, not heretics, who were exceptional by nature. The ability to withstand physical pain was a traditional quality of the martyr, as exemplified in the well-known story of St. Lawrence.[54] When people saw Christians like Lawrence fearlessly accept death, it overturned their expectations of human behavior, which dictated that Christians would "die badly," cowering and begging.[55] Similarly, Dolcino and Michele's fearlessness and conviction convinced the community that they were unjustly put to death. Their attitude was a miraculous gift from God expressed via release from physical suffering. This external sign gained the sympathy and even veneration of observers. In a strange but perhaps expected reversal, it was observers who followed the *inquisitio*'s emphasis on external behavior rather than internal belief.

Negotiation and Consensus

It was dangerous to repudiate inquisitorial decrees and believe a heretic was holy. As a *fautor* or supporter of heresy, one could be exiled from the Christian community and thus bereft of the possibility of salvation. While there might usually be power in numbers, a whole community could suffer the same consequences if inquisitors or the pope placed a town under interdict for venerating a condemned heretic. Rejecting the validity of inquisitorial sentences required negotiation and ultimately majority consensus that the person in question was truly worthy of the community's contumacy. The account of Michele Berti da Calci describes this process. Most sources that inform about holy heretics were composed or recorded by their detractors: inquisitorial sentences, deponent testimony against the suspected individual, or narratives by

---

54. A common theme in the early hagiographical literature is Christ being present and suffering with the martyr, strengthening the idea of martyrs sacrificing their bodies for Christian souls (Delehaye, *Les Origines du culte des martyrs*, 20:5–12; for the medieval account of St. Lawrence, see De Voragine, *Golden Legend*, 2:67.

55. Salisbury, *Blood of Martyrs*, 19.

those who supported the official interpretation of their beliefs and behavior. As a result the texts, such as those that detail Dolcino of Novara's history, generally depict the holy heretic in a negative light as an enemy of Christendom. In contrast, the source that most thoroughly details Michele Berti da Calci's life is positive propaganda, yet it must be used with equal caution. Notwithstanding the one-sided view this particular account provides, the text traces the steps of how communities could construct sainthood out of heresy. It serves as a counterpoint to the examination in the previous chapter of how inquisitors constructed heterodoxy out of sainthood.

During his questioning, Michele Berti da Calci consistently denied that he was a heretic and claimed notaries had twisted his words. The author of his account agreed and portrayed him as a saint, claiming that "striding along with his head bowed, saying the office, he truly seemed like one of the martyrs."[56] The chronicler was convinced of Michele's holiness, but the Florentine citizens were not, at least not yet. Observers went through a process of discernment that occurred within various strata of society. Michele's reactions throughout his incarceration and *inquisitio* engendered controversy even among officials in charge. The author claimed that during his questioning, "the saint responded to all humbly and benignly, so much so that someone, seeing his great constancy and humble speech, said, 'If what you say is true, God give you patience,' and some others, 'he has a devil on his back, and deceives those others.'"[57] According to the author, one of the officials even gave away Michele's remains for burial, an act in direct contradiction to the disposal of the bodies of heretics.[58] Agents of the bishop and the inquisitors disagreed whether his humility and steadfastness should be attributed to God or the Devil.

It is during the walk to his execution that we fully observe the process through which the community became convinced that Michele was holy. There were certain hurdles he needed to overcome. The spatial progression to the site of his execution corresponded with a shift in public opinion. Early in the procession to his death, Michele encountered jeers and questions. Then people gathered in the streets and hung out of their windows, suggesting he tell the authorities whatever they wanted to hear to spare his life. Observers cried, "You don't want to die!" from their windows as he walked past. He responded that he wanted to die for Christ. "You won't die for Christ," the onlookers rejoined. Michele Berti da Calci answered he would die "for the truth."[59] The community continued to test his resolve. In front of the Uffizi

---

56. Piazza, "La passione di frate Michele," 253.
57. Ibid., 246.
58. Ibid., 256; on heretical remains, see the discussion of Peter of Abano earlier in this chapter.
59. Ibid., 253.

some observers jeered, calling out that he did not believe in God, that he had a devil on his back "pulling" him, and that he should repent for his error. Michele responded that he believed in God and the Virgin Mary and the Holy Church, that God protected him against demons, and that "on the contrary [what I believe] is the orthodox faith, in fact it is the truth to which every Christian is bound."[60] By the time he reached the gate of the city, the tone of the remarks had changed. Instead of taunts and questions, "a faithful [individual] began to call out to him, saying, 'remain strong, martyr of Christ, for soon you will receive the crown [of martyrdom].'"[61] The drama culminated in the piazza, where inquisitors enclosed the friar in a wooden box. When the officials asked him one last time, "What is this [thing] for which you are willing to die?," the friar responded with the same sense of purpose he had shown throughout his incarceration: "This is a truth that resides in me, to which I cannot bear witness if I do not die."[62] At the last possible moment, Michele still refused to stray from his beliefs. His death led to discussion and debate in the community, culminating in the assertion that the Florentines badmouthed the inquisitors and secreted his bones away to protect them, perhaps as relics.

Da Calci's supposed heterodox beliefs are not what is contested in this account; rather, it is his saintly behavior in the face of immanent immolation. Both those who initially thought he was possessed by a demon and those who thought he was sacrificing his body for Christ were impressed by the manner in which he approached his death and struggled to understand his behavior in spiritual terms. The text describes how the onlookers attempted to fit Michele's demeanor within a recognizable framework and then debated among themselves whether he was truly a heretic or actually a saint. By the end of the ritualized procession, the deliberations of the Florentine community were complete, removing the friar from the zone of ambiguity. The final event, the securing of his remains, suggests just how impressive Michele Berti da Calci's behavior was to all of those who observed him in his last hours. It also highlights how communal consensus brought pressure to bear upon others, in this case a secular official carrying out the orders of inquisitors and the bishop.

The account of the Dominican friar Marcolinus of Forlì (d. 1397), while not a condemned heretic, illustrates the power of this consensus.[63] The local community's overwhelming conviction that he was holy eventually persuaded

---

60. Ibid.
61. Ibid., 255.
62. Ibid.
63. *Riti*, proc. 773 (Marcolinus of Forli, 1624–1625), and the epistolary account by Johannes Dominici (*Epistolam memorat*, in Corner, *Ecclesiae Venetae, antiquis monumentis*, 7:186–92); see discussion in Kleinberg, "Proving Sanctity," 193–95, and Vauchez, *Sainthood in the Later Middle Ages*, 405–7.

even his reluctant Dominican brethren to accept the town's view of his merits. After Marcolinus's death, a cook noticed that he had had calluses on his knees, a sign to him that the friar must have engaged in long hours of prayer. A carpenter then came forward and claimed Marcolinus healed him. Citizens of Forlì already were predisposed to consider Marcolinus a saint since they believed he was a prophet. For two days they lobbied his Dominican brothers, who considered Marcolinus just a simple man, to allow them to venerate his body. The Dominicans relented, subsequently recasting their assessment of Marcolinus as "simple" to one that championed his simplicity as a manifestation of his virtuous, and saintly, humility. Although initially unwilling to recognize one of their own as a holy man, the Dominicans bowed under the community's pressure. The negotiation that turned a person into a saint prompted a reevaluation of the saint's past. Aviad Kleinberg used Marcolinus of Forlì as an example of this process: "The popular 'canonization,' then, often started with a rash identification: 'Marcolinus is a saint.' The proposition then resisted attempts, either official or unofficial, to defeat it. . . . If the saint successfully passed public trial, his holy essence spread over his person and his actions acquired a new meaning. . . . The concept of sanctity broadened to include 'that which Marcolinus was, or did.'"[64] People reinterpreted the actions of a person like Marcolinus—or Michele Berti da Calci or any other saint—in light of the new perspective and reinscribed them with symbolic meaning.

Communities constructed holy heretics through a process similar to how inquisitors constructed heretical saints. When an inquisitor deemed a local holy person like Guglielma or Armanno Pungilupo to be heterodox, he in effect forged a new identity for the individual. So did a community when it judged a sentenced heretic, like Peter of Abano or Dolcino of Novara, to be holy. Communities had to work hard to achieve a consensus regarding whom they should consider holy. They carefully selected individuals for veneration who met specific criteria and fit into a conventional model of sanctity whose identifiers, such as the signs of martyrdom, had been sanctioned by Rome itself. Late medieval holy heretics thus demonstrate how members of communities reinterpreted a traditional category of the holy, the martyr, and applied it to contemporary examples of spirituality. The characteristics of martyrdom, such as persecution, resolve, and release from bodily pain, indicated someone's innocence and, further, suggested that the person's behavior was divinely inspired. When Christians prosecuted ostensible Christians, communities relied on their own experience to determine if it was actually persecution and if the condemned had the virtues that marked holiness. Consequently, orthodox

64. Kleinberg, "Proving Sanctity," 195.

citizens venerated some condemned heretics. While this devotion functioned like that toward any other saint, it was predicated on the belief that inquisitors were in error. The acceptance of some sentenced heretics as holy saints resulted from increasing intolerance of papal agents interfering in the regulation of local communities during the century and a half after the creation of the inquisitorial office. Orthodox citizens contested the right of inquisitors to govern what were "correct" forms of belief and to monitor the external signs of religious obedience in their communities. By championing the cult of the condemned heretic, citizens "interrupted the circuit of power" of papal agents and "articulate[d] a competing theory of power," just as early Christians did when originally ascribing salvation to those persecuted by Roman officials.[65]

The various manifestations of contested saints emerged through a complex process. Since the determination that someone was a saint, a heretic, or an ordinary person was subjective, there was plenty of room for dispute. Inquisitors and papal emissaries, as literal or de facto outsiders, often had to cope with obdurate citizens during their interpretative quest. The result was a dynamic and dialectical struggle over how to distinguish the holy from the heretical. The disputed assessment led inquisitors to prosecute saints as heretics, hostile observers to denigrate saints as ordinary people, and communities to raise heretics to the status of martyrs. The tenacity of citizens in seeking to retain the right to determine who was orthodox and who heterodox and who was saintly and who heretical was a direct challenge to papal agents and a rejection of the pope's authority. As is clear from the examples in chapters 1–4, these communities included local clergy, especially those who customarily had been in charge of sanctioning cults, and included bishops, canons of cathedrals, and parish priests. They could also include members of the traditional monastic orders and even mendicants who wanted to distance themselves from papal policy. This aspect of clerical involvement demonstrates that one of the boundary markers for disputed sanctity was between those who identified with local interests and those who acted as papal agents, rather than between the laity and clergy or between the elite and so-called popular culture. The process of constructing sainthood thus functioned as a means for communities to shape their religious experiences, build communal solidarity, and articulate displeasure with papal policies. These are some of the motives, among others, that are explored in part II.

---

65. Castelli, *Martyrdom and Memory*, 48.

PART TWO

Why

CHAPTER 5

Economics, Patronage, and Politics

There were a number of motives beyond religious devotion that played a part in local veneration. Salimbene de Adam discussed some in the context of the cults of Albert of Villa d'Ogna and Armanno Pungilupo:

> Here are many reasons for the devotion to this Albert [of Villa d'Ogna]: because the infirm wished to regain their health, because the curious merely wanted to see novelties, because the clerks had envy toward the modern religious Orders, and because the bishops and canons wished to gain money. This latter reason is made clear in the bishop and canons of Ferrara, for they were greatly enriched through Armanno Punzilovo [i.e., Pungilupo]. Another reason is that the exiled of the Imperial party hoped to arrive at a peace settlement with their fellow citizens [of Parma] through these new miracles [of Albert] so that they might come again into their own and not have to travel through the world as vagabonds.[1]

Salimbene's first observation, that people became devoted to a regional saint because they believed the person was holy and could intercede on a supplicant's behalf, was inarguably at the basis of all veneration. He identified four additional reasons in his remarks about thirteenth-century cults: the desire for

---

1. *Chronicle of Salimbene de Adam*, 514.

the new and the spectacular, the jealousy of secular clergy toward the mendicants, greed, and exiled factions' hope of reconciliation. What drove the merely curious to visit the site of a new cult was akin to that of the sick who wanted to be healed. Both wanted to see a miracle performed. The resulting attention heightened the likelihood that other groups might achieve the further desires Salimbene identified.

There were economic, social, and political considerations that motivated segments of society to support regional cults even with the threat of papal or inquisitorial censure, as we have seen occurred with contested saints such as Armanno Pungilupo and Guglielma of Milan. Earthly rewards included the wealth that accrued to a church or a town, the prestige of establishing a cult, and the benefits of promoting a new saint as a holy patron for resolving political disputes, either between rival factions within a town, between towns, or between a town and the papacy. In this chapter's first two sections, on wealth and patronage, the cult of Guglielma of Milan serves as a centerpiece to demonstrate this concatenation of motives. The focus then shifts to examining a saint's role in promoting peace in war-torn late medieval Italy. The chapter therefore moves from economic to political motives and from a narrower focus on individuals and institutions to broader considerations of community and region. It shows that economics and politics, besides spiritual conviction, were primary factors in persuading members of communities to support the cults of their saints, even when inquisitors suspected those saints of heterodoxy or condemned them for it.

Money, Prestige, and Patronage

Milan's veneration of the disputed saint Guglielma illustrates how economic and political processes, such as those Salimbene described, encouraged both support for her cult and opposition to the inquisitorial process into her radical devotees, the Guglielmites, among segments of the orthodox population. Although Guglielma's following is memorable due to the beliefs of the sectarians, a crucial point is that the orthodox public also venerated her in various Milanese churches. The two most distinguished ecclesiastical foundations involved in the process of promoting Guglielma's sainthood were the Cistercian abbey of Sta. Maria di Chiaravalle and the female Humiliate house of Sta. Caterina di Brera, later known as Sta. Maria di Biassono (or just Biassono, as referred to throughout). St. Bernard of Clairvaux founded Chiaravalle, one of the earliest Cistercian monasteries, in 1135. Biassono began as a house for both men and women and was one of the first Humiliati establishments in

Milan; surviving institutional documents date back to 1178.[2] Chiaravalle and Biassono became intimately involved with the Guglielmites through Andrea Saramita and Maifreda da Pirovano, the leaders of the Guglielmite sect. Chiaravalle derived economic benefits from being the site of Guglielma's resting place. Biassono had political ties through its membership to the ruling Visconti family (as discussed in the next section). These factors contributed to their complicity in promoting Guglielma's cult while protecting the sectarians.

Andrea Saramita had a close association with Chiaravalle that stretched back twenty-five years before the inquisitorial inquiry into the sectarians in 1300. While the basis for this relationship is unknown, there is evidence that Andrea acted on behalf of the monastery in some business transactions, probably as its lay procurator, dating to well before Guglielma died in 1281. For instance, Andrea represented Chiaravalle in 1274 when the monks purchased a house in the parish of S. Pietro all'Orto for Guglielma to live in during the last years of her life. In return for this abode, Chiaravalle obtained Guglielma's body after her death. The fact that the abbey purchased a home for her to live in out of its own funds suggests that the monks negotiated for, and expected benefits from, getting her remains as saintly relics.[3]

The monks clearly hoped to profit from the public veneration of Guglielma by both the local Milanese and pilgrims to their house. Andrea and Maifreda anticipated large numbers of pilgrims to her tomb, boasting that the indulgences that would be given would equal those given to pilgrims to Jerusalem.[4] While their hopes of papal recognition did not materialize, one witness in the inquiry of 1300 testified that the monks received "offerings and candles" when their sermons praised Guglielma and that her feast days regularly drew over one hundred participants.[5] Further monetary inducements came from the sectarians themselves. After the purchase of the house for Guglielma in 1274, several members of the sect became oblates of the abbey, bequeathing their own property to the monks. Allegranza and Giovanni Perusio, for example, donated their goods to Chiaravalle in 1277, followed by Carabella and

---

2. The most recent works on Chiaravalle are Facchin, *Chiaravalle Abbey Milan*; Donati, *L'Abbazia di Chiaravalle*; and Ottani, *L'abbazia di Chiaravalle Milanese*. For Biassono, see Andrews, *Early Humiliati*, 49; cf. the early modern history of the Humiliati, "Cronica delle venerando memorie nella congregazione Umiliata," in Milan, Biblioteca Ambrosiana, H inf. 205, f. 112v.

3. The transaction is preserved in Milan, Biblioteca Nazionale Braidense, ms. Bonomi, E. Tabularium monasterii Claravallis, AE XV 20–31, n. 778, 850–53 (incipit "Rugeria uxor Miranisii Miracapitii confirmat . . . Sancti Petri ad Hortum," 9 April 1274). For a discussion of how women functioned as "living saints" and how their supporters prepared to obtain their relics while they were still alive, see Elliott, *Proving Woman*, 71–72; for a discussion of this process in the early modern period, see Zarri, "Living Saints," 219–303.

4. *Milano 1300*, 74.

5. *Milano 1300*, 96. See also discussion in chap. 3 above.

Amizone Toscano.[6] Both were of upper-class families (notaries titled the men "*ser*" in the process) and were powerful patrons. The Garbagnate, a family closely tied to the ruling Visconti and deeply involved with the Guglielmites, were probable patrons of the abbey as well. Chiaravalle's desire to increase its income from relics of a saint was not a new concept, as Patrick Geary's work on the theft of relics in the Middle Ages attests. Recent events in Milanese history made Chiaravalle's tendency to protect a profitable cult even more probable. From 1262 to 1277 two families of Milan, the Visconti and the Della Torre, fought for control of the city. Milan was placed under interdict until Ottone Visconti, archbishop of Milan since 1262, won the title of Lord of Milan in 1277.[7] Following this clash, Milan went to war with the commune of Todi in 1281, a conflict that delayed the translation of Guglielma's body to Chiaravalle, which was situated outside the city walls, until a devotee received safe passage from the Marquis of Montferrato.[8] For about twenty-five years, therefore, continuous political strife drained the coffers of Milan, with little opportunity for passing pilgrims or tradesmen to replenish them. The material benefits of their monastery as a pilgrimage site, especially in these tumultuous times, was not lost on the monks, who had prepared for such an eventuality during the lean years.

The site of a new, flourishing cult brought both wealth and prestige, as a dispute between the Cistercians of Chiaravalle and the clerics of S. Pietro all'Orto over Guglielma's first coffin demonstrates. As noted, in 1274 Guglielma had agreed the monks could bury her body in the abbey in return for allowing her to live in a home they had purchased for her. This home was in the parish of S. Pietro, in the heart of Milan within the old city walls. It is likely that her body remained at the local church throughout delays leading up to her translation to Chiaravalle, outside the city's walls, due to Milan's war with Todi. The translation finally occurred in October 1281. Guglielma's body was placed in a new coffin. Andrea brought the old one to the house of a sectarian, Sibilla dei Malconzati, where representatives from Chiaravalle oversaw the process, which included Andrea washing the body in water and wine (sectarians saved the liquid for use in later rituals) and dressing it in a white scapula given to him by Graziadeo da Operto, a brother of the monastery.[9] Representatives from the church of S. Pietro subsequently requested the first coffin from

---

6. Benedetti, introduction to *Milano 1300*, 39.

7. Muir, *History of Milan*, 8–10; see also Cattaneo, "Ottone Visconti arcivescovo di Milano." Interestingly, the interdict lasted through the reign of Pope Gregory X (r. 1271–1276), who was born Teobaldo Visconti into a different branch of the family and is not to be confused with Ottone's nephew of the same name, who was killed in battle by the Della Torre in 1276.

8. *Milano 1300*, 170.

9. *Milano 1300*, 180.

Sibilla dei Malconzati. The church sought to promote as a second pilgrimage site the parish where this holy woman had spent her last days, wanting to stake a claim to Guglielma's holiness. After becoming cognizant of this plan, the monastery sent two monks to instruct Sibilla not to give the body to S. Pietro because Chiaravalle was its rightful custodian. The monks argued that "[it was] Guglielma herself who chose burial at their monastery" and that they were the ones who had her body.[10] The monks wanted to monopolize Guglielma as their special holy patron, shifting part of Milanese religious life from the urban churches of Milan, such as S. Pietro, to their own monastery in the countryside southwest of the city, near the Corso di Porta Romana (figure 3).

Besides money from supplicants and benefactors, the prestige and power that came from being a recognized pilgrimage site also likely led to the monastery's support of Guglielma's questionable cult. The Guglielmites were inclusive and included servants, young professionals, and members of Milanese nobility. Maifreda da Pirovano, the woman who was the group's chosen future pope after Guglielma's anticipated Second Coming, was a cousin of Matteo Visconti, the nephew of the scion of the house, Ottone Visconti, and the *capitano del popolo* of Milan from 1287 and Imperial Vicar of Lombardy from 1294.[11] Ties between the sectarians, the abbey of Chiaravalle, and the Visconti family permeate the records. Matteo Visconti was charged with protecting the sectarians years after the inquiry of 1300. Pope John XXII stated in a letter of 1324 that Matteo had worked to release Maifreda during the Guglielmite trial of 1300, a charge first brought against Matteo in his trial for heresy in 1322. He also claimed that Matteo's son Galeazzo, also cited for heresy, had been a member of the Guglielmite sect. While there is no surviving evidence in the inquisitorial process that Matteo ever came to Maifreda's aid during the investigation, Francesco Garbagnate, a sectarian questioned in 1300, was Matteo's advocate on a mission to Emperor Henry VII in 1309, demonstrating the continued ties between the Visconti family and those involved with the Guglielmites.[12] Members of the rival Guelph Della Torre faction also were implicated in the heresy. The most prominent Guelph family involved in the Guglielmite sect, the Carentano, had a member, Feliciano, who functioned as one of Matteo

---

10. *Milano 1300*, 128. Cf. Barbara Newman, who interpreted these passages as Chiaravalle arranging for Sibilia to keep the coffin so that S. Pietro would not obtain it (Newman, "Heretic Saint," 13).

11. Muir, *History of Milan*, 10.

12. Muraro, *Guglielma e Maifreda*, 91; the letter is in BAV, ms. 3937. The inquisitorial process against Matteo and his son was edited by Michel, "Les procès de Matteo et de Galeazzo Visconti." The process against the Guglielmites is incomplete since the register of one of the notaries is missing. In the trial of Matteo Visconti, the inquisitors accused him of complicity with both the Guglielmites and the Order of Apostles, who were also persecuted around 1300 (Goodich, *Vita Perfecta*, 205).

Visconti's counselors.[13] Undoubtedly the influence of such a powerful net-
work within the ranks of the devotees was an inducement for the monks of
Chiaravalle to promote the veneration of Guglielma. Moreover, this patronage seemed to protect the monks closely involved with the cult when the inquisitorial process began. For example, Marchisio da Veddano, the monk most
often named as being involved with the Guglielmites, successfully avoided remonstrance and became abbot in 1303.[14]

Could wealth, power, and prestige be enough to make members of a notable Cistercian house turn a blind eye to suspect activities among a cult's devotees? The evidence strongly suggests the answer is yes. As the site of
Guglielma's tomb, Chiaravalle became a locus for Guglielmite activities. The
cumulative testimony suggests that the Guglielmites had a number of questionable practices of which it is hard to believe that the monks were ignorant.
Sectarians would "consecrate" hosts on Guglielma's tomb at Chiaravalle, and
then Maifreda, the so-called future pope, would distribute them to sectarians
in the course of the group's own stylized mass.[15] Even though the cemetery
is about a ten- to fifteen-minute walk from the abbey's church and cloister, one
has to assume the monastery knew these gatherings were taking place on its
own property. In addition, on Pentecost of 1300, the Guglielmites held a feast
because they believed it was the day of Guglielma's Second Coming. The testimony of Gerardo da Novazzano regarding this feast is intriguing, since he
seems to imply that it took place at Chiaravalle, just as the two usual orthodox feasts in her honor, although inquisitors surprisingly did not press him on
this point.[16] The sectarians had been planning for this celebration for some
years. Maifreda da Pirovano dressed in sacerdotal vestments, and they set up
an altar with candles, hosts, water, and wine. After Andrea read the "gospels"
and Franceschino Malconzato the "epistles" (presumably new scriptural works
we know sectarians had composed), Maifreda said mass, distributed hosts, and
gave a benediction.[17] Additional evidence that suggests monks of Chiaravalle
knew of the group's unorthodox views is the fact that they allowed the sectarians to paint an unconventional fresco on their grounds above Guglielma's
tomb. In the scene, as reproduced by Michele Caffi in the first half of the nineteenth century, the Virgin Mary sits on the right with the baby Jesus on her

---

13. Newman, "Heretic Saint," 20.

14. For references to him in the testimony, see *Milano 1300*, 138, 144, 146, 184, and 208; for discussion, see Benedetti, *Io non sono Dio*, 37, and Newman, "Heretic Saint," 14; cf. Wessley, who dated his
election to 1305 (Wessley, "Enthusiasm and Heresy," 141).

15. Andrea Saramita, Albertone da Novate, and Franceschino Malconzato consecrated the hosts
and brought them to Maifreda (*Milano 1300*, 72).

16. *Milano 1300*, 268.

17. *Milano 1300*, 214 and 216.

lap. St. Bernard, on the left, presents a kneeling Guglielma and an unidentified Humiliata sister (probably Maifreda da Pirovano) to the Virgin and Child. While the fresco was an innocuous and pious portrayal on the surface, according to Caffi, Guglielma's face was painted red, the color associated with the Holy Spirit in medieval art.[18] The monks of Chiaravalle, a prominent monastery full of educated Milanese, could hardly have been ignorant of this symbolism.

There is no indication that most of the monks or the wider circle of Milanese devotees believed, as did the sectarians, that Guglielma was the Holy Spirit incarnate rather than "merely" a saint. There is also no evidence that Chiaravalle attempted to distance itself from the Guglielmite sectarians, while there is evidence that a few monks knew of Guglielmite beliefs. The *converso* Marchisio Secco and the oblate Ubertino, both of Chiaravalle, were present at one sectarian lunch when Maifreda declared that Guglielma was the Holy Spirit and a miracle involving a knotted belt occurred.[19] Papal inquisitors questioned Marchisio Secco in 1302, showing that authorities thought Chiaravalle's ignorance of the heresy might be feigned. Even if most monks were not cognizant of the details of Guglielmite beliefs, there were clues that the devotional practices of the sectarians were out of the ordinary. Instead of questioning or admonishing them, the abbot of the monastery invited members of the Guglielmites to luncheon and served them wine, bread, and beans.[20] Furthermore, when the sectarians heard they would be the focus of an inquisitorial investigation, several members of the abbey, including the future abbot Marchisio da Veddano, aided the Guglielmites. Chiaravalle appealed to the archbishop of Milan at the request of the sectarians, presenting him with evidence on the Guglielmites' behalf in hopes that he would intervene and stop the inquiry (see chapter 8).[21] The attempt to forestall the questioning was in vain. Chiaravalle, therefore, not only overlooked devotional aspects that pointed to unorthodox beliefs within the Guglielmite circle but also actively helped the group after inquisitors cited some of them for heresy. The monastery's role should

---

18. Caffi, *Dell'Abbazia di Chiaravalle*, 10 and 69; for the identification of the color red with the Holy Spirit, see "Holy Spirit," in Metford, *Dictionary of Christian Lore*, 122.

19. *Milano 1300*, 234 and 242 for Marchisio; 274 for Ubertino. The miracle is discussed above in chap. 3.

20. *Milano 1300*, 144. The sharing of beans, like that of bread, was an expression of fraternity. In her introduction to the Guglielmite process, Marina Benedetti stated, "Presso l'abbazia venivano celebrati convivi per I quail l'abate di Chiaravalle forniva pane, vino e ceci: i ceci, un alimento alla base del pasto confraternale" (Benedetti, introduction to *Milano 1300*, 43). The inquisitorial register of Bologna also demonstrates the significance of beans as a symbol of some kind of union or bond, as the inquisitors regularly asked deponents if they brought or shared beans with heretics (*Acta S. Officii*, vol. 1). See also Dalarun, *"Dieu changea de sexe,"* 296.

21. *Milano 1300*, 208.

be understood in the context of the wealth, prestige, and power that came from being a pilgrimage site for a new cult and having as patrons powerful families whose members participated in the heterodox activities of the sectarians.

The money that Chiaravalle received from sectarians, other Milanese devotees, and pilgrims from further afield who went to Guglielma's shrine suggests the benefits a contemporary saint that excited attention could provide a church or town. The income generated by pilgrimages and the offerings of the faithful could be impressive, as is clear in the studies of Italian civic cults, such as Augustine Thompson's opus *Cities of God* or Diana Webb's *Patrons and Defenders*. One can well imagine the gifts that poured into the cathedral of Foligno when Peter Crisci's body was laid out in the church of San Feliciano, where "on account of the multitude of people from all over gathering to touch him, for many days he was unburied and not carried to burial."[22] The same situation purportedly occurred after the death of Zita of Lucca, when "for a few days [her body] was not able to be buried [in the church of S. Frediano] because of the great concourse of people who came there to venerate her."[23] The church that held a saint's body had monetary benefits and prestige that came from being the site of the holy person's internment.

Getting a holy benefactor could also provide leverage for that church in the local rivalries that permeated Italian towns. Chiaravalle's efforts to secure Guglielma's first coffin so that the monks would be in control of all her relics and have her as their special patron demonstrates this concern. Conversely, the parish church of S. Pietro's efforts to retain control of that coffin and so share in the saint's glory and all of the benefits that would ensue also shows this aspiration. There are many additional examples that demonstrate the desire to obtain control of a saint's cult in order to increase local prestige vis-à-vis another institution. For instance, the Franciscan convent in Cortona fought with the parish church of S. Basilio to gain control of Margaret of Cortona's body, which was buried in the small parish church on the hill overlooking the city.[24] The Franciscans finally were granted the privilege to oversee the church in 1392.

A similar spirit of competition incited the bishop and canons of Ferrara to support the former admitted Cathar, Armanno Pungilupo. The local Benedictine convent of St. Anthony had received the remains of Beatrice II d'Este

---

22. Gorini, "Beati Petri de Fulgineo Confessoris," 369.

23. *Riti*, proc. 1315 (Zita of Lucca, 1694–1695), f. 132r. Henry of Bolzano, also, remained unburied for eight days in the cathedral of Treviso because of the number of people who came to view his remains (*Riti*, proc. 3021, articulo IX, modern pagination p. 40).

24. Coakley, *Spiritual Power*, 134; and Doyno, "Particular Light of Understanding," 76.

(d. 1262), whom they were promoting as a saint.[25] Beatrice was a member of the local ruling family, the Estes, and so was an auspicious patron. Since the Estes only recently had taken control of Ferrara, the Benedictines' appropriation of Beatrice was an obvious attempt to link themselves with this powerful Guelph family. Yet although Beatrice was admitted into the Benedictine order at the end of her life, she also was associated with the Franciscans, who had promoted her sanctity.[26] Rather than become involved in the tug of war over Beatrice d'Este's spiritual benefaction, the cathedral chapter of Ferrara instead became committed to Armanno's cause. The rapid acceptance of Armanno's sanctity only heightened the canons' dedication to his cult. That ecclesiastical rivalry was a prevailing motive is shown by the fact that while the canons were engaged in sponsoring Armanno's canonization in the 1270s, they also tried to promote the sainthood of the recently deceased bishop, Alberto Prandoni (d. 1274). Prandoni was the same bishop who collected testimony regarding Armanno's miracles and who had thwarted inquisitorial attempts to exhume and burn Armanno's remains in 1272.[27] Unfortunately for the canons, support for Prandoni's sanctity was not strong or widespread. Armanno's cause also was doomed to fail. The tenacity of the Ferrarese canons in promoting Armanno's canonization, however, demonstrates just how much importance was accorded to the patronage of a prospective popular saint.

These few examples of many show that saint's cults were in a certain sense a business. The town, church, and/or religious house that established a cult attained prestige and profit from the pilgrims and offerings that followed. As Diana Webb noted, "Stories told of patron saints of the Italian cities show them . . . displaying their day-to-day concern for their constituents while also earning prestige for themselves and the church and city who claimed their relics."[28] Local rivalries and jealousies also contributed to a strong desire to secure a holy patron. As Aviad Kleinberg argued, "A cult was not just a body of beliefs, but a source of pride and income that strongly resisted being 'forgotten,' rejected, or even reinterpreted."[29] These motives, in conjunction with a belief in the miracle-working power of the saint, often led members of a community to promote and protect a cult even in the face of inquisitorial opposition, as Chiaravalle did for Guglielma and the bishop and canons of Ferrara did for Armanno Pungilupo.

---

25. Wessley, "Enthusiasm and Heresy," 202n4.

26. Benati, "Armanno Pungilupo nella storia religiosa," 90–91.

27. *AASS* III, August 14, col. 177B–178F.

28. Webb, *Patrons and Defenders*, 17.

29. Kleinberg, "Proving Sanctity," 191.

Civic Identity and Political Patronage

Local and contemporary saints' cults brought prestige but also helped to construct or revise a civic identity. This was of particular importance in the thirteenth and fourteenth centuries, when many Italian towns experienced turmoil as communal forms of government shifted to autocratic rule, leading to political factionalism. Some parties also recognized the political expedient of maintaining the patronage of a ruling family by supporting individuals and promoting cults, as seems to have occurred with Biassono's support for the Guglielmites. A brief overview of the political context of late medieval Italy highlights this powerful motive for forming or supporting saints' cults. Papal support was the goal, but even without it, cults allowed their promoters to attain, or retain, the power of patronage.

The disputed election of the Holy Roman Emperor after the death of Frederick Barbarossa of the Hohenstaufen dynasty led to the factionalism that pervaded north-central Italy in the thirteenth and fourteenth centuries. A power vacuum occurred when Barbarossa died in 1190 leaving a young child, Frederick II (d. 1250), as his heir. A rival family, the Welfs, contested Frederick II's claim to the title of emperor. Pope Innocent III eventually backed the Welf cause. "Guelph," the Italian form of "Welf," came to designate those who supported the papally backed claimant. The opposing side took the name "Ghibelline," supposedly derived from "Waiblingen," the name of a castle and the battle cry of the Hohenstaufen heirs. The terms "Guelph" and "Ghibelline" subsequently became the catchwords for Italian partisanship. When Frederick II finally gained the throne in 1215, he broke his promise to the pope to leave the Italian peninsula alone and instead tried to regain control of the territory in northern and central Italy that he had lost during his minority. The ensuing struggle between papal and imperial factions continued for over a century.[30] Popes were doubly involved as the ideological catalyst for asserting the papal monarchy, which justified their authority over secular rulers, and as temporal lords concerned with gaining and maintaining land in the area.[31] Although ostensibly a conflict between papal and imperial advocates, the Guelph-Ghibelline conflict quickly devolved into general civic discord between various party leaders.

Florentine chroniclers attribute the origin of internecine war to an incident between two aristocratic families in 1216, just one year after Frederick II be-

---

30. Hyde, *Society and Politics*, 132.

31. Pope Gregory VII, the first major promulgator of the concept, supported the papal monarchy as an outgrowth of his clash with the Holy Roman Emperor over the nature of papal authority over secular rulers (Morris, *Papal Monarchy*, 79–108).

came emperor. Giovanni Villani, who gave the fullest account, claimed that a drunken party which ended in a knifing and a subsequent betrayal of a peace agreement sparked the factionalism in the Italian cities that quickly became subsumed under the aegis of the Guelph-Ghibelline controversy.[32] Writing from hindsight almost a century after the events, Villani described this act of revenge as the trigger for the political partisanship that was to subsume the peninsula. He was not the first to make this connection between Florence and larger peninsular factionalism. Salimbene, writing a generation earlier, identified Florence as the epicenter of the conflict, although he did not trace it to the source. According to Salimbene, disputes in Tuscany soon became couched in terms signifying this larger dispute. He explained, "In Florence, the Guelphs ruled for the Church; the Ghibellines for the empire; and the names of these two parties became synonymous for the Church and Imperial factions throughout Tuscany, and they still are."[33] The personal vendetta, part of aristocratic Italian culture, became thinly disguised as partisanship and wrangling over political jurisdiction.[34] As power oscillated, the identification of a town as "Guelph" or "Ghibelline" denoted if it was a safe haven for political exiles of a particular persuasion or an opportunity for career-minded officials and *podestà*, who traveled among cities looking for their next prospect in this perilous region of shifting alliances.[35]

The Guelph-Ghibelline dispute was a convenient cover to justify territorial warfare and banish enemies. Those in power tried to extend their control into the *contado* to secure food and resources. In doing so they came into conflict with neighboring rivals who were also attempting to expand their borders, providing a ready-made excuse to attack and thus possibly to obtain the desired material benefits.[36] As parties tried to consolidate their authority, local ruling bodies expelled whole factions from cities, as occurred in Parma in 1279 during the furor over Albert of Villa d'Ogna's sanctity. In that year the Guelphs in power exiled all of the Ghibelline faction while the pope placed the town under interdict. This event was a result of the Guelph-Ghibelline conflict in Bologna in 1274, when the Guelph Geremei faction exiled the Ghibelline Lambertazzi. In 1279 the exiled Lambertazzi from their new base at Faenza initiated a war against the Geremei. The whole Po plain descended into chaos. Pope Nicholas III, despite his efforts, failed in his attempt to restore order before his death

---

32. Villani, *Nuova cronica*, VI.38.267–69; on implications for peacemaking, see Jansen, *Peace and Penance*, 5–8.

33. *Chronicle of Salimbene de Adam*, 381.

34. Larner, *Italy in the Age of Dante and Petrarch*, 64–65.

35. Hyde, *Society and Politics*, 134.

36. Ibid., 43–44; Lansing, "Magnate Violence Revisited," 40–42.

in 1280.[37] Individuals who spoke out against the prevailing party faced a similar fate. For instance, in 1250 the saint Rose of Viterbo (d. 1251) and her family were exiled after she vocally supported the pope when the city was under Ghibelline rule.[38] These regional conflicts encouraged civic patriotism of the sort expressed by the Genoese chronicler Jacopo Doria. Writing circa 1291, Doria explained that the purpose of his chronicle was "that every Genoese by reading this may learn more about the excellent deeds of the commune and his own predecessors; and that through their example and the acceptable rewards which they deservedly gained, he may be the more eagerly inspired to work for and maintain the honor and advantage of the commune."[39] Wars inspired local pride; conversely, pride provoked wars. The legacy of the later Middle Ages, still present in Italy to an extent today, is the regionalism and intense sense of place called *campanilismo*.

During the height of the contest between pope and emperor in the early thirteenth century, many of the towns of northern and central Italy had communal governments. Communes, which developed in the twelfth century, incorporated citizens of the *popolo*, those who were not members of the traditional landed elite, into civic structures.[40] Communes under the rule of the *popolo* elected officials and issued laws collectively.[41] Yet their attempts to focus aggression outward against other communities did not erase the deep fractures within society. Civic discord remained, and perhaps increased under communal governments. It was prompted in part by class conflict, in part by papal and imperial partisanship, and in part by the type of aristocratic feuds that Villani described in Florence. While in theory communes had republican rule, in practice the government limited the pool of officials to the wealthiest members of the most powerful guilds. The *popolo grasso* controlled the communes: not the artisans and lesser merchants that republican rule professed to include, but an oligarchy of "knights by birth" and "knights by fortune" (*cavalieri da natura e cavalieri d'aventura*).[42]

Attempts at territorial expansion increased in the last quarter of the thirteenth and the first quarter of the fourteenth century with the rise of autocratic rulers, or *signori*. Constant warfare and factionalism within communes opened the door for members of wealthy elite families to take control of towns and build their power bases. Ultimately they established dynasties that controlled

---

37. Partner, *Lands of St. Peter*, 276.
38. *AASS* II, September 4, cols. 433A–442A; Weisenbeck and Weisenbeck, "Rose of Viterbo," 148.
39. Doria, *Annales Genuenses*, translated in Waley and Dean, *Italian City-Republics*, 147.
40. For a discussion of the economic and commercial causes of the rise of communal government and a description of city life under the communes, see Jones, *Italian City-State*, 152–332.
41. Coleman, "Cities and Communes," 28.
42. Jones, *Italian City-State*, 222–23.

large tracts of northern Italy. Citizens seeking relief from strife, corruption, and confusion accepted the change in government, some more readily than others. Ferrara came under the control of the Este family in the mid-thirteenth century. Although there were two attempts on the life of the reigning Este lord in 1273 and 1288, there was little public support for the malefactors.[43] Two nearby towns, Modena and Reggio, voluntarily offered Obizzo II d'Este the lordship of their cities in return for his protection.[44] In contrast, some towns, such as Padua, fought against signorial rule until it fell to the da Carrara family in 1328. Most famously Florence remained essentially an oligarchy, albeit sporadically punctuated by brief lordships.[45]

Ultimately *signori* gained control of almost all the cities in north-central Italy either through violent takeovers or by making official the autocratic rule they already had achieved in roles such as the *capitano del popolo*, as the Visconti did in Milan. The chronicler Galvano Fiamma (d. 1344), an ardent supporter of the Visconti *signori*, described how Luchino and Giovanni Visconti brought stability and order to Milan in 1339, instituting laws to the great benefit of citizens. They swore to protect the cities and roads under their command and make them safe; outlawed the vendetta; made it a crime to injure a *popolano*; pledged that people could stay home and work rather than being dragged out into war; and promised they would preserve the residences of traitors and exiles for the good of the city, rather than destroying them. They rescinded a yearly tax, made the *contado* directly responsible to the commune rather than to various lords, swore not to spend the city's money profligately, and promised that, if needed, they would assess taxes across the board, excepting no one.[46] This was the apex of the Visconti's climb to power after gaining control of communal offices, the imperial vicariate, and the archbishopric during the previous century. As Guido Cariboni argued, this path to signorial rule consciously fused the political and religious spheres and included each of these offices held by members of the family being identified with the traditional patron saint of Milan, St. Ambrose. This strategy solidified their overarching power in Milan and bolstered the predominantly Ghibelline family's power against the pope.[47]

---

43. Dean, "Rise of the Signori," 119.

44. Larner, *Italy in the Age of Dante*, 139.

45. Ibid., 138 and 148.

46. Fiamma does not limit his concept of the *popolani* to the wealthy merchants, since he included lower-class citizens in his use of the word. He specifically mentioned a fishmonger and a traveling merchant as examples of those persons who should not be harassed (Fiamma, *Opisculum de rebus gestis ab Azone*, 34–45, partly translated in Dean, *Towns of Italy in the Later Middle Ages*, 235–38).

47. Cariboni, "Symbolic Communication and Civic Values."

Fiamma's panegyric to Milan notwithstanding, the process of creating *signorie* was full of conflict. The resulting political factionalism did not just pit dynastic family against dynastic family; it also was rampant within the individual communes whose attempts to remain faithful to republican ideals struggled under the burden of internecine fighting and external pressures from nearby *signori*. Dino Compagni's (d. 1324) characterization of Florence in the late thirteenth century illustrates the divisiveness that prevailed:

> The city was divided anew: the great, middling, and little men and even the clergy could not help but give themselves wholeheartedly to these factions. . . . All the Ghibellines sided with the Cerchi because they hoped to receive less harm from them, and so did all those who had been of Giano della Bella's mind, since the Cerchi had appeared to mourn his exile. Also of their party were Guido di messer Cavalcante Cavalcanti, because he was an enemy of messer Corso Donati, messer Manetto Scali and his family, because they were relatives of the Cerchi[,] . . . messer Berto Frescobaldi, because he had received large loans from them; messer Goccia Adimari, because he was their business associate; messers Biligiardo, Baschiera, and Baldo della Tosa, out of dislike for their kinsman messer Rosso, because thanks to him they had been deprived of their honors.[48]

Compagni described horizontal social networks based on common cause and self-interest as well as blood ties that aided in destabilizing the region due to the urban milieu, in comparison to a place like Languedoc in southern France.[49]

It was in this context that saint's cults became important for healing the fractures in social networks through communal rituals. All Italian towns had their special patron saints connected to their past and usually a particular veneration to one of the more universal saints, such as the Virgin Mary or one of the apostles.[50] Carrie E. Beneš persuasively argued that towns also promoted classical symbols to develop *campanilismo*, the localized civic pride.[51] Contemporary saints' cults joined these traditional devotions and foundation myths as markers of a town's identity as forged in the recent past. For instance, Michelina of Pesaro (d. 1356) joined the Virgin Mary and Terence, the mythical first bishop of the town, as guardian of Pesaro by the late fourteenth

---

48. *Dino Compagni's Chronicle of Florence*, 26.
49. Given, *Inquisition and Medieval Society*, 121–24.
50. Webb, *Patrons and Defenders*, 7–8.
51. Beneš, *Urban Legends*.

century, based on a fresco dated to that period.[52] The creation of a regional saint's cult was a source to renew civic pride, since acts of communal veneration, such as feast day celebrations, came to represent the might of a community, often under a new ruler. A public exhibition of devotion could be a unifying force because, as Miri Rubin explained, such practices were "cemented by the promise of intercession and independence in moments of crisis, as well as through shared experiences in prayer, feasts, and administration."[53] Ritual acts were an outward expression of loyalty and bonded the participants, even if this feeling of *communitas* was fleeting.[54]

Public and ceremonial acts followed the consensus that someone was a saint. First, a religious institution had to erect a tomb or chapel for the saint. Thus the monks of Chiaravalle built one for Guglielma of Milan, the cathedral chapter of Ferrara for Armanno Pungilupo, the cathedral chapter of Foligno for Peter Crisci, the cathedral chapter of Cremona for Facio of Cremona, and the parish of S. Matteo of Cremona for Albert of Villa d'Ogna. The tomb served as an offering to the saint, expressing the community's loyalty and support, and as a pilgrimage site and gathering place for the saint's devotees. Celebrations such as feast days quickly followed, and the city government officially recognized them. Statutes of Foligno from 1340 and 1381 mention the feast of Peter Crisci and include the expenses paid by the commune for the festivities.[55] Padua issued a statute suspending work on the feast day of Anthony Peregrinus, while André Vauchez argued that the *vita* of Facio of Cremona was composed originally as a sermon for his communal feast day.[56] Processions, such as those that occurred in Parma for Albert of Villa d'Ogna, were another way to glorify the saint and display local pride. Probably one of the clearest connections between new cults, civic rituals, and political patronage is that of the cult of Margaret of Cortona. Cardinal Napoleone Orsini formally approved Margaret's *vita* by her former confessor Giunta Bevignati, the *Legenda de vita et miraculis beatae Margaritae de Cortona*, on 15 February 1308 in the home of the Casali family. The Casali were promoting her as patroness of the town as

52. Dalarun, *"Dieu changea de sexe,"* 368–69. The fresco is in the Museo civico de Pesaro. Her role as "protector" was made official in a 1566 civic statute (ibid., 368).

53. Rubin, *Corpus Christi*, 239.

54. For a discussion of how the saint's cult creates communal identity, particularly in regard to the lay confraternities that emerged in the late Middle Ages, see Paoli, "Nobile depositum Tuderti"; Benvenuti-Papi, "San Zanobi"; and Terpstra, *Lay Confraternities and Civic Religion*. For the impact of political regimes on the practices of confraternities, see Cossar, "Quality of Mercy."

55. Gorini, "Beati Petri de Fulgineo Confessoris," 360–61.

56. *AASS* I, February 1, col. 265A; Polenton, "Vita Beati Antonii Peregrini," 420; and Vauchez, "Sainteté laïque aux XIIIe siècle," 17, respectively.

they also fought to gain formal control over Cortona.[57] The Casali supported the emperor yet had close ties to Orsini. In 1325, when Pope John XXII officially recognized Cortona as an episcopal seat and no longer under the control of the bishop of Arezzo as it formally had been, Ranieri Casali emerged as the new *signor*.[58] That same year, civic statutes laid out festivities for Margaret's feast day as the town's patron.[59]

Rituals had the effect of creating a community of believers in which those who did not participate became the outsiders. Salimbene claimed that people who did not take part in the veneration of Albert of Villa d'Ogna "[were] considered to be simply envious or even heretical."[60] Those who refrained from following the status quo were excluded and censured. Sometimes, however, social solidarity was purchased at the expense of unwelcome attention from religious figures and authorities, particularly inquisitors, which could threaten the very core of community life. The public expressions of veneration that exhibited unity and cohesiveness were what drew Salimbene's attention, leading him to criticize the paintings of Albert of Villa d'Ogna that graced the churches, city walls, and castles of the Po plain, the processions of singing citizens carrying crosses in his celebration, and the veneration of Albert's relics. Similarly, historians have argued that it was the Paschal mass of 1300 that precipitated the inquisitorial process into the Guglielmites and that it was the public veneration at Armanno Pungilupo's tomb in the cathedral and the bishop's collection of miracles that hastened his inquisitor's posthumous investigation. Yet while public rituals could result in undesired attention (as discussed in chapter 3), that attention could further unify citizens against outsiders. While defending a cult, the civic identity of a town became more connected both to the saint and the new ruling elite and was articulated in a formal and public manner.[61] These ties of patronage—between devotee and saint, town and cult, cult and ruler—are the reason why so many contested saints ended up with "immemorial cults" that persisted far beyond the Middle Ages, even when the cults were very local and perhaps even censured. There was a rush of canonization processes for these saints in the seventeenth and eighteenth centuries, testifying to the power of these cults for social solidarity; a short list includes Amato Ronconi (1733–1734), Albert of Villa d'Ogna (1744), Zita

---

57. Coakley, *Women, Men, and Spiritual Power*, 132; Pryds, *Women of the Streets*, 50–51; Cannon and Vauchez, *Margherita of Cortona*, 15.

58. Benvenuti Papi, "*In castro poenitentiae*," 143.

59. Doyno, "Particular Light," 69; statute in Cannon and Vauchez, *Margherita of Cortona*, 227–30.

60. *Chronicle of Salimbene de Adam*, 513.

61. See the various examples in Webb, *Patrons and Defenders*, 135–97.

of Lucca (1694–1695), Henry of Bolzano (1768), Michelina of Pesaro (1737), and Clare of Rimini (1782).

Besides the creation of civic identity, patronage and political relations under the new *signori* also influenced religious institutions to support a saint's veneration. The way in which these motives operated, merely suggested in the case of Chiaravalle's promotion of Guglielma of Milan, is clearly delineated in the story of how Biassono, a female Humiliate house in Milan, became involved with the saint's inner circle of devotees known as the Guglielmites. In the desire to raise Guglielma to the status of a saint, members of Biassono tacitly accepted the Guglielmite heresy. In Biassono's case, ties of dependence and patronage were the major consideration in the community's decision to allow the sectarians to use their house as a base of operations. Biassono had close ties with both of the leading sectarians. Andrea Saramita's daughter, sister, and mother had been members of the community. Maifreda da Pirovano herself was a sister of Biassono and lived there until just a few years before the initiation of the inquisitorial process in 1300.

Like Chiaravalle, Biassono appears to have ignored the questionable activities taking place on its grounds. While living there Maifreda held meetings during which she preached (*praedicat*) to gatherings of both male and female sectarians.[62] Many of the female witnesses testified to accepting hosts from Maifreda at various times, often distributed during gatherings at Biassono after she spoke to the "congregation."[63] Following Guglielma's translation to Chiaravalle, the Humiliate erected a shrine for a vial that contained the water and wine used to wash Guglielma's body. Maifreda used the liquid to anoint the Guglielmite faithful and dispensed it to others to heal various illnesses.[64] As at Chiaravalle, Biassono was the site of an unorthodox painting of Guglielma. This one was above the shrine and depicted Guglielma and Jesus freeing captives, presumably Jews and Saracens, from prison.[65] The fresco was a representation of one of the central tenets of the Guglielmites: that Guglielma and Jesus were one in the Trinity, and that after the Second Coming of Guglielma/ the Holy Spirit/Christ, all the Jews and Saracens would be saved. Maifreda told inquisitors she could not remember if she, Andrea Saramita, or the sisters painted it, but she admitted they had completed it before the first inquiry in

---

62. See, for example, *Milano 1300*, 66, 80, 84, 92, 106, 110, 114, 118, and 120. On female preaching, see the essays in Kienzle and Walker, *Women Preachers and Prophets*, especially those by Anne Brenon, Beverly Mayne Kienzle, and Carolyn Muessig. For an overview of female Humiliate houses and their social composition, see Brasher, *Women of the Humiliati*, 43–76.

63. *Milano 1300*, 230.

64. *Milano 1300*, 180.

65. *Milano 1300*, 80; see also Wessley, "Thirteenth-Century Guglielmites," 298.

1284. Inquisitors had questioned Maifreda that same year.[66] This means that the community at Biassono allowed the painting to remain above the shrine of Guglielma even after Maifreda herself was investigated for heresy. In fact, Biassono permitted both the depiction and Maifreda to remain in the house for another sixteen years despite a second questioning in 1296.

Biassono may have been supportive of Guglielma's cult out of a desire for a female patron saint. The male Humiliati community in Milan had a special devotion to Peter Martyr, the Dominican inquisitor murdered in the city's streets, who had supported their order.[67] The contrast is notable: while the male Humiliati prayed to their patron inquisitor saint, the women harbored a female sectarian that inquisitors would soon execute as a relapsed heretic and fostered the veneration of a woman they would soon posthumously brand a heresiarch. It is not surprising, however, that the sisters of Biassono would feel more devotion toward a pious laywoman who advocated a communal lifestyle than a vocal Dominican preacher and inquisitor. Noblewomen of Milan founded Biassono and erected it "in honor of St. Catherine the Martyr."[68] Sectarians appear to have conflated Guglielma with St. Catherine, so that the early Christian martyr served as an orthodox cover for devotion to the later disputed saint. Besides Chiaravalle and Biassono, the Guglielmites painted images of Guglielma in three local churches; two of these, Sta. Maria Minore and Sant'Eufemia, contained frescoes of Guglielma "under the name of St. Catherine."[69] Sectarians also testified that when Maifreda, Guglielma's "vicar on earth," preached at Biassono, she "sometimes said good words about the Gospels and about St. Catherine and St. Margaret."[70] Although the exact reason for the association between Catherine and Guglielma remains obscure, Barbara Newman has argued that Maifreda used the examples of these female saints, who were themselves associated with preaching to male authorities, to justify her own preaching.[71]

Although Biassono's support of Guglielma may have had a gendered element, the community's motives for overlooking Maifreda's unorthodox activities were likely more political than spiritual. While in Chiaravalle's case the

---

66. *Milano 1300*, 80.

67. Prudlo, *Martyred Inquisitor*, 56; and Andrews, *Early Humiliati*, 252.

68. "Cronica delle venerando memorie nella congregazione Umiliata," Milan, Biblioteca Ambrosiana, H205 inf., f. 112v.

69. There was a portrayal of her in Sta. Maria fuori di Porto Nuovo as well, for which there is no existing description (*Milano 1300*, 72, 236, and 240).

70. *Milano 1300*, 86. Sts. Catherine and Margaret were female martyrs known for their learning. St. Catherine is said to have convinced fifty philosophers that Emperor Maxentius's persecutions of Christians were tyrannical, while Margaret converted many pagans during her martyrdom (De Voragine, *Golden Legend*, 1:334–41 and 232–33, respectively).

71. Newman, "WomanSpirit, WomanPope," 191.

wish to sponsor an important saint and thus increase its prestige and revenues was a motivating factor for aiding the Guglielmites, patronage may have played a more prominent role for Biassono. As noted earlier, Maifreda da Pirovano was a cousin of Matteo Visconti, the *capitano del popolo* of Milan from 1287. Familial connections made Maifreda an imposing figure. The fact that inquisitors questioned at least six of the Humiliate sisters of Biassono during the process of 1300, and burned one as a relapsed heretic, implies that Maifreda's proselytizing within the community was successful and her influence strong. The influence of the Visconti, however, was not the only political factor that may have exerted pressure on the community. Subsequent trouble for the order led Biassono to distance itself from the Guglielmites before the final inquiry of 1300, as Chiaravalle did not. The Milanese Humiliati communities had become engaged in a quarrel with the new, non-Visconti archbishop of Milan only a few years prior to the inquisitorial process, and five members of the community were punished for rebellion.[72] Concomitantly, the inquisitor Tommaso da Como questioned one of the Guglielmite sectarians, Gerardo da Novazzano, in 1296. It was a dangerous time for Biassono to be tolerant of sectarian activity. While the community may have readily acquiesced to Maifreda's activities due to Visconti influence, in 1297 its own concerns proved the *force majeur*. Maifreda left the Humiliate community and moved in with the Cotica family. She did so because, as she testified, the sisters of Biassono reprimanded her for the gatherings she had held at their house.[73] Belatedly Biassono realized that Guglielma's devotees had become too conspicuous, and hence hazardous, to the community's survival regardless of the protection that the Visconti name might afford. Nevertheless, for many years Biassono had taken the path of least resistance and allowed unauthorized activities to take place in its house, undoubtedly due to the political dependence of the Humiliate and the goodwill of the ruling Visconti, who were connected to the sectarians. Other implicated Humiliate sisters continued to live at Biassono after Maifreda's departure, and there is no evidence that they destroyed the painting or altar before the 1300 investigation.

The political situation of late medieval Italy fostered the phenomenon of contested sanctity in several ways. During frequent wars and changing governmental systems, contemporary saints had a particular appeal. Citizens wanted new holy persons in addition to traditional saints who could serve as their intercessors in times of turmoil. Local authorities promoted civic cults

---

72. Under Francesco I of Parma in 1296 (Wessley, "Thirteenth-Century Guglielmites," 298).

73. *Milano 1300*, 80, 124; see also the appendix, "Tavola Sincronica," in Muraro, *Guglielma e Maifreda*, 170.

to regain some of their authority that had been undermined by the Guelph-Ghibelline conflict and the frequent interdicts that it generated. Ruling lords promoted saints as an exposition of an alliance between a holy protector and a terrestrial ruler of a city and welcomed the rituals that accompanied a saint's veneration as a show of communal solidarity, at least on the surface. Finally, the shifting power relations and the rise of the *signori* led to the support of cults and the protection of their aberrant devotees when those cults and devotees were connected to the ruling elite, as we see in the example of Guglielma of Milan.

Reconciling Factions

The saint's role in reconciling factions makes clear the political benefits of a new cult in thirteenth- and fourteenth-century Italy. The existence of a popular cult could strengthen or fix the relationship between a town and the papacy and pave the way for exiled groups to be allowed back into their hometowns. People also could venerate a saint for his or her activities as a peacemaker. This role is apparent in the saints' lives of this period and undoubtedly influenced the view that after death the person would be beneficial as a holy patron. The gift of smoothing relations within towns, between towns, and between a town and the papacy had immediacy and importance in the historical context. An example of each will show why so many communities adopted a contemporary man or woman as a new saint to add to their "urban pantheon," in Vauchez's term, and why devotees obstinately clung to veneration even in the face of papal indifference, open refusal of a canonization inquiry, or an inquisitorial condemnation.

The partisan nature of late medieval Italian politics meant that towns often were fractured based on political identity, even if other ties of dependence (e.g., kinship, business, social) remained intact. Reconciliation, or peacemaking, was extremely important and a process that governments tried to encourage in various ways and ritualize in order to add to the solemnity of the process. Katherine Ludwig Jansen and Glenn Kumhera's recent studies on this practice in medieval Italy have situated private peacemaking within the framework of Christian ideas of penitence. This relationship between peace and penitence is most clear in Jansen's work, which sees both as an act of reconciliation leading to inner tranquility. She explicitly connected the varied religious movements of the later Middle Ages, which "should be understood collectively as peace movements that took the form of penitential processions," with civil concord and the upholding of social order.[74] By this equation, Gerard Segarelli's penitential movement of the *pauperes Christi*, or Raniero Fasani's (d. circa 1285) flagellants, would fit into this framework of upholding social order by reconciling one's inner peace. This is a view that medieval authors who described these processions did not appear to consider based on their descriptions (see chapter 2). In contrast, Kumhera focused more on the political context of peacemaking and how it worked in instances and was helped in practice by religious authorities, rather than how they theoretically conceived of it. His emphasis, however, is on the agency of the individuals who embarked on the making of concord and how governments appropriated that within a criminal justice system that involved the whole community, clerical and secular.[75]

Religion also affected peacemaking on a larger, communal scale. As mentioned, blanket condemnations frequently led to whole segments of the population being exiled from the church. A successful saint's cult could alter this situation drastically, as Salimbene notes in his condemnation of the motives for the Parmeggiani's veneration of Albert of Villa d'Ogna. The government expelled citizens identified as Ghibelline from Parma in 1279, the same year that people in the town began to support Albert's cult. The pope had also imposed an interdict and excommunicated the remaining citizens after a riot in which some attacked the Dominican convent, killed a friar, and forced the rest of the brothers to flee to Reggio.[76] Parma had become an economic, social, religious, and political disaster: income from trade and travelers waned, social networks were torn apart abruptly, the political situation was unstable, and Pope Nicholas II deprived the Parmeggiani of the sacraments, leaving their salvation at stake. The city and its citizens as a whole could have benefited from a new guardian saint, but the exiled partisans had a particular interest in promoting Albert's cult. If the pope could be convinced of the veracity of his miracles, the saint's intercession could get the interdict lifted and mend the town's spiritual relations with the papacy, allowing the Ghibellines to return to their city. General amnesty customarily was given to those who traveled to a town for devotional reasons.[77] Friends, family, business associates, and sympathizers of the exiled citizens knew how religious piety and ritual could aid political factions, an inducement to support Albert's cult.

---

74. Jansen, *Peace and Penance*, 24.

75. Kumhera, *Benefits of Peace*, esp. chaps. 4–5.

76. The riot was prompted by Dominican inquisitors burning two female Cathars (*Chronicon Parmense ab anno 1038 usque ad 1338*, 35; *Chronicle of Salimbene de Adam*, 511 and 514).

77. Vauchez, *Sainthood in the Later Middle Ages*, 235.

A saint could also serve as a peacemaker between rival towns. The *vita* of Facio of Cremona explains how he was the moderator between the warring towns of Cremona and Verona. The context for the struggle between Verona and Cremona was economic profit shrouded in the cloak of the usual contest between the Guelphs and Ghibellines. In Verona during the 1230s, Ezzelino III da Romano exiled the Guelph count, Richard of San Bonifacio. Ezzelino was a member of the established nobility of the Trevisan March and an ally of Emperor Frederick II. A feud between his own family and that of the Camposanpiero family led to factionalism, which provided an opportunity for Ezzelino to use the feud as the justification for territorial conquest. He subjugated Verona, which became his base of operations, and captured various nearby towns. Although officially an imperial administrator, he seems to have been concerned with the accumulation of power.[78] He reportedly terrorized the towns of northern Italy, and his activities became the stuff of legend. For instance, there is a story that he once burned 11,000 Paduans in a building while he sat outside playing games. The contemporary Salimbene, never at a loss for colorful description, claimed, "Ezzelino was feared more than the devil himself, for he would have men, women, and children killed for no reason at all, and would commit the most incredible atrocities. Not even those great tyrants, Nero, Domitian, Decius, or Diocletian approach his like for cruelties. . . . It would take too long to relate all his cruelties, for that would take a huge book."[79] Unsurprisingly, his actions—even if what is recorded is minimally accurate—led to conflict. The cities of Verona and Cremona, led by da Romano and another Ghibelline leader named Uberto II Pallavicino, respectively, became allies of the Holy Roman Emperor Frederick II and his son Manfred, prompting Innocent IV to declare a crusade against the two local leaders in 1250. In 1259, however, Pallavicino switched sides and forged an alliance with the Guelph "crusaders" when Ezzelino da Romano took over Brescia, a town that Pallavicino himself wanted to control. As a result, hostilities between Verona and Cremona increased, and a Guelph party composed of the followers of Azzo d'Este of Ferrara and some exiles from Verona attacked the town of Cremona and killed Ezzelino in battle.[80]

Facio was uniquely situated to serve as peacemaker between the towns. He was born in Verona during these chaotic years but at about age thirty moved to Cremona, his city's archrival. He was loyal to the Guelph cause in Verona. His hagiographer claimed he moved because "he had sustained many perse-

78. Larner, *Italy in the Age of Dante*, 129–31.
79. *Chronicle of Salimbene de Adam*, 186.
80. Larner, *Italy in the Age of Dante*, 39–40.

cutions and afflictions through Verona's lords, or through other citizens of the partisan [i.e., Ghibelline] cause, or through some other reason."[81] After his *fama* as a holy man increased and he had a prophecy in which he predicted peace between the towns, Facio returned to Verona for a reconciliation attempt. Veronese authorities hastily imprisoned him. He remained in custody for four years until he obtained his release with the help of the Cremonese.[82] André Vauchez suggested that perhaps Uberto Pallavicino, the lord of Cremona and ostensibly by then part of the "Guelph" faction, allied his troops with those of d'Este and participated in the attack on Verona, a by-product of which was Facio's release from prison.[83]

Regardless of the success of Facio's efforts at reconciliation, which may fall short of miraculous, the fact remains that Cremona claimed him as its local saint, recognizing his holiness and virtue in attempting to serve as peacemaker between his hometown and adopted town.[84] His hagiography does not fail to capitalize on the treatment he received in Verona as an example of the relative merit of his adopted town. Ultimately, though, it was Facio's attempt to reconcile the rivals that advanced the claim that he was holy and that he was Cremona's protector. In a similar spirit of reconciliation, Margaret of Cortona worked to establish peace between the leaders of Cortona (effectively, the Casali family) and the bishop of Arezzo, Guglielmino degli Ubertini (d. 1289). Cortona was spiritually under the rule of the Arezzese bishop, and tension between city officials of Cortona and the Arezzo diocese came to a head in the mid-1270s. In 1277 Margaret's efforts, which primarily consisted of admonishing the bishop to live in peace with the Cortonese, helped to diffuse the situation.[85] There are other notable examples in which she served as peacemaker between rival groups. As a result, her confessor claimed she had a vision in which Christ called her a *clamatrix pacis*.[86]

A local saint could even function as a means for reconciliation with the papacy, as evidenced in the story of Siena's St. Ambruogio. According to one chronicler, Siena was under interdict in 1286 because the Guelph nobles of the town had killed their bishop. The anonymous chronicler, writing not long after the purported event, explained only that the partisans did not

---

81. Vauchez, "Sainteté laïque aux XIIIe siècle," 36.

82. Gorini, "Beati Petri de Fulgineo Confessoris," 366–67; Vauchez, "Sainteté laïque aux XIIIe siècle," 37–38.

83. Vauchez, introduction to "Sainteté laïque aux XIIIe siècle," 21–23; see also 38.

84. Ibid., 37.

85. Benvenuti Papi, "*In castro poenitentiae*," 143; Schlager, "Foundresses of the Franciscan Life," 159.

86. Bevignati, *Margaret of Cortona*, 216–17, 205, 218, and 256; for the vision, 91. For an example outside of the Italian peninsula, see Goodich, "Foreigner, Foe, and Neighbor."

want his governance and had subsequently elected their own bishop.[87] Siena had a Guelph communal government at the time of the bishop's murder, which had come into power in 1277. Yet the city's Ghibelline sympathies, epitomized in its war with the Florentine Guelphs that culminated at the battle of Montaperti in 1260, remained alive in the traditional Ghibelline nobility, from whose ranks the murdered bishop would most likely have descended. Although theoretically the Guelph government was ruled by the *popolo* and supported by the merchant class, in reality the Sienese commune was a long-standing oligarchy.[88] The men who held government positions were predominantly descended from or related to old feudal families: the Cacciaconti, Berardenghi, Ardenghesca, and Alberti. Bishops were active participants in Italian urban life. Before the rise of communes, the governance of a cathedral town almost invariably devolved to the bishop.[89] This official political role disappeared in the early to mid-thirteenth century as cities transformed into independent communes ruled by the people. The bishop retained a vestige of his prior civic function by serving as the representative of his city: "The model of a good bishop in the communal period," explained Augustine Thompson, "included a role as protector of city independence."[90] During the Guelph-Ghibelline controversy, this role could put the bishop in peril if he was partisan to the losing side in a local battle. Such a situation could have been the case in Siena, hence prompting the bishop's premature death.

The chronicler of Siena explained how the pope, Honorius IV (d. 1287), issued an interdict once he heard the news of the supposed assassination. The commune of Siena "saw the loss of their souls" and in fear for their salvation sent ambassadors to the pope, but Honorius refused them entrance. The Sienese had a local holy man named Ambruogio Sansedoni (or de' Codenaci) who they knew the pope wanted to meet, having heard of the man's miraculous powers. The Sienese "elected" Ambruogio as their "ambassador" to the pope to ask for his benediction and to facilitate reconciliation. Impressed by Ambruogio's sanctity, Honorius told the man during their conference that he should move from Siena and resettle in Rome. Ambruogio responded that he would never consent to move unless the pope lifted the interdict. Honorius IV responded, "'Since you have showered me with so much luminous grace,

---

87. *AASS* III, March 20, col. 180A–241C; *Cronache Senesi*, 71.

88. Even into the early fourteenth century when members of the *popolani grassi*, or important guildsmen, held offices, only sixty families out of a population estimated at perhaps 50,000 participated in the government (Larner, *Italy in the Age of Dante*, 122; for an overview discussion of the social composition of the Italian communities and the complicated relationships among the different classes, see ibid., 83–210).

89. Foote, *Lordship, Reform*, 37–38.

90. Thompson, *Cities of God*, 45.

I want to grant you [your wish] as I promised you.' And raising his hand he said: 'I bless Siena and all of those who are under interdict for the death of their innocent shepherd and bishop.'"[91] The intervention of Ambruogio reconciled the Sienese and the papacy. This story may be more legend than fact, although he attained a public cult as a result of this "miracle." Whether the murder actually occurred, and whether Siena even was under interdict during this period, is disputed.[92] Regardless of the veracity of the account, it highlights how politics impacted the religious life of communities, and more specifically, how local saints functioned within the political venue as negotiators between representatives of church and state to resolve a conflict between estranged parties.

The Sienese tale of Ambruogio is not an isolated incident. The commune of Padua requested a canonization inquiry in 1267 for Anthony Peregrinus, possibly a member of the eremitical Camaldolese Order. His first *vita*, thought to have been written by a cleric with the purpose of prompting an inquiry, is lost. Nevertheless, it was the basis for another *Life* written by Sicco Pollentone in the fifteenth century.[93] That *vita* promoted Peregrinus as a faithful Guelph who fought against the notorious tyrant of the Po plain, and accused heretic, Ezzelino III da Romano. Since Padua in the late thirteenth century was itself a predominantly Guelph community, Peregrinus seemed a likely contender for the role of the city's patron saint. Michael Goodich noted, however, that although Peregrinus's cult flourished in Padua soon after his death, the commune did not grant him public honors until 1324, when Ghibellines gained control of the town.[94] Two possibilities could explain this unusual chronology. If Peregrinus's opposition to Ezzelino da Romano was present in the original thirteenth-century *vita*, the newly aligned Ghibelline Paduans probably were hoping to mend their own relationship with the pope through the hoped-for canonization. A successful inquiry could mitigate any bad feelings by showing that the Paduans would accept a man who exemplified the Guelph cause as holy. If Peregrinus was not a clear enemy of Ezzelino in the 1250s, by the 1320s civic officials could still ride the coattails of a saint who

---

91. *Cronache Senesi*, 71.

92. Most historians doubt this account, since the series of Sienese bishops and their fates is documented. The editor of the Sienese chronicle, however, noted, "Ma coloro che negano l'uccisione del vescovo, non sanno però indicare, nè la causa, nè l'anno dell'interdetto, nè il Papa che l'avrebbe pronunciato; pure tutti ammettendo che l'assoluzione dale censure ecclesiastiche contro i Senesi sarebbe avvenuta per le istanze di questo beato. Ma la controversia è rimasta ancora insoluta" (ibid., 71n1).

93. Polenton, "Vita Beati Antonii Peregrini," 417; Vauchez, *Sainthood in the Later Middle Ages*, 198n137. Vauchez identified Peregrinus as a member of the laity, but the *Acta Sanctorum* claimed he was a Camaldolese monk (*AASS* I, February 1, col. 264).

94. Goodich, *Vita Perfecta*, 195.

was established in a Guelph city to insinuate themselves with the papacy when memories of specifics might have become blurred. In either case, Peregrinus served as mediator after his death.

Rose of Viterbo seemed to fulfill the same promise for a city that had become Ghibelline around the time she was born in the 1230s. Her account survives in two lives: the *Vita Prima*, written soon after her death, and the *Vita Secunda*, composed 150 to 200 years after her death.[95] The two texts focus on different parts of Rose's life and emphasize distinct aspects of it. They both stated that Rose, who died in 1251 around the age of nineteen, was from a Guelph family. Rose preached to people about their vices in the streets of Viterbo, carrying a cross in a very public manner. According to her *Vita Prima*, civic officials first placed her under house arrest and then exiled her family in 1250 at the behest of what the hagiographer called some "heretics" (i.e., Ghibelline officials in open revolt against the pope). Her family moved back in late 1250, when the city was nominally put under papal protection. Soon after the Clarissan monastery of San Damiano refused Rose entrance, she had a prophetic vision of the death of Emperor Frederick II. When she died just a year later, Innocent IV immediately opened a canonization inquiry into her merits in 1252 at the behest of a joint petition of the clergy and the people. While the canonization process fell by the wayside due to a focus on the process of Clare of Assisi who had died in 1253, the next pope, Alexander III, fixed Rose's translation to San Damiano and feast day in 1258 after he had a series of three visions of her. Rose, who had been treated badly due to her vocal piety and her Guelph associations in a Ghibelline town, quickly became a papal favorite for just those reasons. When the bishop and citizens of Viterbo found themselves under a government supportive of the pope, the promotion of Rose's cult became a means to reconcile with the papacy.

When all the benefits were added up, the odds were overwhelmingly in favor of a community obstinately clinging to a local saint. At the basis of all veneration was the conviction that the person was holy. Other considerations, however, were contributing factors. A new saint's cult could provide material benefits to the church and town in which the saint's body resided. It could be used as leverage in local rivalries between ecclesiastical institutions or through patronage attached to political factions. Conversely, it could aid in quelling the tiresome factional quarrels that interrupted thirteenth-century life in Italian towns and even promote the return of exiled factions. Those con-

---

95. The two different *vitae* are in *AASS* II, September 4, col. 433A–442A, both edited by P. Giuseppe Abate in "S. Rosa di Viterbo, Terziaria Francescana." For discussion, see Pryds, *Women of the Streets*, 23–29; Weisenbeck and Weisenbeck, "Rose of Viterbo"; and Rollo-Koster, *Raiding St. Peter*, 156–57.

sidered saints often actively tried to heal the social body no less than the physical bodies of supplicants. Finally, these saints and their cults could promote peace with the papacy. In none of these cases was an official canonization a required outcome to achieve these goals. Belief in the saint, and the saint's beneficial role in the town as a homegrown holy person, trumped papal recognition. The result was contested saints that ran the gamut from those whose supporters willfully challenged inquisitorial condemnations to those whose devotees continued to venerate them even after canonization inquires were forgotten, failed, or rejected.

CHAPTER 6

Anti-Inquisitorialism to Antimendicantism

Anti-inquisitorial attitudes were rife throughout most of the Italian peninsula, in part because inquisitors were plentiful there. While there may have been no organized institution of the inquisition in the Middle Ages, as Richard Kieckhefer famously argued, soon after the inception of the office popes culled inquisitors from the ranks of the new mendicant orders, first the Dominicans and then the Franciscans.[1] In 1254 the papacy organized inquisitors into regional districts divided between the friars. The Franciscans were in charge of the Marches of Treviso and Ancona, the southern half of Romagna, the Duchy of Spoleto, the Province of St. Francis, Tuscany, and Rome and its custodials (the city of Rome, the Patrimony of St. Peter, Sabina, Campania, and the Maritimma). The Dominican inquisitors had authority over Lombardy; the northern part of Romagna, including Bologna, Ferrara, and Parma; the March of Genoa; and, from about 1268 on, the Kingdom of Sicily.[2] More troubling to some than the number of inquisitors was the number of inquisitors thought to be overstepping their bounds and engaging in vindictive persecution rather than justified prosecution.

---

1. Kieckhefer, "Office of Inquisition and Medieval Heresy"; cf. Alan Friedlander's discussion of Bernard Delicieux and his oppositional force in France (Friedlander, *Hammer of the Inquisitors*, 270–72).

2. D'Alatri, *L'inquisizione francescana*, 17–18.

Angelo Clareno recorded concerns about mendicants in the role of inquisitors and inquisitorial abuse of power. Discussing one inquisitorial dragnet, he claimed:

> Then the Lord Andrea [di Isernia] wrote the inquisitor informing him trustworthy people had told him that among all those the inquisitor had captured there was only one [Poor] Lombard. He advised him to attend to the dignity of his inquisitorial office. He advised him as a good friend to stick to the truth in carrying out his duties, because without it neither human nor divine judgment is justly performed. When the inquisitor read Lord Andreo's [sic] letter, he was furious and vengefully turned all his indignation and wrath on the poor brothers he had arrested. . . . The next day he visited them and, binding himself with a terrible oath, said, "Unless you confess to me that you are heretics, may God do thus and so to me if I don't kill all of you right here with a variety of tortures and torments. If, as I ask, you do confess to me that you do or did err in something or other, I'll give you a light penance and set you free immediately." The brothers replied that he should not ask them to say something that wasn't true. Telling such a wicked lie would cause death to their souls and offense to God. The furious inquisitor selected one of them who seemed more fervent than the others, and [who] was a priest, and ordered that he be tortured.[3]

In this troubling account, a lay lord counseled the Franciscan inquisitor to show mercy. From his own sources of knowledge, Andrea di Isernia claimed there was only one potential heretic, a Poor Lombard (or Waldensian), in the bunch of people the inquisitor detained. The inquisitor, presumably drunk on power, regarded the noble's advice as an affront and took out his rage on innocent prisoners. At this point, prosecution becomes persecution and, according to Clareno, inquisitorial authority jeopardized the salvation of Christian souls. Whether or not the events happened as described, this account highlights concerns over the ramifications of inquisitorial power.

Inquisitors were the ones who had the power to destroy the cult of a regional holy man or woman through an official condemnation of heresy. Since all inquisitors were friars, at times lay observers viewed the mainstream members of the wealthy and powerful mendicant orders as less spiritually worthy than those they prosecuted. Inquisitorial activity in local communities therefore consistently fueled the flames of acrimony. In addition, mendicant inquisitors often clashed with other members of the ecclesiastical hierarchy, in

---

3. Clareno, *Chronicle or History of the Seven Tribulations*, 170–71.

particular the secular clergy and the traditional monastic orders. Some of these other clerics viewed the mendicants as upstarts who interfered with their spiritual authority and received seemingly excessive and unwarranted papal favors. Local clergy often banded together with the community to challenge their inquisitorial powers (see chapter 8). This chapter examines the process by which laypeople's anti-inquisitorial attitudes became antimendicant ones, as well as how other clerics' antimendicant views led them to support anti-inquisitorial actions. Both lay and clerical members of communities united against the perceived interloper, the mendicant inquisitor, giving impetus to challenge any of their suspicions or condemnations of hometown saints. Furthermore, antipathy toward the pope or the institutional church became projected onto the mendicants as emissaries of papal power, specifically because of their inquisitorial functions.

Anti-Inquisitorialism and the Sin of Avarice

The mendicants' descent from models of admiration to figures of perturbation was fairly swift. The Dominicans and Franciscans had originally been part of a wider apostolic movement that included the Humiliati and the Waldensians and other mendicants like the Augustinian Friars, the Carmelites, the Friars of the Sack, and the Pied Friars. By the mid-thirteenth century the former two had become incorporated into the church hierarchy, whereas some of the latter groups had a more vexed relationship with the papacy. It was difficult to obtain or retain papal approval. Pope Innocent III deemed the Waldensians heterodox, the Humiliati waited fifty to a hundred years for papal approval, and the Council of Lyons disbanded the Sack and Pied Friars in 1274. In contrast, the Dominicans and Franciscans had a special relationship with the papacy from their inception. The Dominicans were approved as an order specifically to combat heresy. They subsequently conceived of their role as a "sacralized" office. The Franciscans had the charismatic leader St. Francis, who caught the imagination of Innocent III and Cardinal Ugolino, later Pope Gregory IX (d. 1241). Neslihan Şenocak showed that the order early on placed emphasis on education. This focus opened the door for popes to use Franciscans as inquisitors side by side with the Dominicans, as occurred by the 1250s in Italy.[4] Herbert Grundmann characterized the development of the mendi-

---

4. On Humiliati and Waldensians, see Bolton, "Innocent III's Treatment of the Humiliati," and Tourn, *Waldensians*, respectively. For the other mendicant orders, see Andrews, *Other Friars*, esp. 173–230. For the Dominicans, see Ames, *Righteous Persecution*, 23–56; for the Franciscans, see Şenocak, *Poor and the Perfect*, esp. 76–143.

cants into rich and powerful orders as a retreat from their original goal of evangelical poverty and a move toward mainstream monasticism, which ended their radical attitude toward the religious life.[5] Itinerant and educated, Dominicans and Franciscans were bound to papal obedience and functioned somewhat outside the traditional church hierarchy. The Orders of Preachers and Friars Minor were agents that popes could oversee, trust, and mold into instruments for subjecting Christendom to papal control and ensuring orthodoxy. Friars who refused to conform by curbing their commitment to live strictly in accordance with the *vita apostolica*, such as the Spiritual Franciscans (called *fraticelli* in Italy), were first chastised and then persecuted. There had to be clear delineation between the mendicant orders and other groups bent on living an apostolic life. Appointing mainstream Franciscans and Dominicans as inquisitors and punishing those of the orders who deviated, especially on the charge of absolute poverty, was the papacy's crucial move to differentiate orthodox friars from heterodox elements that they were charged to investigate after the creation of the inquisitorial office.

Within sixty years of the inception of the friars, there is proof that many of the *popolo* considered the dominant mendicant orders as the lowest rung on the ladder of an ecclesiastical hierarchy desperately in need of repair. Laypeople held the friars to a higher standard than other clerics because of their mission to follow stringently the *vita apostolica*. Citizens measured mendicant behavior against the original models of Francis and Dominic (and other apostolic leaders whose movements did not fare as well) and found some later friars deficient. Yet it was their position as inquisitors, and the authority that role afforded them to become even wealthier and more powerful at the expense of local humble penitents, that led to the perception that mendicant inquisitors were corrupt. Inquisitorial registers, such as that of Bologna from 1291 to 1310, include numerous testimonies demonstrating that citizens believed those who held the position were avaricious and lustful and that they abused their authority to feed their desires. Specific examples will be discussed in the next section; in short, citizens accused inquisitors either of burning individuals who did not have the money to pay bribes or, conversely, had money the inquisitors wanted to confiscate. Others testified that vice-ridden inquisitors used the threat of an inquiry to persuade women to sleep with them.

Although inquisitorial opponents made these accusations, contemporary events support these opinions. The inquisitorial office had the ability to cow stubborn citizens through fear. Some inquisitors became wealthy through misuse of that power. Excessive prosecution could mean monetary remuneration.

---

5. Grundmann, *Religious Movements*, 226; also Friedlander, *Hammer of the Inquisitors*, 236.

When inquisitors condemned someone as a heretic, they confiscated his or (more rarely) her property and divided it between the secular and religious authorities, including inquisitors themselves. Although mendicant convents housing inquisitors were not the only ones who benefited, in Italy as opposed to other regions the mendicants were the ones who took charge of the confiscated property.[6] Recorded cases show that concerns about aggressive prosecution for monetary gain were valid.

The inquiries into Meco del Sacco, discussed in chapter 2, provide an example of inquisitorial corruption. To reiterate, Meco was a local holy man in Ascoli, widely revered for his charitable and spiritual endeavors. The bishop, the nearby Augustinian convent, and a large segment of the laity were among his many admirers even though inquisitors condemned him for heresy three times. After being released on bail in 1338 after his second condemnation, he appealed to the pope. His argument was that the Franciscans had falsely accused him of heresy to the inquisitor of the same order, Giovanni da Monteleone. Meco claimed they were "moved by jealousy and hatred against him, and because his said hospital and church were more frequented by the faithful of Christ and His mother than their [own] place."[7] He won his appeal, but during his absence the inquisitor, armed and accompanied by clergy from the ancient parish church of S. Maria Intervineas (in the quarter of S. Emidio near the Tufilla gate) destroyed Meco's buildings, including the church attached to the hospital, and confiscated the valuables they contained. Bishop Rainaldo IV showed his support of the local holy man by granting Meco license to rebuild and naming him and his heirs patrons of the hospital for perpetuity.[8] The Augustinians, acting on Meco's behalf, brought charges against these clerics. In 1341 the treasurer of the general vicar of the March of Ancona sentenced the culprits to a heavy monetary fine for reparations.[9] A bull of Pope Clement VI from August 1344 shows that a new inquisitor, Peter da Penna S. Giovanni, condemned Meco for a third time and sentenced him to a fine of sixty gold florins and two years in exile. Meco appealed once again on the same grounds. The pope ordered the recently appointed new bishop, Isacco Bindi, to examine the case. Peter da Penna S. Giovanni ignored the bishop's order to take no further action and excommunicated Meco, claiming that the bishop was biased in Meco's favor. This was an injudicious argument, as the

---

6. Lea, *History of the Inquisition*, 1:501–33, esp. 505–6.

7. *Meco*, appendix 4, 285.

8. *Meco*, appendices 6 and 5, respectively. Interestingly, the church of S. Maria Intervineas is situated only six blocks away from a major thoroughfare now named the via Sacconi, after the followers of Meco del Sacco.

9. *Meco*, appendix 6, 290–93.

pope himself had appointed Bindi to the bishopric, choosing him from the Benedictine convent of S. Michele di Candiana in distant Padua. The inquisitor then led his own armed following to confiscate Meco's goods. These actions prompted Clement VI to order a special commission chaired by Cardinal Guglielmo de Curtè.[10] In 1345 the commission decided that Meco be given restitution, and in 1346 he was posthumously absolved and reinstated in the church. Meco seemingly died of natural causes in the interim, sometime between 1344 and 1346. Meco had at least two sons with his wife, Clarella, before turning to the spiritual life. One of them, Angelo, was named rector of the church and the hospital in 1344. After his death the oratory passed into the hands of the Augustinians and survived under their control until the Napoleonic suppression.[11]

Meco's success at drawing recruits to his penitential lifestyle meant that he had become a powerful figure, and his establishments became wealthy foundations. His complaint about inquisitorial greed is persuasive, given the evidence. He gathered the money necessary to travel to Avignon and launch two appeals. Authorities released him on bail after his second condemnation and also were uncharacteristically kind in the punishment for his third condemnation. On both occasions Meco could have been executed as a relapsed heretic. Instead, he was able to make bail, although he also lost property in the raids and nearly missed being exiled and fined. The records demonstrate that he had a certain amount of wealth and that others were interested in acquiring it through inquisitorial judgments. Luckily, he also had powerful supporters who stymied those efforts. Meco's accusations of inquisitorial avarice were not an isolated incident. The hagiographer of the suspect saint Peter Crisci attributed the same motive to the Franciscans inquisitors of Assisi and Spoleto, as mentioned in chapter 2. The mid-fourteenth century saw at least three other significant and embarrassing inquiries into Franciscan abuse of inquisitorial power for monetary gain. In 1333–1334 the inquisitor of Tuscany, Mino da San Quirico, was investigated on charges of extorting money and of excessive zeal in prosecuting heretics to profit from the confiscation of their goods.[12] The Franciscan convent of Tuscany was soon humiliated again in 1344–1346, when the inquisitor Peter of Aquila faced a similar accusation. According to Giovanni Villani, Peter used his position to collect business debts for his patron, Cardinal Piero of Spain, falsely accusing debtors of heterodoxy.[13] Another episode of

---

10. *Meco*, appendix 11, 296–99.

11. *Meco*, appendices 12–13, 300–306; see also 36, 53, and 187.

12. D'Anvers and Callaey, "Un épisode de l'Inquisition franciscaine en Toscane."

13. Process in ASV, Collectoriae 421.A. For a contemporary description, see Villani, *Nuova cronica*, III, 429–32 (XIII.58), translated in Dean, *Towns of Italy*, 94–96; for discussion, see Mariano d'Alatri,

corruption quickly followed in 1346–1347 when the archbishop of Vercelli (who also served as papal vicar) initiated an inquiry into the Franciscan inquisitor of the March of Ancona, Peter da Penna S. Giovanni. He was the very same man Meco del Sacco criticized for misconduct during his second appeal. Authorities sentenced the inquisitor for extortion, with a fine of five hundred florins, although it is likely he fled soon after his condemnation.[14]

Interestingly enough, these prominent cases of corruption occurred on the heels of the 1322 condemnation of the Spiritual Franciscans. The Franciscans were industrious in promoting saints from their order and had reaped the accompanying material benefits of cults. The consequent wealth they attained was intrinsic to the divide between the Conventuals and the Spirituals. Perhaps increased prosecution of those who remained in the Spiritual camp—or at least sympathy for anyone who subsequently seemed to adhere closely to a more rigorous interpretation of the apostolic life—prompted growing accusations of avarice. In 1302, when the term "Spirituals" was just coming into use prior to the Council of Vienne, Pope Boniface VIII replaced the Franciscan inquisitors of the March of Treviso and the Romagna with Dominicans because of widespread charges of abuse.[15] Accusations, however, were not confined to the Friars Minor. The Dominicans also accrued such charges, although they did not experience the high-profile cases like the Minorites, and many of the complaints against them had more to do with hubris than avarice. For example, the inquisitor of Milan Tommaso da Como excommunicated a man named Pagano of Petrasancta against Boniface VIII's order to withhold further sentencing, clearly overstepping the bounds of his authority. The pope suspended the inquisitor while he examined Pagano's case. Moreover, many citizens of Bologna were vocal regarding their belief that the Dominican inquisitors in that town engaged in misconduct.

A wider perspective suggests that the corruption cases cited above were related to where inquisitors were functioning rather than which order was in charge of the inquisitorial office in the region. The rebuke of the Tuscan inquisitors in the 1340s occurred in Florence. That city, with its many bankers and merchants, provided ample opportunities for extortion. In addition, the political climate in Florence during the 1330s and 1340s was in turmoil. A protracted war with Lucca led to a shift in government, with the citizens voluntarily

"L'inquisizione a Firenze negli anni 1344–46 da un'istruttoria contro Pietro da l'Aquila," in *Eretici*, 1:41–68.

14. ASV, Collectoriae, 384, f. 1r–12r; a transcription and discussion are in Mariano d'Alatri, "Un processo dell'inverno 1346–1347 contro gli inquisitori delle Marche," in *Eretici*, 2:77–107.

15. Burr, *Spiritual Franciscans*, 6; and Lea, *History of the Inquisition*, 1:477.

abandoning communal rule in 1342 and naming Walter of Brienne, titular duke of Athens, a life *signore*. Brienne's pandering to wealthy merchants resulted in a revolt when the lesser guildsmen realized they had no influence with the duke. The *popolo* overthrew Brienne in August 1343, and further problems descended on Florence. An economic depression, caused in part by the fall of the three great Florentine banks, prompted the people to riot.[16] The power vacuum that occurred because of these events provided an opening for men who occupied positions of authority, such as inquisitors, to take advantage. Only one year later the Florentine inquisitor was under a microscope. While the political and economic situation in the March of Ancona was much different, during the years of inquisitorial scandal it also had suffered from a lack of centralized control. The region was troublesome for the Papal States, as many towns chafed under the authority of a terrestrial lord who lived far away in Avignon. Particularly after the death of Pope John XXII in 1334, skirmishes increased as towns sought autonomy. Ascoli itself engaged in an on-again, off-again war with Spoleto and consequently was under interdict from 1324 to 1346. The interdict added to the instability of the region and in its own way created opportunities for some men, like the inquisitor Pietro, to prey on the public.

The inquisitorial office provided an opportunity to sate the earthly desire for both money and power. Inquisitors could attain high office within the church when they successfully prosecuted papal enemies. Citizens of Bologna reviled Guido of Vicenza, the inquisitor who prosecuted many Bolognese in 1300 and oversaw the ultimate condemnation of Armanno Pungilupo in 1301, for what they described as his excessive zeal and corruption.[17] Pope Boniface VIII, however, appreciated Guido's enthusiasm and rewarded him by appointing him bishop of Ferrara in 1303.[18] Clerics who aided inquisitors in their duties by taking part in tribunals to remove a papal enemy also could climb the ladder of the ecclesiastical hierarchy. Brother Simone Saltarelli is an excellent example of this process. Saltarelli was from a noble Florentine family who started out as a Dominican stationed in the province of Etruria (the area around modern Tuscania, just north of Rome). Soon after ascending to the pontificate, John XXII granted Saltarelli the episcopacy of Parma in 1317. The pope, having created an ally through his beneficence, called on a favor, pressing

---

16. Becker and Brucker, "'*Arti Minori*' in Florentine Politics," 95. The three greatest Florentine banks were the Frescobaldi, the Bardi, and the Peruzzi. All three went bankrupt from overextending loans to foreign rulers (Larner, *Italy in the Age of Dante*, 188).

17. Lansing, *Power and Purity*, 151.

18. Lea, *History of the Inquisition*, 2:242.

Saltarelli into service in 1322 in his heresy trial against Matteo I Visconti and his son, Galeazzo I. In March of that year Saltarelli, along with "the bishops of Asti, Novara, Savona, and Alba, [and] with many abbots and other lay nobles" went to a meeting called by John XXII. In the presence of the papal legate, the council "declared that Galeazzo Visconti, *signore* of Milan, was a heretic through his wicked [actions] and the impudent propositions he had made and on account of his engagement in necromancy and extortion and cruelty to religious [persons], having also [had] Bosio de Zaboli, monk of Fontanaviva, amongst others, killed in prison in Parma, [and] he impeded the income of cardinals, [and] he deflowered nuns."[19] Galeazzo Visconti was the nemesis of John XXII, as his father Matteo had been of popes since Boniface VIII. His close alliance with Louis of Bavaria, the contender to the imperial throne, and the breadth of his territory in Lombardy, was a serious threat to papal interests. At the end of the same year in which Saltarelli participated in Visconti's condemnation, the pope made him archbishop of Pisa and thus also of Corsica and Sardinia, both under Pisan rule at the time.

Saltarelli continued to promote papal interests, sometimes in a more overtly political manner. He opposed Louis of Bavaria and Louis's appointed antipope, Nicholas V, although he fled Pisa when Louis entered the city in 1327. This event was recast by the great Dominican preacher and Saltarelli's friend, Bartolommeo da San Concordio, as "heroism." Bartolommeo's biography moralizes Saltarelli: "[He] abandon[ed] the archbishop's seat to him [i.e., Louis of Bavaria] at the cost of the foretold belongings, and with danger to his life, demonstrating in such actions one whose example of constancy [was] in the favor of truth."[20] Saltarelli's legacy was as a man loyal to the pope who had benefited politically from being a reliable papal ally. He was a papal supporter, but one who put on the inquisitorial cloak in the proceedings against the Visconti. He, like actual inquisitors, derived power and wealth from his willingness to step into the role of a prosecutor. It took a short leap for specific antiinquisitorial sentiment to shift to a more general antimendicant sentiment when citizens recognized this pattern of reward for perceived persecution of their friends and families.

---

19. "Memorie concernenti a Monsignore Fr. Simone Saltarelli dell'Ordine de Predicatori, fù vescovo di Parma, ed quindi Archivescovo di Pisa," ASF, fondo corporazioni religiose soppresse dal governo francese, ser. 102, pez. 95, insert V, record 2.

20. "Memorie a Bartolommeo da San Concordio Domenicano," ASF, corporazioni religiose soppresse dal governo francese, ser. 102, pez. 95, insert V, record 16, para. 16.

Anti-Inquisitorialism to Antimendicantism: Donatism and the Sin of Wrath

In communities where inquisitors were active, the laity viewed inquisitorial power as an unwelcome and unnecessary imposition. They resented that men they considered not to be living up to their role as moral examples, much less as judges of spiritual mettle and orthodoxy, had the authority to determine what were "correct" forms of devotion and belief and to monitor the external signs of religious obedience. Clerical vice was an important issue in northern and central Italy, and accusations of that nature became a weapon to combat inquisitorial power. Thirteenth- and fourteenth-century testimony reveals the recurrent belief that inquisitors were themselves sinners and therefore had no right to hold office and no authority to judge the orthodoxy of citizens. Charges levied against them included avarice, lust, pride, and even heterodoxy. Since inquisitors were mendicants, the distinction between their role for the papacy and their vocation in the church became equated.

The belief that only the virtuous and morally pure had the right to judge other Christians resonates with early Donatist ideas that the church deemed heretical but that did not disappear. In the central Middle Ages they were most clearly articulated first in the eleventh-century reform movement in Milan called the Pataria. Even before the Gregorian Reform, this group endorsed clerical celibacy and revolted against clergy they considered corrupt. The Patarines claimed that sacraments performed by unworthy clergy were not valid. They even gained limited pontifical support during the tumult of the investiture controversy, although in the later Middle Ages the term designated any heretic or religious dissenter.[21] Subsequently, however, Donatist arguments had little effect when used as a method of contesting inquisitorial power. Church teachings since St. Augustine had made it clear that Christians must differentiate between the holiness of the individual and the holiness of any ecclesiastical office and the sacerdotal duties it entailed. As a consequence, popes and inquisitors merely ignored the accusations or punished with monetary fines those who had spread such ideas. Yet this type of bad publicity heightened animosity between communities and inquisitors and led to proactive forms of contestation.

Just as the Patarines criticized priests they perceived to have moral failings, so too did the citizens of late medieval Italian towns denounce the inquisitors

---

21. Pope Gregory VII, for instance, permitted them to refuse sacraments performed by sinful priests, although he maintained that sacraments performed by such men were still valid. On the history of the Patarines, see Lambert, *Medieval Heresy*, 44–45; Moore, *Origins of European Dissent*, 40; and Violante, "I laici nel movimento patarino."

in their midst. During a riot that broke out in Bologna in 1299 after inquisitors executed several men as relapsed heretics and also exhumed and burned a woman's remains, Bolognese citizens denounced the inquisitors, repeatedly accusing in this case the Dominicans of simony, sexual vice, and avarice.[22] Some argued that two of the condemned men, Bompietro and Iuliano, were burned because the inquisitors wanted money. Others asserted it was because they wanted Bompietro's sister.[23] One deponent claimed that in the case of the burning of another man, named Bonigrino, the inquisitors wanted the man's granddaughter.[24] Rather than helping souls, these citizens claimed that friars deceived guileless individuals with assurances of salvation while filling their own purses. Witnesses to the ensuing riot testified that they either said themselves, or heard their friends declare, that the Dominican inquisitors only burned men who were poor and had no money with which to bribe the friars or who had refused to pimp their female kin to the inquisitors.[25] Inquisitorial actions were seen as spiteful, ethically bankrupt, and wrathful against those who did not or could not obey their commands, thought by many to be motivated by earthly desires.

The same inquisitorial register shows the Donatist belief that vice compromised one's ability to judge others. According to a Bolognese woman named Meglore, "many passed by to hear the words" of a rabble-rouser in 1299 who proclaimed that "the brothers, and St. Dominic, are more worthy to be burned, unless they are the picture of holiness . . . and [was saying] many evil words in prejudice of the office of the inquisition."[26] The Bolognese charged inquisitors with being the true heretics, as the distinction between justified inquisitorial prosecution and wrathful inquisitorial persecution collapsed. One observer remarked after the sentence against Bompietro and Iuliano, "The brothers are not able to condemn or judge any men, even if they [Bompietro and Iuliano] were heretics, and release them to secular justice so that they

---

22. These themes run throughout the witness testimony; for an example of each charge, see *Acta S. Officii*, vol. 1, nos. 412, 313, and 139, respectively.

23. The charge that the friars were after money is by far the most popular complaint and one that recurs consistently after the inquisitors had sentenced someone (see *Acta S. Officii*, vol. 1, nos. 130, 140, 142, 154, 155, 161, 168, 186–90, 193, 198, 199, 209, 240, 250, 258, 259, 274, 280, 281, 287, 297, 299, 301, 313, 316, 320, 324, 326, 328, 340, 368, 369, 376, 388, 400, 401, 403, 407, 412, 414, 416, 425, 428, 440, 457, 461, 473, 480, 501, 547, and 560). A man named Gontus asserted, "Inquisitor facit hoc quia dictus Bompetrus noluit ei dare sororem suam, nec consentire eam ipsi inquisitori" (testimony of Iacobinus, *Acta S. Officii*, vol. 1, no. 139, 15 May 1299, p. 158; for other examples, see nos. 250, 349, and 404).

24. Testimony of lady Advenante, *Acta S. Officii*, vol. 1, no. 305, 25 May 1299, p. 213.

25. See, for example, *Acta S. Officii*, vols. 1 and 2, nos. 531, 139, and 305; for discussion, see Geltner, *Making of Medieval Antifraternalism*, 100–102.

26. Testimony of Meglore, speaking of Saviabona, *Acta S. Officii*, vol. 1, no. 26, 20 May 1299, p. 54.

would be killed, because this was against God."[27] His statement emphasizes that he believed it was the friars who were not able to condemn heretics, not that condemning heretics was de facto against God. On the day they executed the men, it was asserted that God countered the inquisitors' usurpation of justice by performing a miracle for Bompietro.[28] The Bolognese made it clear that, in their view, "the inquisitor and the brothers were greater heretics than this man Bonigrino" and that "the brothers were more worthy to be burned than Bompietro" because "the brothers were diabolical men."[29] Some Bolognese deponents went further, claiming the head inquisitor, Guido of Vicenza, was the Antichrist himself.[30]

A related claim came from a certain Ala Raimondini, who admitted she had called the inquisitors the children of wolves.[31] As discussed in chapter 2, wolves in the Middle Ages had a negative connotation as dangerous animals that symbolized vice. Her comment also resonated with the biblical imagery of the wolf in sheep's clothing in Matthew 7:15: "Beware of false prophets, who come to you in the clothing of sheep, but inwardly they are ravening wolves." In applying this image to inquisitors, Ala Raimondini reversed a *topos* that inquisitors frequently used against heretics. For instance, Pope Boniface VIII used the phrase in his 1301 condemnation of Armanno Pungilupo (quoted in chapter 2). Armanno, like Ala Raimondini, also supposedly claimed that Christian clerics were wolves who did not do God's work and deceived souls.[32] Again, in this statement there is a clear articulation of Donatist beliefs regarding the friars' pastoral care. Their morals perverted their vows and rendered them unfit for their office. Mendicant inquisitors did not detect heterodoxy; rather, they "induced heresy" in others through their actions.[33] As a result, it was the inquisitors themselves who outwardly looked pious but who were the true heretics. Melissa Vise argued that the type of confessions made by Ala Raimondini and other women in Bologna constituted a religious performance in which deponents both expressed their displeasure at institutional authority through the *inquisitio* and also showed "tacit support of the processes of inquisition."[34] In

---

27. Testimony of Corbicinus speaking of Reçevutus, *Acta S. Officii*, vol. 1, no. 33, 20 May 1299, p. 60.

28. Testimony of Iacobina, *Acta S. Officii*, vol. 1, no. 238, 19 May 1299, p. 193.

29. Respectively: *Acta S. Officii*, vol. 1, no. 23, p. 51; vol. 1, no. 338, p. 225 (see also nos. 359, 370, 379, 382, 427, 476); and no. 379, p. 240.

30. Testimony of lady Benvenuta, *Acta S. Officii*, vol. 1, no. 158, 18 May 1299, p. 168; see also nos. 351 and 404.

31. Testimony of Ala dei Raimondini of her own words, *Acta S. Officii*, vol. 1, no. 543, 8 July 1299, p. 289.

32. *Itinerari*, 50 and 54.

33. Testimony of lady Luchesa, *Acta S. Officii*, vol. 1, no. 510, 3 July 1299, p. 282.

34. Vise, "Women and the Inquisitor," 359.

contrast, participation through recanting and accepting penance does not mean support. What it does demonstrate is an acknowledgment of the larger penitential framework of Christianity and an understanding of the power the pope gave to those in the office, one that inquisitors made clear to the Bolognese when they set their neighbors Bompietro and Iuliano on fire for all to see. It is the power of the office to cow others that citizens tried to harness when they engaged in what I termed "oppositional inquisitorial culture" in chapter 8.

The Bolognese testimony also reveals how attitudes toward mendicant inquisitors became applied by extension to all members of the mendicant orders. Negative views of specific inquisitors and their personal moral failings led to wider antimendicant sentiment. A certain Oddo told his friends, "These brother preachers . . . are hollow thieves, and keep concubines and lovers and there are few [brothers] who do not keep [them], and they go throughout the city to women and beguile them and say to them, 'If you have money, give [it] to us in salvation,' and the women are simple and give to them."[35] Cursius Nero Bonelle remarked, "The Roman Church is a church of malignant men, and that whatever the priests and their prelates and the brother preachers and the brother minors do and have done is for the extraction and extortion of money from simple men of the world who are called Christians and for keeping them under their feet, by telling them good words and seducing them into giving them money, and [he said] that all the works of the prelates and brother preachers and minors and other religious were a pretense and deceptive."[36] A barber, Bertholomeus, supposedly told a group of Dominicans, "You were held at one time to be above [other] orders," with the implication that the Order of Preachers as a whole was no longer admired.[37] A woman named Parta reputedly said "many evil things about the pope and the cardinals and the brothers Preachers and Minors, saying that they were the worst men in the world."[38] Clearly there was more widespread dissatisfaction with members of the mendicant orders than just those who served as inquisitors.

Anti-inquisitorial sentiment stiffened communal resolve to challenge authority over what constituted sanctity or heresy and also contributed to antimendicant attitudes. Animosity toward inquisitors, as verbally articulated in

---

35. Testimony of Bertholomeus de Lanceis, notary, speaking of Oddo, *Acta S. Officii*, vol. 1, no. 232, 3 June 1299, p. 232.

36. Testimony of Manettus Munsirri, notary of Florence, speaking of Cursius, *Acta S. Officii*, vol. 1, no. 89, 8 August 1301, pp. 127–28; see also nos. 87, 88, 573, 578, 817, and 818.

37. The use of the future tense, given the context, is problematic. I have chosen to translate it in the past tense to remain true to the sense of the testimony: "Vos habebitis una vice super clerichatas" (testimony of brother Bonifacius [OP] speaking of what Bertholomeus said, *Acta S. Officii*, vol.1, no. 144, 15 May 1299, p. 161).

38. Testimony of Bertholinus xii de Mançolino, *Acta S. Officii*, vol. 1, no. 35, 21 May 1299, p. 63.

these statements, sometimes resulted in physical attacks. The most famous are the revolts in southern France, mostly in Carcassone, that occurred at the instigation of the renegade Franciscan friar, Bernard Délicieux. In 1295–1296 citizens of Carcassone attacked the Dominican inquisitors and barred them from the churches. A few years later Délicieux led a party that assaulted Dominicans and freed captive heretics.[39] In 1302 people in the town of Albi attacked the Dominicans and expunged images of Sts. Dominic and Peter Martyr, the murdered inquisitor, painted on the city gates.[40] Similar attitudes and actions occurred in Italy. A Bolognese man mocked the Dominicans and their saints, "even saying they made one Peter Martyr a saint, although he should not be a saint and is not one, and he derided St. Peter Martyr and [said] much slander about him."[41] The most remarkable example within the same general time frame occurred in Parma in 1279. After inquisitors handed a woman over to the secular justice to be burned for heresy, the populace pillaged the Dominican convent and killed a friar.[42] When riots broke out in Bologna in 1299, some protesters specifically referred to the Parma instance twenty years prior as a model.[43]

By the late thirteenth century people had lost faith in the friars' ability to unite Christians, strengthen the faith of the orthodox, and inspire heretics to recant. Inquisitorial actions provoked the laity to view the friars overall in a negative light. Attacks on the mendicants were the physical expression of an ethos voiced by one Bondiolus in 1299: "The brothers are evil men and thieves through which, after they came into the world, all faith was lost."[44] It seems a number of people thought that the boundary between prosecution and persecution had disappeared and that mendicant inquisitors took out their anger on those who could not fill their avarice with condemnations of heresy. One scholar of Bologna tragically expressed just how far the mendicants had fallen in the lay population's estimation when he asserted "that he did not have, nor did he want to have, the same faith that the brothers Preachers and Minors had."[45] It is important to note that this perspective occurred in towns where

39. Friedlander, *Hammer of the Inquisitors*, 30–37.

40. Ibid., 105; Geltner, *Making of Medieval Antifraternalism*, 124–26.

41. Testimony of Albertus, servant of Bertholomeus de Lanceis, speaking of Oddo, *Acta S. Officii*, vol. 1, no. 234, 3 June 1299, p. 234; see also no. 366.

42. *Chronicon Parmense*, 35; *Chronicle of Salimbene de Adam*, 511 and 514.

43. Geltner, *Making of Medieval Antifraternalism*, 68–69; Augustine Thompson, "Lay versus Clerical Perceptions of Heresy: Protests against the Inquisition in Bologna, 1299," in *Praedicatores, Inquisitores I. The Dominicans and the Medieval Inquisition*, ed. Wolfram Hoyer (Rome: Istituto Storico Domenicano, 2004): 701–30; and Snyder, "Orthodox Fears," 103.

44. Testimony of Bondiolus speaking of Oddo, *Acta S. Officii*, vol. 1, no. 354, 2 June 1299, p. 230.

45. Testimony of lord Benedictus de Cummis, scholar of Bologna, speaking of Marchus, *Acta S. Officii*, vol. 1, no. 55, 29 June 1299, p. 89.

friars actively engaged in inquisitorial activities against saints described in part I of this study. Certainly many laypersons respected the apostolic goals of the Franciscans and Dominicans, shown by their joining the Third Orders, being part of a confraternity, or monetarily contributing to the orders as individuals, all of which allowed them to become as wealthy and powerful as they did in the latter part of the Middle Ages. Also, it cannot be denied that at times citizens had more base motives for rejecting inquisitorial authority. In Florence, for example, some refused to help inquisitors because they prosecuted widely needed usurers, while others bought property that the government had confiscated and did not want to turn it over to the church.[46] In those areas where inquisitorial prosecution was prevalent, however, lay antipathy toward inquisitors, who personified vice and wrathful persecution, tarnished not just those who held the office but those who could hold the office: any member of the Dominican and Franciscan orders.

Anti-Inquisitorialism to Antifraternalism: The Sin of Pride

The mendicants provoked the indignation of the laity, but they had clerical opponents as well, ones who viewed mendicants as having overweening pride that led them to overstep the bounds of their authority. The secular clergy provided the most vocal and concerted attacks, since the friars legitimately threatened their power. Although at first accepting mendicants as allies in the war against heresy in southern Europe, bishops quickly altered their stance and began to "[have] misgivings as the shower of papal privileges emancipated the new evangelists from the control of the ecclesiastical hierarchy."[47] The best-known conflict between the two ecclesiastical groups took place in the theological faculty at Paris, where William of St. Amour (d. 1273) launched a written crusade against the friars and their principles.[48] Outside the ivory towers of the university of Paris, secular clergy and even members of traditional monastic orders also critiqued and sometimes even overtly challenged mendicant authority.

Secular clergy derived their spiritual authority from their pastoral function as Christ's shepherds rather than withdrawing from the world like regular

---

46. Becker, "Some Implications of the Conflict," 157.

47. Lawrence, *Medieval Monasticism*, 153.

48. See Douie, *Conflict between the Seculars and the Mendicants*, 9–10. For general background about the battle between the seculars and mendicants in Paris, see Lawrence, *Friars*, 134–43 and 153–65; Geltner, *Making of Medieval Antifraternalism*, 15–44.

clergy. Bishops traditionally had authority over uncloistered clerics. The friars lived according to a rule but were deeply involved with pastoral care in the world, although Neslihan Şenocak challenged this view in part by arguing that while the Franciscans were dedicated to education almost from their inception, prestige and material benefits were the initial goals rather than pastoral care.[49] Regardless of the motives for mendicant emphasis on learning, their positioning as an alternative source for pastoral care created a problem for the ecclesiastical hierarchy. Popes released friars from episcopal oversight, leading the secular clergy to believe that their influence over their flock was being undermined. For example, part of the Dominican mission was to preach in order to educate Christians and thus combat heresy.[50] To do so, Dominicans often operated in communities without first getting local approval, a course of action that did little to endear them to the bishops. No one addressed this problem until 1300 when Pope Boniface VIII issued the bull *Super cathedram*, which required that friars obtain the approval of the local bishop to preach.[51] It is hard to determine if citizens really flocked to public squares to hear the fiery mendicant preachers instead of going to hear well-meaning but perhaps rhetorically inept parish priests. It is also difficult to claim with certainty that antifraternal sentiment from within the church hierarchy was as widespread as the mendicants themselves suggest. Guy Geltner examined how mendicant sources often present the friars as victims in the process of constructing "social memory" as part of an order's identity.[52] What is clear from pastoral manuals is that the mendicants considered preaching their main goal. A fourteenth-century Dominican author counseled his *confrères* on the successful formula for luring in audiences: "Know that some story other than a Bible story may be brought forward; say, a tale from Augustine or Gregory or some such author, or from Helinand or Valerius or Seneca or Macrobius. A tale from Augustine, provided it is novel and unusual, is more acceptable than a tale from the Bible, and a tale from Helinand or some other writer who is rarely quoted than a tale from Augustine or Ambrose. And this for no other reason than men's idle curiosity."[53] The fourteenth-century Franciscan preaching manual, the *Fasciculus Morum*, bears witness to this strategy. Biblical accounts in this collection of exempla for sermons are rare and are almost all taken from the Old Testament, while stories in the *Fasciculus Morum* from classical authors

---

49. Şenocak, *Poor and the Perfect*, 144–88.

50. Mulchahey, *"First the Bow Is Bent in Study,"* 6–23.

51. Douie, *Conflict between the Seculars and the Mendicants*, 4.

52. Geltner, *Making of Medieval Antifraternalism*, 103–29.

53. Quoted in Smalley, *English Friars and Antiquity*, 42. Aids for preaching, meant to be utilized instead of read, developed circa 1190–1220 but multiplied exponentially after the coming of the mendicant orders (Rouse and Rouse, *Preachers, Florilegia, and Sermons*, 4).

rival contemporary narratives in terms of numerical supremacy.[54] The papacy implicitly tolerated the resulting popularity contest between secular clergy and the mendicants even after *Super cathedram*, which was meant to allay episcopal concerns but seemingly rarely enforced.

One problem with enforcement was that the mendicants had long abandoned their transient lifestyle to establish fixed convents by the time the pope issued the bull. In 1281 Pope Martin IV gave friars the right to hear confession in *Ad fructus uberes*, further impinging upon traditional episcopal prerogatives and undermining *pieve*, or parish churches.[55] As noted, a foremost concern of the mendicants was pastoral care. The importance of mendicant structures in the urban landscape and how it positioned the mendicants "in between social, religious, and spatial systems," especially in terms of burials, created the wealth and power through donations by individuals, confraternities, and civic governments that challenged the authority of secular clergy.[56] While these efforts are usually thought of as primarily Franciscan endeavors, art historians such as Joanna Cannon remind us that Dominicans also had an important role when it came to lay burials and collaborating with the laity to create altars and images.[57] The privileges and foundations, however, redirected worshippers and funds from parish churches. As Decima Douie noted, "Offerings, legacies, and mortuary dues were diverted from the parish church, for a dying penitent who had made his last confession to a friar generally left money to his confessor's order for Masses on behalf of his soul, and expressed a wish to be buried in its church."[58] Who should retain control over parishioners and their donations was a source of contention within the church structure. Almost a century after the inception of the mendicant orders, John of Pouilly (d. 1328) would claim that God himself had chosen bishops and parish priests to oversee the Christian flock. Thus secular clergy were directly answerable to God just like the pope, and therefore "other persons" (i.e., the friars) were not authorized to perform priestly functions within dioceses or parishes.[59]

---

54. It is thought this text has Franciscan origins. The first sentence of chapter 1 refers to the Franciscan Rule and its instruction to the friars to preach to the laity, and within the text there are three references to Francis as a model of an exemplary life (*Fasciculus Morum*, 4.12, 5.20, and 7.19).

55. Geltner, *Making of Medieval Antifraternalism*, 34.

56. Bruzelius, *Preaching, Building, and Burying*, 4; see also 144–80.

57. Cannon, *Religious Poverty, Visual Riches*, 227–50 and 261–76.

58. Douie, *Conflict between the Seculars and the Mendicants*, 3–4.

59. Published in part in Raynaldi, *Annales Ecclesiastici*, 24:152–61, with the response of Peter de la Palu. See the discussion in Heft, *John XXII and Papal Teaching Authority*, 14–15; and Sikes, "John de Pouilli and Peter de la Palu." In response, mendicant enemies accused Pouilly of heresy in 1318. In 1321 Pope John XXII condemned three of the propositions, which forced Pouilly to recant (Thijssen, *Censure and Heresy at the University of Paris*, 174; Larsen, *School of Heretics*, 95).

According to Amanda Power, to their rivals the mendicants had become "worryingly close to elites, often unscrupulous in their use of patronage, and therefore difficult, even dangerous, for opponents to challenge."[60] There are several examples, however, of secular clergy colluding with citizens to contest inquisitorial sentences and oppose the authority of mendicant inquisitors. A few brief examples demonstrate this point. During the 1299 general inquiry in Bologna, parish priests aided sentenced heretics and were complicit in flouting decrees handed down by the inquisitor Guido of Vicenza. One Bolognese cleric jeopardized his own career, and liberty, by acting as a procurator for a suspected heretic. Another roused the ire of frà Guido and incurred excommunication (later rescinded) because he performed last rites on a suspected heretic named Rosaflora and buried her within sanctified ground after the inquisitor condemned her as relapsed.[61] The reasons these clerics gave for their disobedience was that they knew these men and women intimately and believed they were innately good. Essentially, their justification was that the inquisitors were outsiders. This became more complicated when local clergy were related to suspect citizens or had ties of loyalty to territorial lords who did. Overall, as one scholar noted, some secular clergy "felt that they knew conditions in their own dioceses better than the pope. . . . Still others were temporal lords in their own right or members of local ruling families, and they found it most difficult to dispossess their own flesh and blood of their estates."[62] As a result, local interests tended to trump vocational loyalty. Friars claimed to save souls, but local clergy often viewed them as papal agents who had no true personal connection to parishioners. While the direct action in these cases was against mendicant inquisitors, they also reflect the longstanding concerns regarding the autonomy of the friars and how it affected pastoral care.

Regular clergy also demonstrated active opposition. The Cistercians, perhaps the most powerful and popular order until the advent of the friars, provide a shocking example. The Cistercians of the Milanese abbey of Chiaravalle assisted the Guglielmites, the sectarian devotees of Guglielma of Milan, in their attempt to halt an inquisitorial inquiry. The abbot sent monks as emissaries to the archbishop of Milan. Their purpose was to persuade him that local Dominican inquisitors were suspended from office and therefore did not have the authority to prosecute the sect. In fact, no such suspension was in force. Other monastic orders also supported antimendicant actions. Benedictines assisted in the sacrilegious plunder of the Basilica of S. Francesco at

---

60. Power, "Friars in Secular and Ecclesiastical Governance, 1224–c.1259," 35.

61. For discussion of both instances, see Lansing, *Power and Purity*, 151–52.

62. Shannon, *Popes and Heresy*, 33.

Assisi, the most important Franciscan church because it contained the saint's body. Muzio di San Francesco, the proimperial leader of the March of Ancona, robbed the coffers of S. Francesco. Inquisitors discovered during the subsequent investigation that the abbot and monks of the Benedictine abbey of S. Pietro in Assisi had helped Muzio and his followers.[63] Earlier in this chapter the discussion of Meco of Ascoli showed that Franciscans were jealous of the wealth and popularity of local lay saints who had the support of the bishop and Augustinians. In Assisi we see the opposite process occurring: a traditional monastic order was jealous and so covetous of the wealth and popularity of the Franciscans that it backed an antipapal political revolutionary.

An examination of the combatants in the struggle over the cult of Armanno Pungilupo delineates the chasm that separated the mendicants from other clergy by the end of the thirteenth century. Secular and regular clergy banded together to comprise the group fighting for recognition of Armanno's sanctity: the bishop and canons of the cathedral, several parish priests, and members of the local Cistercian and Benedictine orders. Opposing them were the Dominicans (the lead inquisitor was also the head of the Ferrarese convent of the Order of Preachers), the Franciscans, and members of their respective Third Orders. The two factions waged a protracted war, in which the former fought long and hard for the pope to recognize Armanno as a saint while the latter argued just as intensely that Armanno was a heretic. The hostility intensified when the secular clergy refused inquisitorial demands to exhume and burn the saint's remains. The cathedral housed his remains, and the bishop and canons would benefit economically from a papal imprimatur of his cult. The dispute went deeper, however, and has antifraternal aspects based on jealousy and concerns that the mendicants were overstepping their bounds, as previously discussed. Pope Gregory IX had given the canons possession of the Benedictine monastery of S. Alberto in Pereo in 1230. He also decreed that the Dominican convent of Ferrara should have part of the monastery's yearly proceeds. The canons refused to comply until the Dominicans hired a procurator and appealed to the pope. In Amedeo Benati's assessment, "It is human that the canons [of the parish of Cella Volana], who possessed the important priory of S. Maria in Vado in Ferrara, would consider this division as an abuse of power added to the damage [done] by the invasion of the Dominicans."[64] Economic rivalry between the secular clergy and mendicants manifested itself through the debate about Armanno's holiness. It is notable that when the issue of Armanno's orthodoxy arose, the Benedictines supported the bish-

---

63. Brufani, *Eresia di un ribelle*, 71; Partner, *Lands of St. Peter*, 310.

64. Benati, "Armanno Pungilupo nella storia religiosa," 118–19.

op's efforts even though they had lost their autonomy to the cathedral chapter. Thirty-nine years prior, the Benedictines had been divested of their privilege and their monastery placed under the authority of the bishop of Ferrara. Yet they allied with the bishop to challenge the Dominicans. These actions speak to deeper antifraternal emotions in Ferrara than just a monetary motive could explain.

The mendicants themselves did not always present a united front, as a particularly fitting incident from the Bologna inquisitorial register demonstrates. The Dominican inquisitor, Guido of Vicenza, was prepared to give a general sermon at the Dominican church in Reggio against the Colonna cardinals who had accused Pope Boniface VIII of murder. All citizens within a circumscribed region were required to attend an inquisitor's general sermon, which was the first step in opening a formal procedure against heretics.[65] In this case the heretics were those who supported the Colonna cardinals. In preparation, Guido of Vicenza forbade the Friars Minor of Reggio to preach either at their own church or at the Dominican church or to ring their bells. He also instructed them to attend his sermon. The reason for this personal attention is unclear, but one Dominican friar testified that the inquisitor emphasized that he had never burdened the Franciscans or had made a similar request, suggesting that the inquisitor anticipated recalcitrance from members of the convent.[66] The witness claimed the entire Franciscan community refused to attend, although he saw "other religious men, namely brother preachers, Augustinians, monks, clerics and laypeople who came together for the said sermon."[67] To add insult to injury, another Dominican brother asserted that the Franciscans intentionally rang their bells during Guido of Vicenza's sermon.[68] This behavior was not just a spiteful gesture; because the general sermon was an official act of inquisitorial procedure that the pope specifically authorized, Franciscan disobedience bordered on insurrection. It undermined Guido of Vicenza but also the inquisitorial process as a whole.

While the cause of Franciscan insubordination in Bologna is unknown, the motives for a similar response to inquisitorial power by the Augustinian friars of Ascoli are clearer. As mentioned, the Augustinians became part of Meco del Sacco's protectors after his first abjuration of heresy. In 1338, when the inquisitor took advantage of Meco's absence to destroy his church and hospital,

---

65. Lea, *History of the Inquisition*, 1:371–72.

66. Testimony of brother Anthonius [OP], *Acta S. Officii*, vol. 1, no. 84, 21 November 1299, pp. 119–20.

67. *Acta S. Officii*, 120.

68. Testimony of brother Bartholomeus de Medicis of Reggio [OP], *Acta S. Officii*, vol. 1, no. 85, 21 November 1299, p. 122.

the procurator general of the Augustinians in the March of Ancona, along with the brothers of the convent of S. Agostino in Ascoli, became the plaintiffs in an inquiry into the inquisitor's actions.[69] The inquisitor and his companions on the raid had to pay reparations to the Augustinians, strongly suggesting that Meco's hospital had come under their purview sometime between 1338 when the incident occurred and 1341 when the clerics were sentenced. In this case, deep-seated hostility added fuel to the fire over what the Augustinians must have viewed as Franciscan interference. Pope Alexander IV had granted the Friars Minor permission to build a church in Ascoli in 1257.[70] In 1259 he had to forbid the Augustinians to construct their church and convent in the same place where the Franciscans were building their own structures.[71] The Augustinians losing their case against the mendicant convent laid the foundation for a successful challenge for wealth and power almost a century later in the dispute over the orthodoxy of Meco del Sacco.

Members of both the laity and clergy had distinct reasons for disliking the mendicants. Some citizens believed they were avaricious and corrupt, while some clerics believed they were avaricious and pompous. The friars' role as inquisitors produced more general antimendicant attitudes in laypeople. More general antifraternalism produced anti-inquisitorial sentiments in secular and regular clergy. There are some tantalizing examples of local clergy and laity becoming allies against inquisitors. When Guido of Vicenza excommunicated the Bolognese priest who buried the relapsed heretic named Rosaflora, lay members of the community spoke out, asserting that "it was an evil [thing] that he was suspended from office."[72] Conversely, laity expressed their anger when clergy assisted the mendicants. Paulus Trintinellus of Bologna, for instance, defamed the local Carmelites for not protesting the Dominican inquisitor's judgment against the man named Bompietro. At the reading of Bompietro's sentence Paulus reputedly announced to the crowd, "These Carmelite brothers, who lived in S. Martino, were vile and miserable, because the said Bompietro gave them wine for the sacrifice and they did not defend him nor excuse him, nor help this Bompietro."[73] In a different process, clerics showed their appreciation for their citizens' support by protecting local

---

69. *Meco*, appendix 6, 290–93.

70. Bull of Alexander IV, 13 December 1257, in *Bullarium Franciscanum Romanorum Pontificum*, 2:269.

71. Directive of Alexander IV, 26 August 1259, Archivio di Stato di Ascoli Piceno, perg. 34, noted in *Meco*, 12n31.

72. Testimony of Lady Bella, daughter of Floravantis, *Acta S. Officii*, vol. 1, no. 196, 19 May 1299, p. 179; see also nos. 238, 248, 316, 317, 320–22, 513.

73. Testimony of Nascimbene Adelardi of Bologna speaking of Paulus Trintinellus, *Acta S. Officii*, vol. 1, no. 22, 17 May 1299, p. 49.

cults against mendicant inquisitors. Although the Augustinians were Meco del Sacco's patrons, Meco escaped immolation as a relapsed heretic the first time primarily because of the effort of the bishop, Rainaldo IV, who the Ascolani had the rare privilege to have elected to office.[74] The citizens viewed Meco as a persecuted holy man, and the bishop, listening to his constituency, lobbied on Meco's behalf even though the town was under interdict during the entire course of these events. These examples demonstrate what citizens believed were appropriate relations between laity and clergy. Unlike inquisitors, who were thought of as outsiders regardless of their city of birth, local clerics were part of the community and therefore bound by the same ties of loyalty and patronage as everyone else. Laypeople expected that this bond would remain intact notwithstanding inquisitorial mandates. Growing animosity toward Franciscans and Dominicans, particularly in their capacity as inquisitors, only heightened these expectations of communal solidarity against mendicant interlopers.

As the purview of inquisitors expanded, others increasingly came to suspect the men who fulfilled that role of having as their goals money, prestige, and political power. The statutes of Bergamo reveal how citizens consequently tried to undercut procedures and subject the inquisitor to city ordinances. In 1264 Bergamo's government decreed that anyone cited or excommunicated for heresy would be exonerated after affirming his or her orthodoxy by oath in front of the *podestà* and either the inquisitor or bishop and paying a fine. Thereafter, the person could not be cited for heresy in Bergamo and, if cited elsewhere, the city would pay for magistrates to defend the individual.[75] Antipathy toward inquisitors led to antipathy toward the Franciscans and Dominicans more generally, as seen during a war between the Ghibelline Visconti family and the Guelph Della Torre family in 1310. In the midst of the struggle the people of Cremona, a Ghibelline town, ransacked the mendicant houses.[76] In a similar situation, during a war between forces representing the papal and imperial sides in Spoleto in 1327, the citizens targeted the local mendicant convents and destroyed their goods. In a meeting between representatives of the Franciscans and Dominicans in late September of the same year, the friars jointly decided they should take the moveable goods of the townsmen, called "rebels" in the document chronicling the meeting, in recompense.[77]

---

74. *Meco*, 10. Pope Urban II granted Ascoli this unusual privilege in 1091; it was revoked after the death of Rainaldo IV, although the subsequent appointed bishop also supported Meco in his battle with inquisitors.

75. Lea, *History of the Inquisition*, 2:230.

76. Lawrence, *Friars*, 177.

77. Preserved in an untitled document in ASF, Corporazioni religiose soppresse dal governo francese, ser. 102, pez. 196 secondo, ff. 1r–3r.

It is clear that some citizens saw inquisitors as engaged in persecution, not prosecution. As the pope's agents who policed Christian spirituality, mendicants had come to personify papal power and privilege. Antipapal attitudes also fed into assumptions about inquisitors and resulted in overt challenges to institutional authority when it came to supporting hometown saints.

CHAPTER 7

Papal Politics and Communal Contestation

Inquisitors in Bologna, during a general inquiry that occurred in 1299–1300, asked deponents "if [they knew] any male or female heretic, receiver or defender of heretics . . . or anyone who said anything in support of the Colonna or sympathized with them after they were condemned by the lord Pope Boniface VIII and the Roman Church, or anyone who said anything to the prejudice of the said lord pope."[1] This formulaic question illustrates how the charge of heresy became a weapon in a new war: a battle for temporal and spiritual control over local communities in northern and central Italy. This region was the geographic arena for the political struggle that occurred between popes and Holy Roman Emperors, which divided Italian communities into rival factions. It was also the locus of papal efforts to assert religious authority over independent-minded towns that were responding to papal bureaucratization and consolidation of power. Within this context, the accusation of heterodoxy became one means by which the papacy punished those who refused to support papal aims. As the quote makes clear, those who spoke against the pope, even if they maintained orthodox doctrinal beliefs, were heretics. "Heresy" no longer reflected doctrinal error alone by the late thirteenth century. It had become a characteristic of political orienta-

---

1. Inquisitor Guido of Vicenza questioning lord Franciscus, son of lord and brother Iacobus de Ghixlerius, in *Acta S. Officii*, vol. 2, no. 599, 30 January 1300, p. 375.

tion, an expression of disaffection with the papacy, and an avowal of regional interests that superseded loyalty to Rome.

It was difficult to separate politics or economics from personal devotion. Local needs and concerns often usurped loyalty to the Roman Church, especially under controversial popes such as Boniface VIII or John XXII. The above quote shows an increased papal and inquisitorial eliding of religious and political concerns during the pontificate of Boniface VIII as a way to combat antipapal sentiments. Others, however, appropriated this theoretical shift and terminology and used it against the papacy. Roughly twenty-five years later under the reign of John XXII there is evidence that clergy themselves articulated antipapal sentiments within the same inquisitorial culture framework. Even within the mendicant orders, there were friars like Pietro Nino of Todi, who "preached publicly in the usual pulpit of the aforementioned church of S. Fortunato, while he was present and listening, that Pope John XXII was not pope, rather he was a heretic and a Patarine, and [Pietro] exhorted the people lest they have faith in [the pope]. And this brother Pietro was the first to preach against all the popes in the aforesaid church."[2] Inquisitorial language and the papal conjoining of spirituality and politics was no longer just the purview of popes and inquisitors concerned about the salvation of souls or recalcitrance toward papal interests.

As the head of the Papal States, the pope was the frequent enemy of towns and ruling factions of a different political persuasion. A rejection of the pope's political authority manifested itself through challenges to his spiritual prerogatives, such as his right to canonize saints. The first two sections of this chapter discuss changes in papal philosophy that tried to expand the role of the pope in terrestrial affairs and created inquisitorial culture. While the next chapter addresses this culture in more detail, this chapter traces the steps that led late thirteenth- and early fourteenth-century Italian communities to have political and spiritual antipathy toward the popes and their agents, which became a driving force for these communities to actively contest popes through championing suspect saints, heretical saints, and holy heretics. Moving from the general to the specific, the last part of this chapter provides examples of how popes tried to suppress cults or reject bids for canonization to assert their authority, in the process creating disputed saints.

---

2. Ehrle, "Johannes XXII: Processus habiti . . . provincia S. Francisci," in "Ludwig der Bayer," 160.

The Legacies of Rome: *Lex maiestatis* and *Patria potestas*

In the thirteenth century the papal bureaucracy consolidated its power in various ways. One way was using the *inquisitio*, which allowed popes to control the canonization process and punish those who disagreed with papal directives through the charge of heresy. In order for these accusations to appear feasible, popes had to broaden the definition of heresy to include not only those who held heretical beliefs but also those who undermined papal authority. Innocent III's 1199 bull, *Vergentis ad senium*, provided for such a construction by widening the parameters of heterodoxy, allowing popes to prosecute all kinds of dissenters. Inquisitorial prosecution provided the papacy the means to accuse political dissidents of religious heresy in the battles over who had authority over the towns of north-central Italy: the pope, imperial claimants, or the individual towns and their emerging local lords.

In practice, the medieval conception of heresy could accommodate a broad range of behaviors of which the papacy did not approve. According to theologian James Heft, "Heresy was not limited, as it is today, to the denial of a formally proclaimed truth of revelation, but applied also to the stance of any Christian who out of contumacy refused to submit to the guidance of the Church. The grounds for heresy could not be restricted then simply to matters of doctrine, and still less to matters of revealed doctrine, but included as well universal traditions and customs (*'consuetudines ecclesiasticae'*)."[3] The flexibility of the term "heretic" therefore facilitated its application to a variety of individuals. For instance, if the pope construed one's actions as hostile to him personally, often he drew the conclusion that the person was also hostile to the papacy's authoritative decisions about Christian doctrine. While canon law articulated the "strict" understanding of a heretic as someone who deliberately denied Christian truth, the broad understanding became anyone disobedient to the pope. Since the pope was God's representative on earth, disobedience to his directives constituted contumacy toward God. As one Italian historian explained, "When the social edifice is founded on faith, every opposition resolves itself in heresy, and the pope through his prerogatives, the clergy through their offended privilege, fling out excommunications and interdicts."[4]

In his 1199 bull *Vergentis in senium*, Pope Innocent III equated the religious offense of heresy with the secular crime of high treason.[5] In doing so, he

---

3. Heft, *John XXII and Papal Teaching Authority*, 110; see also Brufani, *Eresia di un ribelle*, 9.

4. Cantù, *Gli eretici d'Italia*, 1:159.

5. Innocent III, *Vergentis in senium*, in *Corpus iuris canonici*, 2:782–83 (XV, 10, 7).

incorporated the Roman law concept of *lex maiestatis* into medieval canon law. *Lex maiestatis* defined treason and forms of punishment for those found guilty of the crime.[6] This application of Roman law is extremely significant. By equating heresy with treason, the papacy expanded its definition of what constituted heresy, legitimized harsh punishment, and effectively proclaimed that the Roman Church was a political entity ruled by the pope.[7] Kenneth Pennington observed that Roman law did not equate heresy with treason because there were different punishments for the two crimes. It was the innovation of Innocent III to apply the penalties for treason to those found guilty of heresy.[8] Another concept derived from Roman law underlying both the idea of the papal monarchy and its articulation in the bull *Vergentis ad senium* was the notion of *patria potestas*, or the power of the father.[9] Just as a father had total control over his wife, children, and servants, so too did the pope, the *papa* or father of Christendom, have full authority over the Christian "children" who were under his protection and not independent (*sui iuris*). In this capacity, the pope could assert his control over those he perceived to have willfully disobeyed the Roman Church in any way that challenged his authority. The pope was responsible for all Christians and could reward and punish at will.

Together, the ideas of *lex maiestatis* and *patria potestas* provided popes with a great deal of power and served as the foundation for the medieval concept of papal plenitude of power or, as the canon lawyer Hostiensis described it, "absolute power" (*potestas absoluta*), which extended papal authority beyond what was available to other rulers. Innocent III asserted, "The pope . . . does not bear the duty of plain man, but of the true God on earth," formulating the concept of the pope's plenitude of power around his role as "vicar of Christ" (*vicarius Christi*).[10] From this perspective Christendom became a single "state" ruled by the pope from the moment Christ gave Peter the keys to the church. The Petrine succession validated the sovereignty of the pope and his ability to "exercise certain prerogatives permitted only to Christ and his vicar."[11] The heretic who flouted the pope did so in the same way as an unruly child disobeyed the parent or a traitor plotted to overthrow a secular monarch, but

---

6. Morris, *Papal Monarchy*, 442; Pennington, "*Pro peccatis patrum puniri*," 1.
7. Ullmann, "Significance of Innocent III's Decretal *Vergentis*," 2:729–43; Pennington, "Innocent III and the Divine Authority," 11–12.
8. Pennington, "*Pro peccatis patrum puniri*," 4.
9. Long, "*Patria potestas*," 873–75.
10. Pope Innocent III, *Tertia compilatio* 1.5.3, cited in Pennington, "*Pro peccatis patrum puniri*," 4 (my translation). See also Southern, *Western Society and the Church*, 102–5.
11. Pennington, "Innocent III and the Divine Authority," 4. Even less than perfect popes retained this authority: "And though the pope as man may not be the best man, he is enabled by the especial grant of divine grace made to Peter and his successors" (Boase, *Boniface VIII*, 322).

the act was even more egregious since it conspired against the authority of God. Furthermore, the pope had even more of a justification to punish any such rebellious spirits, whoever they may be, because, in this understanding, God mandated that the pope was his vicar and superior to anyone else in Christendom. Innocent III's *Vergentis ad senium* fused these Roman and Christian ideas together to formulate papal power in terms of sovereignty, paralleling secular governments, while at the same time superseding them. It provided the means by which the papacy could tangibly enforce the theory of the papal monarchy, which popes had been trying to promote for close to two centuries.[12]

Vergentis was an assertion of the papacy's supreme power, made by a pope well aware of the implications due to his legal training. Innocent III understood that such a foundation for papal authority would provide wide parameters within which to prosecute dissidents and to strengthen control over the Christian flock, particularly the laity.[13] The bull allowed the popes to use the charge of heresy to prosecute a variety of dissidents and enhanced the possibilities for inquisitorial prosecution. "Heretics" came to include those lords who challenged the expansion of the papacy's material interests in northern and central Italy because it encroached upon their own power base and the members of recalcitrant Ghibelline towns who refused to bow to the dictates of a distant church in Rome (or, after 1309, in Avignon). The official assertion of this power coincided with a presumed increase in heterodox thought throughout Europe, or at least a rising concern about heresy, which Innocent III was trying to counteract.[14] It also occurred during the centralization of church administration and papal expansionist efforts undertaken according to the idea of *translatio imperii*. These efforts are revealed in Innocent III's attempt to corral wandering preachers into his stable (to be transformed by later popes into missionaries to convert heretics) and in his role in carving the border and solidifying control over the Papal States. The power accorded by *Vergentis*, and the difficulty in judging internal beliefs by external acts, left the door open for inquisitorial prosecution to be transformed into inquisitorial persecution. As R. I. Moore observed, such persecution became "a weapon in the competition for political influence, and was turned by the victors into an instrument for consolidating their power."[15]

---

12. Morris, *Papal Monarchy*, 2. For general background, see also Pennington, *Popes and Bishops*, and Watt, *Theory of Papal Monarchy*. For a discussion of the issue by a medieval contemporary, see Godin, *Tractatus de causa immediata*.

13. Lansing, *Power and Purity*, 23.

14. On the issue of existence versus identification of heretics, see Moore, *Formation of a Persecuting Society*, 68.

15. Ibid., 146.

The popes who followed Innocent III strove to realize the power accorded them by *Vergentis*, using Innocent's justification of papal sovereignty to assert and extend papal power.[16] For instance, in his 1302 bull *Unam Sanctam*, Boniface VIII claimed papal power was the greatest of all power on earth, above terrestrial authority or that spiritual power given to other clerics. Only God could judge a pope.[17] The debate over papal sovereignty reached its apex during the reign of Pope John XXII. One of this pope's most vehement opponents was Marsiglio of Padua, an educated canon, whose treatise *Defensor Pacis* (1324) maintained that the church was subordinate to the state and that the pope only ruled through the people's assent. One of Marsiglio's boldest conclusions was that "the general council of Christians alone has the authority to canonize anyone or to order anyone to be adored as a saint" and that "no bishop [including the pope, bishop of Rome] has coercive authority or jurisdiction over any layman or clergyman, even if he is a heretic." He finished with the statement that "the bishop of Rome . . . may be advanced to a 'separable' [i.e. solely administrative] ecclesiastical office only by the Christian 'legislator' [i.e. the body politic] . . . and [he] may be suspended from or deprived of office by the same authority."[18] Marsiglio thus argued that the pope gained his authority through popular election and therefore the people could judge and depose the pope. These ideas directly contradicted the assertion that popes could only be judged by God. John XXII excommunicated Marsiglio on 9 April 1327 and declared him a "notorious heretic." A commission the pope appointed condemned five of his propositions on 23 October 1327.[19]

Philip Jones noted that Marsiglio's radical Aristotelian conception of the need for a sole, unifying, secular power divorced from religious authority prefigured such authors as Machiavelli or even Hobbes.[20] Few of Marsiglio's contemporaries went so far in their characterization of the egalitarian relationship between prince and pope. Canonists themselves, however, provided compromise positions between papal absolutists like Innocent III or Boniface VIII and secularists like Marsiglio of Padua. The glosses of Vincentius Hispanus (d. 1248) and Accursius (d. 1260) argued that the power of lay rulers was constrained by the fact that they must obey the law, basing their claims on the

---

16. For a detailed discussion of this process, particularly in the connection between canonizations and papal infallibility, see Prudlo, *Certain Sainthood*, esp. 122–50.

17. Boniface VIII, *Unam Sanctam*, 18 November 1302, translated in Brown, *Canonical Juristic Personality*; see discussion in Boase, *Boniface VIII*, 332.

18. Marsiglio of Padua, *Defensor Pacis*, III, chap. 2, articles 35, 14, and 41, respectively, translated in Thatcher and McNeal, *Source Book for Medieval History*, 317–24.

19. Denzinger, *Enchiridion symbolorum*, 495. A portion of the condemnation is translated in Peters, *Heresy and Authority*, 230–31. See discussion in Heft, *John XXII and Papal Teaching Authority*, 15–16.

20. Jones, *Italian City-State*, 464–66.

Roman law concept of *digna vox*, or that the emperor must submit himself to the law.[21] In a similar vein, when drawing a parallel between a pope and an emperor, commentators logically concluded that a pope also had to be "faithful" to the precepts of the Roman Church, although he was the supreme judge of Christendom.[22] Such a construction of papal authority allowed for differing interpretations of the balance of power between secular and ecclesiastical rulers. Papal power could be construed as limited, just like princely power. Innocent III's bull, through its articulation of papal sovereignty and expansion of the parameters of what constituted heresy, was the foundation for these debates and fostered the conditions under which disputed saints emerged.

Of Popes and Men: Regional Conflict and the *Signorie*

At the same time popes tried to consolidate their authority in the late Middle Ages, the papacy's prestige diminished and challenges to papal authority increased. Two factors eroded the respect accorded popes in the late thirteenth and early fourteenth centuries: their battles with Holy Roman Emperors, which manifested itself in Italy in the division between the Guelphs (propapal) and the Ghibelline (proimperial) factions; and a series of controversial popes, which followed the papal seat's rapid turnover rate from 1250 to 1300. Popes such as Boniface VIII and John XXII became lightning rods because they entered the strife and used the weapon that Innocent III's bull placed at their disposal, the charge of heresy, in the venue of terrestrial politics. Rising animus toward popes acting like the territorial lords they were, as well as severe doubts about the ethics of Boniface and John in particular, led to challenges to papal power. This same period saw many towns switching from communal to signorial governments, creating the perfect storm that produced the majority of cases of contested sanctity. Some emerging lords, or *signori*, used their allegiance to the papacy to garner support to solidify their nascent rule. Others, however, took advantage of the turbulent situation to cement their authority by contesting papal directives and siding with local interests in religious disputes.

The Guelph-Ghibelline controversy, outlined in chapter 5, did not end with Frederick II's death in 1250. The political situation became even more volatile

---

21. Codex 1.14.4 in *Corpus iuris civilis*. The relevant passage in the medieval version of the Codex is 1.17.4. For a general study of the issues, see Pennington, *Prince and the Law*.

22. Tierney, "Prince Is Not Bound by the Laws"; Pennington, "Innocent III and the Divine Authority," 11–14.

when the papacy allied itself with the French count Charles of Anjou in 1266 in order to install someone sympathetic to the papal cause in the kingdom of Sicily and to establish an ally who would defend the church's territorial interests in Italy.[23] The Angevin alliance provoked a new series of local wars. The Guelph elite who financed the pope's endeavors in the region clashed with Ghibelline lords such as the Della Scala, Montefeltro, and Visconti, who had taken advantage of the tired and war-torn Italian communes and were carving out their own dominions.[24] Meanwhile, Rome's efforts to subdue the Papal States and surrounding regions by using French troops inflamed the public. The Perugians burned effigies of the pope and cardinals in 1282, while riots broke out in Civitavecchia and Corneto in the same year over the papacy's attempt to control their food supplies.[25]

These events dictated that towns ruled by a Ghibelline lord, or that had a majority supporting the imperial side, were predisposed to ignore papal decisions that went against local saints and would oppose the work of papal agents, such as inquisitors. It is easy to find examples of contestation in which the intersection of religious and political agendas is so complete that they cannot be disengaged. For instance, when Pope Clement V called a formal crusade against Dolcino and his followers, the citizens of northern Piedmont, led by local Ghibelline leaders in Gattinara and Serravalle, protected the condemned heretics.[26] The survival of the Guglielmite sect until 1300, even though inquisitors had questioned sectarians twice previously, undoubtedly can be attributed to the fact that several devotees were related to or allies of the Lombard *signore* Matteo Visconti. The staunchly Ghibelline Carrara family, lords of Padua for most of the fourteenth century, allowed the cult of Peter of Abano to flourish, although inquisitors posthumously sentenced the physician and astrologer as a relapsed heretic in 1316 for denying God's omnipotence after he narrowly escaped execution by dying of natural causes. These examples are just a few of many showing that local lords allowed, and sometimes even promoted, cults of suspect or condemned saints. New lords used religion for the political expediency of larger opposition to papal authority while currying local favor for the regime, particularly if it was newly established, such as the Carraresi in Padua.

Even towns within the Papal States actively expressed their political opposition to the pope through religious disobedience. The Papal States were the

23. Takayama, "Law and Monarchy in the South, 75–79; Partner, *Lands of St. Peter*, 267–75.

24. On the new Guelph elite, see Partner, *Lands of St. Peter*, 271; on the reemergence of lay territorial lordships, see Dean, "Rise of the Signori," 104–24.

25. Partner, *Lands of St. Peter*, 278–79.

26. Lambert, *Medieval Heresy*, 223.

launching grounds for the Angevin armies to move north against the emperor's forces. Many communities in this region became wholeheartedly Ghibelline as they chafed under the lordship of the pope, who had tightened control to maintain a strong position on the peninsula. The Duchy of Spoleto and the March of Ancona produced several contested saints shortly after the papacy subdued their factions that took the imperial side in the early fourteenth century. Ascoli, a community that had been traditionally Ghibelline from the 1220s, venerated Meco del Sacco in the early fourteenth century, a man who had been charged with heresy three times in ten years. The town, along with Spoleto, also championed Cecco of Ascoli as a holy man, although inquisitors burned him as a sorcerer in 1327 in Florence. The citizens of Foligno selected Peter Crisci as their holy patron, a man that inquisitors questioned during his lifetime. Crisci died in 1323, only one year after the leader Federico I da Montefeltro (the bane of the Roman Church's interests in the Papal States) was ruthlessly cut down in battle and the region forced to submit to the pope's authority.[27] Although Crisci had been a suspected heretic, the Folignese immediately claimed he was a saint and soon built a chapel dedicated to him in the cathedral of S. Feliciano. In choosing to venerate these men as holy despite their run-ins with inquisitors, the people of this region challenged the pope's right to direct their spiritual needs, perceiving it on a continuum with papal efforts to dominate the political horizon.

Antipapal sentiment, stimulated by the havoc wrought by the Roman Church's war with imperial factions, increased during a succession of unpopular popes. The first of these divisive figures was Boniface VIII. The fourteenth-century chronicler Dino Compagni described him as "a man of great boldness and high intelligence; and he ruled the Church as he saw fit and brought low whoever did not agree with him."[28] Boniface championed the concept of *beneficium libertatis*, or that "the church is free from all outside rule, and that in everything the will of the church can be imposed."[29] Such a philosophy resulted in a cadre of opponents, whose ranks swelled as Boniface's perceived abuses mounted during his pontificate. One cause for discontent was his early alliance with France, which infuriated the Ghibelline factions of northern Italy. The pope called on French knights to crush the magnates and the *popolo* of towns that took the imperial side. The reward for the knights was title and jurisdiction to all Italian lands they won, as Dino Compagni described occurred in Florence. Dante Alighieri, no fan of this pope who had exiled him from his

27. Partner, *Lands of St. Peter*, 311.
28. *Dino Compagni's Chronicle of Florence*, 24.
29. Boase, *Boniface VIII*, 142.

beloved city on account of his political affiliation, envisioned Boniface as a future resident of Hell. Dante anticipated, or at least hoped, that Boniface's punishment would be burial headfirst into rock along with simoniacs, with his legs eternally consumed by flames.[30] Many of Dante's readers must have agreed with the appropriateness of this scenario, for Compagni relates that when Boniface died, "many were pleased and delighted, because he ruled cruelly and provoked wars, crushing many people and accumulating much wealth."[31] Compagni's description is better suited to a secular ruler than a spiritual prelate, much less the pope, or so it must have seemed to those who suffered under his heavy hand and who could contrast Boniface's manner of wielding power with the example set by his saintly predecessor, Celestine V (d. 1296).

The mysterious abdication and death of Pope Celestine V was extremely damaging to Boniface VIII and was another cause of estrangement between people and the pope. Celestine, a reluctant successor to St. Peter as bishop of Rome, had abdicated in December 1294, a mere four months after his consecration. The cardinals elected Benedict Caetani, the future Boniface VIII, ten days later. The next year the pope's officials took Celestine, known once again by his given name, Peter of Morrone, into custody. He died within the calendar year, and the event sparked disturbing rumors. Members of the Colonna family, who were powerful Roman rivals of Boniface's Caetani family heritage and so did not benefit from the pope's nepotism, alleged that Boniface had murdered his predecessor. Boniface countered by condemning as heretics those Colonna cardinals who were responsible for the accusation.[32] Boniface's guilt seemed apparent to many individuals who were willing to take the Colonnas' side in the subsequent battle. To those who perceived him as a murderer who had usurped the office of a duly elected pope, Boniface had assumed the pontificate illegally and so could not provide pastoral or doctrinal direction. Even those who did not accuse Boniface of murder, such as the learned theologians of the University of Paris, argued that Celestine V was not able to resign and so Boniface had assumed the pontificate illegally.[33] Political alienation and spir-

---

30. Dante Alighieri, *Inferno*, XIX, in Alighieri, *The Divine Comedy*, vv. 52–57.

31. *Dino Compagni's Chronicle of Florence*, 60–61. Compagni contrasts Boniface's death with the election of his successor, Benedict, who had "few relatives and [was] from an unimportant family, trustworthy and good, discreet and holy" (63).

32. See the discussion of Boniface's nepotism in Peck, *Fool of God*, 119. For an overview of events, see Boase, *Boniface VIII*, 72–78.

33. For example, see the testimony of monk Henricus of Sta. Maria de Monte Armato reporting the words of lord Iacobus Flamenghi of Bologna, *Acta S. Officii*, vol. 1, no. 44, 12 June 1299, p. 73. On the Paris theologians, see Courtenay, "Learned Opinion and Royal Justice," 153–54; for an opposing contemporary argument, see Eastman, "Giles of Rome and Celestine V," 201–4.

itual disaffection thus developed concomitantly during Boniface's reign. Religious disobedience became the vehicle with which people could express opposition. It also provided a pretext upon which the pope could punish vocal adversaries. The refrain "[Boniface] killed Pope Celestine" provided inquisitors with the justification for hauling in citizens on charges of heresy.[34] Inquisitors ordered that anyone who might know anything about Colonna supporters must inform them (see the beginning of this chapter).

The controversy over Boniface's suitability for the pontificate sanctioned other forms of contestation. In Milan, followers of the disputed saint Guglielma argued Boniface did not have the right to appoint the local inquisitor to halt the inquiry into the Guglielmites, since he was not legally pope. Dolcino of Novara, the leader of the religious group known as the Apostles, proclaimed in 1300 that the church under Boniface's leadership had no authority. He predicted an immanent revolution in which Frederick III of Sicily, the Aragonese foe of Boniface and his Angevin allies, would kill Boniface and his corrupt prelates.[35] The number of Dolcino supporters grew as Boniface's enemies, such as the proimperial lords of the Vercelli region, flocked to the radical's banner. Members of the Spiritual Franciscans also mounted opposition to Boniface. Peter John Olivi, a leader of this movement, related how in 1295 some Italian Spirituals asserted that Celestine V was still the pope, that Boniface's supporters were the subordinates of Satan, and that they were going to ask Boniface if they could secede from the Roman Church.[36]

Boniface's harshest critic from within the Italian Spiritual Franciscan ranks was perhaps Jacopone da Todi (d. circa 1306). Jacopone was a Franciscan tertiary with mystical tendencies and an affinity to the concerns of the *fraticelli*. In 1297 he signed a "manifesto" that Cardinals Jacopo and Pietro Colonna wrote against Boniface.[37] The pope imprisoned and excommunicated Jacopone in 1298. The Colonnas were close with other *fraticelli* too, such as John of Parma and Angelo Clareno, the latter of whom mentioned Jacopone in his history of the order, the *Liber chronicarum*, written circa 1323. John of Parma was a retired minister general of the Franciscans who followed apocalyptic Joachimite thought and had close ties with Ubertino da Casale, one of the

---

34. Testimony of Bertholinus Blaxii de Mançolino speaking of Partha, *Acta S. Officii*, vol. 1, no. 35, 21 May 1299, p. 63.

35. *Historia fratris Dulcini*, 21–22. Dolcino's predictions were amended in a second manifesto after Boniface's death in 1303 (ibid., 22–23; Reeves, *Influence of Prophecy*, 245–46).

36. Olivi thought their quest foolhardy (Olivi, "Epistola ad Conradum de Offida").

37. Denifle, "Die Denkschriften der Colonna," 509–29.

future leaders of the Spirituals. Angelo Clareno underwent imprisonment and later voluntary exile in Armenia.[38]

When Jacopone was in prison he wrote three letters to the pope. Although the first two asked for absolution and forgiveness, in the third Jacopone expressed his anger over his unheeded pleas. He directly attacked Boniface:

> Pope Boniface, you've had a lot of fun in this world,
> You'll not be very lighthearted, I suspect, as you leave it.
> . . . .
> Behold, a new Lucifer on the papal throne,
> Poisoning the world with his blasphemies!
> Nothing good is left in you, only sin;
> I'd be ashamed to mention some vices you are accused of.
> . . . .
> I can find no one who can remember
> Any pope of the past who was so vainglorious.
> To have cast aside, as you have, the fear of God
> Is a sign either of heresy or despair.[39]

For Jacopone, it was the pope who had become a heretic through his excessive pride, a charge that would later be formally lodged after Boniface's death. He accused Boniface of blasphemy and of consorting with sorcerers to prolong his life and thus his pontificate.[40] Boniface's politicking had such a detrimental effect on how people perceived the papacy and its role in overseeing the spiritual needs of Christians that in 1299 one learned Bolognese man was provoked to comment in disgust, "I wish that the Sultan (*soldanus*) would come to Rome and submerge the papal seat and the altar of blessed Peter and Paul in such a way that there would never be any altar in the world."[41] This quote suggests that he viewed the enemy Muslims as less morally bankrupt than the papacy. Although prior to the Avignon papacy (also referred to as the "Babylonian Captivity"), this scholar might also be implicitly referring to the biblical depiction of the Babylonians as evil, thus intimating that not even they were as corrupt as Boniface's pontificate.[42]

---

38. See Peck, *Fool of God*, 94–125, and Burr, *Spiritual Franciscans*, 112, on the Colonnas' relationship with the Spirituals.

39. Da Todi, "Third Letter from Jail," vv. 180–82.

40. Ibid., vv. 67–78. On Boniface's heresy charge, see Denton, "Attempted Trial of Boniface VIII," 117–28.

41. Testimony of lord Vanni Ghiandonus of Florence, scholar of Bologna, speaking of lord Andreas Migli of Florence, *Acta S. Officii*, vol. 1, no. 62, 4 November 1299, p. 97; see also no. 236.

42. In the *Greater Life of St. Francis* and the legends in Latin called the *Acts of St. Francis and His Brothers*, Francis's emissaries convert the *soldanus* of Babylon, while in Buoncampagno's *De amicitia* it

Disaffection with the papacy continued virtually unabated after the death of Boniface VIII. Benedict XI succeeded him in 1303 but only reigned for about one year. His successor, Clement V (d. 1312), never set foot in Italy for the entire eight years of his pontificate. He oversaw western Christendom from Avignon, thus beginning the so-called Babylonian Captivity or Avignon exile. The seeming desertion of Rome, the place selected by Christ himself to start his church when he entrusted it to St. Peter, angered Italian citizens. Petrarch, describing the Avignon papacy, bewailed, "Here reign the successors of the poor fishermen of Galilee; they have strangely forgotten their origin. Babylon, the home of all vices and all misery . . . I know by experience that there is no piety, no charity, no faith, no reverence, no fear of God, nothing holy, nothing just, nothing sacred."[43] At Clement's consecration in Lyons, part of a wall collapsed and dislodged the crown from Clement's head, which fell to the ground. Dino Compagni, writing from hindsight, viewed this event as the manifestation of the wrath of God, punishing Clement for not going to Rome. Moreover, Clement's close relationship with Philip IV, king of France, led many to consider him a "puppet" of the secular ruler, according to Giovanni Villani.[44] Finally, the stories of corruption and moral turpitude filtered across the mountain passes did not please the Italian faithful, further connecting the idea of Avignon with scriptural accounts of the evil in ancient Babylon.

The perception of the papacy within Italy deteriorated even more with Clement's successor. After a standoff between the French and Italian cardinals, they finally elected Jean of Cahors, a theologian and canon lawyer aged seventy-two, to be the next pope, who took the name John XXII. He reigned a shocking eighteen years, although it is likely that the cardinals elected him precisely because of his advanced age to provide a temporary solution to the stalemate in the electoral college.[45] John XXII kept the papal seat at Avignon, prolonging the papacy's estrangement from its Italian constituency. This led to more criticism from Italian citizens. Lord Obizzo d'Este, from a traditionally Guelph family, declared, "That man, who is called pope, is not the true pope, because he was not elected at Rome in the seat of blessed Peter, nor ever came to the said seat nor was there, and therefore in the truth of the matter is not pope,

---

is used in this general sense as well as a specific title for Saladin (Bonaventure, *Legenda Maior Sancti Francisci*, in *Legendae duae de vita S. Francisci seraphici*, chap. 8.8; *Actus beati Francisci*, chap. 27; Da Signa, *Amicitia*, chap. 5.3.2 and 6.13.2).

43. Cited in Cheney, *Dawn of a New Era*, 182; see also Rollo-Koster, *Avignon and Its Papacy*, 32–60, and Rusconi, "L'Italia senza papa."

44. *Dino Compagni's Chronicle of Florence*, 75, and Giovanni Villani's account of his election in *Nuova cronica*, 9:80–81; 2:157–64, respectively.

45. Heft, *John XXII and Papal Teaching Authority*, 5.

nor were those things that he did and said of any worth."[46] Lords such as the Este resented that although the pope was in Avignon he took an active part in the politics of the Italian peninsula.

In a manner similar to that of Boniface VIII, John XXII antagonized those who supported the Spiritual Franciscans in their strict adherence to Francis's ideal of poverty. He overwhelmingly ruled in favor of the Conventuals, opposing the Spirituals and denouncing their sympathizers as heretics.[47] In addition, where Louis of Bavaria's allies prevailed, so did hostility for the pope. Upon the king of Bavaria's entrance into the city of Amelia, for instance, citizens shouted in the street, "Long live the holy emperor, death to the Roman Church, death to the heretic Jean de Cahors, Pope John, the Patarine, the dog!"[48] Just as the Colonnas and the Spirituals banded together during the reign of Boniface VIII, so too did John XXII's political adversary, Louis of Bavaria, ally himself with prominent *fraticelli*.[49] Louis used John XXII's decision against the absolute poverty of Christ and his apostles as the basis for his argument that the pope was a heretic. According to an unsympathetic Sienese chronicler, " [Louis the Bavarian said] that Christ did not have belongings as the pope and the clergy, [who] loved belongings, and [that] they were enemies of the holy poverty of Christ, and with reference to this [stated] more articles scandalous in belief, and [though] publicly excommunicated, he and his prelates continued to celebrate the sacred office and to excommunicate pope John [XXII], and through derision they called him priest John, whence a great error was committed in Christianity."[50] The fact that some viewed other aspects of John XXII's theology as shocking only fueled this fire. According to the French continuator of Guillaume de Nangis's chronicle, the pope's claim that saints in heaven neither had the ability to know God nor were perfect until after the general resurrection was met with the following response: "[This pronouncement] scandalized many. But notwithstanding, it is believed he said this more as a matter of opinion than as a declaration, since many people and more important people assert that the statement itself was heretical, and that who-

---

46. Bock, "Der Este-Prozess von 1321," 59–60; see also similar comments on p. 61. Another enemy of John XXII also charged with heresy, Muzio di Francesco d'Assisi, denounced John XXII for the same reasons; see the testimony of *magister* Andrea and Nicolutius Ioli (Brufani, *Eresia di un ribelle*, 146–47 and 190).

47. In his decision of 1318, *Gloriosam ecclesiam*, Pope John XXII condemned the tenets of the Spirituals, later condemning them as heretics in 1322. He alienated one faction of the Conventuals in 1323 with his bull *Cum inter nonnullos*, in which he claimed that Christ and his apostles had held no property either on their own or in common (Heft, *John XXII and Papal Teaching Authority*, 23–28).

48. Fumi, "Eretici e ribelli nell'Umbria," 20.

49. Heft, *John XXII and Papal Teaching Authority*, 35.

50. *Cronache Senesi*, 453.

ever said this with conviction, could not easily be excused of heresy."[51] While some excused John XXII's statements by asserting that he did not seriously hold such views as doctrine, others found his stance convenient to mount an attack against him, a situation that Umberto Eco capitalized on in his novel *The Name of the Rose*. The accusation of spiritual misconduct became the channel through which political enemies could assail John XXII's authority.

Turnover in the papal seat and controversial popes only heightened tensions between the church and many of the new lords intent on expanding their power bases. The dynastic ambitions of new *signori* brought them into direct conflict with the papacy. Regional conflict between the earlier communal governments in some ways had worked to the papacy's advantage. Even Ghibelline communes resisted imperial ambitions to draw northern Italy into the direct control of the Holy Roman Emperor on account of their desire for independent rule.[52] Communes, therefore, unintentionally served papal aims to limit imperial power. If the regional conflict between towns and the factionalism within communes themselves did not allow the papacy to obtain control over individual communes, much less the region, neither did it allow the emperor to do so. After the death of Frederick II and his son Manfred, which resulted in a sixty-year power vacuum within the Holy Roman Empire until Henry VII ascended the throne in 1310, popes could expect that their support of nominally Guelph towns in the latter's regional conflicts would extend the political influence of the papacy.[53]

The rising *signori* dashed papal hopes. Having essentially created small monarchies, *signori* posed a new and more difficult challenge for the papacy.[54] These lords were local, with the ability to raise homegrown armies who knew the terrain, unlike the imperial forces. In battles between papal armies, comprised of mercenaries and French adventurers, and those of the *signori*, the papal side was at a disadvantage. Pope Martin IV discovered this fact when the troops fighting under his banner were massacred in 1282 by Guido di Montefeltro's troops during a battle for control of Forlì.[55] These *signori* were wealthy and powerful men. Many were willing to become opponents of the popes. Even the Guelph lords were untrustworthy allies due to their territorial ambitions. Obizzo II d'Este, for instance, the "pillar of the Church party in the

---

51. *Chronique latine de Guillaume de Nangis*, 2:127.

52. Jones, *Italian City-State*, 336–37. At the forming of the Second Lombard League in 1231, only the cities of Cremona, Parma, Reggio, and Modena were imperial allies (Larner, *Italy in the Age of Dante*, 20). The coalition did not last, and Edward Coleman reminds us that there was no anti-imperial united front ("Cities and Communes," 48).

53. Jones, *Italian City-State*, 341.

54. Dean, "Rise of the Signori," 105–6.

55. Partner, *Lands of St. Peter*, 279.

area," allied himself with the Ghibelline *signore* Alberto della Scala in 1283 to protect his lands from neighboring Guelph lords. In 1295 Obizzo went to war with Bologna, a Guelph commune that was part of the Papal States.[56] Despite the efforts of various popes to curb their authority, signorial dynasties crushed papal hopes of achieving political domination in the region. The political threat that the lords embodied made popes desperate to remove them from the scene by any means possible, including inquisitorial prosecution. The da Romano in Treviso, the Pallavicino in Cremona, the Visconti in Milan, the Montefeltro in Urbino, the da Venosta in Como, and eventually the d'Este in Ferrara all were accused of heresy at the instigation of popes fearful of their power and desirous of obtaining control over their lands.[57]

Northern and central Italy thus became the area upon which popes and emperors played a tug of war for political domination. Although scholars can point to few major battles, Edward Coleman has noted that the bulk of the fighting took place within the cities themselves, in the form of "street skirmishes, assassinations, and the demolition of private fortifications."[58] Communities, therefore, saw the directives of the papacy and inquisitors within a political framework. The political persuasion of the dominant party could impede the effectiveness of inquisitors because citizens viewed inquisitorial prosecution as the papacy's retribution for political opposition. Henry Charles Lea noted that however orthodox a person may have been, if he or she lived in a formerly Ghibelline region and had incurred the wrath of papal officials, it was a foregone conclusion that persecution would follow.[59] Claims of papal plenitude of power provided a justification for such actions. The inquisitorial prosecution of a local noblewoman in Parma, which followed on the heels of a Ghibelline uprising after which partisans had been exiled from the town, seems to support Lea's conjecture.[60] Pope John XXII's battle with the Visconti family in Milan supplies more evidence. During his persecution of Matteo and Galeazzo Visconti and their Ghibelline supporters, inquisitors charged over

---

56. Hyde, *Society and Politics*, 136; Partner, *Lands of St. Peter*, 291.

57. Robert Michel edited the inquisitorial process of the Visconti in "Les procès de Matteo et de Galeazzo Visconti"; see also Besozzi, "I processi canonici contro Galeazzo Visconti"; Cognasso, *I Visconti*; and Muir, *History of Milan*. For Pallavicino, see Lea, *History of the Inquisition*, 2:228–33; for the da Romano, see ibid., 224–27; for Federico da Montefeltro, see Franceschini, *Documenti e regesti*, 1:128–30. For the D'Este process, see Bock, "Der Este-Prozess," 41–111. A comparable though less celebrated situation is the case of Muzio di San Francesco (Brufani, *Eresia di un ribelle*; this work also includes an edition of the inquisitorial process). Another example is that of Corrado da Venosta (see Cavallari, "Eresie e politica").

58. Coleman, "Cities and Communes," 48.

59. Lea, *History of the Inquisition*, 2:236; see also Lawrence, *Friars*, 194.

60. *Chronicon Parmense*, 35; *Chronicle of Salimbene de Adam*, 511 and 514.

1,400 people with heresy.[61] The use of the judicial mechanism of the *inquisitio* as an instrument of political domination, particularly by authoritarian popes such as Boniface VIII and John XXII, increased with the rise of *signori* in northern and central Italy. Yet as the example of Milan suggests, the lords themselves were not the only recipients. Under the expanded interpretation of heresy, whole towns viewed as disobedient—that is, treasonous—could come under fire from the weapons in the pope's arsenal.

Crushing Cults and Destroying Dissidents

The timely crackdown on Armanno Pungilupo's cult is illustrative of how popes used the power of judicial inquisition to punish towns whose loyalty might be suspect. As already discussed, the bishop and canons of Ferrara collected evidence of Armanno's holiness right after his death, making their first bid for his canonization in 1272. Inquisitors questioned deponents about Armanno's heterodoxy almost simultaneously. Due in part to the high papal attrition rate (nine different popes over the intervening years), it was not until Boniface VIII intervened in 1301 that a concerted effort was made to end the dispute over Armanno's cult. The historical context suggests that there was more than a suspect saint's cult at stake, which popes often tolerated if local and seemingly innocuous.

When the canons of Ferrara sent a procurator to Rome in 1300, Boniface VIII refused to grant him an audience. Later that year, when the pope appointed a commission to examine Armanno, he chose men from outside Ferrara, all described as "advocates" (in both the professional and political sense) of the Roman curia.[62] The formerly sympathetic, or at least nonpartisan, response of the papacy to Armanno's cult had altered. The commission condemned Armanno posthumously as a relapsed heretic, destroyed his remains, and dismantled his cult. Stephen Wessley has argued that the shift in attitude resulted from Boniface's desire to make an example of Armanno, in order to "strike a blow" at Frederick III of Sicily, who had sheltered many heretics in direct defiance of papal directives.[63] This scenario seems somewhat unlikely. Frederick III did harbor heretics, though most of them were members of the radical Franciscan reform movement called the Spirituals

61. Partner, *Lands of St. Peter*, 315.

62. Bishop Iohannes and the cathedral chapter of Ferrara sent the canon Bonfamilius to act on their behalf (*Itinerari*, 72). Boniface's advocates included bishop Thomas of Pistoia, *ser* Raphael of Bologna, and *ser* Egidio of Viterbo (*Itinerari*, 48).

63. Wessley, "Enthusiasm and Heresy," 189.

rather than the Cathars, to which Armanno was supposed to belong. The condemnation of Armanno would not have unduly concerned Frederick. He lived outside the peninsula in an ancestral castle in Sicily. While Frederick supported the Colonna against Boniface VIII, even if Frederick had heard of Armanno he would not have been invested in his public cult or viewed its demise as a personal affront.

Boniface's move to end the conflict was more likely a by-product of his attack on the Visconti family, whom he wanted to neutralize to pursue his own territorial ambitions in northern Italy. Matteo Visconti's son, Galeazzo, married Beatrice d'Este, the sister of the Perpetual Lord of Ferrara, in 1300 (figure 5).[64] With this marriage a member of one of the most vocal antipapal families of the time gained entrance into one of the most important propapal homes in northern Italy.

This union was dangerous, for the Estensi had already shown they were less than reliable allies. The region they controlled bordered on the Papal States and served as a buffer between the pope's lands and the territories governed by the Ghibelline lords of the Po plain. If the Estensi switched their alliance, not only would the papacy lose an important associate in the north, but papal lands would be vulnerable to attack from a former friend. Boniface had already tried to check the power of the Visconti in his prosecution of the Guglielmites. The investigation of this Milanese group, occurring the year before Armanno's condemnation, has several parallels to the situation in Ferrara. Inquisitors questioned sectarians in 1284 and 1296, but it was not until 1300 that Boniface focused on abolishing the inner core of devotees of questionable orthodoxy and, consequently, Guglielma's wider orthodox Milanese cult. The investigation coincided with Albert I of Germany renewing Matteo Visconti, the head of the ruling house of Milan, as Imperial Vicar of Lombardy. Matteo was distancing himself from Rome just as his power over northern Italy was waxing. One of the leaders of the Guglielmites, Maifreda da Pirovano, was a cousin of Matteo Visconti. The investigation into the sect was a way to discredit the Visconti and thus weaken their position in Milan.

It seems likely, therefore, that the marriage alliance between the Estensi and the Visconti was the catalyst for papal intervention against Armanno's cult. Boniface VIII punished the Ferrarese for inviting the Visconti into their homes by condemning their saint to eternal damnation. This is not to say that Boniface's allies trumped up charges against Armanno. The investigation began

---

64. Ibid., 212. This is a different Beatrice from the one who died in 1262 and was considered a saint by the Benedictines and Franciscans of Ferrara. This Beatrice's first husband was also a member of the Visconti but from an ancillary line and was only a judge, whereas Galeazzo was heir to what was becoming a dynasty. For further discussion, see Peterson, "Politics of Sanctity," 320.

VISCONTI FAMILY (MILAN)

ESTE FAMILY (FERRARA, MODENA, REGGIO)

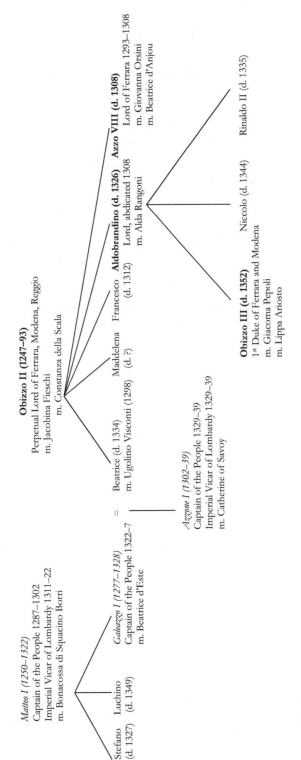

FIGURE 5. Genealogy of the Visconti and Este families in the thirteenth and fourteenth centuries. By author.

long before Boniface ascended to Peter's seat. There was ample cause to warrant an investigation, and the argument could be made that Armanno's ultimate condemnation as a relapsed heretic was justified based on the evidence. Nevertheless, Boniface's adamant refusal even to receive the procurator hired by Armanno's supporters, and the suggestive timing of his decision to end the stalemate in Ferrara, strongly implies that the pope used his power to teach a lesson to those who posed a potential threat to his temporal and spiritual authority. Although the Estensi participated in an offensive that ousted Matteo Visconti from Milan in 1302, the family would become open opponents of the papacy within twenty years of the Visconti-d'Este marriage.[65] The result was that Pope John XXII charged Rainaldo and Obizzo, the scions of the house, with heresy. In this volatile political arena, the cults of local saints like Armanno Pungilupo could get caught in the crossfire.

There were more subtle tactics at the papacy's disposal to punish perceived disobedience. Popes could withhold canonization inquiries when a town's past political orientation displeased them or they questioned its present loyalty. Treviso and Padua are cases in point. The year after a local Camaldolese monk named Parisio died in 1267, Bishop Alberto of Treviso pronounced Parisio a saint through a diocesan inquiry and jointly requested with the commune of Treviso that the papacy open its own formal inquiry into his merits. Little is known about Parisio beyond the fact that he supposedly lived an astonishing 108 years, was an ordained priest, and oversaw the nuns at the convent of Sta. Cristina in Treviso. His *vita* is brief but includes a short list of *miracula* and suggests he had the gift of prophecy.[66] Parisio had counseled the Franciscan bishop when the latter's order charged him with misconduct in 1262. As a result, he obtained an ardent ecclesiastical supporter who rallied citizens around his cause.[67] Although later Trevisan statutes of 1283–1284 record that the commune pledged a significant sum toward the cost of procuring Parisio's canonization and ordained that the *podestà* would make an offering every year at the local saint's altar, further attempts at an inquiry stalled until 1316.[68]

The tumultuous political situation in Treviso was not propitious for a papal canonization. Treviso was tainted by association with the tyrant and anti-papal lord Ezzelino da Romano, whose brother Alberico had controlled the town for years. The exiled Trevisan Guelphs aided in the overthrow and ultimate execution of Alberico in 1260, however, so it would seem logical that

---

65. Dean, "Rise of the Signori," 121.

66. *AASS* II, June 11, col. 484B–485E.

67. *AASS* II, June 11, 484E; *Annales Camaldulenses*, 5:86–87, 91–94, 241–42, 392–93; Webb, *Patrons and Defenders*, 141.

68. *Gli Statuti del Comune di Treviso*, 1:112–13.

the papacy would reward their actions with canonization for their holy hermit saint.[69] Unfortunately, another problem resulted from the political turmoil that ravaged the commune in 1268. That year a member of the city's Ghibelline faction, Gherardo dei Castelli, murdered the bishop's brother. Fighting ensued until 1283 between his allies and the Guelph partisans, including the Azzoni, Avvogaro, and Camino families. In the same year, the Guelph lord Gherardo III da Camino (d. 1306) gained control and established a new signorial government.[70] The murder of a bishop's kinsman was an egregious crime. Moreover, Ghibellines had a foothold in Treviso until Gherardo's rule commenced. While Dante praised him in *Purgatorio* XVI (vv. 121–27 and 133–35) as a paragon of the virtuous ruler of times past, events showed that the *signore* was adept at political posturing and engaged in some activities that would make the papacy look askance at his loyalty. Despite the implicit pro-papal position of the Guelph party, Gherardo clashed with papal interests by taking part in the murder of Jacopo del Cassero (d. 1298), the *podestà* of Bologna and the enemy of the Ghibelline Malatesta family. Following this action the imperial contender Henry VII (soon to be crowned emperor) named Gherardo's son, Rizzardo, Imperial Vicar in 1311. Rizzardo, perhaps unlike his father, was a despot. He married Giovanna Visconti, from the same well-known antipapal Milanese family, but soon was murdered.[71] His half-brother, Guecellone VII, took over as Captain General and Lord of Treviso, only to be deposed on 6 December and exiled on 15 December 1312.

The delay between the 1284 statute acknowledging that renewed canonization efforts for Parisio were to begin and the next request of 1316–1317 demonstrates that not all new signorial rulers tried to ingratiate themselves with their citizens by promoting a saint's cult. Parisio was a ready-made patron if the Camino family wanted to take advantage of the circumstances. Instead, every attempt at his canonization occurred during periods of communal rule, jointly requested by the bishop and the commune. After the Trevisans ousted the Camino ruler in 1312 the town made another bid for Parisio's canonization. The town's Council of Three Hundred decreed in 1316 that it would send men to Rome once again to request a canonization inquiry for Parisio, as well as for Henry of Bolzano (d. 1315), another local saint (figure 6).

---

69. Innocent IV had called a crusade against Ezzelino in 1254; he died in 1259 (Larner, *Italy in the Age of Dante*, 39). For an account of Alberico's death at the hands of the Trevisans, see *Gli Statuti del Comune di Treviso*, 1:110–13.

70. Webb, *Patrons and Defenders*, 141.

71. Giovanna Visconti was the daughter of Beatrice d'Este and her first husband, Nino Giudice di Gallura degli Visconti. Beatrice married Galeazzo I Visconti in 1300 (ibid., 99 and 141–42).

PARISIO OF TREVISO (d. 1267)

1254	1260	1262	1268	1283/4
Crusade called against Ezzolino da Romano, anti-papal lord of the region	Overthrow of Ezzolini's brother Alberico, who controlled Treviso	Bishop of Treviso charged with misconduct; Parisio counsels him	Bishop's brother murdered by anti-papal Gherardo dei Castelli; factional fighting for 15 years	Pro-papal lord Gherardo III da Camino takes control of Treviso **1ST ATTEMPT FOR PARISIO**

HENRY OF BOLZANO (d. 1315)

1298	1311	1312	1316	1317
The da Camino family involved in the murder of the *podestà* of Bologna, a papal ally against the anti-papal Malatesta family	H.R.E. named da Camino heir Imperial Vicar	da Camino overthrown; communal rule restored	**1ST ATTEMPT FOR HENRY** **2ND ATTEMPT FOR PARISIO**	War between Treviso and rising signor Cangrande Scaligeri

1347 – Canonization inquiry request for Henry (2nd attempt), possibly also for Parisio (would be 3rd attempt).
1748 – Canonization process for Henry (3rd attempt). Beatified in 1750.

Figure 6. Timeline of canonization attempts for Parisio of Treviso and Henry of Bolzano. By author.

Henry was extremely charitable and pious and, like Parisio, became the focus of devotion immediately after his death. Miraculous blood ran from his
corpse, and the clamor of citizens led the governing council to order a tomb
built at the cost of one thousand livres and an image of him to be painted on
the communal palace (all at the expense of the commune).[72] Whether the second attempt for Parisio's canonization and the first attempt for Henry's
would have been successful is unknown, for the mission derailed when the
town went to war with Cangrande della Scala (or Scaligeri), a Ghibelline lord
who was subsuming town after town in the Veneto and the March of Treviso
into his dominion. Due to the situation the city's envoys were unable to travel
to champion their saints' merits. Della Scala ultimately prevailed, and Treviso's
hopes were dashed again. He was a major supporter of the imperial claimant
and papal adversary Louis of Bavaria.[73]

Following this lordship, Treviso formed an alliance (or "gave itself to," depending on the source) the Republic of Venice in 1344. One final medieval
attempt to obtain formal papal recognition of these two Trevisan saints occurred in 1347.[74] Treviso lacked the support of the Venetian Republic, since it
was busy fending off eastern attacks from Louis I of Hungary. In 1356 the
city itself was sieged by the Hungarian king with help from another northern
signorial family, the Carrara. Treviso's canonization efforts demonstrate how
saints were at the mercy of the political scene. More importantly, it shows that
new rulers as well as old ones could cause papal reluctance to open an official
canonization inquiry, as is clear from the timeline of Treviso's petitions. The
Trevisans continued to venerate Parisio, considering him a *Prottetore* of the city
well into the eighteenth century, although he was never canonized.[75] Henry of
Bolzano ultimately gained the title *beatus* in 1750.

Similarly, popes rebuffed Padua's efforts at canonization for Anthony Peregrinus. Anthony was probably a Camaldolese monk like Parisio, but he did

---

72. Testimony of Don Pietro Cantinella, prebend of the Cathedral, *Riti*, proc. 3021 (Henry of
Bolzano, 1768), cxxi; see also the second testimony of Pietro Domenico Monigo, p. lx. A descendant
of the Azzoni and Avvogaro families, Nestore degli Azzoni Avvogaro, testified one of his ancestors
was a member of the council that decreed a marble sarcophagus be built for Henry and arranged his
burial in the cathedral (ibid., xxxiv). On the commune's veneration, see Azzoni Avogari, *Memorie del B.
Enrico morto*, 35 and 38. Henry's *vita* and *miraculi* are in *AASS* II, June 10, col. 371B–391C.

73. *Riti*, proc. 3021, p. xli, and testimony of Pietro Domenico Monigo, p. lx. Treviso ultimately
fell to Della Scala in the succeeding decade (Black, "Visconti in the Fourteenth Century," 2–4; Dean,
"Rise of the Signori," 112).

74. Webb states that the last time the Trevisans attempted to get Parisio and Henry canonized
was in 1347, but a papal canonization process for Henry was opened in 1768 (Webb, *Patrons and Defenders*, 141n16).

75. "Fù scelto il Beato Enrico per uno de' santi Protettori di questa città insieme con San Liberale,
e San Parisio, conterminazioni antiche, e perpetue, come hò sempre sentito à dire" (*Riti*, proc. 3021,
p. cxxxi).

not lead the life of a secluded hermit.[76] As his popular surname suggests, Anthony wandered as a pilgrim, traveling to Jerusalem, Compostela, Rome, and Loreto. According to his *vitae*, he was the son of a noble Paduan family named Monzino. Shortly after his death in 1267 the Paduans, prompted by the miracles that occurred at his tomb, requested Anthony's canonization. Their plea was ignored, for an inquiry was never initiated. Anthony's extant hagiographers, both postdating his death by some two hundred years, somewhat defiantly asserted that Anthony was in the ranks of the blessed regardless of the papacy's refusal to recognize that fact officially. The author of one of his *vitae*, Bernardino Scardeonio, remarked, "He was famous because of the many and great miracles after his death, [though] the Roman Church did not permit him to be received into the catalog of the saints. Nevertheless he was held in the greatest veneration from that time in Padua . . . and it was established by municipal decree, that a day was solemnly fixed in his memory for solemn supplication, [which is] observed in all the shops of the city . . . not otherwise than if it had been mandated by the supreme pontiff."[77] His other hagiographer, Sicco Polenton, likewise tried to rationalize the lack of official recognition: "Nevertheless it was not pleasing to the supreme pontiff to have him in the catalog of saints, because he judged it to be sufficient and more than sufficient, that Padua now had one Anthony who is a confessor and held to be a saint."[78] Polenton, of course, is referring to the Franciscan preacher Anthony of Padua, the city's more well-known saint.

Both *vitae* also make a point of noting that Anthony lived in Padua during Ezzelino da Romano's reign of terror. Polenton claimed that Anthony, like his predecessor of the same name, opposed Ezzelino.[79] Polenton thus probably molded the life of Anthony Peregrinus to resemble that of the canonized Anthony of Padua, hoping that formal recognition would likewise follow. In contrast, the author of a sixteenth-century Paduan chronicle claimed that Anthony Peregrinus wandered for five years, returning to Padua only after the death of Ezzelino in 1259.[80] Since the commune of Padua only accorded Peregrinus honors in 1324, after a Ghibelline regime rose to power, his active opposition to Ezzelino as the late chronicler suggested is in question.[81] In sum, there is no evidence except for the fifteenth-century *vita* that describes

---

76. There is a tradition that he belonged to the order, but he was buried in the church of S. Maria de Porcilia outside Padua's walls rather than in the local Camoldense monastery (see *AASS* I, February 1, *Praefatio*, col. 264B).

77. *AASS* I, February 1, *Praefatio*, col. 265A.

78. Polenton, "Vita Beati Antonii Peregrini," 420.

79. Ibid., 417–19. For Anthony of Padua, see *Sancti Antonii de Padua vitae duae*.

80. *AASS* I, February 1, *Praefatio*, col. 264A–B.

81. Goodich, *Vita Perfecta*, 195.

Peregrinus as an adversary of Ezzelino, and perhaps that was why the papacy refused to open an inquiry into his merits. Ezzelino himself was of a Paduan family and used the city as the base for his dynastic aspirations.[82] In addition, as the hagiographer Polenton acknowledged, the commune already had a recent saint at the time of Padua's request in 1267: Anthony of Padua (d. 1231), the Portuguese mendicant who was truly a vocal participant in the church's struggle with Ezzelino in 1230. Loyalty to the papacy's aims resulted in Anthony of Padua's canonization; suspect or even indemonstrable loyalty may have engendered a quashed bid for Anthony Peregrinus's canonization.

The efforts the commune of Perugia made on behalf of its own holy hermit, Bevignate (d. late twelfth century), similarly proved futile, although the reason why popes rejected the Perugians' requests was markedly different from the cases of Treviso or Padua. Almost nothing is known about Bevignate except that he lived in Perugia during the late twelfth or early thirteenth century and that he was a hermit or penitent. Devotion to Bevignate did not arise until 1260 when a hermit, Raniero Fasani (or da Fasoli), had visions in which Bevignate instructed him to start a penitential movement.[83] Raniero gained the support of the bishop, and the commune decreed that it must seek canonization for Bevignate. Every year thereafter the town government read the statute and sent ambassadors to Rome to renew its cause at the election of each new pope, only to be denied for almost fifty years.[84] In the meantime, a church built on an existing structure was dedicated to Bevignate in 1256. In order to strengthen the case for canonization, in 1285 the *podestà* and *capitano del popolo* of Perugia investigated if Bevignate's body was within, presumably because he had been buried in the pre-1256 church.[85] The Knights Templar oversaw the church until their suppression in 1312, when the Knights Hospitaller took over.[86] Although canonization efforts had dwindled away by the early fourteenth century (apparently coinciding with the destruction of the Templars), city statutes of 1342 and 1343 still listed St. Bevignate's feast day, which became a public holiday in 1453.[87] The civic authorities that year justified their decision on the grounds

82. Coleman, "Cities and Communes," 55.

83. Vauchez, *Sainthood in the Later Middle Ages*, 71n33. The following information is from Kern, "Saint Bevignate de Pérouse," unless otherwise noted. For background, see Grundman, *Popolo at Perugia*, 126–29.

84. Webb, *Patrons and Defenders*, 145–46; Vauchez, *Sainthood in the Later Middle Ages*, 71n33.

85. They were instructed to do so by the same council that renewed the 1260 statute, suggesting that it hoped his relics would indeed be found. The outcome of this investigation is unknown (Webb, *Patrons and Defenders*, 146).

86. Roncetti, Scarpellini, and Tommasi, *Templari e ospitalieri in Italia*.

87. *Statuti di Perugia dell'anno 1342*, 2:62 and 349.

that, "although he is not enrolled in the catalogue of saints, it is not to be doubted that he is in celestial glory and among the number of saints."[88] Perugia therefore joined in the same lament of the process and assertion of holiness regardless of papal approval, joining devotees of saints from Padua, Cremona, Treviso, and other cities.

Bevignate had a powerful roster of supporters in the late thirteenth century. The bishop, the city council, the *podestà* and *capitano del popolo*, and the Templars united in their promotion of the saint. Yet this support was not enough. The Perugian cause is a study in how the papacy closely guarded the right to canonize as a means of asserting its spiritual authority and dominating those that only gave nominal obeisance to the papacy, particularly within the Papal States. The canonization attempts failed for several reasons. Foremost is that there was little evidence to bolster Perugia's claims that Bevignate was a saint. Yet other factors were also at work. The impetus for Bevignate's cult was the flagellant movement that emerged in Perugia in 1260, inspired by Raniero Fasani's visions of the prospective saint. The appeal of the flagellants in that year is widely believed to have been a response to Joachimite predictions that the world would end in 1260.[89] The flagellants believed that Christians should punish themselves to expiate sin lest God destroy the world. Although flagellants in general did not err from doctrine, the church reacted strongly against them, particularly in the fourteenth century when their processions were a common occurrence after outbreaks of the plague and were associated with spreading the disease.[90] The fact that they were an unmonitored group of mostly laypersons who had not received the sacrament of penance from priests and so did not have authorization for their actions compounded negative views of their extreme behavior. One chronicler asserted that they believed God sent them to preach, although they did not have official sanction or the proof of a miracle to confirm their election and so were heretics.[91] Pope Clement VI condemned the flagellants in 1349. So while the delayed inquiry into Bevignate's merits and frequent papal interregnums made the failure of his cause a real possibility, his connection with the suspect flagellant movement and Joachimite affiliations rendered it a certainty.

The unforeseen result of the bureaucratization of canonizations was that the papacy fostered a situation in which it had not more, but in fact much less

---

88. Kern, "Saint Bevignate de Pérouse," 52, translated in Webb, *Patrons and Defenders*, 146.

89. Dickson, "Flagellants of 1260 and the Crusades"; Henderson, "Flagellant Movement and Flagellant Confraternities"; and Manselli, "L'Anno 1260 fu Anno Gioachimito?"

90. Dickson, *Religious Enthusiasm in the Medieval West*, chap. 8.

91. *Liber de rebus memorabilioribus*, 283–84, translated in Horrox, *The Black Death*, 152–53.

control over these towns and who they chose to venerate.[92] Popes consequently used these unauthorized saints' cults to impose their will and promote
the idea of the papal monarchy upon disobedient, disloyal, or apathetic communities and/or their rulers. The tools at their command were interdict, inquisitorial prosecution, and rejection of requests for canonization of local
saints. These efforts had mixed results. Communities routinely ignored interdicts, challenged inquisitors, and continued to participate in their local devotions. Sometimes they challenged papal power to the extent of venerating their
saint even after inquisitors posthumously condemned him or her as a heretic.
Cults could even emerge out of the ashes of a burned "martyr," the ultimate
backfiring, as occurred with frà Michele Berti da Calci and Cecco of Ascoli. In
sum, overuse and misuse of the weapons that the broadened definition of heresy provided undercut inquisitorial and papal retribution as deterrents for disobedience. When imposed by the too close yet too distant papacy, and the
seemingly corrupt institution it epitomized, these weapons no longer had the
ability to persuade communities to toe the line. This is not to say that the papacy's efforts were fruitless. On the contrary, its ability to punish was all too
effective at times, and the suffering inflicted on those sentenced as heretics and
their families cannot be underestimated. As tools to enforce obedience within
larger communities, however, the means at the pope's disposal were insufficient and often had the unintended effect of stiffening a community's resolve
to continue supporting its saint(s) and challenging inquisitors.

---

92. Dickson, "115 Cults of the Saints," 15–16.

CHAPTER 8

Methods of Contesting Authority

The deep faith in the miracle-working power of a saint, the conviction that those who experienced the virtues of an individual were most qualified to judge their holiness, the economic and political benefits of promoting local cults, and the anti-inquisitorial and antipapal attitudes of the period in discussion all contributed to local communities contesting the authority of popes and inquisitors. Bishops, civic officials, and devotees often fought hard to keep a saint's cult viable once a majority reached consensus that the person was holy. In some notable cases, they did not fear inquisitors and rejected their authority. Muzio di Francesco of Assisi, an antipapal rebel in the early fourteenth century, purportedly remarked, "I would not fear sentences of excommunication and interdict, any more than I would fear the tail of a donkey."[1] This evidently was a popular saying in late medieval Italy, for it echoed testimony from inquisitorial deponents in Bologna given twenty years prior. This blasé attitude toward papal authority was expressed through citizens routinely contesting inquisitors, who represented papal authority. Sometimes it took the form of riots and physical violence. In cases of disputed saints who were facing possible condemnation, individuals often sought legal

---

1. Testimony of Cello Admanniti, paraphrasing Muzio di Francesco of Assisi in Brufani, *Eresia di un ribelle*, 184–85.

means to beat the system instead, in a process I define as oppositional inquisitorial culture.

A significant aspect of the emerging inquisitorial culture in the later Middle Ages was the implementation of laws and legal procedures to combat heresy, as discussed in chapter 2. Laws and procedures thus became the basis of, and in part a justification for, the prosecution of heretics, but the effects of condemnations had larger significance in society. Ryan Prendergast defined inquisitorial culture as "the control of knowledge, the exclusion of the Other, forced confession and punishment, blood purity, and the public performance of ideology."[2] In contrast, Dyan Elliott chose the term "inquisitional culture," arguing that "the term 'inquisition' (*inquisitio*), even when applied to a particular tribunal, should be understood in the widest sense as a procedure not limited to one forum but the province of many . . . [and] is more reflective of a process than of an institution."[3] The term "inquisitional" refers specifically to the legal procedure, although Elliott uses it for various forms of official "tribunals." Thus I prefer "inquisitorial," which reflects its legal meaning as a procedural system opposed to the accusatory system, but which also encompasses larger social participation and cultural significance. The term also provides more latitude for participation by those outside of the inquisitorial office.

This growing inquisitorial culture could not stay within the purview of papal agents, such as inquisitors. Increasingly, suspect or accused individuals and / or their friends and devotees learned from the *inquisitio* and appropriated aspects of the legal process to challenge inquisitors and protect themselves and cults of local saints. Strategies they used included appealing inquisitorial sentences, attempting canonization inquiries for suspect saints, and questioning the validity of inquisitors to hold office. In doing so, members of communities created their own opposing "inquisitional culture." It is unsurprising that this occurred in the Italian peninsula where there were many inquisitorial inquiries, a long tradition of the study of Roman law, and local men and women—including disputed saints—who needed defending. The first section of this chapter discusses ways in which individuals, such as those I have termed heretical saints, contested heresy convictions. The following two sections discuss the other two methods, canonization inquiries and questioning legitimacy, through which various members of a community colluded to challenge inquisitorial authority on a larger scale and protect local saints' cults.

---

2. Prendergast, *Reading, Writing, and Errant Subjects*, 2.
3. Elliott, *Proving Woman*, 2.

Legal Culture, Inquisitorial Culture, and a Matter of Procedure

Incorporating the *inquisitio* to determine both sanctity and heresy in the early thirteenth century created a new legal culture based on law and procedure. This development was perhaps a natural consequence of the rising interest in Roman law and its influence on canon law. As discussed previously, canon law mandated that it was public behavior that should be examined in cases of orthodoxy and heterodoxy, since only God knew one's internal disposition. The *inquisitio* was to elucidate the truth regarding an individual's acts through *articuli interrogatori*, or articles of interrogation, a list of standard questions that inquisitors would ask. The *inquisitio*'s emphasis on collection and analysis of data by a skilled questioner was supposed to neutralize the problem of exaggerated, biased, or faulty testimony. Manuals for inquisitors, such as the famous fourteenth-century example by Bernard Gui, the *Practica Inquisitionis heretice pravitatis*, included specific questions to ask depending on the heresy of which the individual in question was suspect. The procedure allowed authorities to judge the veracity of deponents' testimonies by comparing the responses of witnesses to their own knowledge of heretics, derived from personal experience or from the descriptions provided in such manuals.[4]

With the *inquisitio* as the foundation, the inquisitorial process became more procedural. There were steps that inquisitors had to follow: a general sermon exhorting people to come forward, official requests for episcopal collaboration, interrogation in front of a notary and witnesses, the opportunity for a person who confessed to examine and confirm the recorded transcripts, an examination of the proceedings by learned representatives, deliberation over the sentences, and steps to impose punishment by secular authorities.[5] Legal procedures became an integral part of inquisitional culture. For papal agents the incorporation of Roman law procedures was the process that detected the "truth" about a person's orthodoxy, or lack of it. For the accused and their relatives the legal process became a source of inspiration of how to beat the inquisitors at their own game, to challenge their power and potentially save lives, property, and reputations.

Most towns had instituted laws addressing heresy by the last quarter of the thirteenth century at the behest of popes. Mendicant inquisitors accelerated their investigation of heresy during this period, especially during the pontifi-

---

4. See Dondaine, "Le manuel d'inquisiteur," for the chronological development and discussion of some of these manuals.

5. Elliott, *Proving Woman*, 121–27; Lea, *History of the Inquisition*, 1:305–49; and Kelly, *Inquisitions and Other Trial Procedures*.

cate of Boniface VIII. Boniface appointed himself inquisitor-general and spearheaded renewed efforts to prosecute heretics. Inquiries against individuals and groups such as the Guglielmites, Armanno Pungilupo, and Gerard Segarelli and his *pauperes Christi*, some of whom had been suspect for years, were brought to fruition during Boniface's reign. Peter Diehl argued for a concomitant shift in local support for inquisitorial efforts, concluding that by the late thirteenth century Italian towns were more likely to enforce antiheretical statutes and to support the prosecution of heretics than they had been in the first quarter of the same century. This change in attitude, he claimed, resulted from a focused mendicant preaching mission against heretics in conjunction with sustained papal pressure on local governments to uphold such statutes. Diehl supported this argument by noting there were only two major examples of what he termed "spontaneous popular" acts against inquisitors in the latter part of the century, in contrast to a significant number in the early thirteenth century.[6] If we extend Diehl's definition and timeframe just a little, however, there are more examples to choose from that undermine this perspective of local communities toeing the line. A short list could include the murders of the inquisitor Peter of Verona (or Peter Martyr) in Milan in 1252 and of the Franciscan inquisitor of Verona, brother Florasio, in the early 1280s.[7] Besides the attack on the Dominican convent in Parma (1279) and riots in Bologna (1299) that Diehl identified, a few (but by no means exhaustive) additional examples include an assault on Franciscan inquisitors in Florence (1297), riots in Ferrara (1301), a battle between the villagers and papal armies in the hills above Novara (1304–1307), and the burning of mendicant property in Spoleto (1327).

There is other evidence to suggest that citizens, including local clergy, did not fully accept inquisitorial culture in the late thirteenth century. Just because towns placed statutes in their books does not prove that civic officials actively supported inquisitorial prosecution within their communities. In fact, the papacy repeatedly had to exhort governments to enact and enforce these regulations. In 1252, 1254, 1258, twice in 1265, and in 1288, popes commanded towns to include laws against heresy in their statutes and reiterated their order that inquisitors had the ability to excommunicate any civic officials who failed to do so.[8] Thus government bodies implemented laws when they bowed to political pressure under duress. While Diehl focused solely on riots as examples of what he calls resistance, challenging inquisitorial culture took many forms beyond large-scale revolts. The usual method on an individual level was

---

6. Diehl, "Overcoming Reluctance to Prosecute Heresy," 49.

7. For Peter of Verona, see Prudlo, *Martyred Inquisitor*, 39–70. On the murder of Florasio, see D'Alatri, "Una sentenza dell'inquisitore," 144.

8. Diehl, "Overcoming Reluctance to Prosecute Heresy," 61.

to thwart inquisitors through evasionary tactics or noncompliance. Perhaps the most famous medieval European example of these strategies was Marguerite Porete's refusal to cooperate with inquisitors questioning her about her work they deemed heretical, *The Mirror of Simple Souls*.[9] Another method was using the appeal process to contest convictions.

The growing inquisitorial culture coincided with a growing legal culture that was permeating the Italian peninsula and affecting all levels of society. Roman law was the special study of universities such as Bologna. The many urban mercantile centers increasingly incorporated legal practices into business endeavors. Notaries were commonplace for contracts, wills, and in civic affairs.[10] The children of merchants were going to new schools to learn basic reading, writing, and arithmetic in the vernacular to aid in their families' businesses.[11] Within this legal culture the procedural elements of inquisitorial culture were recognizable, even if citizens did not accept the official results. As a result, an interesting and unique oppositional inquisitorial culture developed, one that understood judicial procedures and applied these procedures to contest inquisitorial authority. This is not unique to the Italian peninsula. James Givens noted that early in France's inquisitorial history citizens recognized the "technologies of power" that inquisitors used and burned their registers in an attempt to eradicate evidence.[12] Individuals in the Italian peninsula found other methods of contesting inquisitorial authority using the tools provided by the burgeoning legal culture, such as using the appeal process to argue against procedural improprieties.

Then as now, growing recognition of legal procedures prompted individuals to find loopholes in the system, particularly to challenge a conviction, as a posthumous case against a canon of the church of Sta. Maria in Rieti demonstrates. On 30 August 1262 the Franciscan inquisitor of the Patrimony of St. Peter in Tuscany (*Tuscia Romana*), frà Gentilis, sentenced the deceased Palmerio Leonardi as a *fautor*, *credens*, and *receptator* of heterodoxy for sheltering, listening to, and adoring Cathar heretics. The inquisitor claimed Palmerio "had frequently said many heretical words in front of a number of people, damning the church sacraments and asserting many things that destroy the foundation of the catholic faith."[13] The inquisitor denounced Palmerio, posthumously excommunicated him, and ordered that his goods be confiscated. Two days

---

9. Field, *Beguine, the Angel, and the Inquisitor*, 86–88.
10. Foote, *Lordship, Reform*, esp. 145–60.
11. Petrucci, *Writers and Readers in Medieval Italy*, 169–235.
12. Given, "Inquisitors of Languedoc," 349.
13. D'Alatri, *L'inquisizione francescana*, 163.

later Palmerio's son Giovanni successfully appealed this sentence to Rieti's *podestà*, or chief magistrate.[14] The *podestà* explained:

> Giovanni, the natural son of master Palmerio Leonardi, together with his tutor Rainaldo Ranieri, [lodges a] protest in front of the *podestà* so that he will annul the document of the inquisitor frà Gentile, who sanctions the confiscation of goods that [Giovanni] inherited from his father. . . . [Giovanni] presented the motive that the sentence given against his goods is void, having been pronounced when he was absent and he was not cited. Thus it is against the statute of the commune of Rieti. The *podestà* received the protest and, listening to advisors and especially his judge, acknowledges the untouchable right that Giovanni possesses of his sequestered goods. He orders, therefore, that no one anymore dare molest him.[15]

The wily son Giovanni, with the help of his tutor who was knowledgeable about the communal statute that regulated sentencing procedures, used local laws to successfully challenge an inquisitorial conviction. The *podestà*, who was responsible for upholding the city statutes, deemed that proper legal procedure had not been observed and, as a consequence, not only the original sentence of confiscation but also the conviction that justified that confiscation was overturned.

Although Giovanni was successful, the inquisitor struck back by bringing out his big gun: the pope. Pope Urban IV had full authority over communal statutes in Rieti, which was part of the Papal States. As both the spiritual head and terrestrial lord of the city, the pope overrode the *podestà*'s decision and ordered in May 1263 that Giovanni hand over his deceased father's possessions to the cathedral chapter of Rieti. Ultimately Giovanni settled the matter by giving the bishop five hundred Lucchese lire to fulfill his obligation, a transaction documented on 8 July 1263.[16] Although he did not prevail, Giovanni's protest against the legality of the inquisitorial procedure produced results. His efforts meant that for almost a year Palmerio was once again just a deceased canon and not a sentenced heretic. It also postponed Giovanni's having to hand over his inherited possessions to the church. This delay probably allowed Giovanni to sell most of the goods or, more likely, to cut a private deal, since he ultimately paid the bishop in lire instead of in the property listed in the 1262 judgment.

---

14. See similar examples from Orvieto described in Lansing, *Power and Purity*, 147.
15. D'Alatri, *L'inquisizione francescana*, 165.
16. Ibid., 166–67.

The inquisitorial register of Bologna, spanning the years 1291 to 1310, provides evidence on a wider scale that people in Italy understood and appropriated the procedural elements of inquisitorial culture to their own ends. The register provides details of the reaction to the burning of Iuliano, Bompietro, Bonigrino, and the latter's wife, Rosaflora, as relapsed heretics in 1299. Their condemnations sparked a riot, but it is the comments of the observers that prompted the riot that is of particular interest. The testimony records that a number of citizens argued that at least one of the condemnations should be posthumously overturned because the inquisitors had failed in their pastoral duties by refusing to give Bompietro absolution when he sought the host.[17] The bystanders identified this failure, a common part of the execution of a sentence, as a procedural transgression that should have functioned as grounds for an appeal.

Finally, the history of Meco del Sacco documents a more successful example of the use of the appeals process, one specific to contested sanctity. As discussed previously, Meco overturned his own condemnation as a relapsed heretic not once but twice. He was sentenced as a heretic in 1334 and subsequently in 1337. Since he knew that this second conviction left him open to a capital sentence as a relapsed heretic, Meco traveled to the pope at Avignon. He argued that the sentence was invalid due to inquisitorial jealousy and greed at the thought of his forfeited property. The basis of his argument was not exactly a procedural lapse as in the previous examples but a legal infraction, what today one might identify as judicial misconduct. Meco's appeal was successful, and Pope Benedict XII absolved him.[18] When an inquisitor condemned him for a third time in 1344, Meco appealed the conviction on the same grounds as before and again won. In this case the possibility of appeal under Roman-influenced canon law, the presumption of an objective inquest, and the inclusion of official reviews of processes worked in Meco's favor.

Growing recognition of legal procedures prompted individuals to find loopholes in the system, or what might be called chinks in the opposition's armor. Increasingly accused heretics, their friends, and relatives learned from inquisitorial processes, appropriated aspects of legal procedure, and used this knowledge to challenge the prosecution or condemnation of the accused through appealing a conviction on procedural or other grounds. While not widely suc-

---

17. *Acta S. Officii*, vol. 1, no. 156, 18 May 1299, p. 167; see also nos. 166, 167, 173, 174, 184, 208, 211, 218, 219, 226, 227, 233, 234, 239, 248, 249, 260–63, 272, 275, 277, 282–85, 290, 293, 322, 334, 339, 346, 348, 366, 411, 414, 417, 419, 437, 456, 458, 463, 472, 477–79, 481, 490–92, 516, 518–20, 523, 526, 549–51, 553, and 555.

18. *Meco*, appendix 5, 287–89.

cessful, these efforts show that individuals were cognizant of the legal aspects of inquisitorial culture and commandeered parts of that system to contest inquisitors and dismantle the inquisitorial machine. In doing so, an opposing "inquisitorial culture" came to exist. These methods had to be adapted on a larger scale, however, such as when communities contested inquisitors who threatened a saint's cult. In this situation there were two means available: to undermine an inquisitorial process by initiating a canonization process, and to attack the legitimacy of inquisitors to hold office and, by extension, to fulfill their duties. Many of these cases demonstrate that challenging inquisitorial authority cut across the supposed dominant/subordinate divide, as local secular and regular clergy allied with lay members of different social classes to destabilize institutional hegemonic authority and protect their citizens and saints.

Canonization as Contestation

The initiation of a canonization inquiry, firmly within the new juridical *inquisitio* procedure, was a tool used to counteract inquisitorial probes or any rumors that a locally venerated person did not merit that veneration. Sometimes when inquisitors directly challenged the holiness of a person, this act had the potential to officially "redeem" him or her. If a community could gather enough support and money from prominent members for an inquiry, there was the chance that the popularity of the saint and the political influence of his or her supporters would prove the *force majeur*. When a pope agreed to review the merits of a disputed saint, a community had achieved an enormous victory. Although a positive outcome was not assured, the very fact that a pope decided there was enough evidence to initiate an inquiry struck a blow at the potential saint's detractors. In addition, it virtually guaranteed that the cult could continue uninterrupted, at least for the duration of the inquiry and/or possible future canonization process.

The circumstances surrounding the cult of Armanno Pungilupo, posthumously condemned as a relapsed heretic after having recanted Cathar beliefs fifteen years before his death in 1269, already has shown the protective aspect of a canonization inquiry. The bishop, Alberto Prandoni, probably intended to counteract any rumors of Armanno's relapse into heterodoxy by the speed with which he initiated a diocesan inquiry into his canonization.[19] Notwithstanding

---

19. Kleinberg, *Prophets in Their Own Country*, 38.

these efforts, in 1271 the Dominican inquisitor, frà Aldobrandino, placed the town under interdict and excommunicated the canons when they failed to comply with the inquisitor's injunction to exhume and burn Armanno's remains. At this point the Ferrarese became engaged in a battle of competing inquests, one into Armanno's sanctity and one into his heterodoxy. As a brief recapitulation, the cathedral chapter sent evidence of Armanno's miracles and evidence attesting to his orthodoxy to the papal legate in 1272, resulting in an overturning of the inquisitor's excommunication and interdict.[20] The story did not end there, for the debate raged through the later tenures of the Dominican inquisitors Florio, Egidio, and Guido of Vicenza and Bishops Giacomo and Federico of Ferrara. It also forced the intervention of Popes Gregory X, Honorius IV, and Boniface VIII (table 2). After a thirty-year struggle that divided the ecclesiastical community of Ferrara and threatened the peace and spiritual well-being of the city, in 1300 Boniface appointed a judicial council that decided Armanno indeed had been a relapsed Cathar.[21]

Carol Lansing described the documents regarding Armanno as "a sort of *Sic et Non*, since it includes both the Dominicans' excerpt from testimony to the inquisition, selected to prove Armanno's heresy, and the cathedral clergy's collection of depositions of witnesses proving his sanctity and healing miracles."[22] Like Abelard's famed twelfth-century work, in which he presented contrasting viewpoints on Christian doctrine by church authorities with no attempt to resolve the discrepancies, the documents regarding Armanno similarly present contrasting arguments with no resolution that accounts for all the evidence. The salient point, however, is that Armanno's supporters—comprised of both secular clergy and traditional regular clergy of Ferrara, as well as many citizens who attested to his miracles—fought against the inquisitors who tried to destroy Armanno's cult. They did so by turning the inquisitors' own procedure against them. Since the *inquisitio* was used to determine both heresy and sanctity, the bishop successfully appealed the inquisitor's exhumation and interdict in 1272 by requesting a canonization inquiry into Armanno's merits. In doing so, he ensured the continued existence of Armanno's cult for twenty-eight years.

The *vita* of Peter Crisci of Foligno similarly suggests that those who disparaged a disputed saint could be defeated by canonization efforts. After a couple of supposedly jealous friars accused Crisci of heresy, it was necessary for his supporters to assert he was never a heretic and promote his holiness in

---

20. *Itinerari*, 106–7.
21. *Itinerari*, 94–96.
22. Lansing, *Power and Purity*, 93.

order for the cult to survive. Crisci's *vita*, which justified his cult, would only be effective if it reached the proper authorities. The intended audience appears to have been the pope, for besides the life of the saint a list of miracles is also extant. Such documents were the core materials required for a canonization inquiry.[23] The testimony of witnesses about his miracles was notarized, attesting to the validity of the information and transforming the dossier into a legal document, which further demonstrates how the town of Foligno utilized the process of canonization to safeguard the existence of its local saint's cult.[24] A pope never canonized Crisci, but that is not to say that the efforts of his supporters to convince authorities that his cult was warranted were unsuccessful, for no further inquiries into his orthodoxy occurred. There are records of public feasts in his honor starting in 1340, only seventeen years after his death. The city officially recorded the feast in its statutes in 1381 and noted how much money it contributed to the festivities that year. In the mid-fourteenth century the cathedral church of S. Feliciano built a chapel dedicated to Crisci, and in 1385 the cathedral decorated the chapel with his image, complete with aureole. The cult of the once-suspected heretic Peter Crisci finally attained institutional validation in 1391. In that year Pope Boniface IX granted an indulgence to those who traveled to the cathedral of Foligno to celebrate Crisci's feast day on 19 July.[25] By bringing evidence of Crisci's sanctity to the attention of the papacy, the promoters of the cult circumvented the saint's detractors, including inquisitors. The community's efforts liberated Peter Crisci from the shadow of heresy, a process in which the canons of Ferrara, despite their valiant effort on behalf of Armanno Pungilupo, failed.

Those who supported the sanctity of the wine carrier Albert of Villa d'Ogna also availed themselves of the canonization procedure to protect their saint. Albert's cult was well supported across the regions of Emilia Romagna and Lombardy, with the main centers in Parma, Reggio, and Cremona.[26] Supplicants from surrounding towns, such as Pavia, visited his tomb at Cremona. Unlike Armanno Pungilupo or Peter Crisci, Albert of Villa d'Ogna's inquisitors never officially suspected him of heterodoxy. Yet some observers challenged his sanctity and even that he had any particular virtues. Salimbene, for example, asserted people "were made fools of" because Albert was not a true saint but only a "wine drinker" (*potator*) and "sinner" (*peccator*).[27] A formal

---

23. *AASS* IV, July 19, col. 663F; on lists of miracles, see Vauchez, *Sainthood in the Later Middle Ages*, 34–35.

24. Goodich, *Vita Perfecta*, 19.

25. Gorini, "Beatri Petri de Fulgineo Confessoris," 359–61. A copy of the papal letter, issued on 11 May 1391, is included on pp. 363–64.

26. *Chronicon Parmense*, 34–35.

27. *Chronicle of Salimbene de Adam*, 512–13.

canonization inquiry into Albert's merits did not reach the curia until the seventeenth century, when the papacy investigated materials of a number of "saints who enjoyed an immemorial cult."[28] The town of Cremona presented evidence supporting Albert's holiness in 1644 and 1746, without positive results. Nevertheless the existence of these materials, based on medieval documents, demonstrates that Albert's contemporaries expected a canonization inquiry, even though this was not met for some time.[29]

These efforts on Albert's behalf helped to stave off the suppression of his cult. Salimbene's negative opinion of Albert is not the only evidence that suggests his cult might otherwise have faced opposition. The fact that Parma was under interdict the same year that Albert died did not bode well for a new cult, especially if the object of veneration was a poor wine carrier from a family of farmers. Yet Cremona gathered enough support for Albert's cult to flourish without papal or inquisitorial challenges.[30] Thus a Cremonese statute of 1389 formally recognized 7 May as Albert's feast day, to be celebrated with an official ceremony.[31] The Parmeggiani similarly ensured the survival of Albert's cult in their city. The commune and guilds of Parma collaborated to buy a house in order to establish a hospice in Albert's name.[32] At the very least it would be awkward for authorities to seize communal property and destroy a charitable foundation because of unsubstantiated rumors against a local saint's holiness.

The changing political scene at the end of the fourteenth century perhaps explains the long delay in official acknowledgment of Albert's cult in Cremona. Toward the end of the Great Schism, Roman popes such as Boniface IX rewarded towns that had remained loyal to the Roman side by recognizing their local cults.[33] Thus the papal indulgence of 1391 for pilgrimage to Peter Crisci's tomb and Cremona's decision to incorporate Albert of Villa d'Ogna's feast into the civic calendar may have been a result of papal politics. Regardless of the reasons behind the late acceptance of these tolerated saints, whether tacit or explicit, both examples show that taking preliminary steps toward canonization could serve as a preemptive strike against opponents to a cult.

Orthodox devotees were not the only ones to use canonization procedures to challenge claims that their saints might have been heretics. Less-orthodox individuals also recognized that when powerful members of the laity or church

---

28. Vauchez, *Sainthood in the Later Middle Ages*, 567.
29. The process of canonization is in *Riti*, proc. 661 (Albert of Villa d'Ogna, 1744); for the history of the attempts, see Little, *Indispensible Immigrants*, 103–83.
30. *Chronicle of Salimbene de Adam*, 514.
31. *AASS* II, May 7, col. 281A.
32. Vauchez, *Sainthood in the Later Middle Ages*, 236.
33. Ibid., 90n20.

hierarchy supported efforts for a canonization inquiry, a private sect could live on borrowed time shielded by the public cult. There is evidence, for instance, that the Guglielmites might have tried to pave the way for Guglielma of Milan's eventual canonization by garnering support from her royal relatives. The sectarian Andrea Saramita testified that after Guglielma's death in 1281 he traveled to Bohemia, where she supposedly had been born as a member of the ruling house.[34] His companion on the trip was Mirano da Garbagnate, the priest of the church of S. Fermo and the "special secretary" of Andrea and the other leader of the sect, Maifreda da Pirovano. Andrea claimed he verified on this trip that Guglielma had been the daughter of the king of Bohemia, although when the group reached Prague they found that the reigning king had died.[35] This information corresponds to historical facts, for King Ottokar II had died in battle in 1278 when his heir, Wenceslas II, was only a child.[36] Although there is no evidence outside of Andrea's and Mirano's testimonies that any sectarians went to Bohemia, Barbara Newman persuasively argues in favor of the validity of their accounts, noting, "If [Andrea] had not in fact visited Prague in 1282, he could hardly have known in 1300 that there had been a Bohemian interregnum precisely eighteen years earlier."[37] The purpose of the trip was not simply to ascertain Guglielma's heritage. Andrea, questioned on this point, claimed he also went to tell the king that his kinswoman was deceased and to obtain funds from the royal family for Guglielma's proper burial. The inquisitor, either doubting this testimony or having information to the contrary, asked Andrea "if he went to the said king with the intention to acquire the king with him [i.e., on his side] so that Guglielma would be canonized in the Church."[38] Andrea responded that this was not his original aim but, nevertheless, he was unable to secure such support.[39] Regardless of Andrea's initial protests to the contrary, it is likely that one motivation for the trip across the Alps was to garner financial and political assistance from the Bohemian royal house for Guglielma's canonization.

The failed trip did not destroy followers' hopes that the pope would canonize their saint. The witness Bellacara Carentano attested that the group discussed moving Guglielma's remains to her native Bohemia after Andrea and Mirano's unfruitful trip, and the sectarians made clothes for Guglielma's body

---

34. *Milano 1300*, 58, 64, and 70.

35. *Milano 1300*, 58.

36. Polc, *Agnes von Böhmen*, 136–41, cited in Newman, "Heretic Saint," 9–10.

37. Newman, "Agnes of Prague," 562.

38. *Milano 1300*, 58.

39. *Milano 1300*, Otto of Brandenburg was the guardian of the future King Wenceslas. He was acting as regent and was hostile to the royal house (Polc, *Agnes von Böhmen*, 141, cited in Newman, "Agnes of Prague," 559).

for a translation, presumably to follow her canonization.[40] That a number of sectarians were under the apprehension that Guglielma would achieve sainthood is clear from the testimony of Stephano da Crimella, although he did not expect Guglielma's body to be transferred out of the country. Stephano stated "that after [Andrea's trip to Bohemia] he made four ecclesiastical tunics without sleeves in honor and reverence of the said Guglielma, and that he received in his house certain poles from which would be made a certain dais or steps for climbing to the altar [dedicated to] Guglielma, so that there a mass could be celebrated when Guglielma was canonized as the said Andrea stated to this same witness Stephano."[41] The trip to Bohemia occurred before inquisitors ever turned their attention to the sectarians. If Andrea and Mirano made the journey, they must have gone between January 1282, when a war between Milan and Lodi finally ended, causing the roads to reopen, and 1283, when the interregnum in Bohemia ended. The subsequent plans for canonization, however, must have occurred during and/or after the Guglielmites knew they were under suspicion after the questioning of some sectarians in 1284.

The Guglielmites' hope for and attempt to gain support for a canonization process was shrewd. If the king of Bohemia acknowledged Guglielma to be a member of the family, it would verify her relationship to the holy women Margaret of Hungary and Agnes of Bohemia, thus increasing the possibility that an inquiry would occur. If an inquiry led to canonization, Christendom would recognize the woman whom sectarians believed to be the incarnation of the Holy Spirit as a holy woman, even if not divine as the sectarians believed. The group could participate in her public cult, and this recognition could perhaps decrease inquisitorial pressure, allowing the sect to exist unmolested and to venerate Guglielma as they saw fit privately. Or it could be a stepping-stone for the larger aims of the sectarians to put a new pope and cardinals at the helm of a revitalized church with revised Scripture. In either case, canonization efforts justified their public devotion and increased the likelihood that sectarians could function without prosecution.

Clearly citizens were aware of how official recognition of a regional saint could shield the saint, or his or her devotees, from suspicion. The opening of a canonization inquiry did not de facto alter the local perception of a saint, since for an individual to become a saint in the first place there was already a consensus on his or her holiness. Nor did it necessarily mean that these communities were operating within the system and that their attempts showed respect for papal authority. Papal canonization could be a mere tool to ensure

---

40. *Milano 1300*, 64.
41. *Milano 1300*, 234–36.

the survival of a cult, rather than a deep conviction that canonization conferred some special grace on someone that the community had already accepted as a saint. As André Vauchez commented, "Canonization[s] . . . were regarded as . . . largely superfluous procedures, since, in [the community's] eyes, the result was known in advance."[42] We see this in the *vita* that was part of the materials gathered for Facio of Cremona's aborted inquiry, which stated that "although he had not been canonized by the Church militant on earth, he had been received by the Church triumphant in Heaven."[43] The *vitae* of Bevignate of Perugia and Anthony Peregrinus of Padua, among other disputed saints, contain similar statements. In addition, however, canonization inquiries for some questionable groups such as the Guglielmites served another purpose. It allowed their members to proactively contest inquisitorial power when they expected inquisitorial zeal or papal censure of their actions. Overall, the request for papal canonization was a useful tool to allow a saint's cult to flourish unmolested and to challenge inquisitors' authority by adapting one element of their procedural arsenal, the *inquisitio*, for a group or community's own ends.

Questioning Legitimacy

A final juridical method for challenging inquisitorial authority was attacking the validity of specific inquisitors to hold office. As with the other approaches, this technique demonstrated cognizance of the legal aspects of inquisitorial culture. It also showed familiarity with the institutional hierarchy through understanding the chain of command. Specific examples illustrate how very different members of a community, including clergy and laity, could unify in order to protect local cults from potentially threatening outside forces. The inquisitorial process of the Guglielmites in 1300 details a complex yet remarkable example of this strategy. While Guglielma of Milan's inner circle of devotees had joined the Benedictines of Chiaravalle (where Guglielma was interred) in promoting her as a saint, some of those devotees also were struggling for their own survival against increasing inquisitorial pressure. The orthodoxy of the sectarians was directly related to the orthodoxy of Guglielma—who could be, and ultimately was, tainted by association—and therefore by extension to the continued existence of her cult. The sectarians' defiance of the Milanese inquisitors reveals an oppositional inquisitorial culture in which strange bedfellows

---

42. Vauchez, *Sainthood in the Later Middle Ages*, 99.
43. Vauchez, "Sainteté laïque aux XIIIe siècle," 36.

united to stop the process by protesting the inquisitors' institutional authority. Three heterodox devotees, two Cistercian monks, an archbishop, a Franciscan friar, and a renegade tertiary who himself had been condemned for heresy banded together to impede the actions of the Dominican inquisitors. Their plan was to debilitate the inquisitors by contesting their legal right to hold office.

When rumors began to circulate in 1300 that inquisitors once again suspected some sectarians of heresy, one of the group's leaders, Andrea Saramita, along with the sectarian Beltramo da Ferno, a physician, traveled to the local Franciscan convent to consult with Beltramo's brother Daniel, a member of that community. Daniel told the two sectarians that the inquisitors of Milan had been suspended from office. He knew this because another man, Pagano of Petrasancta, had in his possession a copy of a papal decree.[44] Upon their request Pagano searched for but could not locate the document even when the sectarians helped him look for it among his possessions, those of his notary, and those of the archbishop of Milan's notary. Andrea, Beltramo, and Daniel returned to the Franciscan convent. Pagano met them there sometime later and told the sectarians, "It would be worth 25 lire to him, if he had or was able to obtain for sure the official apparatus through which the inquisitors introduced themselves [as such], because if he had this he would send it to the curia and their case [i.e., the legal proceedings] would be terminated."[45] Pagano at some point providentially found the document after two searches through his possessions, although it is not known if any money exchanged hands.

Henry Charles Lea claimed Pagano was a Spiritual Franciscan, but the continuator of Galvano Fiamma's chronicle of the Dominican Order in Milan identified Pagano as a member of the lay confraternity the Order of the Knights of the Blessed Virgin Mary (*Ordo Militiae Beatae Mariae Virginis Gloriosae*), popularly known as the *frati gaudenti*.[46] Pagano had a strong antipathy to the

---

44. *Milano 1300*, 204.

45. *Milano 1300*, 206.

46. Lea, *History of the Inquisition*, 3:37; his conclusion is based on the *Annales Minorum seu Trium Ordinum*, ann. 1295, no. 14; cf. "La cronaca maggiore," 360; see also Wessley, "Enthusiasm and Heresy," 121. On the history of this confraternity in Italy, see Meersseman, "Etudes sur les anciennes confréries dominicaines," 303–5. Although the confraternity was founded by the Dominican Bartholomew of Vicenza and professed members were governed by the Rule of St. Augustine just like the Dominicans, these facts do not preclude the possibility that Pagano was or had been both a Franciscan tertiary and a *frater gaudenti*. The Dominicans' control over this order was not very tight, as Meersseman noted, and the statute of the order, approved by Urban IV in 1261, was drawn up by a Franciscan (304). Salimbene speaks disparagingly of the confraternity, claiming its members did not do any good works though they were wealthy and powerful, were avaricious and pleasure-loving thieves, and were of no use to the church (*Chronicle of Salimbene de Adam*, 477–78).

Milanese inquisitors, who had questioned and condemned him in 1289 for hiding heretics and breaking bread with them.[47] Of the six inquisitors involved in his case, three also later had a starring role in the Guglielmite process: Guido da Cocconato, Rainerio da Pirovano, and Tommaso da Como.[48] Pagano eventually appealed his sentence, and the case was recalled to the pope. While Boniface VIII was examining the matter the presiding inquisitor of Milan, Tommaso da Como, reimposed his sentence. Boniface VIII subsequently suspended frà Tommaso for this action in 1296, although he also arbitrated in 1301 that Pagano had to pay a fine as an aider of heretics.[49] The order suspending the inquisitor undoubtedly was the document that Pagano claimed to have mislaid.

Boniface VIII's letter only suspended frà Tommaso from office. The letter Pagano eventually produced seemingly suspended the authority of all inquisitors operating in Milan. According to the testimony of Beltramo da Fermo, "Reading there the said letter among themselves, this brother Daniel said that he did not doubt that the inquisitors of the Order of Preachers or other inquisitors were unable to perform the inquisitorial office nor to introduce themselves into the inquisitorial office in the city and district of Milan."[50] It is possible that Pagano or his notary altered or forged the document or that the sectarians, in their desire to stop the inquiry, overzealously interpreted its words in their favor. The Franciscan Daniel da Ferno subsequently suggested that Andrea and Beltramo get counsel. Following his advice, they approached the abbot of Chiaravalle and a monk (and future abbot) named Marchisio da Veddano.[51] The relationship between the abbey of Chiaravalle and the leading

----

47. "Cronaca maggiore," 334. The continuator called him "amicissimus tunc ordinis" because he had taken care of a sick friar in 1286 (360).

48. The inquisitors who questioned and condemned Pagano in 1289 were Guido da Cocconato, Rainerio da Pirovano, William de Aquis, Thomas de Mugio, and Julian Reginus (Wessley, "Enthusiasm and Heresy," 121n2). Tommaso da Como became involved with Pagano's appeal in 1296 and was the inquisitor who questioned one of the Guglielmites, Gerard da Novazzano, the same year and who took the testimony of the *converso* Marchisio Secco about the sectarians in 1302.

49. In 1304 Pagano still was complaining to Rome that inquisitors were persecuting him. His will included this statement: "Item dico et protestor et ad memoriam reduco quod inquisitores heretice pravitatis gravissime me molestaverunt et turbaverunt contra deum et iustitiam quia dicebant me esse culpabillem de crimine heresies quod verum non erat" ("Testamentum . . . fratis Pagani de Patra Sancta," Milan, Archivio di Stato di Milano, Archivio Diplomatico, S. Francesco, ms. n. 406, 1304, n. 2, XLVII, [103], f. 1r).

50. *Milano 1300*, 206.

51. The Milanese chronicle of Galvano Fiammo contains an entry for 1247 mentioning a certain lady Petra da Veddano: "Monasterium de Vinea monialium ordinis secundum consilium et ordinationem beati Petri martiris institutum est. Ubi sciendum quod domina Petra da Vedano duas genuit filias de viro suo et patris sui heredes, quas fecit sorores, de quarum bonis temporalibus domus de Vinea fundata est secundum consilium, ut dictum est, beati Petri. In processu autem temporis alique sorores pererexerunt Vedanum ibique habitare ceperunt. Quapropter divisa est prefata hereditas per medium" ("Cronaca maggiore," 327–28). If the monk Marchisio was indeed related to the benefactress

sectarian Andrea Saramita, and the monastery's desire to retain Guglielma as its patron saint, undoubtedly influenced the abbot's decision to help the group. The clerics suggested that the sectarians acquire a copy of the letter from Pagano's notary, which Beltramo and another devotee, Simonino Colliono, proceeded to do. The abbot and Marchisio then brought the case to the archbishop of Milan, Francesco I Fontana of Parma (r. 1296–1308), whom Boniface VIII had appointed in 1296. Upon their return the monks informed the sectarians that the "Lord Archbishop truly would concern himself in the investigation, either in conjunction with the inquisitors or alone."[52] This reaction is notable, for one of the most remarkable aspects of the inquisitorial investigation to this point was that the archbishop and his representatives were conspicuously absent. Integral aspects of the inquisitorial procedure included episcopal cooperation and funding, yet the archbishop of Milan seems to have intentionally distanced himself from the proceedings up to this point.[53] His assurance that he would look into the situation, however, suggests that whatever document Pagano produced seems to have been persuasive. The archbishop, or one of his emissaries, almost certainly apprised the inquisitors of the situation. On 26 July 1300, thirty-two days before Beltramo da Ferno's detailed testimony regarding the efforts to stop the inquisitorial scrutiny of the sect, the inquisitor Guido da Cocconato asked Iacopo da Ferno (the father of Beltramo and Daniel) "if on the preceding Saturday, when the inquisitor had cited him, he said or others said to themselves that this inquisitor could not exercise the inquisitorial office and that the inquisitorial office had been taken away from the inquisitor."[54] The timing shows that inquisitors had knowledge of the Guglielmites' efforts well before the devotee Beltramo informed them of the details.

These events highlight two significant factors regarding inquisitorial culture and how it could be used to protect cults. First, people involved understood the chain of command in the inquisitorial hierarchy and the tools, such as written records, that were part of the inquisitor's arsenal. In this example there was an understanding that inquisitors were under the direct authority of the pope and a recognition of the delicate balance of power between the archbishop and inquisitors that the Guglielmite camp tried to use to its advantage. Community members also appropriated one of the foundational aspects of

---

of Peter Martyr's monastery of Vinea, Petra da Veddano, it is an ironic twist that fifty-three years later he was involved in helping a group antagonistic to the Dominican inquisitors.

52. *Milano 1300*, 208.

53. Elliott, *Proving Woman*, 122–23.

54. *Milano 1300*, 68.

inquisitorial culture: legal documents to confirm authority, gather evidence, and secure official convictions. Guglielma's supporters used such documents to turn the tables and contest inquisitorial authority. Second, the collusion between the parties exhibits how contesting inquisitors produced unexpected relationships. The Guglielmites, in a bid for survival, called on a kinsman who happened to be a Franciscan friar for advice. A disgruntled tertiary with a vendetta against the Milanese inquisitors colluded with the sectarians and provided them with a smoking gun to stop an inquisitorial investigation. The monks of Chiaravalle—in gratitude for Andrea's help in the transference of Guglielma's remains, eager to maintain the flourishing cult surrounding Guglielma, and perhaps out of dislike for the Dominicans—provided the Guglielmites with ecclesiastical support for their endeavor. In this effort, they enlisted the aid of the archbishop of Milan, who himself may have been displeased with the amount of power that the Dominican inquisitors wielded in his city. The local clerical elite's credulity and willingness to get involved with the suspect sectarians (whom inquisitors had already questioned twice) and the somewhat unsavory Pagano suggests that, for them, local concerns and autonomy trumped institutional allegiance.

While the claim that a pope had suspended inquisitors from office might be the most direct means of railroading an inquiry, it was not the only one. Another way potentially to cripple inquisitorial power was to accuse the inquisitor of achieving his office through simony. In 1299 in Bologna a citizen used this allegation to justify a rejection of inquisitorial authority. A Dominican, Pietro Zanchari, testified regarding a certain Filisino: "This man Filisino said that he neither attended to nor feared the inquisitor, nor the office of the inquisition, because the inquisitor held that office unjustly, against God, and that he bought the said office in the Roman curia for two thousand golden florins."[55] The argument is that the means by which the inquisitor attained his post rendered him powerless and tainted the office. This and similar views also demonstrate an understanding of the inquisitorial machine and the hierarchy of institutional authority.

Other strategies evolved that served not just to thwart an individual inquisitor but also to attack the legitimacy of the entire judicial process. One means was to claim the presiding pope, in charge of all inquisitors, had illegitimately obtained his office. This dangerous accusation risked provoking the ire and the full prosecutorial powers of the papacy, but in theory it would dismantle the entire inquisitorial process. The Guglielmites, for instance, accused Boniface

---

55. *Acta S. Officii*, vol. 1, no. 412, 16 June 1299, p. 252; see also nos. 422, 425, 427, and 441.

VIII of not being the true pope as a second means of attack, in case the document they obtained from Pagano, purportedly suspending inquisitors, failed. When inquisitors did challenge the document's authenticity, the group attacked the pope. The sectarian and priest Mirano da Garbagnate testified that Andrea Saramita had told him, "This present pope was not able to absolve or condemn, because he was not justly created, nor can even the archbishop of Milan absolve or condemn, since this archbishop was made by this pope."[56] Inquisitors asked Andrea if he had stated, "The lord Pope Boniface, who is now [pope], is not the true pope."[57] Andrea denied the charge, but the deponent Dionese da Novati attested Andrea and Maifreda da Pirovano often said to many people that Boniface VIII was not the true pope because he ascended to Peter's seat while another pope was still living.[58] The reference here is to Pope Celestine V, who had abdicated the papal seat and ultimately died while imprisoned at the orders of Boniface VIII. The argument was that Boniface had illegally assumed office and hastened the "real" pope's demise; therefore his appointees (the archbishop but also the inquisitors) had no legitimate power. Once the sectarians enlisted the archbishop in their cause, they apparently decided that challenging the inquisitors' right to hold office was a better strategy than alienating the pope by claiming he had no valid authority.

Citizens of Bologna voiced similar concerns about Boniface VIII. One Bolognese deponent articulated some of the reasons why Boniface's election was considered illegal, explaining, "*Ser* Filippo [the son of a Bolognese judge, Aldrevandino de Sala] said that the lord pope Boniface VIII was not the pope in the truth of the matter nor could he be by law because he was elected through simony and he [i.e., Filippo] called him lord Benedict and not the pope lord Boniface. . . . The said lord Boniface or Benedict held lord Celestine or lord Peter of Morrone in prison and caused him to die in prison."[59] Filippo therefore claimed Boniface's election was illegal for two reasons. On the one hand, he had bought his office. On the other hand, he had imprisoned Peter of Morrone (the former Pope Celestine V) and through this act Celestine died, effectively making Boniface a murderer. Another man, Bertolino, testified he had heard a woman named Parta declare, "Pope Boniface, who is now pope, was not nor was he able to be pope, because he caused Pope Celestine to be

---

56. *Milano 1300*, 74.
57. *Milano 1300*, 172.
58. *Milano 1300*, 210.
59. Testimony of Gerard, judge of Bologna, *Acta S. Officii*, vol. 2, no. 598, 30 January 1300, p. 374.

killed."[60] The circumstances of Boniface's election justified a rejection of inquisitorial sentences and vindicated any violence against Boniface or his agents. Another Bolognese witness maintained that "if he had the ability, he would gladly kill lord Pope Boniface and the cardinals, because this lord Pope Boniface had the best man in the world killed, namely Pope Celestine, who was the true pope, and that this Pope Boniface was not pope de jure, although he was pope de facto."[61] The deponent maintained that since Boniface was not lawfully pope, then both he and his appointees should be removed from office. Most interesting in this instance is the exacting legal distinction that was made, showing the appropriation of the juridical inquisitorial culture.

Some twenty years later, other individuals similarly challenged the pontificate of John XXII. Opponents rejected this pontiff's spiritual authority on two premises: he was a heretic and he was illegally elected. Like Boniface VIII before him, John XXII was a divisive force within Italy. The strategy of destroying enemies by utilizing the charge of heresy, first deployed almost a century prior in Pope Innocent IV's crusade against Ezzelino da Romano, was perfected by John XXII. Ghibelline factions subsequently turned the tables, accusing the pope himself of being a heretic. In Todi, when the emperor Louis of Bavaria and the antipope Nicholas V arrived in 1329, the priest of S. Fortunato preached to the public that Nicholas V, the "true" pope, had excommunicated Jean de Cahors (i.e., Pope John XXII), who had been born a heretic.[62] The Spiritual Franciscans in particular frequently justified their dissent by claiming that John XXII's ideas were heretical. When the pope ruled in favor of the Conventuals, asserting Christ and his apostles had in fact owned property, the Spirituals alleged that his decision overturned the ruling of one of his predecessors, Pope Nicholas III. They stated that this act was both illegal and heterodox, since contradicting a previous papal ruling was to suggest papal error. This conflicted with the new concept of papal infallibility that popes would promote but that was also upheld by Peter John Olivi, a Spiritual widely perceived as a saint in those circles.[63] In the late fourteenth century, *fraticelli* such as frà Michele Berti da Calci still invoked this rationale as the basis for rejection of papal authority.

---

60. Testimony of Bertholinus Blaxii de Mançolino, *Acta S. Officii*, vol. 1, no. 35, 21 May 1299, p. 63.

61. Henricus of the monastery of S. Maria de Monte Armato testifying what he heard from his fellow monk Iacobus Flemenghi of Bologna, *Acta S. Officii*, vol. 1, no. 44, 12 June 1299, p. 73.

62. Fumi, "Eretici e ribelli," 13.

63. For an introduction to the concept of papal infallibility see Tierney, *Origins of Papal Infallibility*; for an opposing interpretation, see Heft, *John XXII and Papal Teaching Authority*, 193–201. For Peter John Olivi's life and writings, see Burr, *Olivi and Franciscan Poverty*, and the collected essays in Boureau and Piron, *Pierre de Jean Olivi*. For his cult, see Burr, *Persecution of Peter Olivi*, esp. 87–88, and Burnham, *So Great a Light*, 20–24.

Da Calci claimed that Pope John XXII had become a heretic by rejecting Nicholas III's 1279 bull *Exiit qui seminat*, which stated the Franciscans only had use of the property and goods that had been given to them. The account of his inquisition claimed that "frà Michele, responding [to inquisitors], said that Christ, in the form of a man, showed the way of perfection, nor did his apostles have anything, singly or in common if it was not simple *de facto* usage. And [it was read] how he held Pope John XXII to be a heretic, and his decretals [heretical]. Michele responded, 'It is well, because he did the aforesaid heresy.'"[64] He supposedly then argued that all successive ecclesiastical officials who accepted Pope John XXII's overturning of Nicholas III's bull were devoid of spiritual authority because they were supporters of his heresy.[65]

Opponents of Pope John XXII also used the circumstances of his election to challenge his power and that of the inquisitors who did his bidding. One of the pope's political enemies was the Este family, formerly the leaders of a strong Guelph faction in and around Ferrara. By the first quarter of the fourteenth century, their territorial interests had come into conflict with those of the papacy. Pope John XXII had Rainaldo and Obizzo d'Este charged with heresy in 1321. They countered by arguing "that that man, who is called pope, is not the true pope, because he was not elected at Rome in the seat of blessed Peter, nor ever came to the said seat nor was there, and therefore in the truth of the matter is not pope, nor were those things that he did and said of any worth."[66] Rainaldo and Obizzo thus contended that only popes elected in Rome and who resided there were legitimate. Although there was no real canonical foundation for this argument, it resonated with the emotions of Italian citizens during the Avignon papacy. More importantly, they used it as a strategy to halt an inquisitorial process. Like the Guglielmites, the Este family recognized the links of the inquisitorial chain of command and attempted to thwart inquisitors by attacking the legitimacy of the man who bound them to office.

In sum, by the late thirteenth century there was a robust local understanding of legal and inquisitorial culture, even by those of a lower socioeconomic status who may have been illiterate. Individuals and groups took various tactics to challenge the authority of inquisitors, using elements of the legal pro-

---

64. Piazza, "La passione di frate Michele," 251. The bull is in *Les Registres de Nicolas III*, no. 564.

65. Piazza, "La passione di frate Michele," 227.

66. Bock, "Der Este-Prozess," 59–60; see also similar comments on p. 61. Another enemy of John XXII also charged with heresy, Muzio di Francesco d'Assisi, denounced John XXII for the same reasons. See the testimony of *magister* Andrea: "Mutius dixit quod quilibet papa debet sedere in sede beati Petri Rome et quia presens papa Iohannes non sedit in dicta sede ideo non est papa" (Brufani, *Eresia di un ribelle*, 146–47); see also the remarks of Nicolutius Ioli: "Dixit quod audivit Mutium dicentem quod iste papa non erat papa de iure quia non sedet in sede Petri" (190).

cess to overturn or undermine convictions that could jeopardize cults of local saints. Moreover, these efforts were not limited to the laity. Clerics also voiced opposition to popes and/or their inquisitorial agents or joined with laypeople to thwart inquiries. The desire to protect local cults, along with the antipapal and antimendicant attitudes detailed in previous chapters, became the impetus for direct action against inquisitors, with these instances epitomizing the creation of disputed saints in late medieval Italy.

Conclusion

A variety of factors contributed to the phenomenon of disputed saints in northern and central Italy. As the members of nascent signorial governments gradually defined themselves as communities, partly through conflict and their complicated relationship with the papacy, new local saints emerged as symbols of communal identity. Many of these saints became the focus of a cult precisely because they were believed to have assisted the city in an important battle, assuming the role of protectors in the midst of strife alongside saints connected to their foundation myths. Conversely, Bologna supposedly did not appreciate St. Anthony of Padua, since on his feast day in 1275 the exiled party of the Lambertazzi, sympathetic to the Holy Roman Emperor, defeated the Bolognese faction supportive of the pope.[1] Bonvicino da Riva's 1288 description of Milan attests to this crucial political role of saints' cults. His history of Milan, written shortly after the pope lifted an interdict and when the Visconti and Della Torre families battled for control of the city, argued, "Many foreign tyrants have tried to install here the seat of their tyranny, yet the divine goodness . . . together with that of our patron St. Ambrose . . . has often defended the city from tyrannical rage. . . . [Milan is] the wonderful splendor of the world, the city replete with manifold graces, the venerable city, consecrated by the blood of many martyrs. . . . It

---

1. Webb, *Patrons and Defenders*, 149–50.

not only deserves to be called a second Rome . . . but also [I say] that the seat of the papacy should be transferred here."[2] The late 1280s is also when the cult of the disputed saint Guglielma took shape in Milan, both among her special devotees and in various religious houses across the city. Bonvicino's political propaganda based on holy patrons and the promotion of new cults such as Guglielma's during a contentious time in Milan is a pattern repeated in examples in this book from other towns in other times.

Bonvicino's remarks about how Milan's holiness rivaled Rome because of its saints articulated an aggrandizement and expansionism that created discord between *signori* such as the Visconti and popes, as well as between the various lords themselves who fought for control within towns, such as the Visconti and Della Torre. For Bonvicino, the Milanese shared an identity that set them apart from other citizens, one validated by the graces its saints bestowed upon his city. According to Bonvicino, certain saints chose Milan for the moment of their eternal glory. These holy persons rewarded the Milanese for their merit by granting them protection. Conversely, the worthiness of Milan's local saints contributed to the prestige of the town. Thus, Bonvicino can favorably compare his city to Rome, and even suggest that Rome is no longer qualified to be the seat of Christendom. Milan, because of its many saints and moral integrity, deserved the honor. His characterization illustrates the pride that helped foster repeated wars between the towns of northern and central Italy and that these wars also produced. The demise of the communal form of government in Italy and the reemergence of lay territorial lordships in these centuries, and the economic and social ruptures that resulted, meant that a variety of factions sought cohesion and communal identity in their hometowns. The communal celebration of local saintly patrons contributed to this identity. Public rituals associated with a saint's cult mediated between disparate groups, creating the illusion of a cohesive community. Milan's saints become part of Bonvicino's political propaganda, and new cults fostered loyalty even in the face of papal or inquisitorial disapprobation or condemnation.

A significant aspect of late medieval sanctity that emerges from this study is that both popes and communities used saints as political weapons. Shortly after Bonvicino wrote his panegyric, when the Ghibelline Visconti emerged victorious, they became involved in a decades-long quarrel with the papacy. It is amid such tensions that the phenomenon of the disputed saint flourished, like Guglielma's cult with its connection to the Visconti. As described throughout this study, there were many people in the thirteenth and fourteenth centuries who lived the *vita apostolica* and could fulfill the role of new holy patrons,

---

2. Da Riva, *De Magnalibus Urbis Mediolani*, translated in Dean, *Towns of Italy*, 11–16.

in Milan and elsewhere. The disputed saint was not just a manifestation of a gap between local and papal interests, nor simply a disjunction between popular and official concepts of the holy. Emerging out of the hubs of political unrest in northern and central Italy, disputed saints became central to communities' efforts to achieve religious and political autonomy. Communities used the creation of cults and the canonization process, among other tools available, in a grassroots effort to get things done and cement an independent identity.[3]

Within these towns the support of a powerful Guelph family or the aid of someone directly connected to the papacy increased the odds of one of these saints achieving canonization, such as occurred for Margaret of Cortona. Politics did not supplant spiritual concerns; there is no example, for instance, of an undeserving rapscallion, Boccaccio's literal *ser* Ciappelletto, whom a pope officially endorsed solely because the saint's devotees supported papal interests. Nonetheless, popes repaid loyalty by sanctioning saints. They tended to use canonization as a carrot on a stick, rewarding those who conformed to papal wishes. This process is clear in the relations between the papacy and the mendicant orders. As inquisitors the mendicant friars were answerable only to the pope, which in certain ways circumvented the normal church hierarchy. Their function as papal agents explains the official success and promotion of saints from among these orders in the later Middle Ages.[4] Yet the papacy's largesse in bestowing the honors of sainthood on friars paralleled papal perceptions of mendicant obedience. Richard Kieckhefer noted that although popes favored more Franciscans than Dominicans as saints in the thirteenth century, in the fourteenth century the number of Dominican saints increased under the reform movement of Raymond of Capua, while Franciscan saints declined in the wake of the controversy over the observant Franciscan wing called the Spirituals.[5]

Popes also punished perceived disobedience by obstructing a saint's cult. The papacy's arsenal against potential secular and ecclesiastical rivals included other weapons: inquisitors to suppress cults, interdicts, and withholding requests for canonization inquiries in rebellious towns. The chances of a local saint achieving canonization dropped dramatically if a pope considered the loyalty of a town that was promoting his or her cult to be suspect. The commu-

---

3. For another method, that of using classical symbols and myths, see the examples in Beneš, *Urban Legends*.

4. Mendicant saints were almost exclusively Italian, as compared to the saints who flourished in England and France who were either bishops, members of the traditional monastic orders, or aristocratic laymen (Vauchez, *Sainthood in the Later Middle Ages*, 263; see also 113–22).

5. Kieckhefer, *Unquiet Souls*, 48.

nities that found themselves and their saints the objects of retributive scrutiny did not submit to papal pressures or give up their hopes for official canonization. In fact, the reverse is often true. When a controversy over a prospective saint's merits occurred, towns did not hesitate to use their saints' cults as a vehicle with which to challenge the papal monarchy and its spiritual and political power. The cult of a local saint, which helped to unite disparate groups who sought a patron and protector, was too important for the spiritual and political well-being of these cities that were divided by factionalism and destabilized by changing forms of government. The fact that the papacy canonized or beatified a good number of late medieval disputed saints in the seventeenth and eighteenth centuries amply demonstrates the fortitude of these cities, the significance of saints for communal identity, and the power of collective memory.

Meanwhile, popes tried to crush new magnates and to extend their influence in the north of the Italian peninsula, using both spiritual and political weapons to secure what they regarded as their earthly entitlement. In the north, popes employed mercenaries and Angevin knights to push back their rivals and sent out religious armies, such as crusaders or inquisitors, to strike the final blow at their enemies (e.g., the Visconti or, eventually, the Este). They excommunicated or charged with heresy these lords who were the pope's competitors for land and power, as occurred most notably in the cases of the Visconti in Milan and the Estes in Ferrara. On a larger scale, towns that refrained from acknowledging the papacy's spiritual and/or terrestrial overlordship could soon discover they were under interdict, their patron saints unable to obtain a papal canonization inquiry, and, sometimes, their local holy men and women the object of inquisitorial investigations. Political considerations lessened the chances for official recognition of their cult, irrespective of the saint's spiritual mettle.

Yet when popes became too deeply involved in Italian secular politics, they lost some of their prestige as vicars of Christ. The battles that bore the stamp of papal partisanship, or the use of religious weapons to fight a political war, hastened the identification of the pope as just another aggressive lord. The frequent excommunications and interdicts of whole towns in regions such as the Papal States undercut the value of this spiritual punishment as a deterrent, as in Ascoli. This happened in other areas too; Parma, for instance, was under interdict three times in a thirty-year period. In addition, the inefficacy of inquisitorial tools in Italy undoubtedly aided the creation and continuation of disputed saints and their cults. If inquisitors were unable to enforce their punishments (chapter 8), communities had more power, ability, and incentive to venerate whomever they chose. Notable instances include the town of Nocera, which formed a cult around its local prophet Tommasuccio, although he was imprisoned for heresy three times under the unreliable Guelph family of the Trinci. Another is Ascoli's championing of Meco del Sacco, actually condemned for heresy three times, in the midst of the town being under interdict for three long periods within seventy years. Still another is the small village of Brunate, near Lake Como above Milan, which resurrected the cult of Guglielma of Milan from the vestiges of memory during the height of Visconti rule after inquisitors had burned Guglielma's remains in 1300 to suppress her cult. While these are extreme examples, all of the types of disputed sanctity discussed in this book demonstrate a similar flouting of papal desires to a greater or lesser extent. In addition, the seemingly avaricious and cruel actions of inquisitors further diminished papal authority, as did stories of vice at Avignon, tales of corruption and heresy among the curia, and, for a significant portion of the fourteenth century, anger over the "Babylonian Captivity," or the move of the papal court from Rome to Avignon that lasted from 1309 to 1378. Given these facts, it is significant that the period of the disputed saint came to an end shortly after Pope Gregory XI tried to reestablish the papal seat in Rome. It was the papacy's continuing efforts to consolidate its power in Italy between 1250 and 1400 that produced religious disaffection in the region, rather than what appears in hindsight to be the far more challenging time of the Great Schism that would soon commence.

All these processes—canonization efforts by both the papacy and members of communities and challenges to papal and inquisitorial authority—were hyperlocal. This book, therefore, revises part of the overarching framework of Andre Vauchez's seminal study of late medieval sanctity, as well as Robert Finucane's more recent discussion, by arguing that there was no superideology of the church when it came to canonizations of holy persons in the Italian peninsula. Early leaders of communes were "sleepwalking into a new world," to use Chris Wickham's striking phrase, and perhaps individual popes were too. Thus they were the ones who were forced to react to instances of contestation when they promoted new views of the church's authority in sanctification.[6] As Donald Prudlo argued for the doctrine of papal infallibility, the connection between institutional ideology and experience was symbiotic.[7] Saints became bargaining chips between papal and local forces, influencing both the offering of and resolution to power negotiations. Saints' cults provided a place for local politics to play out, but the papacy's ideology regarding holiness and the canonization process was not the sole driving force.

---

6. Wickham, *Sleepwalking into a New World*, 204.
7. Prudlo, *Certain Sainthood*, 5.

The Janus-like identity of the disputed saint also resulted from divergent conceptions of what behavior constituted sanctity or heresy and differing ideas regarding who should have ultimate authority over the spiritual and political needs of regional towns. The prevalence of contested cases of sanctity cannot be dismissed by claiming that medieval Italians were "semi-Christian" and "voluntary outsiders" to religion, characterized by their "unrelieved contempt for Christian morals and observance and . . . express declarations of unbelief."[8] Italians of the late Middle Ages were deeply pious, attributing their glory and power to their saintly patrons, as Bonvicino asserted for Milan. They believed they had the right to choose those patrons and to judge their saints' merits as witnesses in the ancient Christian tradition to God's power on earth manifested in a local holy man or woman, rather than the pope or his agents who did not personally experience the individual's divine gifts. The factors that created disputed sanctity were thus manifold. Popes waged wars with local communities for power and control. The monastic orders and secular clergy reacted to the papacy's perceived favoritism of the mendicant orders and of their own imperiled prestige and authority. Nobility fought the popes for political power, especially popes such as Boniface VIII and John XXII. Communities refused the spiritual interference of a papacy perceived to be corrupt. In the late medieval cities of northern and central Italy, religious devotion became a highly visible battleground where the right to determine who was a saint and who was a heretic were the principal weapons in a struggle over religious and political autonomy.

---

8. Murray, "Piety and Impiety in Thirteenth-Century Italy," 84.

Bibliography

Primary Sources
Manuscripts

Ascoli Piceno

Pope Alexander IV, letter to Augustinian chapter in Ascoli, 26 August 1259. Archivio di Stato di Ascoli Piceno, perg. 34.

Cremona

"Vita Beati Facii." Cremona, Archivio di Stato di Cremona, Archivio di Santa Maria della Pietà, sez. Iª, cass. 11, ff. 16v–33v.

Ferrara

Account of Dominican chapter meeting at Bologna, 4 June 1272. Ferrara, Biblioteca Comunale Ariostea, MS Cl. I, 445/2, 321–3, 286r–287v.

Florence

Anonymous *vita* of Michele Berti da Calci. Florence, Biblioteca Nazionale Centrale, Magliabechi XXXI. 65, ff. 34r–43v.
Civil process against Michele Berti da Calci, 1389. Florence, Archivio di Stato, Capitano del popolo, n. 1775, ff. 118r–122r.
"Memorie a Fr. Simone Saltarelli a Bartolommeo da San Concordio Domenicano." Florence, Archivio di Stato, corporazioni religiose soppresse dal governo francese, ser. 102, pez. 95, insert V, record 16.
"Memorie concernenti a Monsignore Fr. Simone Saltarelli dell'Ordine de Predica-tori, fu vescovo di Parma, ed quindi Archivescovo di Pisa." Florence, Archivio di Stato, fondo corporazioni religiose soppresse dal governo francese, ser. 102, pez. 95, insert V, record 2.
Record of a meeting of papal legates, Franciscans, and Dominicans at Monte Falconi, 19 August 1327. Florence, Archivio di Stato, Corporazioni religiose soppresse dal governo francese, sec. 102, pez. 196 secondo, ff. 1r–1v.

Record of a riot, 29 January 1328. Florence, Archivio di Stato, fondo corporazioni religiose soppresse dal governo francese, ser. 102, pez. 190, penultimate insert.
Record of questioning of mendicants about rebellion of Assisi and Spoleto at Spoleto, 22 September 1327. Florence, Archivio di Stato, Corporazioni religiose soppresse dal governo francese, ser. 102, pez. 196 secondo, ff. 1r–3r.
Sentence of condemnation of Michele Berti da Calci, 1389. Florence, Archivio di Stato, Capitano del popolo, n. 1782, ff. 25r–29r.

MILAN

"Cronica delle venerando memorie nella congregazione Umiliata." Milan, Biblioteca Ambrosiana, H205 inf.
Life of Tommasuccio of Nocera. Milan, Biblioteca Ambrosiana, cod. I. 115.
"Rugeria uxor Miranisii Miracapitii confirmat . . . Sancti Petri ad Hortum," 9 April 1274. Milan, Biblioteca Nazionale Braidense, ms. Bonomi, E. Tabularium monasterii Claravallis, AE XV 20–31, n. 778, 850–3.
Sacconi, Rainerio. "Tractatus de Catharis sive Paterinis." Milan, Biblioteca Ambrosiana A129 inf., ff. 153r–186v.
"Testamentum . . . fratis Pagani de Patra Sancta," 1304. Milan, Archivio di Stato di Milano, Archivio Diplomatico, S. Francesco, ms. n. 406, n. 2, XLVII, [103].

ROME

Collection of inquisitorial manuals. Rome, Biblioteca Casanatense, ms. 969 [A. III. 34].
List of beliefs of the heresy of the "Spiritus libertatis" (between collection of inquisitorial manuals). Rome, Biblioteca Casanatense, ms. 1730 [A. IV. 49], f. 39r.
Treatise against the *fraticelli*. Rome, Biblioteca Casanatense, ms. 132 [D. III. 34].

VATICAN CITY

Inquisitorial process against Peter of Aquila, 1344–1346. Vatican City, Archivio Segreto Vaticano, Collectoriae 421.A.
Inquisitorial process against Peter da Penna S. Giovanni, 1346–1347. Vatican City, Archivio Segreto Vaticano, Collectoriae, 384, f. 1r–12r.
Philippe de Ferrara, OP. "Liber de introductione loquendi." Vatican City, Biblioteca Apostolica Vaticano, Pal. Lat. 960.
Pope John XXII, letter to the Archbishop of Milan, 1322. Vatican City, Biblioteca Apostolica Vaticano, ms. 3937.
Vatican City, Archivio Segreto Vaticano, *Congregazione dei Riti*, il processo della canonizzazione 89 (Amato Ronconi, 1733–1734).
Vatican City, Archivio Segreto Vaticano, *Congregazione dei Riti*, il processo della canonizzazione 661 (Albert of Villa d'Ogna, 1744).

Vatican City, Archivio Segreto Vaticano, *Congregazione dei Riti*, il processo della canonizzazione 773 (Marcolinus of Forli, 1624–1625).

Vatican City, Archivio Segreto Vaticano, *Congregazione dei Riti*, il processo della canonizzazione 1315 (Zita of Lucca, 1694–1695).

Vatican City, Archivio Segreto Vaticano, *Congregazione dei Riti*, il processo della canonizzazione 3021 (Henry of Bolzano, 1768).

Acta Sanctorum

Albert of Villa d'Ogna. II May, day 7, cols. 281A–F.

Alberto Prandoni. III August, day 14, cols. 177B–178F.

Ambruogio Sansedoni. III March, day 20, cols. 180A–241C.

Anthony Peregrinus. I February, day 1, cols. 264A–265D.

Cecco of Pesaro. I August, day 3, cols. 658C–662F.

Elzear of Sabran. VII September, day 27, cols. 576D–594A.

Facio of Cremona. II January, day 18, cols. 210–11.

Henry of Bolzano. II June, day 10, cols. 371B–391C.

Parisio of Treviso. II June, day 11, cols. 483A–486E.

Peter Crisci. IV July, day 19, cols. 663C–668E.

Rose of Viterbo. II September, day 4, cols. 432A–442A.

Seraphina of San Gimignano. II March, day 12, cols. 236C–242E.

Umiliana dei Cerchi. IV May, day 19, cols. 386D–401D.

Zita of Lucca. III April, day 27, cols. 499B–527A.

Printed

Abate, P. Giuseppe, ed. "S. Rosa di Viterbo, Terziaria Francescana (1233–1251): Fonti storiche della vita e loro revisione critica." *Miscellanea Francescana* 52 (1952): 151–53.

Acta S. Officii Bononie ab anno 1291 usque ad annum 1310. 3 vols. Edited by Lorenzo Paolini and Raniero Orioli. Fonti per la storia d'Italia 106. Rome: Istituto storico italiano per il Medio Evo, 1982–1984.

Actus beati Francisci et sociorum ejus. Edited by Paul Sabatier. Paris: Fischbacher, 1902.

Additus ad Historia fratris Dulcini di anonimo sincrono e De secta illorum qui se dicunt esse de ordine Apostolorum di Bernardo Gui. Edited by A. Segarizzi. *RIS* 9, pt. 5. Città di Castello: Tipi della casa editrice S. Lapi, 1907.

Alighieri, Dante. *The Divine Comedy.* 3 vols. Translated by Allen Mandelbaum. New York: Bantam Books, 1980.

Annales Camaldulenses ordinis Sancti Benedicti. 9 vols. Edited by G. B. Mittarelli and Anselmo Costadoni. Farnborough, UK: Gregg, 1970 [1755].

Annales Minorum seu Trium Ordinum a S. Francisco institutorum. 32 vols. Edited by Luke Wadding. Florence: Ad Claras Aquas, 1931–1964 [1625–1654].

Annales parmenses maiores. MGHSS, XVIII. Hanover, 1863.

Armstrong, Regis J., OFM Cap., and Ignatius C. Brady, OFM, eds. and trans. *Francis and Clare: The Complete Works.* Classics of Western Spirituality. New York: Paulist Press, 1982.

Augustine of Hippo. *Confessions, Books I–XIII.* Translated by F. J. Sheed. Indianapolis: Hackett Publishing Co., 1993.

Bartolomeo of Ferrara. *Libro del Polistore ab anno 1287 usque ad 1347.* Edited by L. Muratori. *RIS* 24, pt. 2. Città di Castello: Tipi della casa editrice S. Lapi, 1910–1912.

Beccaria, Augusto, ed. *Le redazioni in volgare della sentenza di Frate Accursio contro maestro Cecco d'Ascoli.* Atti della R. Accademia delle Scienze di Torino XLI. Turin: Carlo Clausen, 1906.

Benedetti, Marina, ed. *Milano 1300: I processi inquisitoriali contro le devote e i devoti di santa Guglielma.* Milan: Libri Scheiwiller, 1999.

Bernard of Luxembourg. *Catalogus haereticorum.* Cologne: Eucharius Cervicornus, 1522.

Bevegnatis, Iunta. *Legenda de vita et miraculis beatae Margaritae de Cortona.* Edited by Fortunato Iozelli. Biblioteca Franciscana Ascetica Medii Aevi 13. Rome: Collegi S. Bonaventurae ad Claras Aquas, 1997. English translation: Bevignati, Giunta. *The Life and Miracles of Saint Margaret of Cortona (1247–1297).* Translated by Thomas Renna. St. Bonaventure, NY: Franciscan Institute Publications, 2012.

Boccaccio, Giovanni. *The Decameron.* Translated by G. H. McWilliam. New York: Penguin, 2003.

Bock, F., ed. "Der Este-Prozess von 1321." *Archivum Fratrum Praedicatorum* 7 (1937): 41–111.

Bonaventure. *Legenda Maior Sancti Francisci.* In *Legendae duae de vita S. Francisci seraphici,* edited by Collegio San Bonaventura. Rome: Quaracchi, 1923.

Brufani, Stefano, ed. *Eresia di un ribelle al tempo di Giovanni XXII: Il caso di Muzio di Francesco d'Assisi: Con l'edizione del processo inquisitoriale.* Florence: La Nuova Italia, 1989.

Bullarium Franciscanum Romanorum pontificum. 4 vols. Edited by Giovanni Giacinto Sbaraglia. Santa Maria degli Angeli: Edizioni Porziuncola, 1983 [1759].

Bullarum diplomatum et privilegiorum sanctorum Romanum pontificum Taurinensis editio 14. Edited by Aloysio Bilio. Turin: A. Vecco et Sociis Editoribus, 1868.

Chartularium universitatis Parisiensis. 5 vols. Edited by Heinrich Denifle et al. Paris: Delalain, 1889–1897.

Chronicon Parmense ab anno 1038 usque ad 1338. Edited by G. Bonazzi. *RIS* 9, pt. 9. Città di Castello: Tipi della casa editrice S. Lapi, 1902.

Chronique latine de Guillaume de Nangis de 1113 a 1300 avec les continuations de cette chronique de 1300 avec 1368. 2 vols. Edited by H. Géraud. Paris: J. Renouard et cie, 1843.

Clareno, Angelo. *Liber chronicarum, sive, tribulationum ordinis minorum.* Edited by Giovanni M. Boccali. Perugia: Porziuncola, 1998. English translation: Clareno, Angelo. *A Chronicle or History of the Seven Tribulations of the Order of Brothers Minor.* Translated by David Burr and E. Randolph Daniel. St. Bonaventure, NY: Franciscan Institute Publications, 2005.

Clement of Alexandria. *Miscellanies, Book VII.* Edited by Fenton John Anthony Hort and Joseph B. Mayor. New York: Garland, 1987 [1902].

"The Conversion of Peter Waldo." In *Readings in European History,* edited by H. Robinson, 381–83. Boston: Ginn, 1905.

Corio, Bernardino. *L'historia di Milano*. Venice: Giorgio de'Cavalli, 1565.

Corpus iuris canonici. 2 vols. Edited by Emil Friedberg. Leipzig: Bernhard Tauchnitz, 1881.

Corpus iuris civilis. Edited by Paul Krueger et al. Berlin: Apud Weidmannos, 1954.

Cronache Senesi. Edited by Alessandro Lisini and Fabio Iacometti. *RIS* 15, pt. 6. Bologna: Nicola Zanichelli, 1931.

Dalarun, Jacques, ed. *"Lapsus linguae." La légende de Claire de Rimini*. Spoleto: Centro italiano di studi sull'alto medioevo, 1994.

D'Alatri, Mariano, ed. *Eretici e inquisitori in Italia: Studi e documenti*. 2 vols. Rome: Istituto storico del Cappuccini, 1987.

——, ed. *L'inquisizione francescana nell'Italia Centrale del Duecento: Con il testo del "Liber inquisitionis" di Orvieto trascritto da Egidio Bonanno*. Rome: Istituto Storico dei Cappuccini, 1996.

——, ed. "Una sentenza dell'inquisitore fra Filippo da Mantova (1287)." *Collectanea Franciscana* 37 (1967): 142–4.

Da Milano, Ilarino, ed. "Disputatio inter catholicum e paterinum haereticum." *Aevum* 14 (1940): 85–140.

——, ed. "La 'Manifestatio heresies catharorum,' quam fecit Bonacursus." *Aevum* 12 (1938): 301–24.

——, ed. "La 'Summa contra haereticos' di Giacomo Capelli OFM e un suo "Quaresimale' inedito (saec. XIII)." *Collectanea francescana* 10 (1940): 66–82.

——, ed. "Le 'Liber supra Stella' del placentino Salvo Burce contro i Catari e alter correnti ereticali." *Aevum* 16 (1942): 272–319; 17 (1943): 90–146; 19 (1945): 281–341.

Da Riva, Bonvicino. *De Magnalibus Urbis Mediolani*. Edited by P. Chiesa. Milan: Libri Schiewiller, 1998.

Da Signa, Buoncompagno. *Amicitia and De malo senectutis et senii*. Translated by Michael W. Dunne. Dallas Medieval Texts and Translations, 15. Leuven: Peeters Publishers, 2012.

Da Todi, Jacopone. "Third Letter from Jail to Pope Boniface VIII." In *The Lauds*, translated by Serge Hughes and Elizabeth Hughes, 180–82. Classics of Western Spirituality. New York: Paulist Press, 1982.

De Adam, Salimbene. *Cronica*. 2 vols. Edited by Giuseppe Scalia. Turnhout, Belgium: Brepols, 1998. English translation: *The Chronicle of Salimbene de Adam*. Edited by Joseph L. Baird, Giuseppe Baglivi, John Robert Kane. Medieval and Renaissance Texts and Studies 40. Binghamton, NY: SUNY Press, 1986.

Dean, Trevor, ed. and trans. *The Towns of Italy in the Later Middle Ages*. New York: Manchester University Press, 2000.

De Luca, Giuseppe. "Il supplizio di frà Michele da Calci (1389)." In *Prosatori minori del Trecento*, vol. 1, *Scrittori di religione*, edited by Giuseppe De Luca, 213–36. Milan: Riccardo Ricciardi, 1956.

Denifle, Heinrich P., ed. "Die Denkschriften der Colonna gegen Bonifaz VIII. und der Cardinale gegen die Colonna." *Archiv für Literatur- und Kirchengeschichte des Mittelalters* 5 (1889): 493–529.

Denzinger, Heinrich, ed. *Enchiridion symbolorum: Definitionum et declarationum de rebus fidei et morum*, 10th ed. Freiburg: Herder, 1908.

De Paramo, Luis. *De origine et progressu officii sanctae inquisitionis*. Madrid: Ex Typographia Regia, 1598.

DeSantis, Antonio, ed. *Meco del Sacco, inquisizione e processi per eresia. Ascoli-Avignone 1320–1346*. Ascoli Piceno: A. DeSantis, 1982 [1980].

De Vitry, Jacques. *The Life of Marie d'Oignies*. In *Two Lives of Marie d'Oignies*, 2nd ed., translated by Hugh Feiss, OSB. Toronto: Peregrina Publishing Co., 1998 [1987].

De Voragine, Jacobus. *The Golden Legend*. 2 vols. Translated by William Granger Ryan. Princeton, NJ: Princeton University Press, 1993.

Die Register Innocenz' III. Edited by Othmar Hageneder and Anton Haidacher. Graz: H. Böhlaus Nachf, 1964.

Dino Compagni's Chronicle of Florence. Translated by Daniel E. Bornstein. Philadelphia: University of Pennsylvania Press, 1986.

Dominici, Johannes. *Epistolam memorat* (Marcolinus de Forlì). In *Ecclesiae Venetae, antiquis monumentis nunc etiam primum editis illustratae et in decades distributae*, 13 vols., edited by Flaminio Corner, vol. 7, 186–92. Venice: Pasquali, 1749.

Dondaine, Antoine, ed. *Un traité néo-manichéen du XIIIe siècle. Le Liber de duobus principiis, suivi d'un fragment de ritual cathare*. Rome: Istituto Storico Domenicano, St. Sabina, 1939.

Doria, Jacopo. *Annales Genuenses*. In *Georgii et Iohannis Stellae Annales Genuenses*, edited by Giovanna Petti Balbi. *RIS* 17, pt. 2. Bologna: Zanichelli, 1975.

Ehrle, Franz, ed. "Die Spirituellen, ihr Verhältnis zum Franziskanerorden und zu den Fratricellen. 3. Die 'historia septem tribulationum ordinis minorum' des fr. Angelus de Clareno." *Archiv für Literatur- und Kirchengeschichte des Mittelalters* 2 (1886): 106–327.

——, ed. "Ludwig der Bayer und die Fraticellen und Ghibellinen von Todi und Amelia in J. 1328." In *Archiv für Literatur- und Kirchengeschichte des Mittelalters* 1, edited by P. Heinrech Denifle and Franz Ehrle, 158–64. Berlin: Wiedmannsche Buchandlung, 1885.

Eymerich, Nicholas. *Directorium inquisitorum*. Venice: Apud Marcum Antonium Zalterium, 1595.

Fasciculus Morum. Edited and translated by Siegfried Wenzel. University Park: Pennsylvania State University Press, 1989.

Fiamma, Galvano. "La cronaca maggiore dell'ordine domenicano di Galvano Fiamma." Edited by Gundisalvo Odetto. *Archivum fratrum praedicatorum* 10 (1940): 297–373.

——. *Opisculum de rebus gestis ab Azone, Luchino et Johane Vicecomitibus*. Edited by C. Castiglioni. *RIS* 12, pt. 4. Bologna: Zanichelli, 1938.

Franceschini, Gino, ed. *Documenti e regesti per servire alla storia dello Stato d'Urbino e dei conti dei Montefeltro (1202–1375)*. 2 vols. Urbino: Argilia, 1982.

Friedlander, Alan, ed. *Processus Bernardi Delitiosi: The Trial of Fr. Bernard Délicieux, 3 September—8 December 1319*. Philadelphia: University of Pennsylvania Press, 1996.

Fumi, Luigi, ed. "Eretici e ribelli nell'Umbria dal 1320 al 1330 studiati su documenti inediti dell'archivio segreto vaticano." *Bollettino della Deputazione di Storia Patria per l'Umbria* 3 (1897): 257–85 and 429–89; 4 (1898): 221–301 and 437–86; 5 (1899): 1–46 and 205–425.

Gli Statuti del Comune di Treviso (sec. XIII-XIV). 2 vols. Edited by Bianca Betto. Rome: Istituto storico italiano per il Medio Evo, 1984–1986.

Godin, Guillaume Pierre. *Tractatus de causa immediata ecclesiastice potestatis.* Edited by William McCready. Toronto: Pontifical Institute of Mediaeval Studies, 1982.

Gorini, Joannes. "Beati Petri de Fulgineo Confessoris." Edited by Michele Faloci Pulignani. *Analecta Bollandiana* 8 (1889): 358–69.

Guidonis, Bernardus. *Practica inquisitionis heretice pravitatis.* Edited by C. Douais. Paris: Picard, 1886. English translation: *The Inquisitor's Guide: A Medieval Manual on Heretics.* Translated by Janet Shirley. Welwyn Garden City, UK: Ravenhall Books, 2006.

The Holy Bible. Douay-Rheims Version. Rockford, IL: Tan Books and Publishers, 1989 [1899].

Holy See Press Office. "Statistics on the Pontificate of John Paul II," 5 January 2005. http://www.vatican.va/news_services/liturgy/saints/ELENCO_SANTI _GPII.htm. Accessed 6 November 2015.

Horrox, Rosemary, ed. *The Black Death.* Manchester Medieval Sources Series. New York: Manchester University Press, 1994.

La leggenda del Beato Tommasuccio da Nocera. Edited by Michele Faloci Pulignani. Gubbio: Scuola Tipografia "Oderisi," 1932.

La profezie del Beato Tommasuccio di Foligno. Edited by M. Faloci Pulignani. Foligno: Feliciano Campitelli, 1887.

Les registres de Boniface VIII. Edited by Georges Digard, Maurice Faucon, and Antoine Thomas. Paris: E. de Boccard, 1904.

Les registres de Grégoire IX. Edited by Lucien Auvray. Paris: A. Fontemoing, 1896.

Les registres de Nicolas III (1277–1280). Edited by Jules Gay. Paris: A. Fontemoing, 1938.

Les registres de Nicholas IV. Edited by M. Ernest Langlois. Paris: Ernst Thorin, 1905.

Les registres d'Honorius IV. Edited by Maurice Prou. Paris: Ernst Thorin, 1888.

Liber de rebus memorabilioribus, sive Chronicon Henrici de Hervordia. Edited by August Potthast. Göttingen: Dieterich, 1859.

Magnus, Albertus. *Questions concerning Aristotle's "On Animals."* Translated by Irven M. Resnick and Kenneth F. Kitchell Jr. Fathers of the Church Mediaeval Continuation. Washington, DC: Catholic University of America Press, 2008.

Malagola, Carlo, ed. *Statuti delle Università e dei collegi dello studio Bolognese.* Bologna: N. Zanichelli, 1888.

Mariano of Florence. *Compendium chronicarum ordinis Fratrum Minorum,* edited by Teofilo Domenichelli. *Archivum Franciscanum Historicum* 1 (1908): 98–107; 2 (1909): 92–107, 305–18, 457–72, 626–41; 3 (1910): 294–309, 700–715; and 4 (1911): 122–37, 318–39, 559–87.

Marsiglio of Padua. *Defensor Pacis.* In *Monarchia Sancti Romani Imperii,* vol. 2, edited by Melchior Goldast, 309. Hanover: C. Biermanni & Consort, 1611–1614. English translation in *A Source Book for Medieval History,* ed. Oliver J. Thatcher and Edgar Holmes McNeal (New York: Scribner's, 1905), 317–24.

"Martyrdom of Polycarp." In *Some Authentic Acts of the Early Martyrs,* translated by B. C. E. Owen. Oxford: Clarendon Press, 1927.

Michel, Robert, ed. "Les procès de Matteo et de Galeazzo Visconti." *Mélanges d'archéologie et d'histoire* 19 (1909): 269–327.

"Miracula Beati Antonii Peregrini." *Analecta Bollandiana* 14 (1895): 108–14.

Molinier, Charles, ed. "Un traité inédit di XIIIe siècle contre les hérétiques cathares." *Annales de la faculté des letters de Bourdeaux* 5 (1883): 226–56.

Nicholas III (pope). *Exiit qui seminat*. Franciscan Archive. https://franciscan-archive .org/bullarium/exiit-l.html. Accessed 28 August 2016.

Olivi, Peter John. "Epistola ad Conradum de Offida." In "Petri Iohannis Olivi de renuntiatione papae Celestini V quaestio et epistola," edited by Cynthia Kilmer and Eliza Marmursztein; rev. Sylvain Piron. *Archivum franciscanum historicum* 91 (1998): 33–64.

Paris, Matthew. *Chronica Maiora*. Edited by H. R. Luard. Rolls Series 57, 5. London: Longman, 1880.

Peter of Abano. *Conciliator*. Edited by Ezio Riondato and Luigi Olivieri. Padua: Antenore, 1985.

Peters, Edward. *Heresy and Authority in Medieval Europe*. Philadelphia: University of Pennsylvania Press, 1980.

Petersohn, J., ed. "Die Litterae Papst Innocenz III zur Heiligsprechung der Kaiserin Kunigunde (1200)." *Jahrbuch für fränkische Landesforschung* 37 (1977): 21–25.

Piazza, Andrea, ed. "La passione di frate Michele; un testo in volgare di fine Trecento." *Revue Mabillon* n.s. 10 (1999): 231–56.

Polenton, Sicco. "Vita Beati Antonii Peregrini." *Analecta Bollandiana* 13 (1894): 417–25.

Raynaldi, Oderico. *Annales Ecclesiastici*. 37 vols. Paris: Ex Typis Consociationis Sancti Pauli, 1872.

Richer of Sens. *Richeri Gesta Senoniensis ecclesiae*. In *MGHSS*, edited by G. Waitz, vol. 25, 249–345. Frankfurt: 1880.

Ronzoni, Cirillo, ed. *Della vita e delle opere di Pietro d'Abano*. Rome: Coi Tipi Del Salviucci, 1878.

Sancti Antonii de Padua vitae duae, quarum altera hucusque inedita. Edited by Léon de Kerval. Paris: Fischbacher, 1904.

Savonarola, Michele. *Libellus de magnificis ornamentis regie civitatis Padue*. Edited by A. Segarizzi. RIS 24, pt. 2. Città di Castello: S. Lapi, 1902.

Scripta Leonis, Rufini, et Angeli Sociorum S. Francisci. Edited by Rosalind Brooke. Oxford: Clarendon Press, 1970.

Statuti di Perugia dell'anno 1342. 2 vols. Edited by G. degli Azzi Vitelleschi. Rome: E. Loescher, 1913–1916.

St. Francis of Assisi: Writings and Early Biographies. 4th rev. ed. Edited by Marion A. Habig. Chicago: Franciscan Herald Press, 1983.

Tanner, Norman P., ed. *Decrees of the Ecumenical Councils*. Vol. 1, *Nicaea I to Lateran V*. Washington, DC: Georgetown University Press, 1990.

Thorndike, Lynn. *University Records and Life in the Middle Ages*. New York: W. W. Norton and Co., 1975 [1944].

Ugolino. *The Little Flowers of St. Francis of Assisi*. Translated by Dom Roger Huddleston. New York: Limited Editions Club, 1930.

Vauchez, Andrè, ed. "Sainteté laïque aux XIIIe siècle: la vie du bienheureux Facio de Crémone." *Mélanges d'École française de Rome. Moyen Âge* 84 (1972): 13–55.

Villani, Giovanni. *Nuova cronica*. Edited by Giuseppe Porta. Parma: U. Guanda, 1990–1991.

Wakefield, Walter L., and Austin P. Evans, eds. *Heresies of the High Middle Ages*. New York: Columbia University Press, 1991 [1969].

Webb, Diana, trans. *Saints and Cities in Medieval Italy*. Manchester: Manchester University Press, 2007.

Zanella, Gabriele, ed. *Itinerari ereticali patari e catari tra Rimini e Verona*. Istituto Storico Italiano per il Medio Evo, Studi Storici, fasc. 153. Rome: Nella Sede dell'Istituto, 1986.

Secondary Sources

Albertazzi, Marco, ed. *Studi stabiliani: Raccolta di interventi editi su Cecco d'Ascoli*. Trent: La finestra, 2002.

Ames, Christine Caldwell. "Does Inquisition Belong to Religious History?" *American Historical Review* 110 (2005): 1–37.

——. *Righteous Persecution: Inquisition, Dominicans, and Christianity in the Middle Ages*. Philadelphia: University of Pennsylvania Press, 2008.

Anagnine, Eugenio. *Dolcino e il movimenta ereticale all'inizio del Trecento*. Florence: La Nuova Italia, 1964.

Andreatonelli, Sebastiano. *Historiae Asculanae*. Bologna: Forni, 1968 [1673].

Andrews, Frances. *The Early Humiliati*. Cambridge: Cambridge University Press, 1999.

——. *The Other Friars: Carmelite, Augustinian, Sack, and Pied Friars in the Middle Ages*. Woodbridge, UK: Boydell Press, 2006.

Arnold, John. *Belief and Unbelief in Medieval Europe*. New York: Bloomsbury USA, 2005.

——. *Inquisition and Power: Catharism and the Confessing Subject in Medieval Languedoc*. Philadelphia: University of Pennsylvania Press, 2001.

Artusi, Luciano. *Le antiche porte di Firenze: Alla scoperta delle mura che circondavano la città*. Florence: Semper Editrice, 2005.

"Ascoli Piceno—A Polesio sulle tracce di Meco del Sacco e dei Sacconi." *VeraTV.it*, 28 June 2012. http://www.veratv.it/index.php/2012/06/28/ascoli-piceno-a-polesio-sulle-tracce-di-meco-del-sacco-e-dei-sacconi/. Accessed 4 March 2019.

Azzoni Avogari, Rambaldo degli. *Memorie del B. Enrico morto in Trevigi l'anno MCCCXV*. Venice: Pietro Valvasense, 1760.

Bahktin, Mikhail. *Rabelais and His World*. Translated by Helene Iswolsky. Blooming-ton: Indiana University Press, 1984.

Bailey, Michael D. *Magic and Superstition in Europe: A Concise History from Antiquity to the Present*. Lanham, MD: Rowman & Littlefield, 2007.

Baker, Nicholas Scott. "The Death of a Heretic, Florence 1389." In *Rituals, Images, and Words: Varieties of Cultural Expression in Late Medieval and Early Modern Europe*, edited by F. W. Kent and Charles Zika, 33–53. Turnhout, Belgium: Brepols, 2005.

Bartlett, Robert. *The Making of Europe: Conquest, Colonization, and Cultural Change 950–1350*. Princeton, NJ: Princeton University Press, 1993.

——. *The Natural and the Supernatural in the Middle Ages*. New York: Cambridge University Press, 2008.

——. *Why Can the Dead Do Such Great Things? Saints and Worshippers from the Martyrs to the Reformation*. Princeton, NJ: Princeton University Press, 2013.

Becker, Marvin. "Some Implications of the Conflict between Church and State in Trecento Florence." *Mediaeval Studies* 21 (1959): 1–16.

Becker, Marvin, and Gene Brucker. "The '*Arti Minori*' in Florentine Politics, 1342–1378." *Mediaeval Studies* 18 (1965): 93–104.

Bell, Catherine. *Ritual Theory, Ritual Practice.* New York: Oxford University Press, 1992.

Bell, Rudolph M. *Holy Anorexia.* Chicago: University of Chicago Press, 1985.

Benati, Amedeo. "Armanno Pungilupo nella storia religiosa Ferrarese del 1200." *Analecta Pomposiana* 2 (1966): 85–123.

——. "Frater Armannus Pungilupus: Alla ricerca di una identità." *Analecta Pomposiana* 7 (1982): 7–57.

Benedetti, Marina. "Il culto di santa Guglielma e gli inquisitori." In *Vite di eretici e storie di frati,* edited by Giovanno Miccoli, 221–42. Milan: Edizioni Biblioteca Francescana, 1998.

——. *Io non sono Dio: Guglielma di Milano e i Figli dello Spirito santo.* Milan: Edizioni Biblioteca Francescana, 1998.

Beneš, Carrie E. *Urban Legends: Civic Identity and the Classical Past in Northern Italy, 1250–1350.* University Park: Pennsylvania State University Press, 2011.

Benvenuti Papi, Anna. *"In castro poenitentiae": Santità e società femminile nell'Italia medievale.* Rome: Herder Editrice e Libreria, 1990.

——. "Mendicant Friars and Female Pinzochere in Tuscany: From Social Marginality to Models of Sanctity." In *Women and Religion in Medieval and Renaissance Italy,* edited by Daniel Bornstein and Roberto Rusconi, translated by Margery J. Schneider, 84–103. Chicago: University of Chicago Press, 1996.

Benvenuti-Papi, Anna. "San Zanobi: Memoria episcopale, tradizioni civiche e dignità familari." In *I ceti dirigenti nella Toscana tardo communale,* edited by D. Rugiardini, 79–115. Florence: Francesco Papafava, 1987.

——. "Umiliana dei Cerchi: Nascita di un Culto nella Firenze del Dugento." *Studi francescani* 77 (1980): 87–117.

Besozzi, L. "I processi canonici contro Galeazzo Visconti." *Archivum storico Lombardo* 107 (1981): 235–45.

Biddick, Kathleen. "The Devil's Anal Eye: Inquisitorial Optics and Ethnographic Authority." In *The Shock of Medievalism,* edited by Kathleen Biddick, 105–34. Durham, NC: Duke University Press, 1998.

Birkett, Helen. "The Struggle for Sanctity: St. Waltheof of Melrose, Cistercian In-house Cults and Canonisation Procedure at the Turn of the Thirteenth Century." In *The Cult of Saints and the Virgin Mary in Medieval Scotland,* edited by Steve Boardman and Eila Williamson, 43–60. Woodbridge, UK: Boydell and Brewer, 2010.

Black, Jane. "The Visconti in the Fourteenth Century and the Origins of Their Plenitudo Potestatis." In *Poteri signorili e feudali nelle campagne dell'Italia settentrionale fra Tre e Quattrocento: Fondamenti di legittimità e forme di esercizio: Atti del convegno di studi (Milano, 11–12 aprile 2003),* edited by Federica Cengarle, Giorgio Chittolini, and Gian Maria Varanini, 1–20. Florence: Firenze University Press, 2004.

Blaher, Damian Joseph. *The Ordinary Processes in Causes of Beatification and Canonization.* Catholic University of America Canon Law Studies 268. Washington, DC: Catholic University of America Press, 1949.

Blumenfeld-Kosinski, Renate. *The Strange Case of Ermine de Reims: A Medieval Woman between Demons and Saints*. Philadelphia: University of Pennsylvania Press, 2015.

Boase, T. S. R. *Boniface VIII*. London: Constable & Co., 1933.

Bolton, Brenda. "Innocent III's Treatment of the Humiliati." In *Popular Belief and Practice*, edited by G. J. Cuming and Derek Baker, 73–82. Studies in Church History 8. London: Cambridge University Press, 1972.

Bonazzi, Luigi. *Storia di Perugia dalle origine al 1860*. Vol. 1. Perugia: Tipografia Boncompagni E.C., 1876.

Bornstein, Daniel. "The Uses of the Body: The Church and the Cult of Santa Margherita da Cortona." *Church History* 62 (1993): 163–77.

Boureau, Alain, and Sylvain Piron, eds. *Pierre de Jean Olivi (1248–1298): Pensée scolastique, dissidence spirituelle et société*. Paris: J. Vrin, 1999.

Bowersock, G. W. *Martyrdom and Rome*. New York: Cambridge University Press, 1995.

Brasher, Sally Mayall. *Women of the Humiliati: A Lay Religious Order in Medieval Civic Life*. Medieval History and Culture 19. New York: Routledge, 2003.

Brown, Andrew. "Civic Religion in Late Medieval Europe." *Journal of Medieval History* 42 (2016): 338–56.

Brown, Brendan. *The Canonical Juristic Personality*. Washington DC: Catholic University of America Press, 1927.

Brown, Catherine. "In the Middle." *Journal of Medieval and Early Modern Studies* 30 (2000): 547–74.

Brown, Peter. *The Cult of the Saints*. Chicago: University of Chicago Press, 1981.

——. "Society and the Supernatural: A Medieval Change." In *Society and the Holy in Late Antiquity*, edited by Peter Brown, 302–32. Berkeley, CA: University of California Press, 1982.

Bruzelius, Caroline. *Preaching, Building, and Burying: Friars and the Medieval City*. New Haven, CT: Yale University Press, 2014.

Burke, Peter. *Popular Culture in Early Modern Europe*. Aldershot, UK: Scolar Press, 1994.

Burnham, Louisa. *So Great a Light, So Great a Smoke: The Beguin Heretics of Languedoc*. Ithaca, NY: Cornell University Press, 2008.

Burr, David. *Olivi and Franciscan Poverty: The Origins of the Usus Pauper Controversy*. Philadelphia: University of Pennsylvania Press, 1993.

——. *The Persecution of Peter Olivi*. Transactions of the American Philosophical Society n.s. 66. Philadelphia: American Philosophical Society, 1976.

——. *The Spiritual Franciscans*. University Park: Pennsylvania State University Press, 2001.

Bynum, Caroline Walker. "The Female Body and Religious Practice in the Later Middle Ages." In *Fragmentation and Redemption: Essays on Gender and the Human Body in Medieval Religion*, edited by Caroline Walker Bynum, 181–238. New York: Zone Book, 1991.

——. *Holy Feast and Holy Fast: The Religious Significance of Food to Medieval Women*. Berkeley, CA: University of California Press, 1987.

——. *The Resurrection of the Body in Western Christianity, 200–1336*. New York: Columbia University Press, 1995.

——. "Women's Stories, Women's Symbols: A Critique of Victor Turner's Theory of Liminality." In *Fragmentation and Redemption: Essays on Gender and the Human Body in Medieval Religion*, edited by Caroline Walker Bynum, 27–51. New York: Zone Book, 1991.

Caciola, Nancy. *Discerning Spirits: Divine and Demonic Possession in the Middle Ages.* Ithaca, NY: Cornell University Press, 2003.

——. "A Guglielmite Trinity?" *California Italian Studies* 6 (2016): 1–20.

Caffi, Michele. *Dell'Abbazia di Chiaravalle.* Milan: G. Gnocchi, 1842.

Camp, Cynthia Turner. "The Sunday Saint: Keeping a Holy 'Merchant's Time' in the Middle English Life of Erasmus." In *Saints as Intercessors between the Wealthy and the Divine: Art and Hagiography among the Medieval Merchant Classes*, edited by Cynthia Turner Camp and Emily D. Kelley, 44–69. London: Routledge, 2019.

Camp, Cynthia Turner, and Emily D. Kelley, eds. *Saints as Intercessors between the Wealthy and the Divine: Art and Hagiography among the Medieval Merchant Classes.* London: Routledge, 2019.

Cannon, Joanna. *Religious Poverty, Visual Riches: Art in the Dominican Churches of Central Italy in the Thirteenth and Fourteenth Centuries.* New Haven, CT: Yale University Press, 2013.

Cannon, Joanna, and André Vauchez. *Margherita of Cortona and the Lorenzetti: Sienese Art and the Cult of a Holy Woman in Medieval Tuscany.* University Park: Pennsylvania State University Press, 1999.

Cantù, Cesare. *Gli eretici d'Italia: Discorsi storici.* 3 vols. Turin: Unione Tipografico-Editrice, 1886.

Capp, Bernard. "Popular Culture(s)." In *The European World: 1500–1800*, edited by Beat Kümin, 226–35. New York: Routledge, 2014.

Capponi, Pietro. *Memorie storiche della Chiesa Ascolana e dei vescovi che la governarono.* Ascoli Piceno: Tipografia Cesari, 1898.

Cariboni, Guido. "Symbolic Communication and Civic Values in Milan under the Early Visconti." In *Languages of Power in Italy (1300–1600)*, edited by Daniel Bornstein, Laura Gaffuri, and Brian Jeffrey Maxson, 65–76. Turnhout, Belgium: Brepols, 2017.

Carlino, Andrea. *Books of the Body.* Translated by John Tedeschi and Anne Tedeschi. Chicago: University of Chicago Press, 1994.

Carniello, Brian. "Gerardo Segarelli as the Anti-Francis: Mendicant Rivalry and Heresy in Medieval Italy, 1260–1300." *Journal of Ecclesiastical History* 57 (2006): 226–51.

Casagrande, G. "Note su manifestazioni di vita communitaria femminile nel movimento penitenziale in Umbria nei secoli XIII, XIV, XV." In *Prime manifestazioni di vita comunitaria maschile e femminile nel movimento francescana della penitenzia (1215–1447)*, edited by R. Pazzelli and L. Temperini, 459–79. Rome: Commissione Storica Internazionale T.O.R., 1982.

Castelli, Elizabeth A. *Martyrdom and Memory: Early Christian Culture Making.* New York: Columbia University Press, 2004.

Cattaneo, Enrico. "Ottone Visconti arcivescovo di Milano." *Contributi dell'istituto di storia mediovale*, s. 3, I (1968): 129–65.

Cavallari, Ugo. "Eresie e politica: Corrado Venosta e Raimondo della Torre." *Archivio storico lombardo* s. 9, 5–6 (1966–1967): 46–50.

Cazanave, Annie. "Aveu et contrition: Manuels de confesseurs et interrogatories d'Inquisition en Languedoc et en Catalogne (XIIIe–XIVe siècles)." In *La piété populaire au moyen âge: Actes du Congrès national des sociétés savantes, Besançon, 1974, tome 1*, edited by Michel Mollat du Jourdin, 333–52. Paris: Bibliothèque nationale, 1977.

Chartier, Roger. "Culture as Appropriation: Popular Cultural Uses in Early Modern France." In *Understanding Popular Culture: Europe from the Middle Ages to the Nineteenth Century*, edited by Steven L. Kaplan, 229–54. New York: Mouton Publishers, 1984.

Cheney, E. *The Dawn of a New Era: 1250–1453*. New York: Harper & Row, 1962.

Chittolini, Giorgio. "Civic Religion and the Countryside in Late Medieval Italy." In *City and Countryside in Late Medieval and Renaissance Italy: Essays Presented to Philip Jones*, edited by Trevor Dean and Chris Wickham, 69–80. London: Hambledon Press, 1990.

Clarke, Peter D. *The Interdict in the Thirteenth Century: A Question of Collective Guilt*. Oxford: Oxford University Press, 2007.

Coakley, John. "Gender and the Authority of Friars: The Significance of Holy Women for Thirteenth-Century Franciscans and Dominicans." *Church History* 60 (1991): 445–60.

——. *Women, Men, and Spiritual Power: Female Saints and Their Male Collaborators*. New York: Columbia University Press, 2006.

Cognasso, Francesco. *I Visconti*. Milan: Dall'Oglio, 1987 [1966].

Coleman, Edward. "Cities and Communes." In *Italy in the Central Middle Ages, 1000–1300*, edited by David Abulafia, 27–57. New York: Oxford University Press, 2004.

Cossar, Roisin. "The Quality of Mercy: Confraternities and Public Power in Medieval Bergamo." *Journal of Medieval History* 27 (2001): 139–57.

Costa, Patrizia Maria. *Guglielma le Boema, l'"eretica" di Chiaravalle: Uno scorcio di vita religiosa milanese nel secolo XIII*. Milan: NED, 1985.

Courtenay, William J. "Learned Opinion and Royal Justice: The Role of Paris Masters of Theology during the Reign of Phillip the Fair." In *Law and the Illicit in Medieval Europe*, edited by Ruth Mazo Karras et al., 149–63. Philadelphia: University of Pennsylvania Press, 2008.

Creytens, Raymond. "Le manuel de conversation de Philippe de Ferrare, OP." *Archivum fratrum praedicatorum* 16 (1946): 107–35.

Dagenais, John, and Margaret R. Greer. "Decolonizing the Middle Ages: Introduction." *Journal of Medieval and Early Modern Studies* 20 (2000): 431–48.

Dalarun, Jacques. *"Dieu changea de sexe, pour ansi dire": La religion faite femme XIe–XVe siècle*. Paris: Fayard, 2008.

——, ed. *"Lapsus linguae": La légende de Claire de Rimini*. Spoleto: Centro italiano di studi sull'alto medioevo, 1994.

Dal Pino, Franco Andrea. *Il laicato italiano tra eresia e proposta pauperistico-evangelica nei secoli XII–XIII*. Padua: CLEUP, 1984.

D'Ancona, Alessandro. *Varietà storiche e letterarie*. 2 vols. Milan: Fratelli Treves, 1883.

D'Andrea, David M. *Civic Christianity in Renaissance Italy: The Hospital of Treviso, 1400–1530*. Rochester, NY: University of Rochester Press, 2007.

Daniel, E. Randolph. "Joachim of Fiore: Patterns of History in the Apocalypse." In *The Apocalypse in the Middle Ages*, edited by Richard K. Emmerson and Bernard McGinn, 72–88. Ithaca, NY: Cornell University Press, 1992.

D'Anvers, Frédégand and F. Callaey. "Un épisode de l'Inquisition franciscaine en Toscane: Procès intenté à l'inquisiteur Minus de San Quirico, 1333–1334." In *Mélanges d'histoire offerts à Charles Moeller*, vol. 1, 527–47. Paris: A. Picard et fils, 1914.

Dean, Trevor. "The Rise of the Signori." In *Italy in the Central Middle Ages*, edited by David Abulafia, 104–24. Oxford: Oxford University Press, 2004.

Deane, Jennifer Kolpacoff. *A History of Medieval Heresy and Inquisition*. New York: Rowman & Littlefield, 2011.

Delehaye, Hippolyte. *Les origines du culte des martyrs*. Subsidia hagiographica, xx. Brussels: Société des bollandistes, 1933.

Denton, Jeffrey. "The Attempted Trial of Boniface VIII for Heresy." In *The Trial in History*, vol. 1, *Judicial Tribunals in England and Europe, 1200–1700*, edited by Maureen Mulholland and Brian Pullan, 117–28. Manchester, UK: Manchester University Press, 2011.

Dickson, Gary. "The Flagellants of 1260 and the Crusades." *Journal of Medieval History* 15 (1989): 227–67.

——. "The 115 Cults of the Saints in Later Medieval and Renaissance Perugia: A Demographic Overview of a Civic Pantheon." *Renaissance Studies* 12 (1998): 6–25.

——. *Religious Enthusiasm in the Medieval West*. Aldershot, UK: Ashgate, 2000.

Diehl, Peter Davidson. "Overcoming Reluctance to Prosecute Heresy in Thirteenth-Century Italy." In *Christendom and Its Discontents*, edited by Scott L. Waugh and Peter D. Diehl, 47–66. New York: Cambridge University Press, 1996.

Dinzelbacher, Peter. *Heilige oder Hexen? Schicksale auffälliger Frauen in Mittelalter und Früneuzeit*. Munich: Artemis and Winkler, 1995.

Donati, Maria Teresa. *L'Abbazia di Chiaravalle*. Milan: Skira, 2005.

Dondaine, Antoine. "Le manuel de l'inquisiteur (1230–1330)." *Archivum Fratrum Praedicatorum* 17 (1947): 85–194.

Douais, C. *L'Inquisition, ses origines, sa procédure*. Paris: Plon-Nourrit, 1906.

Douie, Decima. *The Conflict between the Seculars and the Mendicants at the University of Paris in the Thirteenth Century*. Aquinas Society of London, Aquinas Paper 23. London: Blackfriars, 1954.

——. *The Nature and the Effect of the Heresy of Fraticelli*. New York: AMS Press, 1978.

Douglas, Mary C. *Purity and Danger: An Analysis of Concepts of Pollution and Taboo*. New York: Routledge, 2002 [1966].

Doyno, Mary Harvey. *The Lay Saint: Charity and Charismatic Authority in Medieval Italy, 1150–1350*. Ithaca, NY: Cornell University Press, 2019.

——. "'A Particular Light of Understanding': Margaret of Cortona, the Franciscans, and a Cortonese Cleric." In *History in the Comic Mode*, edited by Rachel Fulton and Bruce W. Holsinger, 68–78. New York: Columbia University Press, 2007.

DuBois, Page. *Torture and Truth*. New York: Routledge, 1991.

Dwyer-McNulty, Sally. *Common Threads: A Cultural History of Clothing in American Catholicism*. Chapel Hill, NC: University of North Carolina Press, 2014.

Eastman, John R. "Giles of Rome and Celestine V: The Franciscan Revolution and the Theory of Abdication." *The Catholic Historical Review* 76 (1990): 195–211.

Elliott, Dyan. *The Bride of Christ Goes to Hell: Metaphor and Embodiment in the Lives of Pious Women, 200–1500*. Philadelphia: University of Pennsylvania Press, 2012.

———. *Proving Woman: Female Spirituality and Inquisitional Culture in the Later Middle Ages*. Princeton, NJ: Princeton University Press, 2004.

———. "Seeing Double: John Gerson, the Discernment of Spirits, and Joan of Arc." *American Historical Review* 107 (2002): 26–54.

———. "Women and Confession: From Empowerment to Pathology." In *Gendering the Master Narrative: Women and Power in the Middle Ages*, edited by Mary C. Erler and Maryanne Kowaleski, 31–51. Ithaca, NY: Cornell University Press, 2003.

Facchin, Laura. *Chiaravalle Abbey Milan*. Cistercian Library. Milan: Sagep Editori, 2013.

Felice, Eugenio Cappelleti. *La Compagnia de' Neri L'arciconfraternita dei Battuti di Santa Maria della Croce al Tempio*. Florence: Le Monnier, 1927.

Field, Sean L. *The Beguine, the Angel, and the Inquisitor: The Trials of Marguerite Porete and Guiard of Cressonessart*. Notre Dame, IN: University of Notre Dame Press, 2012.

Finucane, Ronald. *Contested Canonizations: The Last Medieval Saints, 1482–1523*. Washington, DC: Catholic University of America Press, 2011.

Foote, David. *Lordship, Reform, and the Development of Civil Society in Medieval Italy: The Bishopric of Orvieto, 1100–1250*. Notre Dame, IN: University of Notre Dame Press, 2004.

French, Roger. *Dissection and Vivisection in the European Renaissance*. Aldershot, UK: Ashgate, 1999.

Frend, W. H. C. *Martyrdom and Persecution in the Early Church: A Study of a Conflict from the Maccabees to Donatus*. New York: Anchor Books, 1967 [1965].

Friedlander, Alan. *The Hammer of the Inquisitors: Brother Bernard Délicieux and the Struggle against the Inquisition in Fourteenth-Century France*. Boston, MA: Brill, 2000.

"Furore." *Villa Conca Smeralda*. http://www.villaconcasmeraldo.com/tag/furore/. Accessed 4 March 2019.

Geary, Patrick J. *Furta Sacra: Thefts of Relics in the Central Middle Ages*. Rev. ed. Princeton, NJ: Princeton University Press, 1990 [1978].

Geltner, Guy. *The Making of Medieval Antifraternalism: Polemic, Violence, Deviance, and Remembrance*. New York: Oxford University Press, 2012.

Ginzburg, Carlo. "The Inquisitor as Anthropologist." In *Clues, Myths, and the Historical Method*, edited by Carlo Ginzburg, translated by John Tedeschi and Anne C. Tedeschi, 156–64. Baltimore: Johns Hopkins University Press, 1989.

———. "Microhistory: Two or Three Things That I Know about It." Translated by John Tedeschi and Anne C. Tedeschi. *Critical Inquiry* 20 (1993): 10–35.

Given, James. *Inquisition and Medieval Society: Power, Discipline, and Resistance in Languedoc*. Ithaca, NY: Cornell University Press, 1997.

———. "The Inquisitors of Languedoc and the Medieval Technology of Power." *American Historical Review* 94 (1989): 336–59.

Goodich, Michael. "*Ancilla Dei*: The Servant as Saint in the Late Middle Ages." In *Women of the Medieval World: Essays in Honor of John H. Mundy*, edited by Julius Kirshner and Suzanne F. Wemple, 119–36. Oxford: Basil Blackwell, 1985.

——. "Foreigner, Foe, and Neighbor: The Religious Cult as a Forum for Political Reconciliation." In *Meeting the Foreign in the Middle Ages*, edited by Albrecht Classen, 11–25. New York: Routledge, 2002.

——. *Vita Perfecta: The Ideal of Sainthood in the Thirteenth Century.* Monographien zur Geschichte des Mittelalters 25. Stuttgart: Anton Hiersemann, 1982.

Green, Monica H. "Integrative Medicine: Incorporating Medicine and Health into the Canon of Medieval European History." *History Compass* 7 (2009): 1218–45.

Grundman, J. P. *The Popolo at Perugia, 1139–1309.* Perugia: Deputazione di storia patria per l'Umbria, 1992.

Grundmann, Herbert. *Religious Movements in the Middle Ages.* Translated by Steve Rowan. Notre Dame, IN: University of Notre Dame Press, 1995 [1935].

Hahn, Cynthia. "Speaking without Tongues: The Martyr Romanus and Augustine's Theory of Language in Illustrations of Bern Burgerbibliothek Codex 264." In *Images of Sainthood in Medieval Europe*, edited by Renate Blumenfeld-Kosinski and Timea Szell, 161–80. Ithaca, NY: Cornell University Press, 1991.

Hamilton, Bernard. *The Medieval Inquisition.* New York: Holmes & Meier, 1981.

Head, Thomas. *Hagiography and the Cult of the Saints.* New York: Cambridge University Press, 1990.

Heft, James. *John XXII and Papal Teaching Authority.* Texts and Studies in Religion 27. Lewiston, NY: E. Mellen Press, 1986 [1977].

Henderson, John. "The Flagellant Movement and Flagellant Confraternities in Central Italy, 1260–1400." *Studies in Church History* 15 (1978): 147–60.

Herlihy, David, and Christiane Klapisch-Zuber. *Tuscans and Their Families: A Study of the Florentine Catasto of 1427.* New Haven, CT: Yale University Press, 1985.

Hyde, J. K. *Society and Politics in Medieval Italy.* London: Macmillan, 1973.

Istoft, Britt. "Divinity Manifest in a Female Body: Guglielma of Milan as the Holy Spirit, Female Deity, and Female Leadership in the Later Middle Ages." *Bulletin for the Study of Religion* 41 (2012): 27–35.

Jacquart, Danielle. "Medical Scholasticism." In *Western Medical Thought from Antiquity to the Middle Ages*, edited by Mirko D. Grmek, 197–240. Cambridge, MA: Harvard University Press, 1998.

Jansen, Katherine Ludwig. *Peace and Penance in Late Medieval Italy.* Princeton, NJ: Princeton University Press, 2018.

Jones, Philip. *The Italian City-State: From Commune to Signoria.* Oxford: Clarendon Press, 1997.

Kelly, Henry. *Inquisitions and Other Trial Procedures in the Medieval West.* Aldershot, UK: Ashgate, 2001.

Kemp, E. W. *Canonization and Authority in the Western Church.* New York: AMS Press, 1980 [1948].

Kern, L. "Saint Bevignate de Pérouse." In *Etudes d'histoire ecclésiastique et de diplomatique*, edited by L. Kern, 1–15. Lausanne, Switzerland: Payot, 1973.

Kieckhefer, Richard. "The Holy and the Unholy: Sainthood, Witchcraft, and Magic in Late Medieval Europe." *Journal of Medieval and Renaissance Studies* 24, no. 3 (1994): 355–85.

——. "The Office of Inquisition and Medieval Heresy: The Transition from Personal to Institutional Jurisdiction." *Journal of Ecclesiastical History* 46 (1995): 36–61.

——. "The Specific Rationality of Medieval Magic." *American Historical Review* 99 (1994): 813–36.

——. *Unquiet Souls: Fourteenth-Century Saints and Their Religious Milieu.* Chicago: University of Chicago Press, 1984.

Kienzle, Beverly Mayne, and Pamela J. Walker, eds. *Women Preachers and Prophets through Two Millennia of Christianity.* Berkeley: University of California Press, 1998.

Klaniczay, Gábor. *Holy Rulers and Blessed Princesses: Dynastic Cults in Medieval Central Europe.* New York: Cambridge University Press, 2002.

——. ed. *Medieval Canonization Processes: Legal and Religious Aspects.* Collection de l'École française de Rome 340. Rome: Ecole française de Rome, 2004.

——. *The Uses of Supernatural Power: The Transformation of Popular Religion in Medieval and Early Modern Europe.* Princeton, NJ: Princeton University Press, 1990.

Kleinberg, Aviad. *Prophets in Their Own Country: Living Saints and the Making of Sainthood in the Later Middle Ages.* Translated by Susan Singerman. Chicago: University of Chicago Press, 1992.

——. "Proving Sanctity: Selection and Authentication of Saints in the Later Middle Ages." *Viator* 20 (1989): 183–205.

Knox, Lezlie. "Audacious Nuns: Institutionalizing the Franciscan Order of St. Clare." *Church History* 69 (2000): 41–62.

Kumhera, Glenn. *The Benefits of Peace: Private Peacemaking in Late Medieval Italy.* Leiden, The Netherlands: Brill, 2017.

Kuttner, Stephan. "La réserve papale du droit de canonization." *Revue historique de droit français et étranger,* 4th series, 18 (1938): 172–228.

Lambert, Malcolm D. *The Cathars.* Oxford: Basil Blackwell, 1985.

——. *Medieval Heresy: Popular Movements from the Gregorian Reform to the Reformation.* 3rd ed. Cambridge, MA: Harvard University Press, 2002 [1977].

Lansing, Carol. "Magnate Violence Revisited." In *Communes and Despots in Medieval and Renaissance Italy,* edited by Bernadette Paton et al., 35–45. Burlington, VT: Ashgate, 2010.

——. *Power and Purity: Cathar Heresy in Medieval Italy.* New York: Oxford University Press, 1998.

Larner, John. *Italy in the Age of Dante and Petrarch, 1216–1380.* London: Longman Group UK, 1980.

Larsen, Andrew E. *The School of Heretics: Academic Condemnation at the University of Oxford, 1277–1409.* Chicago: University of Chicago Press, 2011.

Lawrence, C. H. *The Friars: The Impact of the Early Mendicant Movement on Western Society.* 2nd ed. New York: Longman, 1994.

——. *Medieval Monasticism: Forms of Religious Life in Western Europe in the Middle Ages.* 2nd ed. New York: Longman, 1989 [1984].

Lea, Henry Charles. *A History of the Inquisition.* 3 vols. New York: Cosimo, 2005 [1887].

Le Goff, Jacques. *The Birth of Purgatory.* Translated by Arthur Goldhammer. Chicago: University of Chicago Press, 1984.

Lehmijoki-Gardner, Maiju. "Dominican Penitent Women and the Making of Their Regula." *Speculum* 79 (2004): 676–83.

Lerner, Robert E. "Ecstatic Dissent." *Speculum* 67 (1992): 33–57.

———. *The Heresy of the Free Spirit in the Later Middle Ages.* Berkeley: University of California Press, 1972.

Little, Lester K. *Indispensible Immigrants: The Wine Porters of Northern Italy and Their Saint, 1200–1800.* Manchester, UK: Manchester University Press, 2015.

———. *Religious Poverty and the Profit Economy in Medieval Europe.* Ithaca, NY: Cornell University Press, 1978.

Long, George. "Patria potestas." In *A Dictionary of Greek and Roman Antiquities*, edited by William Smith, 873–75. London: John Murray, 1875.

Maire Vigeur, Jean-Claude. *L'Autre Rome: Une histoire des Romains à l'époque communale (XIIe–XIVe siècle).* Paris: Tallandier, 2010. English translation: *The Forgotten Story: Rome in the Communal Period.* Translated by David Fairservice. Rome: Viella, 2016.

Makowski, Elizabeth. *"A Pernicious Sort of Woman": Quasi-Religious Women and Canon Lawyers in the Later Middle Ages.* Washington, DC: Catholic University of America Press, 2005.

Manselli, Raoul. "L'Anno 1260 fu Anno Gioachimito?" *Movimenti dei disciplinati* (1962): 99–108.

Marangon, Paolo. "Per una revisione dell'interpretazione di Pietro d'Abano." In *Il pensiero ereticale nella Marca Trevigiana e a Venezia dal 1200 al 1350*, edited by Paolo Marangon, 66–104. Abano: Francisci Editore, 1984.

Marcucci, Francesco Antonio. *Saggio di Cose Ascolane e de' vescovi di Ascoli nel Piceno.* Bologna: A. Forni, 1984 [1766].

Mariotti, L. *Historical Memoir of Fra Dolcino and His Times.* London: Longman, Brown, Green, and Longmans, 1853.

McCready, William. *Signs of Sanctity.* Toronto: Pontifical Institute of Mediaeval Studies, 1989.

McGinn, Bernard. *The Calabrian Abbott: Joachim of Fiore in the History of Western Thought.* New York: Macmillan, 1985.

McLaughlin, Megan. "On Communion with the Dead." *Journal of Medieval History* 17 (1991): 23–34.

McNamara, Jo Ann. "The Need to Give: Suffering and Female Sanctity in the Middle Ages." In *Images of Sainthood in Medieval Europe*, edited by Renate Blumenfeld-Kosinki and Timea Szell, 199–221. Ithaca, NY: Cornell University Press, 1991.

Meersseman, G. G. *Dossier de l'Ordre de la pénitence au XIIIe siècle.* Fribourg, Switzerland: Editions universitaires, 1982 [1961].

———. "Etudes sur les anciennes confréries dominicaines, 4, Les milices de Jésus-Christ." *Archivum fratrum praedicatorum* 23 (1953): 275–308.

Meiss, Millard. *Painting in Florence and Siena after the Black Death: The Arts, Religion, and Society in the Mid-Fourteenth Century.* New York: Harper & Row, 1964.

Metford, J. C. J. *Dictionary of Christian Lore and Legend.* London: Thames and Hudson, 1983.

Miller, Tanya Stabler. *The Beguines of Medieval Paris: Gender, Patronage, and Spiritual Authority.* Philadelphia: University of Pennsylvania Press, 2014.

Molinari, Paul. "Saints and Miracles." *The Way* 17 (1978): 287–99.

Mooney, Catherine M. *Clare of Assisi and the Thirteenth-Century Church: Religious Women, Rules, and Resistance.* Philadelphia: University of Pennsylvania Press, 2016.

——, ed. *Gendered Voices: Medieval Saints and Their Interpreters*. Philadelphia: University of Pennsylvania Press, 1999.

Moore, R. I. *The Formation of a Persecuting Society: Power and Deviance in Western Europe 950–1250*. Cambridge, MA: Blackwell Publishing, 1990 [1987].

——. "Heresy as Disease." In *The Concept of Heresy in the Middle Ages (11th–13th c): Proceedings of the International Conference, Louvain, May 13–16, 1973*, edited by W. Lourdaux and D. Verhelst, 1–11. Leuven, Belgium: Leuven University Press, 1983.

——. *The Origins of European Dissent*. New York: Allen Lane, 1985.

——. *The War on Heresy*. Cambridge, MA: Harvard University Press, 2012.

More, Alison. "Institutionalizing Penitential Life in Later Medieval and Early Modern Europe: Third Orders, Rules, and Canonical Legitimacy." *Church History* 83 (2014): 297–323.

Mornese, Corrado, and Gustavo Buratti, eds. *Fra Dolcino e gli apostolici tra eresia, rivolta e roghi*. Rome: DeriveApprodi, 2000.

Morreale, Laura. "Chronicle and Community in Northern Italy, 1270–1360." PhD diss., Fordham University, 2004.

Morris, Colin. *The Papal Monarchy: The Western Church from 1050–1250*. Oxford: Oxford University Press, 1989.

Muir, Dorothy Erskine. *History of Milan under the Visconti*. London: Methuen and Co., 1924.

Mulchahey, M. Michèle. *"First the Bow Is Bent in Study": Dominican Education before 1350*. Toronto: Pontifical Institute of Mediaeval Studies, 1998.

Mundy, John Hine. "In Praise of Italy: The Italian Republics." *Speculum* 64 (1989): 815–34.

Muraro, Luisa. *Guglielma e Maifreda: Storia di un'eresia femminista*. Milan: La Tartaruga, 1985.

Murray, Alexander. "Piety and Impiety in Thirteenth-Century Italy." In *Popular Belief and Practice*, edited by G. J. Cuming and Derek Baker, 83–106. Studies in Church History 8. New York: Cambridge University Press, 1972.

Naudé, Gabriel. *Apologie pour Tous les Grands Hommes, soupçonnez de Magie*. Amsterdam: chez Frédéric Bernard, 1712 (1625). Reprinted as *Apologie pour Tous les Grands Hommes: Qui Ont Este Accusez de Magie*. Classic Reprints. London: Forgotten Books, 2018.

Newman, Barbara. "Agnes of Prague and Guglielma of Milan." In *Medieval Holy Women in the Christian Tradition*, edited by Rosalynn Voaden and Alastair Minnis, 557–79. Turnhout, Belgium: Brepols, 2010.

——. "The Heretic Saint: Guglielma of Bohemia, Milan, and Brunate." *Church History* 74 (2005): 1–38.

——. "Possessed by the Spirit: Devout Women, Demoniacs, and the Apostolic Life in the Thirteenth Century." *Speculum* 73 (1998): 733–70.

——. "WomanSpirit, WomanPope." In *From Virile Woman to WomanChrist*, edited by Barbara Newman, 183–223. Philadelphia: University of Pennsylvania Press, 1995.

Oertel, Christian. *The Cult of St. Erik in Medieval Sweden: Veneration of a Royal Saint, Twelfth–Sixteenth Centuries*. Turnhout, Belgium: Brepols, 2016.

Orioli, Raniero. "Ancora su Fra Dolcino: ex condicto et ordinatione et inductione." *La Cultura* 24 (1986): 190–210.

———, ed. *Fra Dolcino: Nascita, vita e morte di un'eresia medievale*. Milan: Jaca Book, 1984.

———. *Venit perfidus heresiarcha: Il movimento apostolicodolciniano dal 1260 al 1307*. Rome: Istituto storico italiano per il Medio Evo, 1988.

Ottani, Giancarlo. *L'abbazia di Chiaravalle Milanese, e la sua storia*. Pavia: Selecta, 2001 [1942].

Palmer, James A. "Medieval and Renaissance Rome: Mending the Divide." *History Compass* 15 (2017): 1–10.

———. *The Virtues of Economy: Governance, Power, and Piety in Late Medieval Rome*. Ithaca, NY: Cornell University Press, 2019.

Paoli, E. "'Nobile depositum Tuderti': Il culto e il tempio di San Fortunato nella vita religiose di Todi." In *Il tempio del santo patrono: Riflessi storico-artistici del culto di San Fortunato a Todi*, edited by M. Castrichini et al., 35–66. Todi: Ediart, 1988.

Paolini, Lorenzo. *Il "De officio inquisitionis": La procedura inquisitoriale a Bologna e a Ferrara nel Trecento*. 2 vols. Bologna: Editrice Universitaria Bolognina, 1976.

Park, Katherine. "The Life of the Corpse: Division and Dissection in Late Medieval Europe." *Journal of the History of Medicine* 50 (1995): 111–32.

Parker, Holt. "Toward a Definition of Popular Culture." *History and Theory* 50 (2011): 147–70.

Partner, Peter. *The Lands of St. Peter: The Papal States in the Middle Ages and the Early Renaissance*. London: Eyre Methuen, 1972.

Paschetto, Eugenia. *Pietro d'Abano: Medico e Filosofo*. Florence: Nuovedizione E. Vallecchi, 1984.

Pazzelli, R., ed. *Il B. Tommasuccio da Foligno terziario francescano ed i movimenti religiosi popolari umbri nel Trecento*. Rome: Edizioni Commissione Storica, 1979.

Peck, George T. *The Fool of God: Jacopone da Todi*. Tuscaloosa: University of Alabama Press, 1980.

Pegg, Mark Gregory. *The Corruption of Angels: The Great Inquisition of 1245–1246*. Princeton, NJ: Princeton University Press, 2001.

Pennington, Kenneth. "Innocent III and the Divine Authority of the Pope." In *Popes, Canonists, and Texts, 1150–1550*, edited by Kenneth Pennington, 1–32. Aldershot, UK: Variorum, 1993.

———. *Popes and Bishops: The Papal Monarchy in the Twelfth and Thirteenth Centuries*. Philadelphia: University of Pennsylvania Press, 1984.

———. *The Prince and the Law, 1200–1600: Sovereignty and Rights in the Western Legal Tradition*. Berkeley, CA: University of California Press, 1993.

———. "'Pro peccatis patrum puniri': A Moral and Legal Problem of the Inquisition." In *Popes, Canonists, and Texts, 1150–1550*, edited by Kenneth Pennington, 1–21. Aldershot, UK: Variorum, 1993.

Peterson, Janine Larmon. "Episcopal Authority and Disputed Sanctity in Late Medieval Italy." In *Saintly Bishops and Bishops' Saints: Proceedings of the 3rd Hagiography Conference*, edited by John S. Ott and Trpimir Vedriš, 201–16. Zagreb: Croatian Hagiography Society, 2012.

———. "Holy Heretics in Later Medieval Italy." *Past and Present* 204 (2009): 3–31.

———. "The Politics of Sanctity in Thirteenth-Century Ferrara," *Traditio: Studies in Ancient and Medieval Thought, History, and Religion* 63 (2008): 307–26.

———. "Social Roles, Gender Inversion, and the Heretical Sect: The Case of the Guglielmites," *Viator: A Journal of Medieval and Renaissance Studies* 35 (2004): 203–19.

Petrucci, Armando. *Writers and Readers in Medieval Italy: Studies in the History of Written Culture.* Translated by Charles M. Radding. New Haven, CT: Yale University Press, 1995.

Piazza, Andrea. "La *via crucis* di frate Michele." In *Vite di eretici e storie di frati,* edited by Giovanni Miccoli, 243–65. Milan: Edizioni Biblioteca Francescana, 1998.

Pierce, Jerry B. *Poverty, Heresy, and the Apocalypse: The Order of Apostles and Social Change in Medieval Italy, 1260–1307.* New York: Continuum Publishing Group, 2012.

Polc, Jaroslav. *Agnes von Böhmen, 1211–1282.* Munich: R. Oldenbourg Verlag, 1989.

Porta, Giuseppe. "L'urgenza della memoria storica." In *Storia della letteratura italiana, 2: Il Trecento,* edited by Enrico Malato, 159–210. Rome: Salerno Editrice, 1995.

"Porta alla Giustizia (Comune di Firenze)." Wikimapia. http://wikimapia.org /16241460/it/Porta-alla-Giustizia. Accessed 24 August 2016.

Power, Amanda. "The Friars in Secular and Ecclesiastical Governance, 1224–c. 1259." In *The English Province of the Franciscans (1224–c. 1350),* edited by Michael J. P. Robson, 28–45. Leiden, The Netherlands: Brill, 2017.

Prendergast, Ryan. *Reading, Writing, and Errant Subjects in Inquisitorial Spain.* Farnham, UK: Ashgate, 2011.

Prioreschi, Plinio. *A History of Medicine.* Vol. 5, *Medieval Medicine.* Omaha, NE: Horatius Press, 2003.

Prudlo, Donald S. *Certain Sainthood: Canonization and the Origins of Papal Infallibility in the Medieval Church.* Ithaca, NY: Cornell University Press, 2015.

———. *The Martyred Inquisitor: The Life and Cult of Peter of Verona (d. 1252).* Aldershot, UK: Ashgate, 2008.

Pryds, Darleen. *Women of the Streets: Early Franciscan Women and Their Mendicant Vocation.* St. Bonaventure, NY: Franciscan Institute, 2010.

Ranft, Patricia. "The Concept of Witness in the Christian Tradition: From Its Origin to Its Institutionalization." *Revue bénédictine* 102 (1992): 9–23.

Reeves, Marjorie. *The Influence of Prophecy in the Later Middle Ages: A Study in Joachimism.* Rev. ed. Notre Dame, IN: University of Notre Dame Press, 1993 [1969].

Ritchey, Sara. "Affective Medicine: Later Medieval Healing Communities and the Feminization of Health Care Practices in the Thirteenth-Century Low Countries." *Journal of Medieval Religious Cultures* 40 (2014): 113–43.

Robson, Michael. *The Franciscans in the Middle Ages.* Rochester, NY: Boydell Press, 2006.

Rollo-Koster, Joëlle. *Avignon and its Papacy, 1309–1417: Popes, Institutions, and Society.* New York: Rowman & Littlefield, 2015.

———. *Raiding St. Peter: Empty Sees, Violence, and the Initiation of the Great Western Schism (1378).* Series in Church History 32. Boston: Brill, 2008.

Roncetti, Mario, Pietro Scarpellini, and Francesco Tommasi. *Templari e ospitalieri in Italia: La chiesa di San Bevignate a Perugia.* Milan: Electa, 1987.

Rosenwein, Barbara H., and Lester K. Little. "Social Meaning in the Monastic and Mendicant Spiritualities." *Past and Present* 63 (1974): 4–32.

Rotelli, Elena. *Fra Dolcino e gli apostolici nella storia e nella tradizione.* Turin: Claudiana, 1979.

Rouse, Richard A., and Mary A. Rouse. *Preachers, Florilegia, and Sermons.* Toronto: Pontifical Institute of Medieval Studies, 1979.

Rubin, Miri. *Corpus Christi: The Eucharist in Late Medieval Culture.* New York: Cambridge University Press, 1991.

——. "Introduction: Rites of Passage." In *Rites of Passage: Cultures of Transition in the Fourteenth Century*, edited by Nicola F. McDonald and W. M. Ormrod, 1–12. York, UK: York Medieval Press, 2004.

Rusconi, Roberto. "L'Italia senza papa: L'età Avignonese e il grande scisma d'Occidente." In *Storia dell'Italia religiosa*, vol. 1, *L'antichità e il medioevo*, edited by André Vauchez, 427–54. Rome: Editori Laterza, 1993.

Russell, Jeffrey. *Dissent and Order in the Middle Ages: The Search for Legitimate Authority.* New York: Twayne Publishers, 1992.

Sabean, David Warren. *Power in the Blood: Popular Culture and Village Discourse in Early Modern Germany.* New York: Cambridge University Press, 1984.

Sackville, L. J. *Heresy and Heretics in the Thirteenth Century.* York, UK: York Medieval Press, 2011.

Salisbury, Joyce E. *The Blood of Martyrs: Unintended Consequences of Ancient Violence.* New York: Routledge, 2004.

Scaramuccia, Luigi P., ed. *Il Movimento dei Disciplinati nel settimo centenario del suo inizio (Perugia, 1260).* Spoleto: Arte grafiche Penetto & Petrelli, 1962.

Schlager, Bernard. "Foundresses of the Franciscan Life: Umiliana Cerchi and Margaret of Cortona." *Viator* 29 (1998): 141–66.

Schmitt, Jean-Claude. *The Holy Greyhound: Guinefort, Healer of Children since the Thirteenth Century.* New York: Cambridge University Press, 1983.

——. "Religion, Folklore, and Society in the Medieval West." In *Debating the Middle Ages: Issues and Readings*, edited by Lester K. Little and Barbara Rosenwein, 376–87. Malden, MA: Blackwell Publishers, 1998.

Scott, James C. *Domination and the Arts of Resistance: Hidden Transcripts.* New Haven, CT: Yale University Press, 1992.

——. *Weapons of the Weak: Everyday Forms of Peasant Resistance.* New Haven, CT: Yale University Press, 1985.

Şenocak, Neslihan. *The Poor and the Perfect: The Rise of Learning in the Franciscan Order, 1209–1310.* Ithaca, NY: Cornell University Press, 2012.

Sensi, Mario. "Anchoresses and Penitents in Thirteenth- and Fourteenth-Century Umbria." In *Women and Religion in Medieval and Renaissance Italy*, edited by Daniel Bornstein and Roberto Rusconi, translated by Margery J. Schneider, 56–83. Chicago: University of Chicago Press, 1996.

Shannon, Albert Clement. *The Popes and Heresy in the Thirteenth Century.* Villanova, IN: Augustinian Press, 1949.

Sikes, J. G. "John de Pouilli and Peter de la Palu." *English Historical Review* 49 (1934): 219–40.

Smalley, Beryl. *English Friars and Antiquity.* London: Basil Blackwell, 1960.

Smith, Lacey Baldwin. *Fools, Martyrs, Traitors: The Story of Martyrdom in the Western World.* New York: Alfred A. Knopf, 1997.

Smoller, Laura Ackerman. *The Saint and the Chopped-Up Baby: The Cult of Vincent Ferrer in Medieval and Early Modern Europe.* Ithaca, NY: Cornell University Press, 2014.

Snyder, Susan Taylor. "Orthodox Fears: Anti-Inquisitorial Violence and Defining Heresy." In *Fear and Its Representations in the Middle Ages and Renaissance,* edited by Anne Scott and Cynthia Kosso, 92–106. Turnhout, Belgium: Brepols, 2002.

Southern, R. W. *Western Society and the Church in the Middle Ages.* New York: Penguin, 1970.

Stantchev, Stefan K. *Spiritual Rationality: Papal Embargo as Cultural Practice.* New York: Oxford University Press, 2014.

St. Lawrence, John. "A Crusader in a 'Communion of Saints': Political Sanctity and Sanctified Politics in the Cult of St. Simon De Montfort." *Comitatus* 38 (2007): 43–67.

Tabacco, Giovanni. "La genesi culturale del movimento comunale italiano." *Atti della Società Ligure di Storia Patria* n.s. 29 (1989): 13–32.

Takayama, Hiroshi. "Law and Monarchy in the South." In *Italy in the Central Middle Ages,* edited by David Abulafia, 58–81. Oxford: Oxford University Press, 2004.

Tangheroni, Marco. "Sardinia and Italy." In *Italy in the Central Middle Ages, 1000–1300,* edited by David Abulafia, 237–50. New York: Oxford University Press, 2004.

Terpstra, Nicholas. "Civic Religion." In *The Oxford Handbook of Medieval Christianity,* edited by John H. Arnold, 148–65. Oxford: Oxford University Press, 2014.

——. *Lay Confraternities and Civic Religion in Renaissance Bologna.* New York: Cambridge University Press, 1995.

Thijssen, J. M. M. H. *Censure and Heresy at the University of Paris, 1200–1400.* Philadelphia: University of Pennsylvania Press, 1998.

Thomasini, Jacobi. *Patavini illustrissimi virorum elogia iconibus exornata.* Padua: Apud Pasquadum, 1630.

Thompson, Augustine, OP. *Cities of God: The Religion of the Italian Communes 1125–1325.* University Park: Pennsylvania State University Press, 2005.

——. "Lay versus Clerical Perceptions of Heresy: Protests against the Inquisition in Bologna, 1299." In *Praedicatores, Inquisitores I. The Dominicans and the Medieval Inquisition.* Edited by Wolfram Hoyer, 701–30. Rome: Istituto Storico Domenicano, 2004.

Thorndike, Lynn. *A History of Magic and Experimental Science.* 8 vols. New York: Columbia University Press, 1923.

——. "Peter of Abano and the Inquisition." *Speculum* 11 (1936): 132–33.

——. "Relations of the Inquisition to Peter of Abano and Cecco d'Ascoli." *Speculum* 1 (1926): 338–43.

Tierney, Brian. *The Origins of Papal Infallibility, 1150–1350: A Study on the Concepts of Infallibility, Sovereignty and Tradition in the Middle Ages.* Rev. ed. Leiden: Brill, 1997 [1988].

——. "'The Prince Is Not Bound by the Laws': Accursius and the Origins of the Modern State." *Comparative Studies in Society and History* 5 (1963): 389–95.

Tocco, Felice. "Gli Apostolici e fra Dolcino," *Archivio storio Italiano* s.v., 19 (1897): 241–75.

——. *Guglielma Boema e i Guglielmiti.* Atti della R. Accademia dei Lincei, Cl. di sc. morali, series 5, vol. 8. Rome: Tipografia dell'Accademia dei Lincei, 1900.

Tourn, Giorgio. *The Waldensians: The First 800 Years (1174–1974)*. Translated by Camillo P. Merlino. Turin: Claudiano, 1980.

Turner, Victor. "Pilgrimages as Social Processes." In *Dramas, Fields, and Metaphors: Symbolic Action in Human Society*, edited by Victor Turner, 166–230. Ithaca, NY: Cornell University Press, 1978.

——. *The Ritual Process: Structure and Anti-Structure*. 2nd ed. L. H. Morgan Lectures, 1966. Ithaca, NY: Cornell University Press, 1977.

Ullmann, W. "The Significance of Innocent III's Decretal *Vergentis*." In *Études d'histoire du droit canonique dediées à Gabriel Le Bras*, vol. 2, edited by Gabriel Le Bras, 729–43. Paris: Sirey, 1965.

Vandenbroucke, François. "Discernement des esprits au moyen âge." In *Dictionnaire de spiritualité, ascétique et mystique*, vol. 3, edited by Charles Baumgartner et al., cols. 1254–66. Paris: G. Beauchesne et ses fils, 1937.

Van 't Spijker, Ineke. "Model Reading: Saints' Lives and Literature of Religious Formation." In *"Scribere sanctorum gesta": Recuiel d'études d'hagiographie médiévale offert à Guy Philippart*, Hagiologia 3, edited by Étienne Renard et al., 135–56. Turnhout, Belgium: Brepols, 2005.

Vauchez, André. *The Laity in the Middle Ages: Religious Beliefs and Devotional Practices*. Edited by Daniel E. Bornstein. Notre Dame, IN: University of Notre Dame Press, 1993.

——. *La sainteté en Occident aux derniers siècles du Moyen Âge (1198–1431)*. Rome: École française de Rome, 1981. English translation: *Sainthood in the Later Middle Ages*. Translated by Jean Birrell. Cambridge: Cambridge University Press, 1997.

——. "Pénitents au Moyen Âge." In *Dictionnaire de Spiritualité ascétique et mystique: doctrine et histoire*, vol. 12, edited by Marcel Viller, cols. 1010–23. Paris: G. Beauchesne, 1984.

Vercellino, Ferruccio. *Frà Dolcino: Il brigatista di Dio*. Milan: Laura Rangoni Editore, 1997.

Vescovini, G. Federici. "Peter of Abano, the 'Conciliator' between Magic and Science." *Medicina nei secoli* 20 (2008): 607–40.

Violante, Cinzio. "I laici nel movimento patarino." In *Studi sulla christianità medio-evale: Società, istituzioni, spiritualità*, edited by Cinzio Violante, 75–120. Milan: Vita e Pensiero, 1972.

Vise, Melissa. "The Women and the Inquisitor: Peacemaking in Bologna, 1299." *Speculum* 93 (2018): 357–86.

Wakefield, Walter L. "Burial of Heretics in the Middle Ages." *Heresis* 5 (1985): 29–32.

Waley, Daniel, and Trevor Dean. *The Italian City-Republics*. 4th ed. New York: Longman, 2010 [1969].

Watt, John. *The Theory of Papal Monarchy in the Thirteenth Century*. New York: Fordham University Press, 1965.

Webb, Diana. *Patrons and Defenders: The Saints in the Italian City-States*. New York: I. B. Taurus Publishers, 1996.

Weinstein, Donald, and Rudolph M. Bell. *Saints and Society*. Chicago: University of Chicago Press, 1982.

Weisenbeck, Joan, and Marlene Weisenbeck. "Rose of Viterbo: Preacher and Reconciler." In *Clare of Assisi: A Medieval and Modern Woman*, edited by Ingrid Peterson, 145–55. St. Bonaventure, NY: Franciscan Institute, 1996.

Wessley, Stephen. "Enthusiasm and Heresy in the Year 1300," PhD diss., Columbia University, 1976.

——. "The Thirteenth-Century Guglielmites: Salvation through Women." In *Medieval Women*, edited by Derek Baker, 289–304. Studies in Church History 14. Oxford: Basil Blackwell, 1978.

West, Delno. "The Education of Fra Salimbene of Parma: The Joachite Influence." In *Prophecy and Millenarianism. Essays in Honor of Marjorie Reeves*, edited by Ann Williams, 191–216. Essex, UK: Longman, 1980.

——. "The Reformed Church and the Friars Minor: The Moderate Joachite Position of Fra Salimbene." *Archivum Franciscanum Historicum* 64 (1971): 273–84.

Wickham, Chris. *The Mountains and the City: The Tuscan Appennines in the Early Middle Ages*. Oxford: Clarendon Press, 1988.

——. *Sleepwalking into a New World: The Emergence of Italian City Communes in the Twelfth Century*. Princeton, NJ: Princeton University Press, 2015.

Wilson, Elizabeth. *Adorned in Dreams: Fashion and Modernity*. London: Virago, 1985.

Zanoni, L. *Gli Umiliati nei loro rapporti con l'eresie, industria della lana ed i communi nei secoli XII e XIII sulla scorta di documenti inediti*. Rome: Multigrafica, 1970.

Zarri, Gabriella. "Living Saints: A Typology of Female Sanctity in the Early Sixteenth Century." In *Women and Religion in Medieval and Renaissance Italy*, edited by Daniel Bornstein and Roberto Rusconi, 219–303. Chicago: University of Chicago Press, 1996.

INDEX

Printed in the USA
CPSIA information can be obtained
at www.ICGtesting.com
CBHW031412210524
8886CB00003B/133